FOR THE MOUTH OF THE
LORD HAS SPOKEN

In a world full of confusion and marked by subjectivism, where the Bible is marginalized even within churches, every generation of God's people needs to be taught and reminded that the Bible is God's living, active, and all-sufficient Word, bearing His authority and power as the sword of the Spirit. With his characteristic careful exegesis and clear teaching, Guy Waters has written an extremely helpful book on the doctrine of Scripture that is bound to be of great benefit and blessing to the Church. *For the Mouth of the Lord has Spoken* faithfully explains not only what the Bible is, but why God has given it to us—what He has designed for His Word to do in and through us. Along the way, Waters also teaches us both how to read the Bible and how to apply it to our daily lives. The Scriptures were central in the life of our Lord Jesus Christ, and Waters' book helps us understand why. I recommend this excellent resource for personal and group study, assured that this book will lead its readers to the Book, with renewed fervor and conviction that it is indeed the very Word—and words—of God.

L. MICHAEL MORALES
Professor of Biblical Studies,
Greenville Presbyterian Theological Seminary, Greenville, South Carolina

The last few decades have seen a plethora of books and essays on the doctrine of Scripture. What does this volume by Guy Prentiss Waters contribute? It is a first-class treatment of the doctrine, rich in the categories of systematic and historical theology. Second, and scarcely less important, it offers convincing reflections on where the doctrine 'fits' in the theological prospectus, over against those who, on the one hand, make it the foundation of everything, and those who, on the other hand, write it off as of incidental importance. Third, it is written with the admirable clarity and deceptive simplicity for which Waters is becoming known. And finally, it ends with courteous but firm engagement with Karl Barth and Peter Enns.

D. A. CARSON
Research Professor of New Testament,
Trinity Evangelical Divinity School, Deerfield, Illinois

In a wide-ranging and timely study, which draws attention to some of the most compelling evidence from church history, Waters shows what it means for the Bible to be the Word of God. He meets challenges head-on, showing how the Reformed doctrine of Scripture, which takes seriously Scripture itself, best answers challenges old and new. Waters helps us see how the Bible is—wonderfully—a book unlike any other.

BRANDON D. CROWE
Associate Professor of New Testament,
Westminster Theological Seminary, Philadelphia, Pennsylvania

This fine book is marked by breadth, depth, and integrity. It is broad in its coverage of biblical foundations, hermeneutical issues, and key contemporary figures. It is deep in historical grounding, theological mooring, and grasp of primary sources. The book's integrity lies in its refusal to minimize the importance of the Bible's own testimony to its revealed and unerring character and content, despite Western trends that do just that. This is an important contribution to a discussion necessitated by what an apostle called 'God's oracles' (Rom. 3:2) in an intellectual atmosphere that prizes human speculation over divine revelation.

ROBERT W. YARBROUGH
Professor of New Testament,
Covenant Theological Seminary, St. Louis, Missouri

What can be more important than understanding the Book that God gave us? Dr. Guy Waters thoroughly, carefully, and winsomely sets before us the riches of the doctrine of Scripture. He alerts us to faulty thinking of the past and the present and also commends to us a faithful and orthodox view of the Bible, the very words of God, which are life itself.

STEPHEN J. NICHOLS
President of Reformation Bible College, Sanford, Florida
Chief Academic Officer of Ligonier Ministries

While Christians put their trust in the Lord, their knowledge of the Lord depends upon His sure and steady Word, the Holy Scriptures. Therefore, the doctrine of the Holy Scriptures is central to the Christian faith. Guy Waters helps us to listen to God's testimony in His Word to the inspired reliability of His Word. This much-needed, well-written book stands firmly in the tradition of Augustine, Calvin, Turretin, and Warfield as it teaches and defends the Bible's inspiration and authority.

JOEL R. BEEKE
President,
Puritan Reformed Theological Seminary, Grand Rapids, Michigan

Given the fact that apart from God's self-disclosure in Scripture, the church has no objective warrant for making theological claims, it is always welcome and necessary to have books that expound and defend Scripture as God's Word written. In this very helpful and readable work, Guy Waters gives us a faithful exposition of what Scripture is by discussing the classic attributes of Scripture in light of the Reformation and contemporary discussions. For Christians today who want to articulate and defend what Scripture is as God's authoritative and trustworthy Word, especially in light of current challenges, this book is a must-read!

STEPHEN J. WELLUM
Professor of Christian Theology,
The Southern Baptist Theological Seminary, Louisville, Kentucky

FOR THE MOUTH OF THE
LORD HAS SPOKEN

THE DOCTRINE OF SCRIPTURE

GUY PRENTISS WATERS

SERIES EDITORS J.V. FESKO & MATTHEW BARRETT

Unless otherwise stated scripture quotations are from *The Holy Bible, English Standard Version*, copyright © 2001 by Crossway Bibles, a division of Good News Publishers. Used by permission. All rights reserved.

Copyright © Guy Prentiss Waters 2020

paperback ISBN 978-1-5271-0607-9
epub ISBN 978-1-5271-0659-8
mobi ISBN 978-1-5271-0660-4

10 9 8 7 6 5 4 3 2 1

Published in 2020
in the
Mentor Imprint
by
Christian Focus Publications Ltd,
Geanies House, Fearn, Ross-shire,
IV20 1TW, Great Britain.

www.christianfocus.com

Cover design
by Pete Barnsley

Printed by
Bell & Bain, Glasgow

All rights reserved. No part of this publication may be reproduced, stored in a retrieval system, or transmitted, in any form, by any means, electronic, mechanical, photocopying, recording or otherwise without the prior permission of the publisher or a licence permitting restricted copying. In the U.K. such licences are issued by the Copyright Licensing Agency, Saffron House, 6-10 Kirby Street, London, EC1 8TS www.cla.co.uk

CONTENTS

Series Preface	9
Preface	11
CHAPTER 1 Revelation: Part 1	13
CHAPTER 2 Revelation: Part 2	39
CHAPTER 3 Inspiration and Inerrancy	71
CHAPTER 4 Our 'Full Persuasion'	115
CHAPTER 5 The Sufficiency of Scripture	151
CHAPTER 6 The Clarity of Scripture	201
CHAPTER 7 Karl Barth and Scripture	233
CHAPTER 8 Peter Enns and the Doctrine of Scripture	271
Scripture Index	307
Subject Index	311

In Memory of My Father,

Elzberry Waters, Jr. (1933–2016)

Series Preface

Reformed, Exegetical and Doctrinal Studies (R.E.D.S.) presents new studies informed by rigorous exegetical attention to the biblical text, engagement with the history of doctrine, with a goal of refined dogmatic formulation.

R.E.D.S. covers a spectrum of doctrinal topics, addresses contemporary challenges in theological studies, and is driven by the Word of God, seeking to draw theological conclusions based upon the authority and teaching of Scripture itself.

Each volume also explores pastoral implications so that they contribute to the church's theological and practical understanding of God's Word. One of the virtues that sets R.E.D.S. apart is its ability to apply dogmatics to the Christian life. In doing so, these volumes are characterized by the rare combination of theological weightiness and warm, pastoral application, much in the tradition of John Calvin's *Institutes of the Christian Religion*.

These volumes do not merely repeat material accessible in other books but retrieve and remind the church of forgotten truths to enrich contemporary discussion.

Matthew Barrett
J. V. Fesko

Preface

There is no book better than the Bible. The reason that the Bible is the best of books is because it is God's own Word. He breathed this book into existence (2 Tim. 3:16). He does wonderful things in and by it. He shows us who He is. He shows us who we are. He convicts us of sin. He points us to the Savior. He tells us of the glorious realities of eternal life, peace, and joy. He teaches us. He corrects us. He directs our lives. He woos us. He warns us. He comforts us. He motivates us. He encourages us. He meets with us.

But there is hardly a book more assailed, mocked, and assaulted than the Bible. We live in a world that is no friend to God and His Word. This enmity is vividly captured in the ministry of Jeremiah, the weeping prophet. As Jeremiah's secretary, Baruch, read aloud the prophecies of Jeremiah from a scroll, King Jehoiakim cut up the scroll and cast the pieces into the fire (Jer. 36).

Within the contemporary church, many do not understand, or do not clearly understand, what the Bible is and why God has given it to us. Perhaps, one will say, these are purely academic matters. In reality, these matters are profoundly practical. As our grasp of them goes, so goes the vitality and stability of our Christian lives.

For all these reasons, it is important that we understand the book that God has given us. What is the Bible? What has God designed for it to do in our lives? How has He intended for us to read it? What challenges present themselves at the dawn of the twenty-first century to a faithful reading, understanding, and application of God's Word?

I have written this book to help answer some of these questions. I am very grateful that the series editors, John V. Fesko and Matthew Barrett, not only invited me to contribute to this series, but also demonstrated heroic longsuffering in awaiting a final draft of this book. Willie Mackenzie, Director of Publishing at Christian Focus, has shown no less patience and kindness toward me as he awaited the manuscript.

Particular thanks are due to the Board of Trustees of Reformed Theological Seminary, and to J. Ligon Duncan III, Chancellor and CEO, for making it possible for me to write as a faculty member of RTS. I am grateful to the support and encouragement of my colleagues on the Jackson campus, particularly Miles V. Van Pelt, the Academic Dean of RTS, Jackson. Present and former students, Nathan Lee and Kevin Vollema, have read through part or all of the manuscript and have spared me many errors and mistakes. My former student, Bryant Park, promptly and capably gathered for me many resources and materials that I used in preparing this book. My RTS colleague, Duncan Rankin, graciously offered wisdom and hard to find source materials as I was drafting the chapter on Karl Barth. My RTS colleague, Mark McDowell, read through the draft chapter on Karl Barth and offered a number of helpful suggestions. James T. O'Brien read through the entirety of the manuscript and lent careful, critical, and invaluable editorial guidance. I am grateful to P&R for its permission to use a portion of the material in Chapter 3 from my *What Is the Bible?* (P&R, 2013). I am also grateful to Jared Hood, editor of the Reformed Theological Review, for permitting my two articles, 'Peter Enns and the Incarnational Analogy, Part 1' *RTR* (2019) 78/3: 197-217, and 'Peter Enns and the Incarnational Analogy, Part 2' *RTR* (2020) 79/1: 29-45 to appear as Chapter 8 of this book.

It seems fitting to close this preface and to commence this book with a statement attributed to the young Martin Luther, 'Let them destroy my works; I desire nothing better; for all I wanted was to lead Christians to the Bible, that they might afterwards throw away my writings. Great God! if we had but a right understanding of the Holy Scriptures, what need would there be of my books?'[1] May God help you, reader, more and more to understand, prize, and cherish His Word, to the glory of its Divine Author.

---

1. As quoted by Theophilus Stork, *The Life of Martin Luther and the Reformation in Germany* (Philadelphia: Lindsay & Blakiston, 1854), 20-1.

Revelation: Part 1

In this chapter, we are going to begin to define 'revelation.' We will first offer a working definition, and then explore two ways in which the Bible speaks of revelation. Theologians have termed these two ways 'general' (or 'natural') revelation and 'special' revelation. These studies in definition will prepare us to think carefully about the nature and character of the Bible.

What Is Revelation?

The core of the idea of revelation is 'disclosure.' The English word, 'reveal,' derives from a Latin verb meaning 'to pull back the veil.'[1] Revelation enables access to that which is otherwise inaccessible. Christianity is predicated upon the self-revelation of God.[2] The concept of revelation,

---

1. The English verb 'reveal' is derived from the Latin verb *revelare,* which, in turn, is composed of two Latin words, the prefix *re-* and the noun *velum, The Compact Edition of the Oxford English Dictionary* (2 vols.; Oxford: Oxford University Press, 1971). The Latin noun *velum* denotes 'a cloth, covering, awning, curtain, [or] veil,' Charlton T. Lewis and Charles Short, *A Latin Dictionary* (Oxford: Oxford University Press, 1879).

2. The last three centuries in particular have witnessed considerable philosophical and theological attention to the idea of revelation, much of it hostile to classical Christianity. For helpful surveys of these discussions, see Warfield, 'The Idea of Revelation and Theories of Revelation,' in *The Works of Benjamin B. Warfield* (10 vols.; New York: Oxford University Press, 1932), 1:37-48; H. D. McDonald, *Theories of Revelation: An Historical Study, 1700-1960* (Grand Rapids: Baker, 1979); J. I. Packer, 'Contemporary Views of Revelation,' in *Honouring the Written Word of God: The Collected Shorter Writings of J. I. Packer, Volume 3* (Carlisle: Paternoster, 1999), 65-80; Ronald H. Nash, *The Word of God and The Mind of Man* (Phillipsburg, NJ: P&R, 1982); and John M. Frame, *The Doctrine*

however, is not unique to Christianity. As Herman Bavinck observed in the early twentieth century, 'the history of religions is proof that the concept of revelation is not only integral to Christianity and occurs in Holy Scripture but is a necessary correlate of all religion.'[3] Judaism, Christianity, and Islam are all founded upon claims to divine, verbal revelation. Many religions throughout human history, however, are not founded upon sacred texts thought to disclose the divine mind. Yet these religions rest, at some level, upon what is thought to be divine revelation. The scholar of ancient Roman religion, John Scheid, insists that ancient Roman religion 'was a religion without revelation, without revealed books, without dogma and without orthodoxy.' Rather, its 'central requirement was ... "orthopraxis," the correct performance of prescribed rituals.'[4] But these elaborate rituals, Scheid observes, were oriented towards the gods whom the Romans regarded as 'liv[ing] in the world alongside men and [striving] with them, in a civic context, to bring about the common good.'[5] These rituals admitted of multiple purposes, but all rituals were undertaken out of a conviction that they would be acceptable or pleasing to the venerated god. In other words, these rituals reflect the practitioners' belief that they are acting in accordance with the mind of the deity.[6] Even religions of orthopraxy, then, require some measure of divine revelation for their functioning and maintenance.

---

of the Word of God (Phillipsburg, NJ: P&R, 2010), 13-43. Helpful Reformed treatments of the subject include Herman Bavinck, *The Philosophy of Revelation* (Grand Rapids: Eerdmans, 1953), and Paul Helm, *The Divine Revelation* (Westchester, IL: Crossway, 1982). Two influential recent Roman Catholic surveys are those of Avery Cardinal Dulles, *Models of Revelation* (Maryknoll, NY: Orbis, 1992) and *Revelation Theology: A History* (New York: Herder and Herder, 1969).

3. Herman Bavinck, *Reformed Dogmatics* (ed. John Bolt; trans. John Vriend; 4 vols.; Grand Rapids: Eerdmans, 2003), 1:284. In the section that follows this statement, Bavinck offers support for this claim from the information about world religions available to him, 1:284-7. As Bavinck elsewhere observes, 'humanity as a whole has been at all times supranaturalistic to the core,' *The Philosophy of Revelation* (Grand Rapids: Eerdmans, 1953), 1. Compare Turretin, 'no nation has ever been found so barbarous as not to have its hierophants engaged in gaining the knowledge of and in teaching divine things,' *Institutes of Elenctic Theology* (3 vols.; Phillipsburg, NJ: P&R, 1992-7), 1:3 (=1.2.1).

4. John Scheid, *An Introduction to Roman Religion* (trans. Janet Lloyd; Bloomington, IN: Indiana University Press, 2003), 18.

5. ibid., 147.

6. This is not necessarily to say, of course, that such beliefs are either accessible in writing to outsiders or consciously informing the ritual actions of the practitioners.

The idea of revelation, then, is not unique to Christianity. Some understanding of revelation persistently informs human religious endeavor. Even so, it would be misguided to construct either a definition or doctrine of revelation by compiling the results of an empirical survey of human religions. This becomes evident when we reflect upon the necessary conditions for revelation. Revelation requires a revealer, recipients of revelation, and something revealed. Christianity makes distinct claims about each of these three dimensions of revelation. The *revealer* is the God whom we encounter both in the world that He has made and upon the pages of Scripture. This God is 'a personal God, possessing the attributes of power, intelligence, and moral excellence.' He is, 'in relation to the universe, … at once immanent in, and transcendent to, the universe.' God's 'moral government over mankind and other intelligent creatures rewards and punishes them according to their moral character.'[7] The *recipients of revelation* are the intelligent, moral creatures whom this God has made for His own glory, particularly, human beings (Gen. 1:26-7, Rom. 11:36).[8] Specifically, people are said to be made after God's own 'image' and 'likeness' (Gen. 1:26, cf. 1:27). Since God is represented in Scripture as a God who speaks, the image must include the capacity to reason.

> Man … is not dumb and uncomprehending, but is endowed with a mental faculty that enables him to use language for the rational expression and communication of his thoughts and wishes, to pursue intellectual studies, to investigate the connection between things, and to appreciate the rationality of God's creation, of which he himself is a part. And man is not dumb because God is not dumb. God is a God who speaks, and his speaking is the declaration of his mind and his will … Being exclusively formed in the divine image, man alone of earth's creatures is endowed with the faculty of rationality which enables him, as a reflector of the Creator's rationality, to think and to plan and to speak.[9]

It is not simply that human beings happen to receive the revelation that God makes to them. It is that human beings are intentionally created with the capacity to understand and to respond to the God who made them.

---

7. Thomas C. Johnson, 'Synopsis of Lectures on Inspiration,' n.p., n.d., 3.

8. For purposes of this discussion, we set aside consideration of another category of intelligent, moral creatures, namely, the angels.

9. Philip Edgcumbe Hughes, *The True Image: The Origin and Destiny of Man in Christ* (Grand Rapids: Eerdmans, 1989), 57.

But the Bible says more about the recipients of revelation than that they are made after the image of God. Human beings are in a state of alienation from and rebellion against God. All human beings have sinned and, therefore, fallen short of the glory of God (Rom. 3:23). That is to say, they, through sin, have failed to answer the purpose for which they were made – to glorify the God who made them.[10] Sin has affected even the workings of the human mind. Humans have become 'futile in their thinking, and their foolish hearts were darkened' (Rom. 1:21). They are 'darkened in their understanding, alienated from the life of God because of the ignorance that is in them, due to their hardness of heart' (Eph. 4:18). Human beings are by nature, therefore, unwilling recipients of God's speech. They have no interest in what God has to say to them. Rather, 'by their unrighteousness [they] suppress the truth' (Rom. 1:18).

This reality, in turn, brings us to the third dimension of Christianity's claims about divine revelation, namely, *that which is revealed*. Whatever God chooses to reveal about Himself is addressed to natively hostile recipients. In other words, the content of God's speech cannot but reflect the antipathy that unrenewed sinners have towards God. His self-revelation is adapted to their condition and state as sinners. But even as God's self-revelation reflects the condition of its recipients, it is still God's *self*-revelation. As Francis Turretin has observed, 'the nature and goodness of God who, since he is the best, is most communicative of himself. He cannot communicate himself more suitably to a rational creature and in a manner more fitting to human nature than by the knowledge and love of himself.'[11] Revelation is not a fundamentally vindictive enterprise. Its most basic end is not to seal the condemnation of sinful recipients. At bottom, revelation is the benevolent expression of a God who is love (1 John 4:9). In revelation, God communicates Himself to His image-bearers.

In saying that God reveals Himself to human beings, we are defining revelation as a fundamentally personal enterprise. This is not to say that revelation is not propositional in nature.[12] On the contrary, revelation

---

10. Douglas Moo, *Romans 1-8* (WEC; Chicago: Moody, 1991), 226-7.

11. Francis Turretin, *Institutes of Elenctic Theology* (3 vols.; Phillispburg, NJ: P&R, 1992-7), 1:3 (=1.2.1).

12. One leading theologian of the twentieth century, Karl Barth, understands revelation as personal but distances revelation from propositional truth. Revelation, he argues, takes place in the interpersonal encounter between God and the individual who responds to God in faith.

is both personal *and* propositional.¹³ Proponents of personal-not-propositional revelation erect a false antithesis between 'personal' and 'proposition.' As Frame has noted, 'there is no reason why someone cannot reveal himself through revealing information about himself. In fact, we regularly do that. It's almost impossible to imagine revealing yourself to someone without at the same time revealing information about yourself. And whenever we reveal information about ourselves, we are to some extent (not exhaustively, to be sure) revealing ourselves.'¹⁴ Furthermore, the word group 'reveal' in the New Testament, as Frame observes, 'present[s] revelation as God's communicating information.'¹⁵ The New Testament writers, following the Old Testament, uniformly understand revelation in propositional terms. God has come to man, but He has come to man along the avenue of speech.¹⁶ Human beings know God, but that knowledge can never be less than propositional in nature.¹⁷

In summary, to speak of revelation is to speak of the self-disclosure of the living, personal God who has made all things for Himself. Because

---

It is a mistake, according to Barth, to identify the Bible with the Word of God. The Bible bears witness to the Word of God, but is not itself the Word of God *simpliciter*. It is the occasion of revelation but not revelation itself. For a fuller discussion of Barth's doctrine of revelation and the Bible, see Chapter 7. See also the summary of Dulles, *Models of Revelation*, 84-97.

13. Nash notes that the theological antithesis between person and proposition frequently posits the conviction that 'cognitive knowledge about God is unattainable. Because God is totally transcendent, because He is unlike anything else in human experience, human language is an unfit instrument to capture ideas or express truths about God. Nor are human rational faculties adequate for knowledge about the transcendent,' *The Word of God and The Mind of Man*, 47. The Bible, however, understands neither divine transcendence nor the mind of divine image-bearers along such lines.

14. Frame, *Doctrine of the Word of God*, 41.

15. ibid. See Frame's helpful discussion of the way in which the New Testament's designation of Christ as 'Word' in no way diminishes the authority of Jesus' words, *Doctrine of the Word of God*, 42-3. On the contrary, Frame observes, 'in God's personal words, Christ himself comes to engage our belief and obedience,' 43.

16. To anticipate our discussion below, we are not saying that God, in natural revelation, audibly and verbally speaks to human beings through the things that are made. General revelation is 'unwritten,' Shedd, *Dogmatic Theology* (3 vols.; 1894; repr. Grand Rapids: Eerdmans, 1969), 1:62. We are saying, however, that human beings inexorably know God through the creation, and that knowledge is irreducibly propositional in nature. For a recent effort to conceive natural revelation in terms of 'personal-word revelation,' see Frame, *The Doctrine of the Word of God*, 78.

17. For a defense of the proposition that human words are capable of being 'words of God, conveying to us the Word – that is, the message – of God,' see Packer, 'The Adequacy of Human Language,' in *Honouring the Written Word of God*, 23-49.

He is a sovereign God, neither constrained nor conditioned by anything outside Himself, He is sovereign in self-revelation. He chooses whether or not to reveal Himself. He chooses when, where, and how to reveal Himself. And He chooses what to make known of Himself. We may only know of God what He chooses to reveal of Himself.[18] The character of the God who reveals Himself necessarily determines the character of His self-revelation. God is all-knowing and He is true. His self-revelation is, therefore, altogether true. God is righteous and holy. His self-revelation, therefore, reflects His pure and upright character.

The living and personal God discloses Himself to His living and personal image-bearers. He has so created human beings that they are constitutionally equipped to receive and to respond to His self-revelation. He has furthermore made people to dwell in a world that He has not only spoken into existence, but also sustains and governs. The world is, therefore, not an environment that is intrinsically hostile to God's project of self-revelation. On the contrary, God has so fashioned the world as to complement His purpose and work of revealing Himself to humanity.

What exactly is it that God reveals to His reasonable creatures? The content of this revelation supremely concerns God Himself, specifically, 'his nature, works, will, or purposes.'[19] God's character, God's decrees, and God's works comprise the substance of God's self-disclosure to His creatures.[20]

Natural Revelation

When reflecting upon what God reveals of Himself to His image-bearers, theologians typically distinguish two kinds of revelation. The first has been termed 'natural' or 'general' revelation. The second,

---

18. 'God can be known only because and so far as he reveals himself,' Warfield, 'The Idea of Revelation and Theories of Revelation,' in *Works*, 1:37.

19. Warfield, 'The Idea of Revelation and Theories of Revelation,' in *Works*, 1:37.

20. There is a sense in which we may speak more broadly still of revelation. W. G. T. Shedd speaks of 'revelation in its general and wide signification' as 'any species of knowledge of which God is the ultimate source and cause,' *Dogmatic Theology*, 1:62. This is so because man's 'axiomatic knowledge,' his 'intellect,' and the 'laws of human intelligence' all find their ultimate source in God, ibid. Theologians typically, however, speak of revelation more narrowly in terms of God's self-disclosure to His rational creatures. And yet, as we shall see in our discussion of natural revelation, Shedd makes an important and welcome observation. Since every datum of knowledge in the world is revelatory of God, it is not in principle improper to speak of 'revelation' in such broad and sweeping terms.

'special revelation.'²¹ Each is revelation from God to human beings. But each is distinct in its content, sphere, and purposes. To appreciate the one kind of revelation, it is important to have a good grasp of the other. For that reason we will explore each in turn, beginning with 'natural' or 'general' revelation.

Terminology

We may begin with the diversity of nomenclature that theologians have employed to characterize this category of revelation. 'Natural' captures the fact that this revelation comes to humans through 'the media of natural phenomena, occurring in the course of Nature or of history.'²² 'General' reflects the scope or sphere of this revelation. It extends to the whole of the human race, across the entirety of human history and wherever in the world that human beings have found themselves.

Taken of themselves, these terms are complementary and not competing. That is to say, each captures a distinct aspect of what theologians understand this species of revelation to be. One should take care, however, to distinguish 'natural revelation' from 'natural theology.'²³ In natural revelation, human beings are 'passive or receptive.'²⁴ They are recipients of the revelation that God is pleased to make of Himself in the world. In natural theology, however, human beings construct arguments premised upon the data that natural revelation supplies.²⁵ The project of natural theology, which is a venerable one in Christian reflection, seeks to 'establish or make probable certain theological propositions about the existence and character of God, from premises of a non-theological character,' that is, from premises not drawn from the explicit statements of Scripture.²⁶

---

21. Bavinck employs the term 'supernatural revelation,' even as he stresses that 'all revelation is supernatural,' *Reformed Dogmatics*, 1:303, 307. Warfield notes the following pairings of terms to characterize these two categories of revelation, 'natural and supernatural revelation ... general and special revelation ... natural and soteriological revelation,' 'The Biblical Idea of Revelation,' in *Works*, 1:6.

22. Warfield, 'The Biblical Idea of Revelation,' in *Works*, 1:6.

23. For what follows, I am partially indebted to Helm, *The Divine Revelation*, 9-12.

24. Helm, *The Divine Revelation*, 10.

25. But it does not follow that natural theology 'assume[s] that there is no revealer,' *pace* Helm, *The Divine Revelation*, 11.

26. Helm, *The Divine Revelation*, 9. For a classical example of natural theology in the Reformed tradition, see Thomas Chalmers, *On Natural Theology* (2 vols.; New York:

Natural theology, then, is an intellectual enterprise in which humans are actively and constructively engaged. Natural revelation is necessarily true, since it is divine revelation. Natural theology is necessarily fallible, or subject to error, since it is the work of human beings who are liable to err.[27]

For the remainder of this chapter, we are going to explore natural revelation along four lines. We will see, first, that the Bible testifies to divine self-revelation in the creation. Second, we will address the content of that revelation. What is it that God makes known of Himself in the world? Third, we will briefly explore the subjective side of natural revelation. That is to say, are humans competent to receive and to understand natural revelation? Fourth, we will explore the purposes of natural revelation.

Biblical Testimony to Natural Revelation

First, the Bible testifies to divine self-revelation in the creation. This line of proof is not, of course, the sole demonstration of the fact that God has revealed Himself in the world. But these passages carry a two-fold importance for our discussion. First, as the Word of God, they speak authoritatively to the existence, nature, and purposes of general revelation. Second, these passages will help us formulate a complete doctrine of revelation. Put another way, to arrive at a proper understanding of special revelation, we need first to have a grasp of natural revelation. As we shall see, special revelation assumes and builds upon the testimony of natural revelation. Warfield perceptively puts the matter more strongly.

> Without general revelation, special revelation would lack that basis in the fundamental knowledge of God as the mighty and wise, righteous and good, maker and ruler of all things, apart from which the future revelation

---

Robert Carter & Brothers, 1857); and Robert L. Dabney, *Syllabus and Notes of the Course of Systematic and Polemic Theology Taught in Union Theological Seminary, Virginia* (5th ed.; Richmond: Presbyterian Committee of Publication, 1871), 5-78. For a recent example of natural theology in the neo-Thomistic tradition, see now Edward Feser, *The Last Superstition: A Refutation of the New Atheism* (South Bend, IN: St. Augustine's Press, 2010); *Aquinas (A Beginner's Guide)* (Oxford, UK: Oneworld, 2009); and *Five Proofs of the Existence of God* (San Francisco: Ignatius, 2017).

27. In analogous fashion, the theology that human beings draw from the infallible Bible is the fallible work of fallible people. We distinguish in each case infallible revelation from the fallible theology that we derive from that infallible revelation.

of this great God's interventions in the world for the salvation of sinners could not be either intelligible, credible or operative.[28]

In special revelation, then, we do not meet a different God than we meet in natural revelation. We meet the same God, more fully revealed.

We may point to at least four passages in which the Bible testifies to the existence and character of natural revelation. The first is Psalm 19:1-4.

> The heavens declare the glory of God,
>   and the sky above proclaims his handiwork.
> Day to day pours out speech,
>   and night to night reveals knowledge.
> There is no speech, nor are there words,
>   whose voice is not heard.
> Their measuring line goes out through all the earth,
>   and their words to the end of the world.

David begins this psalm with 'the heavens' or 'the sky' and proceeds down to 'the earth' or 'the world' (19:1). His concern is with the natural world in all its dimensions, from 'the sky above' to 'the end of the world' (19:1, 4). He uses verbal language to describe the activity of the inanimate creation. The 'heavens declare,' the 'sky above proclaims,' 'night to night reveals' (19:1, 2). David's statement in verse 3 is initially puzzling, 'there is no speech, nor are there words, whose voice is not heard,' what Derek Kidner terms 'the paradox of wordless speech.'[29] This statement certainly confirms the metaphorical character of the heavens' declaration. But it does more. In the words of J. A. Alexander, 'far from weakening the testimony ... the absence of articulate language ... makes [this testimony] stronger. Even without speech or words, the heavens testify of God to all men.'[30]

To what do the heavens testify? To 'the glory of God,' His 'handiwork.' The world testifies to the fact that God has made it and, as such, exhibits

---

28. Warfield, 'The Biblical Idea of Revelation,' in *Works*, I:7.

29. Derek Kidner, *Psalms 1-72* (TOTC; Downers Grove, IL: InterVarsity, 1973), 98. As Peter C. Craigie observes, 'on the one hand, there is no speech, no noise, from a literal or acoustic perspective (v. 4); on the other hand, there is a voice that penetrates to the furthest corners of the earth,' *Psalms 1-50* (WBC; Nashville: Thomas Nelson, 1983), 181.

30. As quoted at Charles Hodge, *Systematic Theology* (3 vols.; New York: Charles Scribner's Sons, 1901), 1:24.

the character and majesty of its Maker.[31] When human beings, who are capable of rational reflection, look at the world that God has made, they necessarily discern the glory of God from the works of His hands.[32] It is for this reason that David can describe this revelation, which is not verbally uttered, in expressly propositional terms ('speech,' 'knowledge,' 19:2). Humans cannot but know God from the creation.

David also testifies to the fact that this revelation is ongoing or perpetual. 'Day to day pours out speech, and night to night reveals knowledge' (19:2). There is, in other words, a perpetual replenishment of the knowledge of God to the minds of those who inhabit God's world. This revelation is not extraordinary or sporadic. It is ordinary and continuing.[33]

Implied in the psalm is that this revelation or testimony is inescapable. It is presented to human beings continually and at every point of creation. There is no location where humans are not exposed to this revelation. In every place and at all times, the works of God's hands confront humans with the existence and character of God. It is in this connection that Bavinck correctly characterizes general revelation as 'supernatural revelation.'[34]

A second passage that addresses general revelation is Romans 1:19-20, 2:14-15.[35] We will give particular attention, first, to Romans 1:19-20.

---

31. John Calvin observes that 'this skillful ordering of the universe is for us a sort of mirror in which we can contemplate God, who is otherwise invisible,' *Institutes of the Christian Religion* (ed. John T. McNeill; trans. Ford L. Battles; 2 vols.; LCC; Philadelphia: Westminster, 1960), 1:52 (= 1.5.1); Kidner suggests that the verb 'pours forth' ('pours out,' ESV) in verse 2 'suggests the irrepressible bubbling up of a spring, and therefore perhaps the unfailing variety with which the days reflect the Creator's mind,' *Psalms 1-72*, 97-8.

32. 'The firmament, while, from the nature of things it is only an announcement by matter of fact, of what God has made, testifies, at the same time, (since doing proceeds from being) of the Creator, what he is, concerning his glory,' E. W. Hengstenberg, *Commentary on the Books of Psalms* (rev. ed.; 3 vols.; trans. P. Fairbairn and J. Thomson; Edinburgh: T&T Clark, 1851), 1:329.

33. Alexander characterizes 'day' and 'night' in 19:2 as 'witnesses in unbroken succession,' quoted at Hodge, *Systematic Theology*, 1:24. Craigie comments that 'day' and 'night' serve 'as the two fundamental perspectives from which the heavens may be perceived,' *Psalms 1-50*, 180.

34. Bavinck, *Reformed Dogmatics*, 1:307-8. For a fuller list of OT testimonies to the self-revelation of God in the world, see Bavinck, *Reformed Dogmatics*, 1:310.

35. Derek Kidner plausibly suggests that the 'thought' of Psalm 19 may 'underlie the argument of Romans 1:18f.,' *Psalms 1-72*, 97, cf. E. W. Hengstenberg, *Commentary on the Book of Psalms*, 1:329.

> For what can be known about God is plain to them, because God has shown it to them. For his invisible attributes, namely his eternal power and divine nature, have been clearly perceived, ever since the creation of the world, in the things that have been made. So they are without excuse.

The conjunction 'for' serves to ground Paul's assertion in Romans 1:18, 'for the wrath of God is revealed from heaven against all ungodliness and unrighteousness of men, who by their unrighteousness suppress the truth.' The reason, then, that Paul provides in Romans 1:19-20 as to why God is now revealing His 'wrath' against human beings is that human beings have responded in rebellion and ingratitude to God's self-revelation in nature.

Paul tells us at least five things about general revelation in these verses. First, the agent of this revelation is God, 'God has shown it to them' (1:19). Paul is not describing a mechanical and impersonal process. He is, rather, stressing that God is disclosing Himself to human beings. Second, the medium of that revelation is the world, specifically, 'the things that have been made' (1:20). Even the human person, created by God, is a medium of God's self-revelation to humanity.

Third, the content of that revelation is the existence and the character of God, specifically, His 'invisible attributes,' 'his eternal power and divine nature' (1:20). The invisible God reveals Himself through the visible world. Fourth, Paul addresses the extent of this revelation in two regards. Spatially, God reveals Himself in nothing less than 'the things that have been made' (1:20). Every creature testifies to God. Temporally, God has been revealing Himself through the creature 'ever since the creation of the world' (1:20). There is, therefore, no human being in the world, nor has there ever been a human being in history, who has not been confronted with this divine revelation.

Fifth, Paul insists that this revelation is subjectively effective. This self-revelation comes to human beings through the mind ('what can be known about God,' 1:19). It is 'plain to them' and 'clearly perceived' (1:19, 20). Paul does not attribute this effectiveness to the intellectual prowess of its recipients. Rather, this revelation successfully reaches its targets because 'God has shown it to them' (1:19). They are therefore 'without excuse' (1:20). Put most simply, human beings 'know God' (1:21).

In a point to which we shall return below, Paul insists that the response of human beings to this revelation is uniformly negative.[36] In spite of this knowledge, people 'did not honor him as God or give thanks to him' (1:21). Paul instances idolatry and immorality as two signal proofs of human rebellion against this revelation. Paul in no way mitigates human responsibility because of this sinful response to God. On the contrary, as Paul's argument in Romans 1:24-32 shows, the fact that human beings respond in the way that they do to divine revelation only renders their condition worse before God. Humans are accountable to God for their rejection of His self-revelation.

A passage that lies in close connection with Romans 1:19-20 is Romans 2:14-15.

> For when Gentiles, who do not have the law, by nature do what the law requires, they are a law to themselves, even though they do not have the law. They show that the work of the law is written on their hearts, while their conscience also bears witness, and their conflicting thoughts accuse or even excuse them.

Whereas, in Romans 1:18-32, Paul was addressing humanity in general, he turns his attention in Romans 2:1f. to the Jew.[37] In both passages, he establishes the unrighteousness of human beings before the righteous God. In Romans 2:12, Paul insists that Jews will be held accountable to 'the law,' that is, the divinely revealed Torah. If they wish to be counted righteous on the basis of their lifestyle, they must be more than 'hearers' of the law. They must be 'doers of the law' (Rom. 2:13).[38] In Romans 2:14-15, Paul speaks of 'Gentiles.' These are not Gentile Christians, but Gentiles who, unlike the Jews, do not have access

---

36. Absent, of course, the intervention of the saving grace of God.

37. See the discussion at C. E. B. Cranfield, *Romans 1-8* (ICC; Edinburgh: T&T Clark, 1975), 137-9; and Arland J. Hultgren, *Paul's Letter to the Romans: A Commentary* (Grand Rapids: Eerdmans, 2011), 111-13. Both Cranfield and Hultgren understand Paul to be engaging a Jewish interlocutor at 2:1f.

38. 'Paul is simply setting forth the standard by which God's justifying verdict will be rendered ... [His] purpose is not to show how people can be justified but to set forth the standard that must be met if a person is to be justified ... Paul affirms the principle that doing the law can lead to salvation; but he denies (1) that anyone can so 'do' the law; and (2) that Jews can depend on their covenant relationship to shield them from the consequences of this failure,' Douglas J. Moo, *The Epistle to the Romans* (NICNT; Grand Rapids: Eerdmans, 1996), 148.

to Torah.[39] Even though they lack Torah, they 'by nature do what the law requires' (Rom. 2:14). In other words, Gentiles, who lack the written, inscripturated Word of God, nevertheless do what that Word commands. Furthermore, they do it 'by nature,' as a function of their created humanity.[40] It is in this way that they are 'a law to themselves, even though they do not have the law' (Rom. 2:14). All human beings have access to and are under the authority of God's 'law.' The Jews access that law through special revelation. Non-Jews have access to it by another means.

In Romans 2:15, Paul addresses how non-Jews (and all human beings) have access to that 'law.' The 'work of the law is written on their hearts.' The expression 'work of the law' distinguishes the 'law' to which Gentiles are subject from Torah. At the same time, Paul's use of the word 'law' in the expression 'work of the law' indicates overlap with Torah.[41] In light of what he has argued in Romans 1:18-32 regarding human depravity, Paul must be thinking of the moral core of the Torah, that is, the Decalogue. Supporting this identification is what Paul goes on to say in Romans 2:15, 'while their conscience also bears witness, and their conflicting thoughts accuse or even excuse them.' By 'conscience' Paul is thinking of the aspect of the human personality that not only informs one of his duty before God but also gives pleasure or inflicts pain when one conforms to or deviates from that duty.[42] To conscience, the inner 'thoughts' of a person join their testimony, either to 'accuse' or 'excuse' that person. The legal terminology that Paul uses ('witness,' 'accuse,'

---

39. James D. G. Dunn, *Romans 1-8* (WBC 38A; Nashville: Thomas Nelson, 1988), 98-9; *Pace* N. T. Wright, 'The Law in Romans 2,' in *Paul and the Mosaic Law* (ed. James D. G. Dunn; Grand Rapids: Eerdmans, 2001), 146. For a survey of recent discussion, see now Colin G. Kruse, *Paul's Letter to the Romans* (PNTC; Grand Rapids: Eerdmans, 2012), 136-40.

40. '"By nature" is contrasted with what is derived from external sources and refers to that which is engraven on our natural constitution. What is done "by nature" is done by native instinct or propension, by spontaneous impulse as distinguished from what is induced by forces extraneous to ourselves,' John Murray, *The Epistle to the Romans* (2 vols.; NICNT; Grand Rapids: Eerdmans, 1959, 1965), 1:73. Compare Hultgren, *Romans*, 117-18.

41. 'There is then an overlap between what God has given through the law (the Torah) and the moral consciousness of the Gentiles,' Hultgren, *Romans*, 117. See also Murray, *Romans*, 1:74-5; Cranfield, *Romans 1-8*, 158.

42. Kruse, *Romans*, 141.

'excuse') anticipates the Last Judgment ('the day when, according to my gospel, God judges the secrets of men by Christ Jesus'). The transactions of conscience are echoes of divine, eschatological judgment.[43] As with the revelation that Paul describes in Romans 1, the revelation of Romans 2:14-15 is continual and successfully reaches all human beings.

Taking Paul's statements in Romans 1 and Romans 2 together, we see that God reveals Himself to all human beings, in every age and place of the world. He reveals not only His being and character but also the moral obligations to which all human beings are subject. We encounter this revelation outside of ourselves, in the world that God made and upholds. We also encounter this revelation within ourselves, in our own persons, which God also made and upholds. No human being is without this revelation since, in Calvin's words, 'men cannot open their eyes without being compelled to see him.'[44] Neither is the effectiveness of this revelation a function of men's native intelligence or education.[45] The great tragedy of the human condition is that human beings, through sin, have turned their backs against this God in willful and culpable rebellion.

A third passage in which the Bible testifies to God's self-revelation in the natural order is Paul's sermon to the Lystrans in Acts 14. After Paul heals a man 'crippled from birth [who] had never walked' (Acts 14:8), the Lystrans conclude that Paul and Barnabas are 'gods [who] have come down to us in the likeness of men' (14:11). As the Lystrans prepare to offer sacrifices to Paul and Barnabas, the missionaries intervene by addressing them in a brief speech recorded by Luke.

> Men, why are you doing these things? We also are men of like nature with you, and we bring you good news, that you should turn from these vain things to a living God, who made the heaven and the earth and the sea and all that is in them. In past generations he allowed all the nations to walk

---

43. What Paul describes in these verses, then, is one way in which the 'wrath of God' is being manifested in the world now, so, rightly, Shedd, *Dogmatic Theology*, 1:62.

44. Calvin, *Institutes of the Christian Religion*, 1:52 (=1.5.1). In the same section, Calvin observes, 'Yet ... wherever you cast your eyes, there is no spot in the universe wherein you cannot discern at least some sparks of his glory.'

45. 'But upon his individual works he has engraved unmistakable marks of his glory, so clear and so prominent that even unlettered and stupid folk cannot plead the excuse of ignorance,' ibid.

in their own ways. Yet he did not leave himself without witness, for he did good by giving you rains from heaven and fruitful seasons, satisfying your hearts with food and gladness. (Acts 14:15-17)

Paul and Barnabas first deny that they are divine or suprahuman – 'we also are men of like nature with you.' Affirming their common humanity, the missionaries point the Lystrans to their Maker. He is the 'living God, who made the heaven and the earth and the sea and all that is in them.' Even though He has permitted human beings to 'walk in their own ways,' that is, in the way of idolatry, He was never 'without witness.' He has shown himself good by doing 'good' to the undeserving. Paul points specifically to God's provision of 'rains' and 'fruitful seasons.' Furthermore, this abundant provision has occasioned a second gift of God to His creatures, namely, the 'satisf[action]' of their 'hearts with food and gladness.'

In this brief speech, Paul identifies God as the Creator and Sustainer of all things. Most of his address is taken up with the providence of God. Paul reflects on divine providence in two ways. First, God is sovereign over 'all the nations,' even in 'past generations.' He directs human affairs. Second, God is good and demonstrates His goodness in amply providing for the physical needs and inward satisfaction of His rebellious creatures. This ongoing and universal display of goodness is a 'witness' to His existence and character. Paul concludes that that goodness should have led human beings to repentance (cf. Rom. 2:4).[46]

A fourth passage in which the Bible addresses the general revelation of God to human beings comes from a slightly later period in Paul's missionary journeys.[47] In Acts 17:22-31, Paul addresses a body of cultured and educated pagans in Athens, namely, the 'Areopagus.'[48] While acts of spontaneous idolatrous devotion had prompted Paul's speech in Lystra, the plurality of entrenched idols in Athens prompts Paul's Areopagus speech. An altar inscribed 'To the unknown god'

---

46. On Paul's characterization of this message as 'good news' to the Lystrans, see my *A Study Commentary on the Acts of the Apostles* (Darlington, UK: EP, 2015), 340-2.

47. Some of the material that follows has been drawn from my *Acts*, 419-25.

48. The 'Areopagus' denoted both a location and a body of persons in ancient Athens. The Areopagus consisted of 'retired magistrates' and assumed the 'role [of] the guardian of traditional Athenian ways,' J. Camp, cited at Eckhard Schnabel, *Early Christian Mission* (2 vols.; Downers Grove, IL: InterVarsity, 2004) 2:1172.

becomes the occasion for Paul's address (Acts 17:23). This altar, for Paul, testifies to the Athenian dissatisfaction with their own idolatrous religion. Paul will proceed to diagnose that dissatisfaction and propose the cure.[49] Paul first addresses the 'truth about God' (17:24-5), then the 'truth about humanity' (17:26-8), and then draws implications of those truths for his Areopagite audience.[50] In Acts 17:24-5, Paul addresses truths about God. God is the Creator of the world and all things in it (17:24). He is the sustainer of all things as well, 'he himself gives to all mankind life and breath and everything' (17:25). As such, He neither dwells in human 'temples' nor stands in need of 'anything,' not least the contributions of 'human hands' (17:24, 25). In Acts 17:26-8, Paul addresses truths about humanity. God has created all human beings who, in turn, descend from 'one man' (17:26). God, in turn, has 'determined allotted periods and the boundaries of their dwelling place' (17:26). In other words, God has sovereignly appointed both the times and places of human habitation. His providence towards humanity has in view the goal of people 'seek[ing] God' who 'is actually not far from each one of us' (17:27). The nearness of God, Paul insists, is something that even pagan writers have acknowledged (17:28).

In Acts 17:29-31, Paul draws two implications for his hearers. The first is that they should not worship idols but worship the true and living God alone. Since, he reasons, we are 'God's offspring,' we should not fashion God after our own image. We must understand God in light of who He truly is and worship Him accordingly. The second is that there is a coming judgment in righteousness. God will hold His 'offspring' accountable for their sin, especially their sin of idolatry.

In this address, Paul makes fundamental observations about God and humanity. Although these observations are taught in Scripture, Paul does not appeal to Scripture to support them. Rather these are truths that are generally accessible to human beings by virtue of their being image-bearers who inhabit a world that God has made and sustains. It is for this reason that Paul is able to cite non-Christian writers in support of crucial planks of his argument.

---

49. For a defense of this interpretation, see my *Acts,* 420-1.

50. The descriptions of the first two sections are those of David Peterson, *Acts* (PNTC; Grand Rapids: Eerdmans, 2009), 495-6, but the versification differs from Peterson's outline.

We have looked at four passages that provide sustained reflection upon God's self-revelation through the media of created things. These media include the natural world as created and sustained by God, the human person, and human history. The Scripture understands this revelation to reach all human beings, regardless of where in the world they live or when in human history they have lived. People receive this revelation regardless of their educational attainments – the unlearned and the educated alike know God from the things that are made. It is not an overstatement to say that a constituent aspect of our humanity is exposure to and reception of this revelation.

Content of Natural Revelation

We are now in a position to reflect further on the content of natural revelation. Since God reveals Himself through the things that are made, then what particularly does God reveal about Himself to human beings? We may look at that revelation along two lines. The first concerns God's own being, attributes, and works. The creation reveals the existence of the God who made and who sustains the works of His hands. In writing to the Romans, Paul identifies the 'invisible attributes' of God, namely, 'his eternal power and divine nature' as being revealed through the creation (Rom. 1:20). It is in his addresses to the Areopagus and to the Lystrans that Paul testifies to God's self-manifestation of His being and attributes in His works of creation and providence. In his Areopagus address, Paul distinguishes God from what He has 'made,' namely, 'the world and everything in it' (17:24). By virtue of His being Creator, He is 'Lord of heaven and earth' and stands in no need of the creature ('[he] does not live in temples made by man, nor is he served by human hands, as though he needed anything,' 17:24, 25). On the contrary, creatures stand in constant need of His sustenance and provision ('since he gives to all mankind life and breath and everything,' 17:25). His providence extends to the world of human affairs. He has not only made humanity to dwell on 'all the face of the earth,' but He has also 'determined allotted periods and the boundaries of their dwelling place' (17:26).

God, then, is the Creator and Sustainer of all things. He exists independently of the creature and is in no way dependent upon the creation. Even so, He is not removed from the creature, but intimately involved in the life and well being of the creation, not least human beings. In his address to the Lystrans, Paul stresses the goodness of God to human beings. God not only provides for our physical needs, but also 'satisfy[ies] ... hearts with food and gladness' (14:17). The remarkable thing about this perpetual display of divine goodness is that its recipients 'walk in their own ways' (14:16). This divine goodness to humanity, then, is properly an expression of God's benevolence. That is to say, it is an expression of His will to do good to His creatures without regard to humanity's desert.[51]

The second line of general revelation concerns the duty that human beings owe to God. It is this dimension of God's self-revelation to which Paul devotes particular attention in Romans. All human beings, Paul argues, know and are obliged to obey what Paul calls the 'work of the law,' that is, the moral core of the law that God revealed to Israel (Rom. 2:15). People have access to this law through 'conscience,' that working of the soul that not only informs one of his duty to God, but also affords pleasure and inflicts pain upon obedience and disobedience, respectively (Rom. 2:15). Coupled with this sense of obligation to divine law is awareness of a future state of rewards and punishments, into which one enters in consequence of final, divine judgment. Peoples' 'conflicting thoughts accuse or even excuse them on that day when, according to my gospel, God judges the secrets of men by Christ Jesus' (Rom. 2:16). Humans 'know God's decree that those who practice such things [i.e., the sins of Rom. 1:18-31] deserve to die ...' (Rom. 1:32).

There are, therefore, distinctly theological and ethical lines of natural revelation.[52] The opening lines of the Westminster Confession of Faith capture the Bible's testimony to the character of God's self- revelation in the world, 'the light of nature and the works of creation and providence do ... manifest the goodness, wisdom, and power of God.'[53] In a similar

---

51. Turretin, *Institutes,* 1:242 (=3.20.5).

52. Just as the study of the theological line of natural revelation is often comprehended under 'natural theology,' so the study of the ethical line of natural revelation is comprehended under 'natural law.' On natural law in the Reformed tradition, see now Susan Schreiner, *The Theater of His Glory: Nature and the Natural Order in the Thought of John Calvin* (Grand Rapids: Baker, 2001); David VanDrunen, *Natural Law and the Two Kingdoms: A Study in the Development of Reformed Social Thought* (Grand Rapids: Eerdmans, 2010); Stephen J. Grabill, *Rediscovering the Natural Law in Reformed Theological Ethics* (Grand Rapids: Eerdmans, 2006).

53. WCF 1.1. Compare the testimony of Belgic Confession, Art. 2; Heidelberg Catechism 122; Gallic Confession Art. 2.

way, Calvin noted in the century before the Westminster Assembly, 'men cannot open their eyes without being compelled to see him ... [the] marks of his glory [are] so clear and so prominent that even unlettered and stupid folk cannot plead the excuse of ignorance.'[54]

For all that God reveals of Himself in natural revelation, it is not a complete or full revelation of God. That is to say, there are objective limitations to natural revelation. We may address three such limitations. The first is that there are some things that God does not reveal about Himself in general revelation. God reveals His existence and His attributes, but He does not reveal, for example, His Triunity. There is no distinct revelation of the Person of the Son or the Person of the Spirit in nature.[55] This limitation does not render untrue what God reveals of Himself in nature. But it does render it incomplete.[56]

Or, we may consider the revelation of God's goodness. We have seen that part of God's self-revelation in nature is His benevolent provision for the physical and inward well-being of human beings. We term this provision 'benevolence' because it is without reference to the character of the recipients. In fact, as Paul testifies elsewhere, human beings are subject to God's wrath for their sin – a matter that is equally a testimony of God's self-revelation in the world. While general revelation reveals the goodness of God, it does not disclose the saving mercies of God that are tendered in the gospel. We might even say that natural revelation provides hints that there may be mercy, in so far as God has thus far

---

54. Calvin, *Institutes,* 1:52 (=1.5.1).

55. Bavinck, *Reformed Dogmatics,* 1:313. Some theologians, notably Jonathan Edwards, have concluded that 'our natural reason is sufficient to tell us that there are these three [i.e., "God, and the idea of God, and the inclination, affection, or love of God"] in God, and we can think of no more,' in *WJE,* vol. 21, *Writings on the Trinity, Grace, and Faith,* ed. Sang Hyun Lee (New Haven: Yale University, 2003), 131-2. Edwards' claim follows his survey of biblical teaching on the Trinity. It is doubtful, then, that he is claiming that natural reason, unaided by special revelation, is capable of arriving at the Triunity of God. Even so, Edwards reflects the outer limits of what Reformed theologians have typically granted regarding natural reason's understanding of the nature of God. For antecedents to Edwards' line of reflection, see the literature cited at *WJE,* vol. 13, *The 'Miscellanies,' a-500,* ed. Thomas A. Schafer (New Haven: Yale University, 1994), 256, n. 1, esp. Heinrich Heppe, *Reformed Dogmatics* (rev. and ed., Ernst Bizer; trans. G. T. Thompson; London: Allen & Unwin, 1950; repr., Grand Rapids: Baker, 1978), 106-8.

56. Speaking of natural revelation generally, Johannes Cocceius observes that while 'true ... it is not adequate,' cited at Heppe, *Reformed Dogmatics,* 3.

delayed final judgment. But natural revelation does not open a door of mercy for sinners.[57]

This observation leads to a second and related limitation of natural revelation, one that is frequently observed by Reformed theologians.[58] Natural revelation offers no way of salvation to sinners. It shows human beings what their duty before God is, and it shows them that obedience is rewarded and disobedience punished (Rom. 2:14-15). But to the one who violates that law, there is no provision in general revelation of mercy or salvation. Specifically, there is no provision of atonement for sin, and 'Natural Theology offers no moral force higher than moral suasion.'[59] Natural revelation has no way to deliver sinners from the guilt of their sin or to rescue them from its bondage and corruption.

We may see the same point advanced, in a different light, from the Scripture itself.[60] The Bible teaches that Jesus Christ is the only way that God has opened to salvation (Acts 4:12). The ordinary way in which sinners are saved is through the preaching of Christ crucified and the reception of Christ in the way of repentance and faith (1 Cor. 1:21; Rom. 10:13-15).[61] The Bible not only closes the door to salvation through non-Christian religions, but it also closes the door to salvation through the light of nature.[62] Therefore, both the silence of natural revelation and the testimony of special revelation concur in denying salvation outside of Jesus Christ, by whom alone one may come to the Father (John 14:6).[63]

---

57. See here the judicious comments of William Cunningham, *Theological Lectures on Subjects Connected with Natural Theology, Evidences of Christianity, the Canon and Inspiration of Scripture* (London: James Nisbet & Co., 1878), 116.

58. See, representatively, Calvin, *Institutes*, 1:69-71 (=1.6.1), and Turretin, *Institutes*, 1:9-16 (=1.4).

59. Dabney, *Syllabus*, 76.

60. For what follows, see Hodge, *Systematic Theology*, 1:29-30.

61. In saying 'ordinary,' we affirm that 'elect infants, dying in infancy' and 'all other elect persons who are uncapable of being outwardly called by the ministry of the Word' are not beyond the reach of salvation (WCF 10.3).

62. A point captured by WLC 60, A. 'They who, having never heard the gospel, know not Jesus Christ, and believe not in him, cannot be saved, be they never so diligent to frame their lives according to the light of nature, or the laws of that religion which they profess; neither is there salvation in any other, but in Christ alone, who is the Savior only of his body the church.'

63. Bavinck, *Reformed Dogmatics*, 1:313.

There is a third limitation to natural revelation. This limitation concerns the authority of natural revelation.[64] Natural revelation, since it is divine revelation, is authoritative in itself.[65] Unlike special revelation, however, natural revelation has not been committed by God to writing. There is no inspired and authoritative record of natural revelation to check or to refute errors that humans may make and have made with reference to its teachings.

Reception of Natural Revelation

This last limitation leads to our third question. The Scriptures everywhere testify to the depravity of human thinking. Paul characterizes Gentile unbelievers as walking 'in the futility of their minds. They are darkened in their understanding, alienated from the life of God because of the ignorance that is in them, due to their hardness of heart' (Eph. 4:17-18). In the context of discussing general revelation, Paul comments that 'although [people] knew God, they did not honor him as God or give thanks to him, but they became futile in their thinking, and their foolish hearts were darkened. Claiming to be wise, they became fools ... they exchanged the truth about God for a lie ... God gave them up to a debased mind to do what ought not to be done' (Rom. 1:21-2, 25, 28). Paul is describing the influence and effect of sin upon human thinking. Have human beings so ruined themselves because of sin that they are thereby incapable of knowing anything about God from the world?

Some theologians have been understood to deny the epistemological competency of human beings, apart from the intervention of saving grace, to come to a true understanding of general revelation.[66] Cornelius Van Til,

---

64. For a different argument in support of this point, see Dabney, *Syllabus,* 76-7.

65. Shedd speaks of 'general or unwritten revelation, though *trustworthy,*' as '*not infallible*' since 'natural religion cannot be any more trustworthy than the human intellect itself is,' and 'the human intellect cannot be infallible, unless it is preserved from all error by an extraordinary exertion of a Divine power,' *Dogmatic Theology,* 1:66 (emphasis original). While the mind, Shedd concedes, may 'reach a high degree of certainty and validity,' it 'never reaches the point of absolute infallibility,' ibid. Ascribing fallibility to revelation, however, invites the confusion of what is objectively revealed with the subjective reception of that revelation. One may agree with Shedd's statements about the human mind without attributing fallibility to revelation proper.

66. To be distinguished from other theologians, such as Karl Barth, who categorically denied general revelation altogether, on which see Bruce A. Demarest, *General Revelation: Historical Views and Contemporary Issues* (Grand Rapids: Zondervan, 1982), 122-9.

for instance, has been understood along these lines.⁶⁷ Without entering into the debates about Van Til's epistemology, we may take up these debates' underlying question – has sin so influenced the mind that the fallen mind is rendered incapable of knowing God through His self-revelation in the world?

Answering this question requires negotiating two classes of statements in Scripture. The first is that human thinking has been profoundly influenced through sin. Paul's statements in Romans 1 and Ephesians 4 are but a few of Scripture's statements testifying to the noetic effects of sin. Such is the depth of the human condition that Paul can say that unbelievers do 'not know God' (Gal. 4:8; cf. 1 Thess. 4:5; 2 Thess. 1:8; 1 Cor. 1:21). The second class of statements insists that sinful human beings do know God – 'although they knew God' (Rom. 1:21). This class of statements is important to Paul's thinking because this knowledge of God renders all people accountable to God (Rom. 1:21, 28-32). If human beings do not in some sense know God as He has revealed Himself in creation, on what basis will God hold them accountable for rebellion against Himself?⁶⁸ How, then, do we reconcile these apparently contradictory statements? Do sinners know God or do they not?

The resolution to this difficulty is to appreciate the distinct senses in which the Scripture speaks of knowledge. At one level, knowledge consists of intellection by the faculty of understanding. At a related but distinguishable level, knowledge involves one's favorable disposition to the person or object known.⁶⁹ Sin leaves the integrity of the faculty of understanding unimpaired. But sin results in the depravity of the

---

67. So R. C. Sproul, John Gerstner, and Arthur Lindsley, *Classical Apologetics: A Rational Defense of the Christian Faith and a Critique of Presuppositional Apologetics* (Grand Rapids: Zondervan, 1984); and Demarest, *General Revelation,* 147-56. For a response to Sproul, Gerstner, and Lindsley, see the review of John M. Frame, 'Van Til and the Ligonier Apologetic,' *WTJ* 47.2 (1985): 279-99, repr. in John M. Frame, *Cornelius Van Til: An Analysis of His Thought* (Phillipsburg, NJ: P&R, 1995), 401-22. Even as Frame critiques Ligonier, he concedes that 'Van Til's writings do pose some difficulty here ... His representations, I think, are not fully consistent. What is more, he has admitted some difficulty in this area,' *Analysis,* 414. For more recent constructions of Van Tilian epistemology, see now K. Scott Oliphint and Lane G. Tipton, eds., *Revelation and Reason: New Essays in Reformed Apologetics* (Phillipsburg, NJ: P&R, 2007).

68. Put differently, denying that unbelievers know God, in this sense, lessens or even eliminates their accountability to God.

69. For a theological articulation of this classical anthropological distinction see, representatively, A. A. Hodge, *Outlines of Theology* (rev. ed.; 1879: repr. Edinburgh: Banner of Truth, 1972), 284.

disposition that governs the soul's faculties. As such, the disposition is implacably hostile to God. Therefore, all human beings 'know' God in the sense that they grasp His existence, attributes, and righteous requirements from natural revelation. But they 'do not know' God in the sense that, out of sinful hatred to Him, they abhor and reject the God made known to them in natural revelation.[70] Therefore, 'they exchange the truth about God for a lie' (Rom. 1:25).

Purposes of Natural Revelation

The effect of natural revelation upon a mind governed by sin, then, is to occasion the aggravation of that person's guilt before God. In light of that state of affairs, we may well ask our fourth and final question, what are God's purposes in natural revelation? We should first register the fact that this circumstance in no way reflects injustice on the part of God. Natural revelation is designed, in Paul's words, that people 'should seek God, in the hope that they might feel their way toward him and find him [who] is actually not far from each one of us' (Acts 17:27). His patient delay of judgment is designed to lead men to repentance (Rom. 2:4). If sinful people misuse natural revelation, that misuse is not God's fault.

What, then, are the purposes or objectives of general revelation? We may identify several purposes. First, general revelation supplies an ongoing testimony to human beings of the character of God, and particularly of the 'goodness of God towards sinners unworthy even of these remains of light.'[71] Second, the revelation of the righteous requirements that God imposes upon men, and of the certainty of a final judgment serve to restrain sin in a fallen world. As such, the world of fallen humanity is not as wicked as it would otherwise be.[72] Third, general revelation serves, as we have seen, to establish the inexcusability of human rebellion against God. Conscience serves now to anticipate the verdict of the judgment of the Last Day (Rom. 2:15, 16).[73] Fourth,

---

70. Correspondingly, in regeneration, what is repaired is not the faculty of understanding, *per se*, but the soul's disposition. The soul now loves what it formerly hated (God), and hates what it formerly loved (sin). Set on this new foundation, the soul's faculties now function properly, in the way that God created them to function.

71. Turretin, *Institutes*, 1:10 (=1.4.4).

72. ibid.

73. ibid.

the incomplete character of general revelation, particularly its silence with respect to an avenue of saving mercy from God to sinners, should incline human beings to seek further revelation from God.[74] Fifth, natural revelation, as we shall see further in the next chapter, provides the necessary context within which special revelation is given and is to be understood by its recipients. Absent natural revelation, special revelation is meaningless.

We may, furthermore, point to ways in which general revelation is helpful to believers in particular. As the seventeenth century scholastic theologian J. H. Heidegger observes, believers 'already taught from God's word about the true God and the way of His salvation' should 'look up more also from God's admirable works to His power, wisdom and goodness, worship His majesty and put all their trust in the one and only God of Israel, who alone doeth such things.'[75] Everywhere the believer goes in this world, and at all times, he sees the works of the God he knows from Scripture. This sight should prompt the believer to respond to his God in renewed trust and devotion. As Bavinck notes, 'Christians find themselves at home also in the world. They are not strangers there and see the God who rules creation as none other than the one they address as Father in Christ.'[76]

Furthermore, attentiveness to God's self-revelation in the world is a help to believers as they bear witness to unbelievers. The fact that we live, as image-bearers, in God's world gives us a 'point of contact with all those who bear the name "human".'[77] Our knowledge of God and of ourselves from general revelation therefore helps us to engage unbelievers apologetically and evangelistically. Under the guidance of Scripture, we may point unbelievers to truths about God, the world, and themselves from general revelation.

Finally, general revelation performs another valuable service to faith.

> The rich significance of general revelation comes out in the fact that it keeps nature and grace, creation and re-creation, the world of reality and the world of values, inseparably connected. Without general revelation,

---

74. So, rightly, Dabney, *Syllabus*, 77-8.
75. As cited at Heppe, *Reformed Dogmatics*, 4.
76. Bavinck, *Reformed Dogmatics*, 1:321.
77. ibid.

special revelation loses its connectedness with the whole cosmic existence and life ... [R]eligion becomes alien to human nature. Christianity becomes a sectarian phenomenon and is robbed of its catholicity. In a word, grace is then opposed to nature ... By contrast, general revelation maintains the unity of nature and grace, of the world and the kingdom of God, of the natural order and the moral order, of creation and re-creation, of *physis* and ethos, of virtue and happiness, of holiness and blessedness, and in all these things the unity of the divine being.[78]

Such an integration, of course, is only possible if one both possesses and rightly understands the nature and content of special revelation. In the next chapter, we will begin to give attention to what the Bible reveals about itself.

---

78. Bavinck, *Reformed Dogmatics,* 1:322. We see this integration biblically reflected in Psalm 19, in which David proceeds from the heavens declaring the glory of God to the Torah and its revelation to human beings. 'The psalmist moves in a climactic fashion from macrocosm to microcosm, from the universe and its glory to the individual in humility before God. But the climax lies in the microcosm, not in the heavenly roar of praise. For the heavens declare the glory of God, but the law declares the will of God for mankind, the creature. And though the vast firmament so high above us declares God's praise, it is the *Torah* of God alone that reveals to mankind that he has a place in the universal scheme of things,' Craigie, *Psalms 1-50,* 183.

Revelation: Part 2

In the last chapter, we began a study of 'revelation.' Revelation is God's sovereign self-disclosure to His reasonable creatures. This revelation, however, admits of an important distinction, that of natural (or general) revelation and special revelation. Natural revelation, we have seen, is God's self-disclosure through the works of His hands. In it, human beings discern the wisdom, power, and goodness of God. This revelation is not a complete disclosure of the being and works of God, but it is a true and accurate one. God reveals enough of Himself to render human beings inescapably aware of His existence. As such, all people are accountable to the God whom they know from the world. But general revelation does not reveal to human beings the way of salvation. Its disclosure of the divine benevolence does not extend to God's saving mercies in Jesus Christ.[1] That disclosure comes through what has been termed special revelation.

In this chapter, we will give consideration to special revelation. First, we will think about special revelation in relation to general revelation, and particularly its necessity in relation to general

---

1. 'Not that we would assert and undertake to prove *positively upon principles of reason,* that God could not, in point of fact, pardon the sins of penitent sinners, or deny that the light of nature affords any grounds for believing that God is placable and ready to forgive. But it has been often proved by the defenders of revelation—and this is sufficient— that it is impossible to reach by the light of nature, without revelation, to a certain and assured conviction that God will pardon sin,' William Cunningham, *Theological Lectures on Subjects Connected with Natural Theology, Evidences of Christianity, the Canon and Inspiration of Scripture* (London: James Nisbet & Co., 1878), 116.

revelation. Second, we will explore special revelation's defining features, and the modes or forms in which God has conveyed special revelation. Third, we will see that special revelation did not come to human beings in scattershot fashion. It assumes, rather, a deliberate redemptive-historical shape and structure. That formal shape and structure, furthermore, is critical to understanding and appreciating the content of special revelation.

The Necessity of Special Revelation

Special revelation is incomprehensible apart from general revelation. That is to say, general revelation provides the context necessary to understand special revelation. But, we have noted, there are some limitations to general revelation. For one thing, general revelation makes an adequate but incomplete revelation of God's character and works.[2] Furthermore, the depravity of humanity twists and corrupts the revelation that people receive through the natural world. As Calvin notes, 'while some may evaporate in their own superstitions and others deliberately and wickedly desert God, yet all degenerate from the true knowledge of him. And so it happens that no real piety remains in the world.'[3]

These limitations are, on the one hand, inherent to natural revelation, and, on the other hand, a consequence of human depravity. When we turn to consider special revelation proper, we may better understand the limitations of natural revelation, and the consequent need for special revelation. One of the virtues of special revelation is that it objectively corrects humans' misapprehensions of natural revelation. Calvin expresses this point in a memorable illustration.

> Just as old or bleary-eyed men and those with weak vision, if you thrust before them a most beautiful volume, even if they recognize it to be some sort of writing, yet can scarcely construe two words, but with the aid of spectacles will begin to read distinctly; so Scripture, gathering up the

---

[2]. 'What natural religion teaches about God, although imperfect is not therefore untrue,' Heinrich Heppe, *Reformed Dogmatics* (rev. and ed., Ernst Bizer; trans. G. T. Thompson; London: Allen & Unwin, 1950; repr., Grand Rapids: Baker, 1978), 3.

[3]. John Calvin, *Institutes of the Christian Religion* (ed. John T. McNeill; trans. Ford L. Battles; 2 vols.; LCC; Philadelphia: Westminster, 1960), 1:47 (=1.4.1). Calvin goes on to say in this same paragraph that human beings are by no means 'free ... from blame' for this 'degenerat[ion].' People 'do not ... apprehend God as he offers himself, but imagine him as they have fashioned him in their own presumption,' ibid.

otherwise confused knowledge of God in our minds, having dispersed our dullness, clearly shows us the true God.⁴

As corrective lenses compensate for the defects of poor vision, so the Scriptures help us to overcome the ways in which sin has adversely affected our understanding of divine things from natural revelation.

Special revelation not only reveals with greater clarity and fullness the truths revealed in natural revelation, but it also discloses truths about the being and works of God that are otherwise inaccessible to human beings. Turretin addresses this characteristic of special revelation well.

> Although natural revelation may hand over different things concerning God and his attributes, will and works, yet it cannot teach us things sufficient for the saving knowledge of God without a supernatural verbal revelation. Indeed it shows that God exists (*quod sit Deus*), and of what nature (*qualis*), both in unity of essence and as possessed of different attributes, but does not tell us who he is individually and with regard to the persons. This will (as contained in the law), it imperfectly and obscurely manifests (Rom. 2:14,15), but the mystery of the gospel is entirely concealed. It displays the works of creation and providence (Ps. 19:1-3; Acts 14:15-17; 17:23-28; Rom. 1:19, 20), but does not rise up to the works of redemption and grace which can become known to us by the word alone (Rom. 10:17; 16:25, 26).⁵

Special revelation is necessary, then, for at least three reasons. It corrects misunderstandings about natural revelation. It further and more clearly reveals truths already revealed in natural revelation. It reveals truths that are not at all revealed in natural revelation.

We may refine this observation further. Reformed writers in the period of the Reformation and post-Reformation particularly emphasized the need for *written* special revelation. They did so, of course, in response to Rome's claims that unwritten traditions stood alongside and (the Reformers maintained) above the written Word of God.⁶ In the

---

4. Calvin, *Institutes*, 1:70 (=1.6.1). Calvin employs the metaphor of 'spectacles' to similar use at *Institutes*, 1:160-1 (=1.14.1). There is an important hermeneutical principle expressed here, to which we shall return in a later chapter. It is that special revelation must govern our interpretation of natural revelation.

5. Turretin, *Institutes of Elenctic Theology* (3 vols.; Phillipsburg, NJ: P&R, 1992-7), 1:56-7 (=2.1.6).

6. See, representatively, Turretin, *Institutes*, 1:57 (=2.2.1). For a fuller discussion of the historical development of these Protestant claims during this period, see Richard

seventeenth century, Reformed theology offered at least three reasons for the necessity of written, that is inscripturated, special revelation. These reasons are the 'preservation of the word,' 'its vindication,' and 'its propagation.'[7] In reflecting on the necessity of special revelation, the nineteenth century theologian Abraham Kuyper proposed four benefits that accrued to a specifically *written* word.[8] The first, he argued, is 'durability.' That is to say, 'writing ... relieves the spoken word of its transitoriness.'[9] In this regard, Kuyper continues, 'writing alone has created the possibility of collecting human thought, of congealing it, of handing it down from age to age, and of maintaining the unity of our human consciousness in the continuity of the generations.' Since special revelation is for 'the *world*, and hence for the generations of all ages until the end is come,' it was necessary that it be committed to writing.[10]

The second benefit of the written word is that it is 'catholic,' that is, 'bound by neither place nor nation it overcomes the limitation of the local.'[11] If durability addresses conceivable limitations afforded by time, then catholicity addresses conceivable limitations afforded by geography or space. This benefit, Kuyper notes, answers the reality that God has

---

A. Muller, *Post Reformation Reformed Dogmatics: The Rise and Development of Reformed Orthodoxy, ca. 1520 to ca. 1725* (4 vols.; Grand Rapids: Baker, 2003), 2:171-6, 200-1. We will revisit the theological issues undergirding this dispute in our discussion of the sufficiency of Scripture in Chapter 5.

7. Turretin, *Institutes*, 1:58 (=2.2.6). These reasons are given expression in the opening paragraph of the Westminster Confession of Faith, 'for the better preserving and propagating of the truth, and for the more sure establishment and comfort of the Church against the corruption of the flesh, and the malice of Satan and of the world, to commit the same [i.e., special revelation] wholly unto writing: which maketh the Holy Scripture to be most necessary ...' (1.1.). Calvin anticipates many of these reasons in his discussion of the subject at *Institutes*, 1:69-74 (=1.6.1-4). For a contemporary statement of many of these reasons, see René Pache, *The Inspiration and Authority of Scripture* (trans. Helen I. Needham; Chicago: Moody, 1969), 32-4.

8. The following derives from Abraham Kuyper, *Principles of Sacred Theology* (trans. J. Hendrik de Vries; 1898; repr., Grand Rapids: Eerdmans, 1954), 405-12.

9. Kuyper, *Principles of Sacred Theology*, 407. Curiously, Kuyper's argument takes a Platonizing turn when he commends writing for 'set[ting] free ... human thought ... from the process of time. By writing, human thought approaches the eternal, the enduring, and to a certain extent, impresses upon itself a Divine stamp,' ibid.

10. Kuyper, *Principles of Sacred Theology*, 408. Emphasis original.

11. ibid.

loved the world (cf. John 3:16) and that He has appointed the gospel to be preached to all the nations (cf. Acts 1:8).[12]

Third, written special revelation carries the benefit of 'fixedness.' 'Unwritten tradition,' on the other hand, is invariably characterized by 'injurious multiformity.'[13] Since the gospel calls us 'to hold true to what we have attained' (Phil. 3:16), then our 'rule' of faith and practice must be fixed. It must not be subject to the vicissitudes of change.[14]

A fourth and related virtue of written special revelation is 'purity.' Special revelation is not only addressed to sinners but it 'directs itself against the mind and inclination of the sinner.'[15] In other words, sinful recipients of special revelation have a vested, sinful interest in corrupting or otherwise adapting that revelation to accommodate their love for sin. Non-written revelation would be particularly susceptible to such modifications.[16]

Kuyper notes that the Reformed doctrine of the necessity of a written special revelation highlights an important difference between Protestantism and Rome.

> So long as the revelation is handed down by oral tradition only, the great multitude was and ever remained dependent upon a priestly order or hierarchy to impart to them the knowledge of this revelation. Hence there ever stood a man between us and God. For which reason it is entirely natural that the Roman hierarchy opposes rather than favors the spread of the printed Bible. And it behooves us, in the very opposite sense, to confess, that the Divine revelation, in order to reach immediately those who were called to life, *had* to assume the form of writing, and that only by *printed* writing could it enter upon its fullest mission of power.[17]

Roman Catholicism, of course, does not categorically reject written revelation. In supplementing this revelation with unwritten revelation, however, it necessarily interjects a *medium* between the individual

---

12. Kuyper, *Principles of Sacred Theology*, 409.

13. Kuyper, *Principles of Sacred Theology*, 410. Kuyper recognizes that the transformation that tradition undergoes may in fact 'occur unconsciously or without ill intent, but in every case it breaks the working power of the transmitted revelation,' ibid.

14. ibid.

15. ibid., 411.

16. ibid.

17. ibid., 412. Emphasis original.

and God. Even within Protestantism, there have been attempts to supplement the Bible with what are said to be later and additional revelations, whether through dreams, prophecies, or other modes of alleged revelation. It is important to recognize, with Kuyper, that all such claims to unwritten revelation effectively compromise the Protestant principle of the soul's unmediated access to God through Jesus Christ.[18] The form of special revelation as written complements and is in fact necessitated by the leading concern of the material content of special revelation, that is, the salvation of sinners through Jesus Christ alone.[19]

Before we turn to the nature and contents of special revelation, we should offer some concluding reflections on the relationship between general and special revelation.[20] As Warfield has noted, the 'two species or stages of revelation should not be set in opposition to one another,' for 'they constitute together a unitary whole, and each is incomplete without the other.'[21] The 'relation is not one of contrast and opposition, but rather one of supplement and completion.'[22] General revelation, Warfield continues, 'is rooted in creation and the relations with His intelligent creatures into which God has brought Himself by giving them being. Its object is to realize the end of man's creation, to be

---

18. We will address such claims more fully in Chapter 5.

19. This is not to say, of course, that all special revelation within redemptive history has been committed to writing. As we will see, God has given special revelation to His people through modes other than writing. God, furthermore, did not purpose to preserve all the special revelation that He delivered through non-written modes. But, in the progress of redemptive history, God proceeded to commit His self-revelation to writing. Note the perceptive observation of Calvin, '[I]n order that truth might abide forever in the world with a continuing succession of teaching and survive through the ages, the same oracles he had given to the patriarchs, it was his pleasure to have recorded, as it were, on public tablets. With this intent the law was published, and the prophets afterward added as its interpreters,' *Institutes*, 1:71 (=1.6.2). On the circumstances that permitted the 'church before Moses' to flourish without the 'written word,' and that required the church in subsequent times to have written revelation, see Turretin, *Institutes*, 1:58-9 (=2.2.7).

20. What follows is dependent on the reflections of Benjamin B. Warfield, 'The Biblical Idea of Revelation,' in *The Works of Benjamin B. Warfield* (10 vols.; New York: Oxford University, 1932), 1:7.

21. ibid. Compare the almost identical statement at Warfield, 'Christianity and Revelation,' in *Selected Shorter Writings of Benjamin B. Warfield* (ed. John E. Meeter; 2 vols.; Phillipsburg, N.J.: P&R, 1970-3), 1:27.

22. Warfield, 'Christianity and Revelation,' in *SSW*, 1:27.

attained only through knowledge of God and perfect and unbroken communion with Him.'²³ For Warfield, special revelation was necessitated upon 'the entrance of sin into the world, destroying this communion with God and obscuring the knowledge of Him derived from Nature.'²⁴ (In fact, we will observe below the presence of special revelation *before* the fall.) Furthermore, it is not as though special revelation has obviated general revelation. 'Without general revelation, special revelation would lack that basis in the fundamental knowledge of God as the mighty and wise, righteous and good, maker and ruler of all things, apart from which the further revelation of this great God's interventions in the world for the salvation of sinners could not be either intelligible, credible, or operative.'²⁵ Special revelation is necessary, but that necessity in no way suggests that general revelation is either intrinsically defective or dispensable given the advent of special revelation.²⁶ Grace perfects or completes nature. It does not obliterate or bypass nature.²⁷

Definition of Special Revelation

We may now turn to the nature and contents of special revelation. It is important to stress at the outset that special revelation is revelation no less than general revelation is revelation. That is to say, it is the

---

23. Warfield, 'The Biblical Idea of Revelation,' in *Works*, 1.7.

24. ibid.

25. ibid., 1.7.

26. The indispensability of this connection is evident in the classical distinction between 'simple (pure) articles' and 'mixed articles.' The former 'rest purely upon [special revelation],' while the latter find testimony in both general and special revelation, Heppe, *Reformed Dogmatics*, 11. The doctrine of the Trinity would be a classical and generally undisputed example of the former. The doctrine of divine benevolence, of the latter. God's goodness is evident in general revelation, but His goodness finds supreme expression in the cross which is alone revealed in special revelation. As Turretin notes, 'to be able to know God as merciful by a general mercy tending to some temporal good and the delay of punishment is far different from being able to know him as merciful by a mercy special and saving in Christ after a satisfaction has been made. To be able to know him as placable and benign is different from being able to know him as actually appeased or certainly to be appeased,' *Institutes* 1:12-13 (=1.4.11). See the brief and general articulation of the doctrine at Turretin, *Institutes*, 1:8 (=1.3.10).

27. 'Nature precedes grace; grace perfects nature. Reason is perfected by faith, faith presupposes nature,' Herman Bavinck, *Reformed Dogmatics* (ed. John Bolt; trans. John Vriend; 4 vols.; Grand Rapids: Eerdmans, 2003), 1:322.

sovereign self-disclosure of the personal God to His reasonable creatures. The content of this disclosure is otherwise inaccessible to human beings.

But, within the framework of that similarity, there are important differences. We may define special revelation in at least four respects, each of which highlights important distinctions between general and special revelation. We will devote most of our attention to the first distinction and address the remaining ones in brief. First, whereas general revelation reaches all people in all ages at all times, special revelation has limitations of audience. The medium of general revelation is 'the things that have been made' (Rom. 1:20). General revelation, therefore, extends to every rational creature. General revelation, furthermore, is 'clearly perceived,' thus rendering all humans 'without excuse' (Rom. 1:20). Since general revelation has been coming to human beings 'ever since the creation of the world' (Rom. 1:20), there is no generation of humanity that has ever been without access to it.

Special revelation, however, only comes to particular recipients. This is a point that is frequently emphasized in relation to Israel under the law. Through Moses, God tells Israel that they are unique in their nearness to God and in their possession of His law, 'For what great nation is there that has a god so near to it as the LORD our God is to us, whenever we call upon him? And what great nation is there, that has statutes and rules so righteous as all this law that I set before you today?' (Deut. 4:7-8; compare Deut. 4:32-4, 7:6, 10:15). The Psalmist declares, 'He declares his word to Jacob, his statues and rules to Israel. He has not dealt thus with any other nation; they do not know his rules' (Ps. 147:19-20). Through the prophet Amos, God tells Israel, 'you only have I known of all the families of the earth ...' (Amos 3:2).[28] Jesus affirmed this principle to the Samaritan woman when He told her, 'You worship what you do not know; we worship what we know, for salvation is from the Jews' (John 4:22). And the apostle Paul

---

28. When God says that He 'knows' Israel here, He is not saying that He is cognizant or merely aware of them. The verb 'know' here denotes the self-commitment of God to the people whom He has chosen, redeemed, and set apart as holy. Compare, in this context, Hosea 5:3, 13:5. This 'knowledge' entails God's unique self-revelation to Israel. This sense of personal communion and intimacy is reflected in the use of the verb to express the marital act (Gen. 4:1, for example).

enumerated among the many outward privileges of Israel the fact that 'the Jews were entrusted with the oracles of God' (Rom. 3:2). The Israelites uniquely possessed 'the giving of the law, the worship, and the promises' (Rom. 9:4).[29]

Such testimonies as these highlight two important characteristics of special revelation. First, special revelation is predominantly given in Scripture in *covenantal* context.[30] As we shall see in the next section, the Bible reflects a covenantal structure to human history. It is within the context of this covenantal structure that special revelation comes to human beings. The passages we have surveyed above join special revelation to Israel, God's covenant people. This is not to say that the entirety of special revelation documented in the Bible is directly addressed to the covenant people of God. God speaks, for instance, to the pagan king Abimelech in a dream (Gen. 20:3); to Balaam, a pagan prophet who was not part of Israel and whom the Scripture denounces for his sin of seeking financial profit through prophetic activity (Num. 22-4; 2 Pet. 2:15-16); and to the Babylonian king Nebuchadnezzar in a dream subsequently interpreted by the prophet Daniel (Dan. 4:1-27). But these three instances underscore an important point. Although none of these individuals is a member of God's covenant people, the revelation that they receive is for the benefit of God's covenant people. God's self-revelation to Abimelech preserves the chastity of Sarah and, therefore, the divine promise to raise up through Abraham and Sarah

---

29. For Paul, this principle is reinforced by his consistent characterization of Gentiles (apart from saving grace) as 'darkened in ... understanding, alienated from the life of God because of the ignorance that is in them, due to their hardness of heart' (Eph. 4:18; cf. Rom. 1:18-32). Compare Peter's characterization of Gentiles as bound to 'the futile ways inherited from [their] forefathers' (1 Pet. 1:18).

30. On the covenantal character of special revelation, see now Matthew Barrett, *God's Word Alone: The Authority of Scripture* (Wheaton, IL: Crossway, 2016). Compare Frame, *The Doctrine of the Word of God* (Phillipsburg, NJ: P&R, 2010), 117. Some authors have attempted to argue that Scripture is formally 'covenant canon,' so Michael S. Horton, *The Christian Faith: A Systematic Theology For Pilgrims on the Way* (Grand Rapids: Zondervan, 2011), 151-5. Horton argues 'there can be no covenant without a canon or canon without a covenant. In fact the covenant *is* the canon and vice versa ... The covenant Lord creates a people out of nothing by his speech and shapes, regulates, and defines the covenantal life of his people by his canon,' *The Christian Faith*, 155. Even if one stops short of drawing such a close connection between covenant and canon, one must recognize that God has intended the canon of Scripture to regulate the faith and practice of His covenant people.

a promised offspring.[31] Through Balaam, God brings blessing on His people and frustrates the intentions of the Moabites to curse Israel.[32] Nebuchadnezzar's dream impresses upon Israel that their covenant God is sovereign over the affairs of kings and empires.[33] God intends special revelation, then, to benefit His covenant people whom He has redeemed and has set apart in unique relationship with Himself.[34]

A second and related important characteristic of special revelation to which the passages referenced above testify is that special revelation is fundamentally *communal* or *corporate* in orientation. That is to say, God does not intend special revelation to benefit or profit individuals in isolation from one another. He directs special revelation for the benefit of the covenant community as such. To be sure, God's covenant people is comprised of individuals who, as such, have individual obligations before God. Special revelation certainly speaks to individuals in light of their individual necessities and commitments. But throughout redemptive history special revelation has not come to an aggregate of disassociated individuals, but to individuals whom God has enfolded or incorporated into His people. Even when God reveals Himself to an individual prophet, that revelation is intended for the covenant community to whom God has sent that prophet. During the apostolic age, when prophecy was active in the local churches, Paul could remind the Corinthians that God intended prophecy for the edification of the church, 'the one who prophesies speaks to people for their upbuilding and encouragement and consolation ... the one who prophesies builds up the church (1 Cor. 14:3, 4). Furthermore, Paul stressed, 'prophecy is not for unbelievers but for believers' (1 Cor. 14:22, AT).[35] Contrary

---

31. G. Ch. Aalders, *Genesis* (2 vols.; trans. William Heynen; BSC; Grand Rapids: Zondervan, 1981), 2:31-2.

32. A. Noordtzij, *Numbers* (trans. Ed van der Maas; BSC; Grand Rapids: Zondervan, 1982), 201, 210.

33. Dale Ralph Davis, *The Message of Daniel* (TOTC; Downes Grove, IL: InterVarsity, 2013), 63-7.

34. Citing the examples of the 'dreams sent to Abimelech ... Pharaoh ... Nebuchadnezzar ... and to the soldier in the camp of Midian,' Warfield notes, 'it was in the interests, not of the heathen world, but of the chosen people that they were sent; and these instances derive their significance wholly from this fact,' 'The Biblical Idea of Revelation,' in *Works*, 1.10.

35. The ESV renders this verse, '...prophesy is a sign not for unbelievers but for believers,' noting in its margin, 'Greek lacks *a sign*.'

to popular misconception, God has not intended prophecy either to disclose to particular individuals the answers to the private questions that they may have or to provide individualized guidance to people in the specific circumstances in which they may find themselves. God sends prophets to speak God's own words to the entire covenant community for that community's edification or building up.[36]

It is important at this stage of our discussion to avoid two misunderstandings. In the first place, to say that God has intended special revelation for the covenant community is not to say that God intends that revelation be the exclusive property of His people. The intention of the covenant that God made with Abraham was to bring blessing to 'all the families of the earth' (Gen. 12:3). The New Testament writers stress that this promise has come to fulfillment in the extension of the gospel to the Gentiles (Gal. 3:1-9). In like fashion, God's purpose in specially revealing Himself to His people was that that knowledge would be diffused to the world. In Deuteronomy, after reminding Israel of the privilege of receiving special revelation from God, Moses tells Israel the result of this reception.

> Keep [the LORD's statutes and rules] and do them, for that will be your wisdom and your understanding in the sight of the peoples, who, when they hear all these statutes, will say, 'Surely this great nation is a wise and understanding people.' For what great nation is there that has a god so near to it as the LORD our God is to us, whenever we call upon him? And what great nation is there, that has statutes and rules so righteous as all this law that I set before you today? (Deut. 4:6-8)

The prophets anticipate a wider and intentional diffusion of the saving knowledge of God in connection with the ministry of Christ. In Isaiah, God says to His Servant, 'it is too light a thing that you should be my servant to raise up the tribes of Jacob and to bring back the preserved of Israel; I will make you as a light for the nations, that my salvation may reach to the end of the earth' (Isa. 49:6; cf. Isa. 42:6). This prophecy comes to fulfillment in Jesus Christ. John characterizes the incarnation in these terms, 'the true light, which enlightens everyone, was coming

---

36. Of course in making this point, we affirm and in no way deny that the communal or corporate character of this revelation is suited, by divine intention, to the myriad of circumstances in which individual believers find themselves, 2 Peter :3-4, 2 Timothy 3:16-17.

into the world' (John 1:9). Strikingly, this prophecy also finds fulfillment in the ministry of the Servant's servant, the apostle Paul (see Acts 13:47). Through the apostle to the Gentiles, whom Jesus has commissioned to preach the gospel, 'light' and 'salvation' extend to the 'end of the earth' (cf. Acts 1:8). In this way the prophetic promise comes to pass, 'the earth shall be full of the knowledge of the LORD as the waters cover the sea' (Isa. 11:9; cf. Hab. 2:14).

This extension of the saving light of the world is not accidental. Jesus concludes His ministry on earth with commissions to the apostles. Each of these commissions entails the proclamation of the good news to the nations (see Matt. 28:18-20; Luke 24:44-9; John 20:19-23). The last book of the Bible documents the outcome or fruit of this work. Heaven is populated with 'a great multitude that no one could number, from every nation, from all tribes and peoples and languages, standing before the throne and before the Lamb ... and crying out with a loud voice, "Salvation belongs to our God who sits on the throne, and to the Lamb"' (Rev. 7:9-10).

There is a second misunderstanding to avoid when one affirms that special revelation has the covenant community as its destination. This characteristic of special revelation does not mean that the contents of special revelation are esoteric mysteries into which one must be initiated to understand their meaning. Paul's words to Agrippa, who accused the apostle of madness (Acts 26:24), are instructive, 'I am not out of my mind, most excellent Festus, but I am speaking true and rational words. For the king knows about these things, and to him I speak boldly. For I am persuaded that none of these things has escaped his notice, for this has not been done in a corner' (Acts 26:25-6). Neither the redemptive events to which Paul testifies nor Paul's public proclamation of those events are the private possession of the covenant community. Paul's testimony is 'true and rational' and he testifies to what 'has not been done in a corner.' Paul's ministry in Athens confirms Christianity's willingness not only to proclaim the Christian message to unbelievers, but also to engage unbelief's objections to that message (see Acts 17:16-34). The biblical message advances public claims about objective realities that admit of verification.[37]

---

37. None of this is to deny that an illuminating work of the Holy Spirit is necessary to come to a saving understanding of biblical truth. We will address this work of the Spirit in Chapter 4.

We now turn to a second way in which special revelation differs from general revelation. The content of special revelation differs from that of general revelation. This difference, we have seen, surfaces in two respects. First, where general and special revelation overlap in content, special revelation provides fuller and clearer testimony.[38] Second, special revelation makes known certain truths that are otherwise inaccessible through general revelation. These truths include the Triunity of God, the Incarnation of Christ, the atonement, and the nature of and necessity for the regenerating work of the Holy Spirit.

A third and related point of difference between general and special revelation is that special revelation alone reveals the way in which sinners may be saved. General revelation, we have seen, discloses the holiness and righteousness of God, on the one hand, and the depravity of human beings, on the other. It even points to a general benevolence of God. But it is special revelation alone that reveals the mercies of God in Jesus Christ to sinners. The only revealed way of salvation is provided in special revelation. J. I. Packer helpfully summarizes the heights and limitations of general revelation in this respect.

> General revelation ... lacks redemptive content. It indicates that God punishes sin, but not that he pardons it. It shows forgiveness to be needed without showing it to be possible. It preaches the law without the Gospel. It can condemn, but not save. Any unbeliever who rightly understood it would be driven to despair. However clearly the content of general revelation was grasped, it would by itself provide no adequate basis for fellowship with God.[39]

It is only the cross of Christ, revealed in the gospel, that can provide the salvation that sinners need (1 Cor. 1:20-4).[40] This is a point that Paul

---

38. See our discussion of 'mixed articles' at note 26.

39. J. I. Packer, *God Has Spoken: Revelation and the Bible* (3d ed.; Grand Rapids: Baker, 1994), 55.

40. Note in this connection Westminster Larger Catechism Question and Answer 60, for which 1 Cor. 1:20-4 has been supplied as a prooftext, 'Q. Can they who have never heard the gospel, and so know not Jesus Christ, nor believe in him, be saved by their living according to the light of nature? A. They who, having never heard the gospel, know not Jesus Christ, and believe not in him, cannot be saved, *be they never so diligent to frame their lives according to the light of nature, or the laws of that religion which they profess;* neither is there salvation in any other, but in Christ alone, who is the Savior only of his body the church' (emphasis added).

emphasizes even within his exposition of general revelation in Romans 1.[41] In general revelation, there is the revelation of the wrath of God to disobedient sinners (Rom. 1:18). It is in the gospel alone that 'the righteousness of God is revealed from faith for faith' for 'salvation' (Rom. 1:16-17). Apart from special revelation, then, sinners ordinarily cannot be saved.[42]

A fourth and final point of difference between general and special revelation has reference to the goal of each. Each body of revelation has as its supreme end the glory of God. But general and special revelation realize this goal in distinct ways.

> [General revelation's] object is to realize the end of man's creation, to be attained only through knowledge of God and perfect and unbroken communion with Him. On the entrance of sin into the world, destroying this communion with God, and obscuring the knowledge of Him derived from Nature, another mode of revelation was necessitated, having also another content, adapted to the new relation to God and the new conditions of intellect, heart and will brought about by sin ... Revelation ... in its double form was the Divine purpose for man from the beginning, and constitutes a unitary provision for the realization of the end of his creation in the actual circumstances in which he exists.[43]

General revelation, considered in itself, glorifies God as the Creator, Sustainer, and Judge of the world. Sharing these goals, special revelation furthermore glorifies God as the Redeemer of sinners.

This latter characteristic of special revelation relates to the way in which Reformed writers in the sixteenth and seventeenth centuries spoke of the 'scope' of special revelation, that is, 'what Scripture as a whole means or signifies.'[44] The scope of the Scripture, taken as a

---

41. Packer, *God Has Spoken*, 63.

42. In saying 'ordinarily,' we mean that God is quite capable of saving people whose minds are either too immature (infants) or too damaged (the mentally handicapped) to be able to be 'outwardly called by the ministry of the Word' (WCF 10.3). That is to say, they are in these respects incapable of understanding special revelation. This incapacity does not prevent us from entertaining the possibility of their salvation. The same may not be said, however, of people 'not professing the Christian religion ... be they never so diligent to frame their lives according to the light of nature, and the laws of that religion they do profess' (WCF 10.4).

43. Warfield, 'The Biblical Idea of Revelation,' in *Works*, 1:7.

44. Muller, *Post-Reformation Reformed Dogmatics*, 2.206. I am indebted, for what follows, to Muller's survey of this point at *Post-Reformation Reformed Dogmatics*, 206-23.

whole, is the revelation of God's mercies in Jesus Christ.[45] Christ is 'at the doctrinal center of Scripture and, therefore, at the doctrinal and specifically soteriological center of Christian theology.'[46] Reformed theologians were careful to insist that this principle did not mean that 'Christology ... impinge[d] interpretatively on every exegetical issue or point of doctrine.'[47] The particular goal of special revelation (the glory of God in Christ, the Savior of sinners) suits the scope of that revelation (the person and work of Christ) in such a way that 'all Scripture and all doctrine point toward the person and work of Christ as the core of the Christian message, the central soteriological truth, but not the overarching meaning of all Scripture, confession, and system.'[48]

In summary, special revelation is the self-revelation of the triune God to His people. Special revelation has a fullness and clarity that general revelation does not have. Special revelation particularly and uniquely sets forth the way in which sinners may be saved, through faith in the Lord Jesus Christ. In this way, special revelation glorifies God in His works of creation, providence, *and* redemption.

The Modes of Special Revelation

We may now take up the question in what modes or forms God reveals Himself to His people in special revelation. This is related to but distinct from the question of the means or instruments of special revelation.[49] General revelation, we have seen, comes to human beings 'through the media of natural phenomena, occurring in the course of Nature or of history.'[50] Since special revelation is verbal and propositional in nature, it frequently comes to people through the means of rational creatures, such as angels and human beings.[51]

---

45. Muller, *Post-Reformation Reformed Dogmatics*, 2.207.

46. ibid., 2.212.

47. ibid. In this respect, Reformation and Post-Reformation Reformed theologians parted company with their Lutheran contemporaries.

48. ibid. Compare the complementary observations of Bavinck, *Reformed Dogmatics*, 1:344-6.

49. For a recent treatment of the media, or means, of special revelation, see Frame, *Doctrine of the Word of God*, 71-4.

50. Warfield, 'The Biblical Idea of Revelation,' in *Works*, 1:6.

51. Special revelation may, of course, come immediately (apart from means), that is, from God Himself. On one extraordinary occasion, that of Balaam's donkey in Numbers 22, a (speaking) animal may be the instrument of revelation.

But what are the modes or forms through which God specially reveals Himself to His people?[52] Bavinck identifies three such modes that he argues are common to other religions, namely, 'manifestation, prediction, and miracle.'[53] These three categories appear in biblical revelation in the form of 'theophany, prophecy, and miracle,' respectively.[54] One virtue of Bavinck's presentation of these three modes of revelation is the way in which he shows their culmination in the person and work of Christ.[55] Theophany 'reach[es] its climax ... in Christ, who is the *angelos, doxa, eikon, logos, huios tou theou,* in whom God is fully revealed and fully given.'[56] The New Testament presents Christ as 'the supreme, the unique and true prophet ... the full and complete revelation of God,' and 'the absolute miracle, descended from above, and yet the true and complete human.'[57] The modes of special revelation, on this presentation, evidence special revelation's fundamentally eschatological character.[58]

A complementary and arguably more satisfying taxonomy of the modes of biblical revelation appears in Warfield's reflections on Scripture.[59] Warfield identifies what he terms 'three well-marked modes of revelation ... (1) external manifestations, (2) internal suggestion, (3) concursive operation.'[60] The first two of these three modes broadly

---

52. Discussions of the modes of revelation include Warfield, 'The Biblical Idea of Revelation,' in *Works*, 1:3-34; Bavinck, *Reformed Dogmatics*, 1:326-39; and John S. Feinberg, *Light in a Dark Place: The Doctrine of Scripture* (FET; Wheaton, IL: Crossway, 2018), 79-105. Warfield and Bavinck employ the term 'mode;' Feinberg, the term 'form.'

53. Bavinck, *Reformed Dogmatics*, 1:326.

54. ibid., 1:328.

55. In light of Bavinck's conviction that 'the person and work of Christ is the central revelation of God; all other revelation is grouped around this center,' *Reformed Dogmatics*, 1:339.

56. Bavinck, *Reformed Dogmatics*, 1:329.

57. ibid., 1:335, 339.

58. Note how Bavinck argues that each mode admits of an as-yet consummate expression in history, *Reformed Dogmatics*, 1:329-30, 336, 339.

59. Warfield approvingly references the three-fold distinction that Bavinck develops, 'it is customary to say that in the course of his redemptive work, God makes himself known in three modes – theophany, prophecy, miracles – or more broadly phrased, in appearing, speaking, doing – in his person, speech, deeds,' 'Christianity and Revelation,' in *SSW*, 1:29.

60. Warfield, 'The Biblical Idea of Revelation,' in *Works*, 1:15.

correspond to 'theophany' and 'prophecy,' respectively. 'External manifestation' refers to 'all of those mighty works by which God makes himself known.' For Warfield, 'theophany' is the 'typical form' of this category, but this category also includes miracles.[61] 'Internal suggestion' includes 'visions and dreams ... and with them the whole "prophetic word."'[62] The third category, 'concursive operation,' refers to 'that form of revelation illustrated in an inspired psalm or epistle in history, in which no human activity – not even the control of the will – is superseded, but the Holy Spirit works in, with and through them all in such a manner as to communicate to the product qualities distinctly superhuman.'[63]

Warfield is careful to stress two qualifications in advancing this three-fold categorization of the modes of revelation. The first is that each mode is present in every epoch of redemptive history. 'One or the other may seem particularly characteristic of this age or of that; but they all occur in every age. And they occur side by side, broadly speaking on the same level.'[64] The second is that each mode is the equal of the others in terms of 'worthiness' or 'purity' as revelation from God.[65] To suggest a gradation in the quality of revelation is to confuse the very nature of revelation, 'the intellectual or spiritual quality of a revelation is not derived from the recipient but from its Divine Giver.'[66]

With those qualifications in mind, these three modes of special revelation admit of a particular historical succession. These three modes correspond to historical 'periods at least characteristically of what we may somewhat conventionally call theophany, prophecy and inspiration.'[67] Theophany predominates from the Patriarchs up to the ministry of Samuel. Prophecy predominates from the ministry of Samuel

---

61. ibid.

62. ibid. For Warfield, visions and dreams are the 'typical forms of prophecy,' but share with the spoken prophetic word the 'essential characteristic' of 'com[ing] not by the will of man but from God,' ibid.

63. ibid.

64. ibid.

65. ibid.

66. Warfield, 'The Biblical Idea of Revelation,' in *Works*, 1:16.

67. ibid., 1:14.

to the close of the Old Testament. Inspiration, or concursive operation, characterizes the apostolic writings of the New Testament.[68]

And yet, Warfield insists, there is a single and singular category of revelation that defies classification in one of these three categories. That category is 'the culminating revelation, not through, but in, Jesus Christ ... the revelation accumulated in Him stands outside all the diverse portions and diverse manners in which otherwise revelation has been given and sums up in itself all that has been or can be made known of God and of His redemption. He does not so much make a revelation of God as Himself is the revelation of God ...'[69] How, then, does the revelation given through the apostles of Jesus Christ relate to this unique category of revelation? 'The entirety of the New Testament is but the explanatory word accompanying and giving its effect to the fact of Christ.'[70] Apostolic revelation does not so much succeed the revelation in Christ as explicate it.

The Redemptive-Historical Shape of Special Revelation

Warfield's observation that the modes of special revelation in part correspond to a succession of historical epochs in the history of redemption prompts an important observation about the character of special revelation. The totality or aggregate of special revelation is not a random assortment of scattershot divine self-disclosures. Special revelation has its own intrinsic shape or structure. This shape or structure is not only inherent to special revelation but also fundamentally historical in character.

We have already seen one hint of this characteristic of special revelation in our earlier survey of special revelation. Special revelation, we have seen, is not given for the benefit of human beings, in general. God, rather, reveals Himself to His covenant people. That revelation,

---

68. ibid.

69. Warfield, 'The Biblical Idea of Revelation,' in *Works*, 1.28.

70. ibid. In the following sentence, Warfield draws a crucial implication from this state of affairs, 'And when this fact was in all its meaning made the possession of men, revelation was completed and in that sense ceased. Jesus Christ is no less the end of revelation than He is the end of the Law.' We will return to this observation when we argue for the cessation of special revelation in Chapter 5.

of course, is intended under the New Covenant to go to the nations. But the ever-expanding covenant people of God are the initial recipients and the intended beneficiaries of that revelation. God, furthermore, administers His promises to His covenant people through a succession of covenantal administrations.[71] Reformed theology has understood pre-redemptive human history to be structured according to a covenant that God made with humanity in Adam.[72] 'Covenant,' then, formally shapes the history of humanity documented in the Bible. Our expectation is that divine self-revelation would in some way reflect this historical shape or structure.

The Omega of Special Revelation

Before we look at the particular shape of special revelation, however, we need to show that there is form or shape to special revelation. We may begin by looking at the *telos* or goal of special revelation, the person and work of Jesus Christ. Two New Testament books, the Epistle to the Hebrews and the Gospel according to John, are particularly emphatic in the way in which they present Christ as the goal of special revelation.

The writer to the Hebrews introduces his epistle with an affirmation that Christ is the intended culmination of God's self-revelation in history.

> Long ago, at many times and in many ways, God spoke to our fathers by the prophets, but in these last days he has spoken to us by his Son, whom he appointed the heir of all things, through whom also he created the world (Heb. 1:1-2).

In these verses, the writer periodizes history in a particular way. 'These last days' have dawned with the appearing of God's 'Son,' that is, the Lord Jesus Christ (see Heb. 9:26). In company with other New Testament writers, the author to the Hebrews understands the person and work of Christ to inaugurate a new epoch in human history (compare Acts 2:17,

---

71. For a recent survey and defense of Covenant Theology, see Guy Prentiss Waters, J. Nicholas Reid, and John R. Muether, eds., *Covenant Theology: Biblical, Theological, and Historical Perspectives* (Wheaton, IL: Crossway, 2020).

72. On the Covenant of Works, see my 'The Covenant of Works in the New Testament' and 'Covenant in Paul' in Guy Prentiss Waters, J. Nicholas Reid, and John R. Muether, eds., *Covenant Theology: Biblical, Theological, and Historical Perspectives* (Wheaton, IL: Crossway, 2020), 79-97, 227-45.

1 Pet. 1:20). The terminology 'last days' denotes 'eschatological finality.'[73] That is to say, the 'last days' admit of no successive era or epoch. They represent the climax and consummation of God's purposes in history.[74]

To this periodization corresponds God's speech in history. Hebrews characterizes God's pre-'last days' speech in Hebrews 1:1, 'long ago, at many times and in many ways, God spoke to our fathers by the prophets.' Tellingly, whatever differences may obtain between pre-'last days' and 'last days' speech, both are the self-revelation of God. Pre-'last days' speech is no less divine revelation than 'last days' speech is.

What, then, characterizes and distinguishes 'last days' speech from pre-'last days' speech? First, the recipients of pre-'last days' speech are 'our fathers,' that is, the people of God prior to the coming of Christ; the recipients of 'last days' speech are 'us,' that is, the New Covenant community. Second, the instruments of pre-'last days' speech were the 'prophets,' God's spokespeople. God's 'last days' speech, however, has come by the Son of God, who is 'the radiance of the glory of God and the exact imprint of his nature' (Heb. 1:3). Christ, then, is set forth as God's Prophet, but He differs in important respects from the prophets of old. In light of the unique character of His person (Heb. 1:3) and redemptive work (Heb. 1:4), it would be improper to see Him as an instrument of revelation along the lines of the Old Testament prophets. Christ is not one more in an ongoing succession of prophets.[75] Nor is Christ the final installment in a sequence of prophets with whom He is equal. Christ is both the consummator and *sui generis*.

Third, pre-'last days' speech is characterized by diversity.[76] During that period of time, God spoke 'at many times and in many ways,' that is, 'different times and places' and 'different modes and genres.'[77] Such

---

73. Richard B. Gaffin, Jr., 'The Redemptive-Historical View,' in *Biblical Hermeneutics: Five Views* (ed. Stanley E. Porter and Beth M. Stovell; Downers Grove, IL: InterVarsity, 2012), 94.

74. As Gaffin perceptively notes, Hebrews 8-10 understands this periodization of pre-last days and last days to correspond to the historical eras of the Old and New Covenants, respectively, ibid. Hebrews' eschatological structuring of human history is fundamentally covenantal in orientation.

75. Islam contends that Christ is a prophet, but is succeeded by Mohammed.

76. As Gaffin observes, 'the diversity of God's speaking is a function of its taking place "through the prophets,"' 'The Redemptive-Historical View,' 96.

77. Gaffin, 'The Redemptive-Historical View,' 95.

a range of diversity was suitable to the period of history leading up to Christ. There is, to be sure, diversity within 'last days' revelation. That diversity, however, does not define or characterize that revelation in the manner that it does pre-'last days' speech.

Fourth, the content of 'last days' speech is Christ, His Incarnate person and His finished, redemptive work (Heb. 1:3-4). We may fairly infer from these opening verses that Hebrews understands Christ to be the goal of God's pre-'last days' speech. Such an inference is warranted by the way in which Hebrews will later relate Moses (Heb. 3), the Aaronic Priesthood (Heb. 5–7), and the Tabernacle with its attendant festivals and sacrifices (Heb. 8–10) to Christ. The tabernacle was 'a copy and shadow of the heavenly things,' and 'the law has but a shadow of the good things to come' (Heb. 8:5, 10:1). But Christ has 'appeared as a high priest of the good things that have come' (Heb. 9:11). The leading contents of pre-'last days' speech, as Hebrews develops the matter throughout his epistle, are so much as one great shadow that Christ has cast backwards into history (cf. Col. 2:16-17).[78]

In summary, all special revelation is divine speech. That divine speech admits of a progressive character.[79] It assumes 'the form of a regular historical development.'[80] That history admits of two basic epochs or phases – that which is prior to Christ, and the dawn of the 'last days' in Christ. Pre-'last days' special revelation, for all its diversity, advances

---

78. The contrast, Packer explains, is 'not between crude and refined, "primitive" and "evolved", partly false and wholly true, but between promises and their fulfillment, types and the antitype, shadows and substance, incompleteness and perfection, in the two successive dispensations of divine grace under which God's covenant people have lived. It is a contrast to be expounded in terms, not of better conceptions of God, but of the better covenant (Heb. 7:22), the better priest (7:26ff.), the better sacrifice (9:23), the better promises (8:6), the better hope (7:19), the fuller access (9:8f., 10:19ff.), and the livelier foretastes of glory (6:4f.), that Christians have through Christ as compared with Old Testament believers …,' *God Has Spoken*, 80-1.

79. Although not 'progressive' in the sense that modern critical scholarship has employed the term, namely, 'to express the idea that the history of revelation is really the history of how Israel's thoughts of God evolved from something very crude (a tribal war-god) through something more refined (a moral Creator) to the conception of God taught by Jesus (a loving Father); and has set forth this idea in such a way as to imply that Christians need not bother with the Old Testament at all, since all that is true in its view of God can be learned from the New Testament, and all the rest of what it says about Him is more or less false,' Packer, *God Has Spoken*, 81.

80. Warfield, 'The Idea and Theories of Revelation,' in *Works*, 1:46.

towards its appointed goal, the person and work of Christ. 'Last days' special revelation is characterized by its declaration of the facts and significance of the person and work of Jesus Christ. The unity of special revelation consists, then, of two basic realities. Its author is God, and its content is the Lord Jesus Christ. What Bavinck describes of history may be rightly attributed to special revelation, 'just as up until this time everything had been prepared with a view to Christ, now everything is traced back to him.'[81]

The opening verses of the Fourth Gospel confirm what we have seen about special revelation from Hebrews. In his Prologue (John 1:1-18), the apostle John helps us to see the way in which the person and work of Christ offer definition to the contours of special revelation. In the first place, John titles Jesus 'the Word' (John 1:1, 14). This appellation, unique to the Prologue, has been the subject of considerable academic discussion.[82] The sense of the term is best determined from the context of the Prologue. 'The Word' describes the Second Person of the Godhead, the 'only begotten Son' (1:14, NASB) in distinction from but consubstantial with and equal in power and glory to the Father. The Word is coeternal with the Father. 'Through him,' John tells us, 'all things were made ... and without him was not anything made that was made' (1:3). The Father, through the Son, brought all things into being. The title, 'Word,' then conveys the idea of the creative power that belongs to God alone.[83] The title also denotes God's self-disclosure or self-revelation, a point to which John is attentive at the close of his Prologue, 'No one has ever seen God; the only begotten God, who is at the Father's side, he has made him known' (1:18; ESV, 'the only God'). It is not that Jesus is *a* revealer of the Father, but He is *the* revealer of the Father. His unique identity, coupled with His unique relationship with the Father, means that His disclosure of the Father is *sui generis* (see John 14:1-11).

---

81. Bavinck, *Reformed Dogmatics*, 1:347.

82. And yet, note the title 'word of life,' which arguably refers to Jesus (1 John 1:1), and 'the Word of God' (Rev. 19:13), which certainly refers to Jesus. On the literature addressing the denotation of the title 'Word' in John's Prologue, see Craig Keener, *The Gospel of John: A Commentary* (2 vols.; Peabody, MA: Hendrickson, 2003), 1:339-63.

83. An idea that is found in the Old Testament. In Psalm 33:6-7, the Psalmist conjoins God's creative Word with His divine power, 'By the word of the Lord the heavens were made, and by the breath of his mouth all their host. He gathers the waters of the sea as a heap; he puts the deeps in storehouses.'

The Word, then, did not begin to be. He is eternal (John 1:1-3). He did, however, 'become flesh and dwelt' among His people (John 1:14). He disclosed His 'glory ... full of grace and truth' to His apostolic witnesses (1:14). In this way He revealed the Father to human beings (1:18). The span of time between creation and the Incarnation, however, is not a space empty or void of Jesus Christ, according to John. In John 1:6-8, (the apostle) John summarizes the ministry of John (the Baptist).[84] John the Baptist is a 'man sent from God' (1:6). He is, therefore, a true prophet and spokesman of God. While 'not the light,' he bore 'witness about the light' (1:8). In fact, God 'sent' him 'to bear witness about the light' (1:8). John's ministry, then, is one of pointing to and bearing testimony about Christ, the Light (see 1:4).

Neither John the Baptist nor his ministry is singular. Just as the narrative of the Fourth Gospel will go on to show, it was not only John the Baptist who pointed human beings to Jesus (John 1:29-42). The whole of the Old Testament economy pointed to Jesus Christ.[85] For this reason, Jesus tells His opponents, 'the Scriptures ... bear witness about me' (5:39); 'If you believed Moses, you would believe me; for he wrote of me' (5:46). The entirety of the economy prior to the Lord Jesus Christ anticipated and pointed towards Christ. This characteristic of this period of history pertained to the revelation that God provided His people at this time. John the Baptist represents the apex or culmination of an era of preparation and, particularly, of preparatory witness towards Jesus Christ.[86]

We may summarize the Gospel of John's teaching about the structure and progression of special revelation. The goal of special revelation is the person and work of the Incarnate Christ. What renders Christ unique is

---

84. Tellingly, the only 'John' mentioned by name in the Fourth Gospel is John the Baptist. The apostle John refers to himself by the title, 'the disciple whom Jesus loved' (John 13:23, *et pass.*).

85. Jesus makes this point globally in John 2 when He declares that the purification waters prescribed by the Mosaic Law and the temple itself found their intended fulfillment in Him (John 2:1-12, 13-25). That is to say, the Temple (and, before it, the Tabernacle) and all its attendant rites and festivals find their meaning and fulfillment in Jesus Christ (cf. John 1:14). Furthermore, Jesus can say that 'Abraham rejoiced that he would see my day' (John 8:56), and John can say that 'Isaiah saw his glory and spoke of him,' that is, Jesus (John 12:41). In these ways, John tells us, the entirety of the Old Testament economy was by design oriented towards and finds fulfillment in the person and work of Christ.

86. Compare here the statement of Jesus in Matthew 11:13, 'for all the Prophets and the Law prophesied until John.'

His unique relationship with the Father and, on that basis, His unique disclosure of the Father to human beings (1:1-3, 18). This disclosure transpired consummately at the Incarnation (1:14). The period of history subsequent to the creation but leading up to the Incarnation is a period of preparation. John the Baptist is not only the climactic voice of that period but also its exemplar. In company with others whom God 'sent' and by whom God spoke, John 'came to bear witness about the light' (1:6, 8).

The Alpha of Special Revelation

In light of our studies in Hebrews 1:1-4 and John 1:1-18, we may conclude that Jesus Christ is the *telos* or goal of special revelation. We may now ask the question, 'When did special revelation commence?' If special revelation encompasses the span of redemptive history and finds its consummation in the person and work of Christ, what is its alpha point? We certainly must point to the *Protoevangelium*, the first announcement of the gospel in Genesis 3:15, as the initiation of 'redemptive revelation.'[87] But redemptive special revelation, while perhaps the primary or leading species of special revelation, is not the only kind of special revelation to which Scripture testifies. Geerhardus Vos has spoken of 'pre-redemptive special revelation.'[88] By pre-redemptive special revelation, Vos has in mind the revelation of God to Adam and Eve in the Garden, prior to their fall into sin. This revelation consists of 'four great principles,'

1. the principle of life in its highest potency sacramentally symbolized by the tree of life;
2. the principle of probation symbolized in the same manner by the tree of knowledge of good and evil;
3. the principle of temptation and sin symbolized in the serpent;
4. the principle of death reflected in the dissolution of the body.[89]

While it is beyond the scope of our work to summarize Vos's findings, we may draw three summary observations. First, the revelation in view,

---

87. Warfield, 'The Biblical Idea of Revelation,' in *Works*, 1:13.
88. Vos, *Biblical Theology: Old and New Testaments* (Edinburgh: Banner of Truth, 1975), 27.
89. ibid.

contained in Genesis 2, is *special* revelation.[90] It is above and beyond the revelation that God makes of Himself generally to human beings in nature and providence. The superadded quality of this revelation warrants its inclusion in what we call 'special revelation.' Second, the revelation of Genesis 2 informs us that, even in the estate of innocency, general revelation was insufficient with respect to God's purposes for Adam and Eve. The fact that God revealed Himself in Genesis 2 as He did testifies to the necessity of this revelation for Adam and Eve's fulfilling or realizing the purposes for which God had created them. Third, what is the content of this pre-redemptive special revelation? As Warfield observes, God spoke, in Genesis 2, to Adam in his created integrity.

> Man dwelt with God in Eden, and enjoyed with Him immediate and not merely mediate communion. In that case, we may understand that if man had not fallen, he would have continued to enjoy immediate intercourse with God, and that the cessation of this immediate intercourse is due to sin.[91]

The purpose of pre-redemptive special revelation, moreover, was not to maintain the *status quo ante*. It was, as Vos stresses, to bring the creation to its purposed consummation.

> Man had been created perfectly good in a moral sense. And yet there was a sense in which he could be raised to a still higher level of perfection ... The advance was meant to be from unconfirmed to confirmed goodness and blessedness; to the confirmed state in which these possessions could no longer be lost, a state in which man could no longer sin, and hence could no longer become subject to the consequences of sin. Man's original state was a state of indefinite probation: he remained in possession of what he had, so long as he did not commit sin, but it was not a state in which the continuance of his religious and moral status could be guaranteed him. In order to assure this for him, he had to be subjected to an intensified, concentrated probation, in which, he remained standing, the status of probation would be forever left behind.[92]

---

90. Note that, while Warfield materially agrees with Vos concerning the contents of pre-redemptive revelation, he opts to term it 'general revelation,' reserving 'special revelation' for the redemptive revelation that commences in Genesis 3, 'The Biblical Idea of Revelation,' in *Works*, 1:7-8.

91. Warfield, 'The Biblical Idea of Revelation,' in *Works*, 1:8.

92. Vos, *Biblical Theology*, 22. Compare his equally perceptive remarks at *Redemptive History and Biblical Interpretation: The Shorter Writings of Geerhardus Vos* (ed. Richard B. Gaffin, Jr.; Phillipsburg, NJ: P&R, 1980), 242-5.

God intended for the fellowship and communion that Adam enjoyed with Him in the Garden of Eden to be advanced in two related respects. The first is that it would be rendered permanent and beyond forfeiture. The second is that it would thereby be heightened or intensified. It was to that end that God revealed Himself to Adam in Genesis 2.

It would be a mistake to conclude that the question of the precise identification of the revelation in Genesis 2 (general or special) is a purely academic question. As Vos observes, 'what we inherit in the second Adam is not restricted to what we lost in the first Adam; it is much rather the full realization of what the first Adam would have achieved for us had he remained unfallen and been confirmed in his state.'[93] In this respect, pre-redemptive special revelation and redemptive special revelation stand in the closest relationship. In pre-redemptive special revelation, we learn how God had called Adam to bring humanity to the realization of the divine purpose for humanity, namely, confirmed and consummate communion with Himself. Through his first sin, Adam, and we in Adam, failed to bring that purpose to realization. In that failure, we forfeited the fellowship that Adam enjoyed in the Garden, before the fall. It is in redemptive special revelation that we learn how God will bring His purpose for humanity to fruition. It will not be through the person and work of the First Adam, but through the person and work of the Second and Last Adam, Jesus Christ. Christ will undo what Adam has done, and Christ will do what Adam has failed to do. In so doing, He advances redeemed humanity to the goal that God had set before Adam at the creation. Just as God's work of redemption in Christ finds its pattern and foundation in the covenant that God made with Adam, so His redemptive special revelation finds a corresponding foundation in pre-redemptive special revelation.[94]

Continuing Revelation?

We have reflected on both the alpha and omega points of special revelation. Special revelation finds its beginnings in the Garden, when God spoke

---

93. Vos, *Redemptive History and Biblical Interpretation*, 243. Vos follows with this theological observation of pastoral importance, 'Someone placed in that state can never again fall from it. As truly as Christ is a perfect Saviour, so truly must he bestow on us the perseverance of the saints,' ibid.

94. For the details of which, see Vos's whole discussion at *Biblical Theology*, 27-44.

to Adam in Genesis 2. Special revelation finds its consummation in the Second and Last Adam, the Lord Jesus Christ (Heb. 1:1-4; John 1:1-18). Although we will address this question more fully in Chapter 5, we may now broach the question whether God continues to reveal Himself to the church, or whether 'those former ways of God's revealing His will unto His people [are] now ceased.'[95] In other words, does special revelation continue after the apostolic age, until the return of Christ, or did special revelation cease with the apostolic generation?

Our survey of the redemptive-historical shape of special revelation points decisively to the cessation of special revelation with the close of the apostolic generation. In making this claim, we do not deny that the Spirit continues to work by and with the Word throughout the history of the church and, individually, in the lives of God's people. We are, rather, making the claim for the finality of special revelation as it has come to us in God's written Word. How is this evident from the redemptive-historical shape of special revelation?

In the first place, we have observed that Jesus Christ is the consummation of divine special revelation. He is, furthermore, the *sui generis* self-disclosure of God to humanity. In this respect, Warfield observes, 'the entirety of the New Testament is but the explanatory word accompanying and giving its effect to the fact of Christ.'[96] Once 'this fact was in all its meaning made the possession of men, revelation was completed and in that sense ceased. Jesus Christ is no less the end of revelation than He is the end of the law.'[97] Given, as we shall see further in a later chapter, the character of the New Testament writings as the unique, apostolic witness to Jesus Christ, we may regard special revelation as having come to its intended completion with the completion of the apostolic witness to Christ.

It is telling that when the apostle Paul, in the twilight of his life and ministry, is preparing Timothy and Titus for ministry in the post-apostolic church, he never once prepares them to receive further revelation from God. On the contrary, he repeatedly and emphatically calls them to read and to preach the Scriptures of the Old Testament before the

---

95. Westminster Confession of Faith, 1.1.
96. Warfield, 'The Biblical Idea of Revelation,' in *Works*, 1:28.
97. ibid.

church (1 Tim. 4:13; 2 Tim. 3:15-17), and adhere to the 'deposit' they have received from the apostle Paul, that is, the New Covenant revelation that Christ has made to His church through His apostles (see 2 Tim. 1:14, 2:2). The church stands on the once-for-all foundation that Christ has laid through His apostles and prophets, namely the Scriptures of the New Testament, coupled with the Scriptures of the Old Testament (Eph. 2:20). As Bavinck succinctly states the matter, 'The Scripture was completed; now it is worked out.'[98]

The Movement of Special Revelation

Before we draw to a close our consideration of the shape and structure of special revelation, we have one further observation to register. We have reflected on both the alpha and omega points of special revelation and the implications of those *termini* for the content and concern of that revelation. We may now attend to an aspect of special revelation that not only characterizes the whole of it but lends an important window into its nature.

Special revelation has as its prevailing concern the communion or fellowship of human beings with God. After the fall, special revelation maintains that concern – now only through the redeeming work of Christ, the Last Adam. Human history after the fall begins with the message of the gracious provision of Christ for the salvation of sinners (see Gen. 3:15). The closing words of the Bible emphasize that message as well, 'the grace of the Lord Jesus be with all. Amen' (Rev. 22:22). The whole of redemptive special revelation, we have seen, has as its chief and leading concern the person and work of the Lord Jesus Christ, the only Savior of sinners. In this respect, the Bible is not cacophonic but symphonic.

Just as symphonies frequently consist of distinct and progressive movements, so also we may identify discrete epochs or eras within redemptive history. To help us identify those epochs we need first to

---

98. He continues, 'No new constitutive elements can any longer be added to special revelation now, because Christ has come, his work is finished, his Word completed ... Scripture clearly teaches that God's full revelation has been given in Christ and that the Holy Spirit who was poured out in the church has come only to glorify Christ and take all things from Christ (John 16:14),' *Reformed Dogmatics*, 1:347. One should note, however, Vos's speculation that, when Christ returns in glory, there will be an added renewal of special revelation to the church, *Biblical Theology*, 6.

appreciate a standing feature of the redemption that the Bible documents. There is a particular contour or pattern to special revelation, namely the conjunction of 'redemptive deed' and 'redemptive word.' God typically acts in history and accompanies that action with an explanatory word. While God's redemptive deeds are by no means mute, they require divine explanation in order to profit people.[99] In fact, apart from God's redemptive words, human beings would be, at best, left in uncertainty about the meaning and significance of God's redemptive deeds.[100]

Redemptive deed and redemptive word, or redemptive special revelation, therefore appear conjunctively in Scripture. Special revelation does not appear scattershot, and is not administered randomly. Special revelation, rather, appears alongside of the progressive succession of the redemptive deeds of God.[101] In fact, the Old and New Testaments document a handful of major, redemptive deeds of God, around which redemptive special revelation clusters. These redemptive deeds of God stand not only in progressive relationship, but also in organic relationship.[102] In this light we are able to identify epochs or eras of both redemptive history and redemptive revelation.

At the risk of oversimplification, we may identify three major or primary epochs in biblical history and revelation.[103] The first is the

---

99. 'Revelation thus appears, however, not as the mere reflection of the redeeming acts of God in the minds of men, but as a factor in the redeeming work of God, a component part of the series of His redeeming acts, without which that series would be incomplete and so far inoperative for its main end,' Warfield, 'The Biblical Idea of Revelation,' in *Works*, 1:12.

100. And, as Warfield rightly notes, seen from one perspective, God's redemptive words are themselves redemptive acts, 'Thus the Scriptures represent it, not confounding revelation with the series of the redemptive acts of God, but placing it among the redemptive acts of God and giving it a function as a substantive element in the operations by which the merciful God saves sinful men. It is therefore not made even a mere constant accompaniment of the redemptive acts of God, giving their explanation that they may be understood. It occupies a far more independent place among them than this, and as frequently precedes them to prepare their way as it accompanies or follows them to interpret their meaning. It is in one word, itself a redemptive act of God and by no means the least important in the series of His redemptive acts,' 'The Biblical Idea of Revelation,' in *Works*, 1:12-13.

101. 'Revelation is the interpretation of redemption; it must, therefore, unfold itself in instalments [*sic*] as redemption does,' Vos, *Biblical Theology*, 6.

102. On which, see Vos, *Biblical Theology*, 7.

103. Following Vos, *Biblical Theology*.

Mosaic era, the historical centerpiece of which is the Exodus. God's dealings with His people prior to the Exodus anticipate this great redemptive act, and His dealing with His people subsequent to the Exodus follow from it. The Pentateuch, or the first five books of the Old Testament, centers around the Exodus, and serves to explicate that great and typological redemptive work of God. The second is the Prophetic era, the historical centerpiece of which is the Exile of Israel and Judah and the Restoration of God's people to the land of promise. There is a flourish of written prophetic activity before, during, and after the Assyrian and Babylonian Exiles. All the prophetic books of the Old Testament may be traced to this general period of time and serve to explicate God's actions in removing His people from and subsequently returning them to the land. The third is the New Testament, the incarnation, life, death, and resurrection of the Lord Jesus Christ. The twenty-seven books of the New Testament serve not only to document the facts of the life and ministry of Christ, but also to explicate their saving significance for human beings.

These three epochs stand in progressive and organic relationship with one another. The Exodus becomes the pattern and paradigm by which God saves His people from sin in Christ. The Exile and Restoration demarcate the beginning of the end of the Mosaic era and point to the coming work of God in Christ. The New Testament declares that the 'last days' have dawned in Christ and, in Him, His accomplished salvation is offered to all people. Within the New Testament particularly, the Gospels concentrate upon documenting the historical factuality of the incarnation, death, and resurrection of Christ. Acts and the Epistles concentrate upon explicating those facts' saving significance for human beings.[104]

Importantly, the succession of epoch upon epoch does not entail replacing or obviating the revelation given in conjunction with prior epochs. Both Christ and the apostles testify to the fact that the Old Testament points to and speaks of the life and ministry of Christ (Luke 24:25-7, 44-9). As Packer has observed, 'these later items [in the

---

104. Note the pattern identified by Vos, 'the usual order is: first word, then the fact, then again the interpretative word. The Old Testament brings the predictive preparatory word, the Gospels record the redemptive-revelatory fact, the Epistles supply the subsequent final interpretation,' *Biblical Theology*, 7.

series of God's words] can only be interpreted in the light of the series as a whole,' a dynamic, he goes on to stress, that applies no less to 'God's Word spoken by His Son.'[105] Consequently, Packer concludes, 'the very nature of the revelatory process itself made it necessary that a unified record of God's words should be provided.'[106] The very diversity of special revelation, then, testifies to its unity and unbroken cohesiveness.

Of course, this is not the only way in which we may understand and appreciate the unity of Scripture. Special revelation, as we have seen Hebrews claim, is the very speech of God (Heb. 1:1-4). In the next chapter, we will give closer attention to this aspect of Scripture by reflecting on both the inspiration and inerrancy of the Bible.

---

105. Packer, *God Has Spoken*, 82.
106. ibid.

Inspiration and Inerrancy

One of the most insightful treatments of the doctrine of the inspiration of Scripture is Reformed theologian B. B. Warfield's 'The Real Problem of Inspiration.'[1] Authored at the close of the nineteenth century, during the rising tide of historical critical assaults upon the doctrine of inspiration, this piece does more than defend the doctrine. It clarifies the implications of denying the doctrine.

> If criticism has made such discoveries as to necessitate the abandonment of the doctrine of plenary inspiration, it is not enough to say that we are compelled to abandon only a 'particular theory of inspiration,' though that is true enough. We must go on to say that that 'particular theory of inspiration' is the theory of the apostles and of the Lord, and that in abandoning *it* we are abandoning *them* as our doctrinal teachers and guides ... The real issue is to be kept clearly before us, and faced courageously ... Are the New Testament writers trustworthy guides in doctrine? Or are we at liberty to reject their authority, and frame contrary doctrines for ourselves? If the latter pathway be taken, certainly the doctrine of plenary inspiration is not the only doctrine that is 'destroyed,' and the labor of revising our creeds may as well be saved and the shorter process adopted of simply throwing them away.[2]

Put succinctly, if the New Testament writers teach the doctrine of plenary, verbal inspiration, then to reject that doctrine necessarily

---

1. Benjamin B. Warfield, 'The Real Problem of Inspiration,' in *The Works of Benjamin B. Warfield* (10 vols.; New York: Oxford University, 1932), 1:170-226.
2. ibid., 1:180, emphasis original.

overthrows their authority as teachers of doctrine. 'If we may not accept [the Bible's] account of itself ... why should we care to ascertain its account of other things?'[3]

Warfield is not saying that Christianity is suspended upon the doctrine of inspiration. In fact, he strenuously insists that this is not the case.

> Let it not be said that thus we found the whole Christian system upon the doctrine of plenary inspiration. We found the whole Christian system on the doctrine of plenary inspiration as little as we found it upon the doctrine of angelic existences. Were there no such thing as inspiration, Christianity would be true, and all its essential doctrines would be credibly witnessed to us in the generally trustworthy reports of the teaching of our Lord and of His authoritative agents in founding the Church, preserved in the writings of the apostles and their first followers, and in the historical witness of the living Church. Inspiration is not the most fundamental of Christian doctrines, nor even the first thing we prove about the Scriptures. It is the last and crowning fact as to the Scriptures.[4]

This is not at all to say that inspiration is a matter of indifference. It is simply to assign the doctrine its proper importance. Inspiration is neither the basis of nor theoretically necessary to Christianity. But because Christ and the apostles teach the doctrine of inspiration, 'we must trust these writings in their witness to their inspiration ... and if we refuse to trust them here, we have in principle refused them trust everywhere.'[5]

With an appreciation of the importance of and the stakes involved in the doctrine, we are now prepared to address the inspiration of Scripture. First, we will advance a definition of inspiration. In the course of advancing that definition we will give particular attention to the question of the divine and human authorship of Scripture. Second, we will explore the proofs for the inspiration of Scripture. We will see how the Bible testifies to itself as a book given by divine inspiration. Third, we will reflect upon and respond to some alternative views of the Bible's origins. Finally, we will see that the inerrancy

---

3. George Purves, 'St. Paul and Inspiration,' *Presbyterian and Reformed Review* (Jan 1893): 21, cited at Warfield, 'Real Problem,' in *Works*, 1:214.

4. Warfield, 'Real Problem,' in *Works*, 1:209-10.

5. ibid., 1:212.

of Scripture is both a necessary correlate of inspiration and a positive teaching of Scripture.

The Reformed Doctrine of Inspiration – a Definition

The doctrine of the Bible's inspiration is not an invention of the modern era. It is a longstanding confession of the Christian church. Representative is the statement of the Westminster Confession of Faith that the sixty-six books of the Bible are 'all ... given by inspiration of God to be the rule of faith and life.'⁶

But what does it mean to say that the Bible is 'inspired'? At the most basic level, it is to restate the testimony of Scripture to itself, 'all Scripture is given by inspiration of God ...' (2 Tim. 3:16, AV). We will give further attention to this verse below. To begin, we must venture a theological definition of the term 'inspired.' In defining and explaining 'inspiration,' our debt to the Old Princeton writers, and particularly B. B. Warfield, will be evident. After we venture this definition and explanation, we may proceed to show its biblical warrant.

A. A. Hodge and B. B. Warfield have advanced a comprehensive definition of the term 'inspiration.'

> [Inspiration is] God's continued work of superintendence, by which, his providential, gracious and supernatural contributions having been presupposed, he presided over the sacred writers in their entire work of writing, with the design and effect of rendering that writing an errorless record of the matters he designed them to communicate, and hence constituting the entire volume in all its parts the word of God to us.⁷

In light of this definition, we may predicate two qualities of 'inspiration.' First, inspiration is plenary. That is to say, 'the whole of Scripture is given

---

6. Westminster Confession of Faith, I.2. On the doctrine of Scripture in the writings of representative theologians across the history of the church, see the discussion of Herman Bavinck, *Reformed Dogmatics* (ed. John Bolt; trans. John Vriend; 4 vols.; Grand Rapids: Eerdmans, 2003), 1:402-22 and especially the essays in John D. Hannah, ed., *Inerrancy and the Church* (Chicago: Moody, 1984).

7. A. A. Hodge and B. B. Warfield, *Inspiration* (Philadelphia: Presbyterian Board of Publication, 1881), 17-18. Compare the similar definitions at Charles Hodge, *Systematic Theology* (3 vols.; New York: Charles Scribner's Sons, 1901), 1:154; J.I. Packer, *'Fundamentalism' and the Word of God* (Grand Rapids: Eerdmans, 1958), 77. See the collation of nineteenth century definitions at Benjamin B. Warfield, 'Inspiration,' in *Selected Shorter Writings of Benjamin B. Warfield* (ed. John E. Meeter; 2 vols.; Phillipsburg, NJ: P&R, 1970-3), 2:616.

by divine inspiration.'[8] The whole of the Scripture, from beginning to end and inclusive of all its parts, is inspired.[9] Second, inspiration is verbal. The inspiration of Scripture extends down to its very words. The doctrine of inspiration says more than that the thoughts or ideas of Scripture are inspired. It affirms that each word of the original was given by divine inspiration.[10] Therefore, in affirming plenary, verbal inspiration, we are saying that 'the Scriptures not only contain but ARE, THE WORD OF GOD, and hence that all their elements and all their affirmations are absolutely errorless, and binding the faith and obedience of men.'[11]

We may note a few dimensions of this definition of plenary, verbal inspiration. First, inspiration is fundamentally objective and not subjective. That is to say, inspiration does not describe the effect that Scripture may have on a person. The doctrine is not affirming that the Bible is a document that inspires its readership.[12] Neither does inspiration predicate something of the experiences of the biblical authors in response to a teaching or act of God.[13] Inspiration does not describe something contained within the realm of subjective experience. The term, rather, predicates an objective quality of the Scripture itself.

Furthermore, in saying that inspiration is objective, we are making a claim about the *verbal text* of Scripture. Some understand 'inspiration' to denote the work of God in revealing Himself to the biblical authors

---

8. R. C. Sproul, *Scripture Alone: The Evangelical Doctrine* (Phillipsburg, NJ: P&R, 2005), 136.

9. And yet note the stricture of Thomas Cary Johnson, 'the word plenary adds nothing [to inspiration]; but may be affirmed,' 'Synopsis of Lectures on Inspiration' (n.p., n.d.), 7. Compare the concurring judgment of Hodge and Warfield, who, while approving of the use of the word 'plenary,' nevertheless comment that 'the word ... is in itself indefinite, and its use contributes nothing either to the precision or the emphasis of the definition,' Inspiration, 18.

10. See Article VI of the Chicago Statement on Biblical Inerrancy (1978), quoted at Sproul, *Scripture Alone*, 136.

11. Hodge and Warfield, *Inspiration*, 10. Emphasis original.

12. This is not to deny, of course, that God intends for the Scripture to have a profound subjective influence on the lives of His people. It is to say that the term 'inspiration' does not denote that influence.

13. 'In this view, the biblical authors were inspired in the same sense that a pupil might be inspired by his teacher and therefore pass on what he has learned,' Matthew Barrett, *God's Word Alone: The Authority of Scripture* (Wheaton, IL: Crossway, 2016), 227.

who, 'having been divinely helped to certain knowledge were left to the natural limitations and fallibility incidental to their human and personal characters, alike in their thinking out their several narrations and expositions of divine truth, and in their reduction of them to writing.'[14] On this view, inspiration extends only so far as God makes Himself known to the authors of Scripture.

Others understand 'inspiration' in a higher sense. This view holds that 'while the thoughts of the sacred writers concerning doctrine and duty were inspired and errorless, their language was of purely human suggestion, and more or less accurate.'[15] God has not only revealed Himself to the biblical authors, but He has also supplied them with thoughts or ideas relating to belief and practice. It was left, however, to these authors to commit these ideas to words. These words fallibly express the infallible ideas they have received from God.

Neither of these views adequately rises to the definition of the doctrine of inspiration set forth above. To be sure, with respect to the first view, inspiration presupposes the self-revelation of God. Inspiration, however, denotes a work of God distinct from revelation.[16] As Charles Hodge observes, 'the object of revelation is the communication of knowledge. The object or design of inspiration is to secure infallibility in teaching ... the effect of revelation was to render its recipient wiser. The effect of inspiration was to preserve him from error in teaching.'[17]

Inspiration, with respect to the second view, stresses that the thoughts of the biblical writers come from God, but it is equally concerned to stress that the *words* in and by which those thoughts come to expression in the

---

14. Hodge and Warfield, *Inspiration*, 20.

15. ibid., 21.

16. Even as inspiration and revelation 'were often enjoyed by the same person at the same time,' Hodge, *Systematic Theology*, 1:155. Thus, while distinguishable, revelation and inspiration were in some instances inseparable, and in some instances separable, on which see further James Bannerman, *Inspiration: The Infallible Truth and Divine Authority of the Holy Scriptures* (Edinburgh: T&T Clark, 1865), 151-3. Note, as well, Warfield's proper insistence that inspiration is a 'mode of revelation,' 'The Biblical Idea of Inspiration,' in *Works*, 1:106. Inspiration and revelation 'differ [not] ... as genus from genus, but as a species of one genus differs from another,' since inspiration 'is one of the modes in which God makes known to men His being, His will, His operations, His purposes,' 'The Biblical Idea of Inspiration,' in *Works*, 1:107.

17. Hodge, *Systematic Theology*, 1:155. Compare Warfield, 'Inspiration,' in *SSW*, 2:615.

biblical text are no less given from God. For this reason, the doctrine is concerned to stress that inspiration extends to the very words of the text of Scripture. Any effort, furthermore, to erect a wall between inspired thought and uninspired words is an ultimately futile one, since 'infallible thought must be definite thought, and definite thought implies words.'[18] To posit inspired thought expressed in uninspired words, moreover, means that we have no more 'certainty for the foundation of our faith as is guaranteed by the natural competency of the human authors, and neither more nor less. There would be no divine guarantee whatever. The human medium would everywhere interpose its fallibility between God and us.'[19] As J. I. Packer rightly stresses, 'if the words were not wholly God's, then their teaching would not be wholly God's.'[20]

Inspiration, then, is the superintending work of God with respect to the human authors of the Bible in 'their entire work of writing' so as to guarantee that each of the words they authored were the very words of God, words that were and are true and without error.[21] The doctrine of inspiration makes a two-fold claim about the authorship of Scripture. It insists that God is the author of the whole of the Bible. It furthermore insists that human beings are the authors of each of the books of the Bible. This state of affairs raises the question how we are both to understand and to relate the divine and human authorship of the Bible.[22]

Warfield has influentially and compellingly articulated the relationship between the human and divine in Scripture, employing the term 'concursus' to characterize it.[23]

> According to this mode of conception the whole of Scripture is the product of divine activities, which enter it, however, not by superseding the activities of the human authors, but confluently with them; so that the Scriptures are the joint product of divine and human activities, both of which penetrate

---

18. Hodge and Warfield, *Inspiration*, 22.
19. ibid.
20. Packer, *Fundamentalism*, 90.
21. Warfield, 'Inspiration,' in *SSW*, 2:615.
22. For a helpful collation of Warfield's writings on this subject, see Anthony N. S. Lane, 'B. B. Warfield and the Humanity of Scripture,' *Vox Evangelica* 16 (1984): 77-94.
23. For a concise and more recent treatment of concursus with respect to Scripture, see Packer, *Fundamentalism*, 81-2.

them at every point, working harmoniously together to the production of a writing which is not divine here and human there, but at once divine and human in every part, every word, and every particular.[24]

Here Warfield insists that the Scripture is entirely divine and entirely human with respect to its authorship. One may not compartmentalize the Bible into divine and human sections. Nor may one conceive the Bible as the authorial product of human beings whose humanity was suspended or overruled by divine influence in the act of writing.[25] Divine authorship and human authorship are to be understood in concursive operation, God working 'confluently' with humans to produce the inspired text of Scripture. The Bible is 'a divine-human book, in which every word is at once divine and human.'[26] Or, 'the whole Bible is recognized as human, the free product of human effort, in every part and word. And at the same time, the whole Bible is recognized as divine, the Word of God, his utterances, of which he is in the truest sense the Author.'[27]

It is important to remember that the divine participation in the production of Scripture does not begin when the human author commences the act of writing the biblical text.[28]

---

24. Warfield, 'Inspiration,' in *SSW*, 2:629. Compare the similarly worded statement at 'The Divine and Human in the Bible,' in *SSW*, 2:547.

25. The Scriptures are 'given through men after a fashion which does no violence to their nature as men,' 'The Biblical Idea of Inspiration,' in *Works*, 1:99.

26. Warfield, 'The Divine and Human in the Bible,' in *SSW*, 2:546. Warfield grounds this conception in the Reformed doctrine of God, who is 'immanent as well as transcendent in the modes of his activity,' ibid. Warfield locates the concursus of inspiration particularly within the doctrine of divine providence, 'Why should we accept a theory of inspiration which is the analogue of the deistic rather than one which is the analogue of the divine-immanence theory of God's relation to the universe? Why may we not believe that the God who brings his purposes to fruition in his providential government of the world, without violence to second causes or to the intelligent free agency of his creatures, so superintends the mental processes of his chosen instruments for making known his will, as to secure that they shall speak his words in speaking their own?,' 'Review of Three Books on Inspiration,' in *SSW*, 2:611.

27. Warfield, 'The Divine and Human in the Bible,' in *SSW*, 2:547. The Bible, Warfield continues, is 'one single and uncompounded product' with 'two elements ... as [its] inseparable constituents,' ibid.

28. Neither is this divine work without reference to that human author's situation in time and place, 'These books were not produced suddenly, by some miraculous act – handed down complete out of heaven, as the phrase goes; but, like all other products of

> If asked where and how the divine has entered this divine-human book, [the Christian] must reply: 'Everywhere, and in almost every way conceivable.' Throughout the whole preparation of the material to be written and of the men to write it; throughout the whole process of the gathering and classification and use of the material by the writers; throughout the whole process of the actual writing, – he sees at work divine influences of the most varied kinds, extending all the way from simply providential superintendence and spiritual illumination to direct revelation and inspiration.[29]

Divine activity extends back to the preparation not only of the matters that will form the subject of the biblical book but also of the author himself – his character, mental habits, education, influences, predilections – in short, the whole of who he is as a writing agent.

In another article, Warfield elaborates the extensiveness and intricacy of this divine work of preparation leading up to the production of Scripture.

> There is to be considered, for instance, the preparation of the material which forms the subject-matter of these books: in a sacred history, say, for example, to be narrated; or in a religious experience which may serve as a norm for record; or in a logical elaboration of the contents of revelation which may be placed at the service of God's people; or in the progressive revelation of Divine truth itself, supplying their culminating contents. And there is the preparation of the men to write these books to be considered, a preparation physical, intellectual, spiritual, which must have attended them throughout their whole lives, and, indeed, must have had its beginning in their remote ancestors, and the effect of which was to bring the right men to the right places at the right times, with the right endowments, impulses, acquirements, to write just the books which were designed for them ... If God wished to give His people a series of letters like Paul's, He prepared a Paul to write them, and the Paul he brought to the task was a Paul who spontaneously would write just such letters.[30]

For this reason, there is no inherent tension or conflict between the divine and the human in the production of Scripture. To be sure, Warfield insists

---

time, are the ultimate effect of many processes cooperating through long periods,' 'The Biblical Idea of Inspiration,' in *Works*, 1:100.

29. Warfield, 'The Divine Origin of the Bible,' in *Works*, 1:429.

30. Warfield, 'The Biblical Idea of Inspiration,' in *Works*, 1:101. In succeeding pages, Warfield goes on to illustrate this principle with other genres of biblical literature.

that inspiration is a distinct and 'additional Divine operation' to the aforementioned work 'of the production of Scripture.'[31] But the divine work of inspiration does not face the limitations and obstacles posed by recalcitrant and flawed humanity.[32] Inspiration, rather, builds upon an earlier divine work, one that had been molding and preparing both the author and his subject matter from their inception. Inspiration works upon materials that God Himself has prepared from the very beginning, and has prepared according to His specific purposes for the text of Scripture.

To be sure, 'concursus' admits of further specification.[33] But, for purposes of defining inspiration, it is sufficient to note the fundamental harmony and cooperation of the divine and the human in the production of Scripture. The result is a book that, down to its very words, is entirely human and entirely divine, the very Word of God.

The Biblical Testimony to Inspiration

With a working definition of inspiration in place, we are now prepared to proceed to the biblical testimony for inspiration, the doctrine 'that inspired men were the organs of God in such a sense that their words are to be received not as the words of men, but as they are in truth, as the words of God (1 Thess. 2:13).'[34] We will first look at two important passages that figure into an understanding of the Bible's testimony about itself. They are 2 Timothy 3:16-17 and 2 Peter 1:19-21. We will then look at classes or categories of biblical evidence that corroborate the witnesses of these particular texts.

---

31. Warfield, 'The Biblical Idea of Inspiration,' in *Works*, 1:104.

32. The illustration that Warfield cites to describe the position that he critiques is that of pure light shining through a colored window, 'so any word of God which is passed through the mind and soul of a man must come out discolored by the personality through which it is given, and just to that degree ceases to be the pure word of God,' 'The Biblical Idea of Inspiration,' in *Works*, 1:102.

33. Warfield's three modes of revelation (external manifestation, internal suggestion, concursive operation), surveyed in the last chapter, require, as Lane observes, a nuanced understanding of concursus in relation to the particular type of revelation in question, 'B. B. Warfield and the Humanity of Scripture,' 85-8. Warfield recognizes, for instance, that, in prophecy, the human author is engaged differently than, say, in an epistle or a history, Hodge and Warfield, *Inspiration*, 16-17, 'Inspiration,' in *SSW*, 2:631. Concursus, in other words, looks different in the epistles of Paul than it might, say, in the prophecy of Jeremiah.

34. Hodge, *Systematic Theology*, 1:157.

(1) 2 Timothy 3:16-17

The *locus classicus* of the biblical doctrine of inspiration is 2 Timothy 3:16-17, 'All Scripture is breathed out by God and profitable for teaching, for reproof, for correction, and for training in righteousness, that the man of God may be competent, equipped for every good work.' The Greek word (*theopneustos*) that the AV renders 'given by inspiration of God' is rendered by the ESV, 'breathed out by God.'[35]

Considerable lexical attention has been devoted to the meaning of the Greek word *theopneustos*.[36] The word appears only once in the Greek New Testament, and is comprised of two parts, one denoting the noun 'God,' the other denoting the verb 'to breathe.'[37] The word denotes neither the 'nature' of Scripture nor 'its effects.'[38] It denotes, rather, the 'origination of Scripture.'[39] The classical English translation, 'inspired' (breathed into) is misleading. This English word can suggest that God appropriated an existing set of books and set, in some fashion, His divine authority upon them. But that is not the denotation of the underlying Greek word. The word, as it is used in context, refers to the fact that the text in question is 'breathed out by God.' God is the author and the producer of the books to which Paul refers in 2 Timothy 3:16. As J. I. Packer has rightly noted, 'just as God made the host of heaven "by the breath of his mouth" (Ps. 33:6), through

---

35. To note a sampling other modern renderings of this word: 'inspired by God' (NAS, NRSV, NAB, HCSB, NET); 'God-breathed' (NIV).

36. Foundational, although dated, is the work of Warfield, 'God-Inspired Scripture,' in *Works*, 1:229-80. This article was Warfield's critical response to the proposal of the late nineteenth-century lexicographer, Hermann Cremer, that the meaning of *theopneustos* is 'inspiring its readers,' 'God-Inspired Scripture,' in *Works*, 231. For more recent lexicographical discussion of this term, see William D. Mounce, *Pastoral Epistles* (WBC 46; Nashville: Thomas Nelson, 2000), 565-6; I. H. Marshall, *The Pastoral Epistles* (ICC; Edinburgh: T&T Clark, 1999), 793-5; Philip H. Towner, *The Letters to Timothy and Titus* (NICNT; Grand Rapids: Eerdmans, 2006), 589; Robert W. Yarbrough, *The Letters to Timothy and Titus* (PNTC; Grand Rapids: Eerdmans, 2018), 429-30.

37. On the occurrences of the term outside the Greek New Testament in literature contemporary to the Greek New Testament, see BDAG, s.v. *theopneustos*. The second part of the word *theopneustos* should be translated passively, 'breathed,' since 'objective verbals compounded with *theos* most frequently – though not always – have a passive meaning...,' Bavinck, *Reformed Dogmatics*, 1:425.

38. Warfield, 'God-Inspired Scripture,' in *Works*, 1:280.

39. ibid.

His own creative fiat, so we should regard the Scriptures as the product of a similar creative fiat.'[40]

To what body of literature does Paul attribute the quality 'breathed out by God'? It is 'all Scripture' (*pasa graphe*). There is a syntactical question attending Paul's expression in 2 Timothy 3:16. Some translators and commentators have urged that the first part of verse 16 should be translated, 'every scripture inspired of God is also profitable ...' On this translation, the adjective *theopneustos* is attributive. But the adjective *theopneustos* is best taken not attributively but predicatively.[41] The translation adopted by most translations and commentators, 'all Scripture is breathed out by God ...,' is the correct one. Even so, the doctrine of inspiration does not necessarily stand or fall upon this translation question.[42]

If 'all Scripture' is 'breathed out by God,' what, then, does Paul understand 'all Scripture' to be? The context supplies the answer in verse 15, 'how from childhood you have been acquainted with *the sacred writings*.'[43] The 'sacred writings,' a phrase that appears only here in the Greek New Testament, refers to the books of the Old Testament. Since Paul places no limitation or qualification upon them, we are bound to take the 'sacred writings' to refer to the entirety of the Old Testament.[44]

Paul, then, is saying that the whole of the Old Testament has its origin in God speaking its words. It is the distillation of the breath of God, as it were. God is the Divine Author of each of the books of the Old Testament. Although Paul refrains here from detailing 'what particular books enter into the collection which he calls Sacred Scriptures, or by

---

40. Packer, *God Has Spoken*, 92.

41. So Towner, *The Letters To Timothy and Titus*, 585, 7; George W. Knight, *The Pastoral Epistles* (NIGTC; Grand Rapids: Eerdmans, 1992), 445-8.

42. Were the adjective attributive, then Paul could be making a claim about a particular class of 'Scripture,' namely, 'the Scripture that is inspired.' Such an expression would then suggest that Paul recognizes a class of 'uninspired Scripture.' The attributive reading, however, need not yield such a conclusion. It could be paraphrased, 'every Scripture, seeing that it is God-breathed, is as well profitable,' an 'assertion' made 'distributively of all [Sacred Scriptures'] parts,' Warfield, 'The Biblical Idea of Inspiration,' in *Works*, 1:80.

43. Bavinck, *Reformed Dogmatics*, 1:437.

44. Compare here Romans 15:4, 'For *whatever was written in former days* was written for our instruction, that through endurance and through the encouragement of *the Scriptures* we might have hope,' ibid.

what precise operations God has produced them,' his main point is clear, to declare 'the value of the Scriptures, and the source of that value in their Divine origin.'[45]

(2) 2 Peter 1:19-21

A second passage that is important for understanding the Bible's testimony to itself is 2 Peter 1:19-21, 'And we have something more sure, the prophetic word, to which you will do well to pay attention, as to a lamp shining in a dark place, until the day dawns and the morning star rises in your hearts, knowing this first of all, that no prophecy of Scripture comes from someone's own interpretation. For no prophecy was ever produced by the will of man, but men spoke from God as they were carried along by the Holy Spirit.'

In the immediately preceding verses (2 Pet. 1:16-18), Peter recounts the Transfiguration of Christ and the voice of God the Father in connection with that event. It is with respect to that occurrence that Peter declares, 'we have something more sure, the prophetic word.' The prophetic word here refers at least to the prophetic books of the Old Testament and likely to the whole of the Old Testament.[46] What does it mean, then, that, in light of the events relayed in verses 16-18, the apostles of verse 18 have the prophetic word 'more sure'?[47] It is doubtful that Peter is saying that the Transfiguration and the divine voice are inherently less certain than the prophetic word. After all, the God who spoke on the Mount of Transfiguration is the same God who spoke through the prophets (Heb. 1:1-3). Likelier is that Peter testifies to the fact that, for him and the other apostles, the events of the Transfiguration have lent a degree of heightened subjective certainty to the Old Testament Scriptures.[48] That

---

45. Warfield, 'The Biblical Idea of Inspiration,' in *Works*, 1:81.

46. So Schreiner, *1, 2 Peter, Jude* (NAC 37; Nashville: B&H, 2003), 319, and the literature cited at 319n.51.

47. Given the appearances of the second person personal pronoun and the second person possessive in the rest of verse 19 and in verse 20, it is almost certain that the first person plural pronoun ('we') is exclusive and not inclusive of the readers, so Schreiner, *1, 2 Peter, Jude*, 318-9. The pronoun, then, refers to Peter, James, and John, the three apostles with Jesus on the Transfiguration mount.

48. So Schreiner, who understands, however, the 'prophetic word' more narrowly in terms of the Old Testament's teaching 'that there is a future coming of Christ for judgment and salvation,' *1,2 Peter, Jude*, 319. See the helpful discussion at Warfield, 'The Biblical Idea of Inspiration,' in *Works*, 1:81-2.

is, the apostles' confidence in the Old Testament Word of God was only intensified and confirmed by the Transfiguration, which 'provide[d] a confirmatory interpretation of that word.'[49]

It is to this 'prophetic word' that Peter points his readers ('to which you will do well to pay attention,' 1:19). He underscores the necessity of the Scripture to the believer. It is a 'lamp shining in a dark place' (1:19). We are bound to give heed to the Old Testament Scripture, Peter tells us, 'until the day dawns and the morning star rises in your hearts' (1:19). For all the difficulties presented by this statement, its basic reference is clear – the return of Christ at the end of the age.[50] The Old Testament Scripture norms the faith and lives of believers until the consummation.

After impressing on the church the reliability, necessity, and perpetuity of the Old Testament Scriptures, Peter turns in the following verse to reflect upon their inherent authority. Translators have differed in their rendering of 2 Peter 1:20. The difference concerns whether the Greek word translated 'one's own' (*idias*) refers to the prophet or the reader of prophecy. Contextual reasons support the latter reading. Peter is stressing that the meaning of Old Testament Scripture is not the product of the will or whim of its readers, not least the 'false teachers' (2:1, cf. 2:1-22).[51]

One reason that the meaning and interpretation of Scripture is not legislated by its readership appears in the following verse. Since prophecy did not originate from 'the will of man,' its meaning and interpretation is not determined by the will of man either (1:20).[52] On the contrary, Peter continues, 'men spoke from God as they were carried along by the Holy Spirit' (1:21). As Warfield paraphrases Peter's statement, 'speaking thus under the determining influence of the Holy Spirit, the things they spoke were not from themselves, but from God.'[53]

---

49. Schreiner, *1, 2 Peter, Jude*, 320.
50. See the helpful discussion of Peter H. Davids, *The Letters of 2 Peter and Jude* (PNTC; Grand Rapids: Eerdmans, 2006), 209-10.
51. On which, see Schreiner, *1, 2 Peter, Jude*, 322-3. For a defense of the former view, see Davids, *Letters*, 210-3.
52. This point, of course, would have been uncontroversial among Peter's readers since the Old Testament clearly and frequently insisted that 'the characteristic of a false prophet was that he prophesied out of his own mind (Jer. 14:14; 23:16; Ezek. 13:3; [Deut. 18:20]),' Davids, *Letters*, 213.
53. Warfield, 'The Biblical Idea of Inspiration,' in *Works*, 1:82.

Peter's words are important for our understanding of the Old Testament Scripture in at least two respects. The first is that he offers unambiguous testimony to the authorship of Scripture. While fully affirming human authorship of the Scripture ('men spoke …'), he at the same time affirms divine authorship of the same ('… as they were carried along by the Holy Spirit'). The second is that Peter's words offer insight into the way in which the Scripture came into being, the intersection of divine and human in the production of Scripture.

> God has produced the Scriptures … through the instrumentality of men who 'spake from him.' More specifically, it was through an operation of the Holy Ghost on these men which is described as 'bearing' them. The term here used is a very specific one. It is not to be confounded with guiding, or directing, or controlling, or even leading in the full sense of that word. It goes beyond all such terms, in assigning the effect produced specifically to the active agent. What is 'born' is taken up by the 'bearer,' and conveyed by the 'bearer's' power, not its own, to the 'bearer's' goal, not its own. The men who spoke from God are here declared, therefore, to have been taken up by the Holy Spirit and brought by his power to the goal of his choosing. The things which they spoke under this operation of the Spirit were therefore his things, not theirs.[54]

Without destroying, much less compromising, the humanity of the human authors of Scripture, God the Spirit, in this work of inspiration, guarantees that these authors' words are God's own Word. We have, then, 'an immediately Divine word.'[55] Peter does not dwell on the details of this concursive work that yields the inspired Word of God. What he does is to affirm both the divine and the human authorship of Scripture, and to do so in such a way as to show that the entirety of the product is God's own Word.

(3) Other Testimonies

As we have noted earlier, 2 Timothy 3:16 and 2 Peter 1:19-21 are by no means the only testimonies that we have to the divine origin and authority of the Scripture. They are distinguished, to be sure, by the fullness and clarity of their testimony. But they sit alongside a host of other passages that bear witness to the same truth.

---

54. ibid., 1:83.
55. ibid., 1:83.

It will be beneficial to expand our review of the biblical evidence for the inspiration of Scripture, if only to confirm our earlier findings. In the above two passages, Paul and Peter have in view the canonical books of the Old Testament. What may be said of the books of the New Testament? What do these twenty-seven books say about their own authority, and how do these statements compare to those that they make about the Old Testament's authority and to those statements that the Old Testament itself makes regarding its own authority?

Both the biblical testimonies to the inspiration of Scripture, and the secondary literature addressing those testimonies are voluminous.[56] A thorough review is beyond the scope of our work here. We may offer, however, a brief survey of some of the leading testimonies pertaining to the Old Testament and to the New Testament.

Testimonies Pertaining to the Old Testament

We have observed above the apostolic statements of 2 Timothy 3:16 and 2 Peter 1:19-21 testifying to the inspiration of the entirety of the text of the Old Testament. The Old Testament writers also bear witness to their own divine origin and authority.[57] There is 'direct speech from God to men and women,' such as we find at Exodus 20:1-4.[58] The prophets frequently and routinely invoke the formula 'thus says the LORD,' indicating that their words originate from the mouth of God Himself. The distinction between a true prophet and a false prophet is that the words of the former proceed from the mind of God; the words of the latter proceed from the mind of man.[59] The Old Testament furthermore frequently testifies to the writing activity of Moses and the Prophets who followed him. The fact that Moses is said to write at the command of God (Exod. 17:14) and that what Moses writes is said to be the Word

---

56. Two recent works that provide structured and useful points of entry into the biblical material are those of Wayne A. Grudem, 'Scripture's Self-Attestation and the Problem of Formulating a Doctrine of Scripture' in *Scripture and Truth* (ed. D. A. Carson and John D. Woodbridge, Grand Rapids: Baker, 1983), 19-59, and Barrett, *God's Word Alone*, 238-62. Still valuable is the work of Bavinck, *Reformed Dogmatics*, 1:389-402, and Warfield, 'The Biblical Idea of Inspiration,' in *Works*, 1:86-99, 109-11.

57. The following is indebted to the outline of Grudem, 'Scripture's Self-Attestation.'

58. ibid., 19.

59. ibid., 22-5. See also the texts cited at n.52 above.

of God (Exod. 24:4) should govern the many other passages in which we are informed that prophets subsequent to Moses engaged in writing activity.[60] In other words, they also wrote at the command of God, and what they wrote is the Word of God.

Strikingly, both Jesus and the apostles in their use of the Old Testament testify to the divine origin and authority of the Old Testament.[61] J. I. Packer explains the importance, in particular, of Jesus' testimony to the Old Testament.

> The Old Testament is to be received on [Jesus'] authority (over and above its own witness to itself as the authoritative written utterance of God, abidingly true and trustworthy). Its divine authority and His confirm each other, so that not to accept both would be to accept neither.[62]

A. A. Hodge and B. B. Warfield summarize the significance of the apostles' testimony to the Old Testament.

> Christ sent out the apostles with the promise of the Holy Ghost, and declared that in hearing them men would hear him. The apostles themselves claimed to speak as the prophets of God, and with plenary authority in his name binding all consciences. And while they did so God endorsed their teaching *and their claims* with signs and wonders and divers miracles. These claims are a universal and inseparable characteristic of every part of Scripture.[63]

With this understanding of the significance of both Jesus' and the apostles' teaching with respect to the Old Testament in place, we may now explore the contents of their respective testimonies. First, we offer a couple of examples from the teaching of Jesus. At the end of His public ministry, Jesus provides an explanation of Psalm 110:1.

---

60. On these passages, and others, see Grudem, 'Scripture's Self-Attestation,' 25-7.

61. It often goes without saying, but it is worth stating explicitly, that the teaching of the New Testament is regulative for the Christian church. If the New Testament makes certain claims about the origin and authority of the Old Testament, then those claims are binding upon the Christian church.

62. Packer, *Fundamentalism*, 59. Packer goes on to note that, 'in conjunction with Christ's teaching, the written word of the Old Testament retains its full, divine authority,' ibid. That is to say, Jesus does not advance His own teaching and authority at the expense of the authority of the Old Testament.

63. Hodge and Warfield, *Inspiration*, 29. Compare the remarks of Warfield, 'Inspiration,' in *SSW*, 2:634-5.

And as Jesus taught in the temple, he said, 'How can the scribes say that the Christ is the son of David? David himself, in the Holy Spirit, declared, "The Lord said to my Lord, 'Sit at my right hand, until I put your enemies under your feet.'" David himself calls him Lord. So how is he his son?' And the great throng heard him gladly (Mark 12:35-7).

In introducing this statement of David, Jesus says, 'David himself, in the Holy Spirit, declared.' Jesus recognizes that David is the author of this Psalm. But David is not the sole author of this Psalm. What he utters, he uttered 'in the Holy Spirit.' The Holy Spirit is the author of this text no less than David is. David wrote by inspiration of the Holy Spirit.

Also towards the end of His public ministry, Jesus quotes the teaching of Genesis 2 in relation to the creation of Adam and Eve and the institution of marriage.

[Jesus] answered, 'Have you not read that he who created them from the beginning made them male and female, and said, "Therefore a man shall leave his father and his mother and hold fast to his wife, and they shall become one flesh"? So they are no longer two but one flesh. What therefore God has joined together, let not man separate' (Matt. 19:4-6).

Jesus identifies the author of the words of Genesis 2:24 ('Therefore a man shall leave his father and his mother and hold fast to his wife, and they shall become one flesh') with the One who created Adam and Eve. Jesus explicitly identifies this author as 'God.' As Warfield observes, however, 'this passage [i.e., Gen. 2:24] does not give us a saying of God's recorded in Scripture, but just the word of Scripture itself, and can be treated as a declaration of God's only on the hypothesis that all Scripture is a declaration of God's.'[64] The fact that Jesus can point to the descriptive statement of Genesis 2:24 as God's utterance is reflective of His general conviction that the whole of Scripture has God as its author.

The apostles share precisely the same commitment as Jesus with respect to the origin and authority of Scripture. The epistle to the Hebrews, when quoting from Psalm 95, identifies the author of the psalm as 'the Holy Spirit,' 'Therefore, as the Holy Spirit says, "Today, if you hear his voice..."' (Heb. 3:7). Hebrews does not, of course, deny that Psalm 95 is a human composition. But it affirms that the anonymous

---

64. Warfield, 'The Biblical Idea of Inspiration,' in *Works*, 1:89.

author wrote the psalm by inspiration of the Holy Spirit. The apostle Peter declared in the upper room, after the ascension, 'Brothers, the Scripture had to be fulfilled, which the Holy Spirit spoke beforehand by the mouth of David concerning Judas ...' (Acts 1:16). Peter proceeds, in verse 20, to quote from Psalm 69 and Psalm 109, both psalms that are attributed to David. Once again, we see not only an affirmation that David is the human author of these psalms, but also that the Holy Spirit is the author of these psalms. The words of these psalms are no less the Holy Spirit's than they are David's. Furthermore, as Peter says, the 'Holy Spirit spoke ... by the mouth of David.' These portions of Scripture are at one and the same time the compositions of God the Spirit and His human instrument, David.[65]

We may also register a pattern of locution that appears across the New Testament writings with respect to the Old Testament Scripture. The New Testament authors are entirely comfortable interchanging 'God' with 'Scripture.' For example, in Romans 9:17, Paul says, 'For the Scripture says to Pharaoh, "For this very purpose I have raised you up, that I might show my power in you, and that my name might be proclaimed in all the earth."' What is striking is that in the verse that Paul quotes (Exod. 9:16), 'the Lord' is the one identified as the speaker of these words (see Exod. 9:13). When Paul quotes this verse, however, it is 'Scripture' that is said to speak these words. As Grudem notes, 'there is in Paul's mind an equivalence between the nature of what Scripture says and the nature of what God says.'[66] Paul does the same thing in Galatians 3:8, when he cites the text of Genesis 12:3. As Warfield demonstrated with clarity and fullness over a century ago, the expressions 'it says,' 'Scripture says,' and 'God says' are interchangeable expressions.[67] There is, Warfield argued, 'an absolute identification, in the minds of [the New Testament] writers, of "Scripture" with the speaking God.'[68] The reason that the New Testament writers make this equation is not difficult to discern. This manner of speaking arises

---

65. Compare precisely the same pattern at Acts 4:24-6, in which the early believers quote Psalm 2 as the Holy Spirit speaking 'through the mouth of our father David ...'
66. Grudem, 'Scripture's Self-Attestation,' 39.
67. Warfield, '"It Says:" "Scripture Says:" "God Says"' in *Works*, 1:283-332.
68. ibid., 1:284.

directly from their conviction that the whole of Scripture is authored by God.

The New Testament

When we come to the writings of the New Testament, we may ask the same question of them that we have asked of the writings of the Old Testament: How did the New Testament writers regard their own writings? Did their commitment to the divine origin, inspiration, and authority of the Old Testament translate to the New Testament? We may initially explore how the New Testament writers viewed their own writings. We may identify at least two ways in which the New Testament writers provide an answer to this question. First, we will see that the New Testament writers understood their writings to be the equivalent of the Old Testament with respect to divine authorship and authority. One important way in which they demonstrate this conviction is by conjoining their writings with the books of the Old Testament as regulative of the church's faith and practice. In other words, the authors of the New Testament reveal an awareness that, under the supervision of the apostles, the canon of Scripture was expanding. New books – the books that we call the 'New Testament' – were being added to the existing corpus of Scripture. We are not yet prepared to address the question, 'which books constitute the canon of the New Testament?'. But we will here show that within the New Testament there is an awareness that the canon is expanding, which in turn demonstrates how the New Testament writers regarded their own writings and how these writers taught the church to regard these writings.

Second, we will see that the New Testament authors understood their writings to carry the authority of Jesus Christ Himself. That is to say, a statement of Peter or Paul in their letters has precisely the same authority as a statement of Jesus Christ recorded for us in the Gospels. To reject an apostolic teaching or to disobey an apostolic command, then, is to reject the teaching or command of Christ Himself.

Foundational to the consideration of the origin and authority of the New Testament writings is the teaching of Jesus in the Upper Room on the eve of His crucifixion. The Upper Room discourse is designed to prepare the apostles for life and ministry after the death, resurrection, and ascension of Jesus Christ. One of the ways in which Jesus prepares the apostles is by apprizing them of the ministry of the Spirit whom He will send upon His exaltation. One way in which the Spirit will minister to the apostles is by furnishing them with the teaching of Jesus that they will provide to the church.

> But the Helper, the Holy Spirit, whom the Father will send in my name, he will teach you all things and bring to your remembrance all that I have said to you (John 14:26).

> I still have many things to say to you, but you cannot bear them now. When the Spirit of truth comes, he will guide you into all the truth, for he will not speak on his own authority, but whatever he hears he will speak, and he will declare to you the things that are to come. He will glorify me, for he will take what is mine and declare it to you. All that the Father has is mine; therefore I said that he will take what is mine and declare it to you (John 16:12-15).

We will return to these important statements in the next chapter. We may simply register a few observations at this juncture of our reflection. First, Jesus is speaking to the eleven apostles. He is not directly addressing Christians in every time and place. As such His words apply to the apostles in a way that they do not to other Christians.[69] One way in which this specificity of application becomes clear is from the content of the promise that Jesus makes. Jesus promises that the Father will send the 'Holy Spirit,' the 'Spirit of truth' to the apostles. The Spirit will come to teach them. He will 'bring to your remembrance all that I have said to you,' and He will also 'speak' and 'declare' to the apostles words of Christ that they have not yet heard, since they 'cannot bear them now.' Christ, then, generates the expectation that the Spirit will verbally reveal Christ's mind to the apostles. This promise is a promise of revelation that is written by inspiration. When the apostles subsequently deliver writings to the New Testament church by way of imposition, our expectation is that these compositions have been produced by inspiration of the Holy Spirit. As such, these books will give an indication of their character as the inspired Word of God.

While the writings of the New Testament are not saturated with these explicit indications, they are nevertheless present. In some passages, the

---

69. D. A. Carson, *The Gospel According to John* (PNTC; Grand Rapids: Eerdmans, 1991), 541, 542.

apostles relate the writings of the New Testament to the Old Testament Scripture. In others, they relate the writings of the New Testament to the teaching of Jesus. We may look at five particularly striking examples, three from the letters of Paul, and two from the letters of Peter.[70]

In 1 Corinthians 14:37, Paul is addressing the disorder within the worship of the Corinthian church. One of the problems in Corinth centers around the activity of some who are speaking in tongues and others who are actively prophesying. Paul does not deny but affirms that what they are bringing to the church is 'revelation' (see 1 Cor. 14:30). His concern is that the way in which these individuals are exercising their gifts does not promote the edification of the church (1 Cor. 14:26). Paul therefore lays down explicit guidelines for the way in which tongue-speaking and prophesying are to transpire in the assembly.[71] Paul asserts not only these guidelines but his authority in laying them down, 'If anyone thinks that he is a prophet, or spiritual, he should acknowledge that the things I am writing to you are a command of the Lord' (1 Cor. 14:37).[72] Paul here identifies his instructions with 'a command of the Lord,' that is, of the Lord Jesus Christ. He insists in the following verse that 'if anyone does not recognize this, he is not recognized' (1 Cor. 14:38). To disobey these instructions (that is, this 'command of the Lord') and Paul's Christ-given authority in giving them is therefore to forfeit recognition within the Christian church. The question arises whether this claim (and the authority of the person who administered this claim) is anomalous for Paul's teaching in general. The answer is a firm 'no.' As Grudem has astutely observed,

---

70. Four of these five passages surface in compositions whose authenticity has been questioned. That is to say, many historical-critical scholars doubt that Paul authored 2 Thessalonians or 1 Timothy and that Peter authored 2 Peter. In what follows, we regard these letters as authentic compositions of those apostles. This understanding is based upon the testimony of the letters themselves and reflects the early, widespread, and unchallenged judgment of the early church tasked with discerning genuine from spurious writings that claimed to be authored by the apostles. For a concise defense of the authenticity of each of these letters, see D. A. Carson and Douglas J. Moo, *An Introduction to the New Testament* (2d ed.; Grand Rapids: Zondervan, 2005).

71. In a later chapter, we will address the question whether the gifts of tongues and prophesy continue into the contemporary church.

72. Were Paul's authority not clear to the congregation, it could appear to uninformed onlookers an act of presumption to lay down guidelines and restrictions governing the dissemination of the 'word of God' to the congregation (1 Cor. 14:36).

'it is inconceivable that all the instructions in 1 Corinthians 12-14 are based on words of the earthly Jesus handed down to Paul through oral or written tradition ... Rather, Paul has here instituted a number of new rules for church worship at Corinth and has claimed for them the status of "commands of the Lord."'[73] These commands, in other words, arise in unmediated fashion from Paul's apostolic authority. If these commands carry intrinsic dominical authority, our presumption is that all of Paul's teaching bears such authority.[74]

This presumption finds confirmation in Paul's teaching in 2 Thessalonians 3:14, 'If anyone does not obey what we say in this letter, take note of that person, and have nothing to do with him, that he may be ashamed.' This claim follows an extended chain of commands, beginning in verse 6. There Paul tells the church that he 'command[s]' them 'in the name of our Lord Jesus Christ,' a point he repeats in verse 12, 'Now such persons we command and encourage in the Lord Jesus Christ ...' The commanding authority that Paul invokes is not grounded in his person, but in the Lord Jesus Christ. In this context, Paul understands no practical distinction between the authority of his command and the authority of the Lord Jesus Christ. In verse 14, Paul stresses the consequences of disobedience to the apostolic command. Such disobedience subjects one to the severe discipline of the church.

---

73. Grudem, 'Scripture's Self-Attestation,' 48.

74. Note Grudem's handling of the objection, frequently raised, from 1 Cor. 7:12, 'To the rest I say (I, not the Lord),' in which Paul appears to be distancing his teaching from that of the Lord Jesus Christ, 'It is undeniable that such a distinction is made, but it must be evaluated in the light of verses 25 and 40. In verse 25, Paul says that he has no command (*epitage*) of the Lord concerning the unmarried, but will give his own opinion. This means at least that he had possession of no earthly word of Jesus on this subject and probably also that he had received no subsequent revelation about it. In verse 12, then, the meaning must be that in this area Paul had no earthly words of Jesus that he could quote,' 'Scripture's Self-Attestation,' 47. Such an approach to the text is confirmed by Paul's words in 1 Cor. 7:10, 'To the married I give this charge (not I, but the Lord) ...' The charge that follows is a summarization of Jesus' earthly teaching about divorce. Paul is taking care in 1 Cor. 7:10 to reference the earthly teaching of Jesus. He is taking care in 1 Cor. 7:12 to uphold the integrity of the written record of Jesus' earthly teachings by stressing that the command that follows was not one uttered by Jesus in the course of His earthly ministry. The particular distinction that Paul draws here in verses 10 and 12 in no way precludes the teaching of verse 12 from being the teaching of the risen Christ through His servant, the apostle Paul. There is, therefore, no inherent contradiction between what Paul says in 1 Cor. 14:37 and what he says in 1 Cor. 7:10, 12.

The implication is that persistence in disobedience subjects one to formal removal from the church.

Paul's claim here, however, is not limited to the sequence of commands beginning in verse 6. On the contrary, the warning of verse 14 extends to 'what we say in this letter.' The whole of Paul's teaching in 2 Thessalonians, therefore, is regulative of the church's belief and obedience and carries the authority of the risen Lord Jesus Christ. What Paul says to the church in this letter is what Jesus Christ says to the church. Once again, there is no indication that Paul understood himself to be doing something extraordinary with respect to his teaching ministry as an apostle. On the contrary, Paul's claims in these verses emerge organically from his teaching in these verses. Our expectation is that Paul's claim in verse 14 is not singular but is representative of his teaching preserved in the letters that bear his name.[75]

In 1 Timothy 5:18, Paul makes a claim not about his own writings but another portion of what we now call the New Testament, 'For the Scripture says, "You shall not muzzle an ox when it treads out the grain," and, "The laborer deserves his wages."' In this verse, Paul provides grounds for his command in verse 17.[76] These words are two quotations that both fall under the heading, 'the Scripture says.' The first quotation derives from Deuteronomy 25:4, a verse that Paul had previously quoted in 1 Corinthians 9:9. The second quotation is a quotation from the teaching of Jesus Christ. It appears in two places in the Gospels, Matthew 10:10 and Luke 10:7. Strikingly, the Greek text of 1 Timothy 5:18 and of Luke 10:7 are identical. This identity has prompted the conclusion that Paul is not merely placing Jesus' teaching alongside the Old Testament and within the category of 'Scripture.' He is equally placing the Gospel according to Luke in the same category.[77] Towards

---

75. This point helps to shed light on the importance of Paul's claim in 2 Thessalonians 2:15, 'So then, brothers, stand firm and hold to the traditions that you were taught by us, either by our spoken word or by our letter' (cf. 2:2, 'not to be quickly shaken in mind or alarmed, either by a spirit or spoken word, or a letter seeming to be from us, to the effect that the day of the Lord has come'). The fact that Paul's letters carried the divine authority that they did accentuated for Paul the importance of the church's discerning authentic from spurious compositions of Paul.

76. Though it should be stressed that the claim of verse 17, as an apostolic command, bears intrinsic or inherent authority.

77. Knight, *Pastoral Epistles*, 234.

the close of his apostolic ministry, then, Paul testifies to the expanding canon of Scripture. Writing with divine authority, Paul testifies to Luke's Gospel as the Word of God, no less than the books of the Old Testament are the Word of God.

In two passages, the apostle Peter testifies both to the expanding canon of Scripture and to the inherent divine authority of the writings of the New Testament. An important statement comes in 2 Peter 3:1ff., 'remember the predictions of the holy prophets and the commandment of the Lord and Savior through your apostles.' While it is possible that Peter refers to New Testament prophets in this verse, the context suggests that he has Old Testament prophets in mind.[78] To the 'predictions of the holy prophets,' Peter conjoins 'the commandment of the Lord and Savior ...' He understands, then, the teaching of Jesus Christ to carry the same divine authority as the prophetic teaching referenced here. This 'commandment,' furthermore, is given 'through your apostles.'[79] 'The point is that the words of Jesus Christ had been transmitted by the apostles.'[80] Likely in view is not a subset of Jesus' teaching but 'the teaching of Jesus in general as a command.'[81] Peter, therefore, is pointing to the authoritative transmission of Jesus' teaching to the church by the apostles. It is this teaching, in its apostolic form, that shares the same authority as the prophetic teachings that Peter references in this same verse. Peter, then, testifies to an expanding canon in which the writings of the apostles are being incorporated into the existing Scriptures of the

---

78. So, rightly, Schreiner, *1,2 Peter, Jude*, 370; Davids, *The Letters*, 260. Schreiner notes that in 1:16-21, Peter conjoins 'apostolic (1:16-18) and prophetic (1:19-21) testimony to verify the future coming of the Lord,' and references in 'revers[e] ... order' the same two groups in 3:2, ibid.

79. Commentators debate the precise identity of 'your apostles.' Some take it to refer to 'the "college" of the apostles, that is, the original apostles thought of as a group,' Davids, *The Letters*, 261. Some commentators who adopt this view point to this expression ('your apostles') as 'evidence for the post-apostolic date of 2 Peter,' ibid. But this conclusion is hardly a necessary inference from such a denotation of the phrase. Others, as Schreiner and Green, take the phrase 'your apostles' more narrowly, to refer to a subset of the apostles. For purposes of our discussion, however, it is not important to resolve the question whether 'your apostles' is to be construed broadly or narrowly. Peter is making a point that pertains to the office and work of an apostle, however many apostles may be in view numerically.

80. Schreiner, *1, 2 Peter, Jude*, 371.

81. Davids, *The Letters*, 261.

Old Testament. Those writings, no less than the Old Testament, are the Word of God.

A few verses later, in verses 15-16, Peter makes this point explicit. He mentions 'our beloved brother Paul' who wrote to Peter's audience 'according to the wisdom given him, as he does in all his letters when he speaks in them of these matters. There are some things in them that are hard to understand which the ignorant and unstable twist to their own destruction, as they do the other Scriptures.' The reference to 'all his letters' suggests that, even in Peter's lifetime, Paul's letters were being collected and circulated within the early church.[82] The phrase 'according to the wisdom given him' suggests an awareness that Paul's letters are not merely human compositions. His letters evidence a wisdom not his own, one that God has given to him. It is at the end of the verse that Peter makes an extraordinary claim that lends depth to his declaration that Paul wrote according to divine wisdom. Peter classifies Paul's letters with what he calls 'the other Scriptures.' Peter thus testifies to the church's recognition that the letters of Paul are the Word of God, that they belong to the expanding canon of Scripture.[83] It is in light of this classification, then, that we may fairly conclude that the grant of wisdom to which Peter refers in verse 15 denotes the work of inspiration in connection with the composition of Paul's letters.

In summary, we have seen indications from within the New Testament writings that the authors regarded themselves as writing with divine authority. Paul was conscious of writing with dominical authority (1 Cor. 14:37), an authority that was non-negotiable in the Christian church (2 Thess. 3:14). Peter not only points to the fact that the apostles authoritatively transmit the teaching of Jesus to the church, but also that this apostolic teaching carries the same authority as the prophetic teaching of the Old Testament. Each is the Word of God. In the wake of this assertion, Peter classifies the collection of Paul's letters

---

82. J. N. D. Kelly, *The Epistles of Peter and Jude* (HNTC; New York: Harper & Row, 1969), 371; *Pace* Schreiner, *1, 2 Peter, Jude*, 396; Moo, *2 Peter, Jude*, 310-11. It is fair to say, however, we do not know how many letters were at this time compiled and in circulation. What is important, for our purposes, is that there was an existing collection that was known by and familiar to more than one congregation of the church (cf. 1 Pet. 1:1).

83. For a lexical defense of the Greek word translated 'other' denoting 'another of the same kind,' see Schreiner, *1, 2 Peter, Jude*, 398.

as 'Scripture' and acknowledges that they were given by inspiration of the Holy Spirit.

For these reasons, everything that the apostles predicate of the Old Testament (see 2 Tim. 3:16, 2 Pet. 1:19-21) applies equally to the writings of the New Testament. There are no degrees of authority or divinity when one compares each of the two Testaments. Each body consists of human compositions, but not mere human compositions. Human beings authored these books by inspiration of the Holy Spirit. As such, each book in its entirety and from its inception is the very Word of God.

We should also appreciate how recognition of the authority of the books of both Testaments brings us back to the authoritative teaching of Jesus Christ. We recognize the authority of the Old Testament in light of the authoritative teaching of Jesus Christ about the Old Testament.[84] It is, furthermore, to the authority of Jesus Christ that the apostles appeal in their own writings. And it is by the authority that Christ has granted to the apostles that they testify to the expanding canon of Scripture, specifically, the inclusion of our New Testament writings in the church's Bible.[85] The divine origin, inspiration, and authority of the Bible, then, rests upon the authority of the apostles and, correspondingly, the authority of the head and king of the church, Jesus Christ.

Alternative Views to Plenary, Verbal Inspiration

Within the church and academy, however, there have arisen views of the Bible that either deny or compromise the Bible's testimony about itself.

---

84. Acknowledging, of course, that Jesus did not lend to the Old Testament something that it did not previously have. Its authority was and remains inherent to itself. One benefit of Jesus' testimony is not only that it is rendered with divine authority itself, but that it also addresses the Scriptures of the Old Testament in comprehensive fashion. It is from the teaching of Jesus that in especially clear fashion we understand that the entirety of the Old Testament is the Word of God.

85. 'Apostolicity thus determines the authority of Scripture; and any book or body of books which were given to the Church by the apostles as law must always remain of divine authority in the Church. That the apostles thus gave the Church the whole Old Testament, which they had themselves received from their fathers as God's word written, admits of no doubt, and is not doubted. That they gradually added to this body of old law an additional body of new law is equally patent ... [A]ll the books which now constitute our Bible, and which Christians from that day to this, have loyally treated as their divinely prescribed book of law, no more and no fewer, were thus imposed on the Church as its divinely authoritative rule of faith and practice,' Warfield, 'The Authority and Inspiration of the Scriptures,' in *SSW*, 2:538-9.

Although we will not offer a full and comprehensive survey or critique of such views, we will sketch here three of the leading alternatives to plenary, verbal inspiration.[86] The first argues for a partial or limited inspiration of the Bible. The second argues against plenary, verbal inspiration by arguing that one should understand the Scripture along the lines of analogy of the theanthropic person of Christ. As Christ has two distinct natures, the divine and the human, so also the Scripture is said to have two natures, divine and human. The third is a view that is thought to have been embraced by many conservatives and, in this respect, differs from the previous two views. It understands the Bible to have been given by dictation or mechanical inspiration.

The first view is really a family of views. Instead of seeing the whole Bible as the inspired Word of God, it limits inspiration in some fashion. This limitation admits of a number of forms.[87] We may mention two of these forms. The first limits inspiration to what are said to be the 'doctrinal teaching[s]' of the Bible.[88] This view often claims that there are historical, geographical, or scientific errors within the Bible. These alleged errors are not attributed to the Spirit but to the human authors in distinction from the Spirit. Without exploring this view in detail, we may identify at least two problems with it. The first is that it requires the reader to partition the Bible into portions for which the Spirit assumes authorial responsibility and portions that are alleged to be the product of fallible and errant human composition. But this is not the testimony of the Bible to itself. If this view were correct, that is, if there were proven errors in the Bible, then the solution is not to alter our view of inspiration

---

86. In Chapters 7 and 8, we will engage more comprehensively two influential alternatives to the Bible's teaching about itself.

87. The following taxonomy is indebted to that of Hodge, *Systematic Theology*, 1:181-2.

88. Hodge, *Systematic Theology*, 1:181. One classical expression of this view is Henry Preserved Smith, *Inspiration and Inerrancy: A History and a Defense* (Cincinnati: Robert Clark & Co., 1893), on which see the review by B. B. Warfield, 'Professor Henry Preserved Smith, On Inspiration' *Presbyterian and Reformed Review* V (1894): 600-53, repr. *Limited Inspiration* (Phillipsburg, NJ: P&R, 1962). A more recent articulation of this view is Richard Coleman, 'Reconsidering "Limited Inerrancy,"' *JETS* 17 (1974): 207-14. For responses to Coleman's view in particular, see Vern S. Poythress, 'Problems for Limited Inerrancy,' *JETS* 18/2 (1975): 93-102, and John Frame, *The Doctrine of the Word of God* (Phillipsburg, NJ: P&R, 2010), 167. For a brief critical response to limited inerrancy, see John S. Feinberg, *Light in a Dark Place: The Doctrine of Scripture* (Wheaton, IL: Crossway, 2018), 303-7.

by delimitation. The solution is to reject inspiration altogether. The second problem with partial or limited inspiration is that it runs into an insuperable practical difficulty. The line between doctrinal teaching and historical, geographical, or scientific errors is not as clear as it is sometimes alleged.[89] The resurrection, for instance, is equally doctrinal and historical (see 1 Cor. 15:1-11).[90] If the resurrection is not a fact of history, then it is a false doctrine and our faith is vain (15:14).

The second way in which some attempt to limit inspiration is by claiming that inspiration extends to the thoughts of the biblical writers but not to their words. That is to say, the text of Scripture is the human authors' fallible attempt to verbalize those infallible thoughts that they have received from the Spirit of God. There are at least two problems with this view. The first is that it is counter to the Scripture's testimony that inspiration extends to the words of the Bible. This testimony, for instance, accounts for the way in which the New Testament writers can suspend an argument on a single word of the text of the Old Testament, a text they regard as given by inspiration of God (see Gal. 3:16, Heb. 4:7; Rom. 15:9-12).[91] The second problem with this view is that it requires us to conceive inspiration in terms of wordless or non-verbal thoughts. But, as John Feinberg has recently observed, 'how can concepts be communicated to biblical writers (or anyone else) without using language? And if a concept requires pristine clarity, then the words used to divulge it to the biblical writer will need to be precise. This idea that anyone could inspire thoughts without the use of actual words goes contrary to the most fundamental intuitions of philosophy of language, and of common sense.'[92] It is not simply that this view of inspiration is contrary to the testimony of Scripture. It is fundamentally contrary to the way in which God has structured the human mind.

---

89. 'Who is to say what is faith and what is not? Those who claim that the Bible is infallible only as a rule of faith do not define where faith begins and where it ends,' E. J. Young, *Thy Word Is Truth: Thoughts on the Biblical Doctrine of Inspiration* (1957; repr. Edinburgh: Banner of Truth, 1963), 101.

90. See Frame, *Doctrine of the Word of God,* 177-8.

91. In the last text, Paul is supporting his claim in Romans 15:8-9a from the texts of Scripture cited in Romans 15:9, 10, 11, 12. Each of these four texts has the word 'Gentiles,' a word that is crucial to his claim in 15:8-9a ('... in order that the Gentiles might glorify God for his mercy').

92. Feinberg, *Light in a Dark Place,* 215.

A second proposed alternative to plenary, verbal inspiration argues for an analogy between the two natures of Christ and the Bible. Just as the divine Word became flesh, so also we may understand the Scripture as incarnate. To be clear, an analogical understanding of Scripture is not necessarily antithetical to plenary, verbal inspiration.[93] Many of its recognized proponents, however, have presented their views in opposition to plenary, verbal inspiration. With this qualification in mind, we may reflect on those forms of the analogical understanding of Scripture that consciously reject plenary, verbal inspiration. One such form has surfaced in a recent and influential treatment of the doctrine of Scripture.[94] We will explore this proposal more fully in a later chapter. For now, we may reflect on analogical understandings of Scripture in more general fashion.

It is important, in the first place, to note that there is nothing inherently objectionable to the observation that there is an analogy between the 'divine-human personality' of Christ and the Scripture.[95] The stalwart inerrantist, Warfield, observes that such an analogy 'calls attention to an important fact, and the analogy holds good at a certain distance. There are human and Divine sides to Scripture, and, as we cursorily examine it, we may perceive in it, alternately, traits which suggest now the one, now the other factor in its origin.' [96] The problem, Warfield continues, is that there are a host of points at which Christ and Scripture are not analogous.[97] The analogical relation, he concludes, is ultimately a 'remote' one and not particularly well-suited to elucidating the nature of Scripture.[98]

---

93. Some have appealed to this view in support of plenary, verbal inspiration, so Nigel M. de S. Cameron, 'Incarnation and Inscripturation: The Christological Analogy in the Light of Recent Discussion,' *SBET* 3 (1985): 35-46, as cited at Feinberg, *Light in a Dark Place,* 220n.26. We will explore orthodox Reformed statements and assessments of the Incarnational Analogy in Chapter 8.

94. Peter Enns, *Inspiration and Incarnation: Evangelicals and the Problem of the Old Testament* (Grand Rapids: Baker, 2005), and *Inspiration and Incarnation: Evangelicals and the Problem of the Old Testament* (2d ed.; Grand Rapids: Baker, 2015).

95. Warfield, 'The Biblical Idea of Inspiration,' in *Works,* 1:108.

96. ibid.

97. On which, see Feinberg, *Light in a Dark Place,* 224-8.

98. Warfield, 'The Biblical Idea of Inspiration,' in *Works,* 1:108. Compare the concurring judgment of Packer, 'at best the analogy between the divine-human person of

The problem, however, with some proposals arguing for an analogy between Christ and the Scripture is that they suffer from defective Christology, a defective view of the Bible, or both. Certain proponents have pled for errors in the Bible in light of the fact, they reason, that the Bible is human. A genuinely human document, they argue, is fallible and will contain errors. Just as the deity of Christ does not overwhelm His humanity, so also, it is claimed, the divine element of Scripture does not overwhelm the human element.[99]

What are the difficulties with this particular rendering of the analogy? One concerns its poor Christology. This analogy suggests that the humanity of Christ is fallible and possibly even sinful. It suggests that the divine Son of God took into personal union with Himself fallen humanity. Both its understanding of the humanity of Christ and the relationship between the two natures of Christ are contrary to the Scripture's teaching about the person of Christ.

It is also mistaken to say that that the biblical books, because they are human compositions, contain errors. Sin, of course, is a pervasive aspect of our fallen human experience, and the doctrine of Scripture does not claim that the human authors were immaculate people. But sin is not a necessary attendant of humanity and human experience.[100] Furthermore, because the Bible is a divinely authored book and because the Spirit worked upon the human authors to produce the inspired text of Scripture, we may and must insist that the Bible, a fully human composition, is without error.

Those who have pressed the analogical view in service of an errant Bible, then, face two problems. One is that the person of Christ and the Bible are not strictly or precisely analogous with respect to the matter under consideration, that is, the interrelation of the divine and the human.[101] The other is that this particular analogical view yields

---

the Word made flesh, who is Christ, and the divine-human product of the Word written, which is Scripture, can be only a limited one,' *Fundamentalism*, 82-3.

99. See the discussions at Packer, *Fundamentalism*, 82-4; Feinberg, *Light in a Dark Place*, 225.

100. Adam and Eve, after all, were created in righteousness. The saints in heaven are now righteous and without sin.

101. 'There is no hypostatic union between the Divine and the human in Scripture; we cannot parallel the "inscripturation" of the Holy Spirit and the incarnation of the

a defective Christology, specifically in its predication of the fallen humanity of Christ. In point of fact, and this is where the analogy properly holds, in both Christ and the Bible, the fully human nature and the fully human text are entirely free from sin.[102]

A third and final view that departs from plenary, verbal inspiration has been termed mechanical inspiration or the theory of dictation. This view has a particular understanding of the way in which the human authors composed the text of Scripture.

> [T]he mental activity of the writers was simply suspended, apart from what was necessary for the mechanical transcription of words supernaturally introduced into their consciousness.[103]

In this respect, according to this view, 'the human writers have contributed no quality of their own to the product, save as a musical instrument may contribute a quality to the music played upon it.'[104] They are 'passive instruments or amanuenses – pens, not penmen, of God.'[105] This view minimizes, even eliminates, the authorial contribution of the human writers in the interests of safeguarding the text of Scripture as divinely authored.

How may we respond to this understanding of the Bible? First, it should be noted that critics of plenary, verbal inspiration frequently confuse that view with mechanical inspiration. In point of fact,

---

Son of God. The Scriptures are merely the product of Divine and human forces working together to produce a product in the production of which the human forces work under the initiation and prevalent direction of the Divine: the person of Our Lord unites in itself Divine and human natures, each of which retains its distinctness while operating only in relation to the other. Between such diverse things there can exist only a remote analogy; and, in point of fact, the analogy in the present instance amounts to no more than that in both cases Divine and human factors are involved, though very differently. In the one they unite to constitute a Divine-human person, in the other they cooperate to perform a Divine-human work,' Warfield, 'The Biblical Idea of Inspiration,' in *Works*, 1:108.

102. So rightly, Warfield, 'The Biblical Idea of Inspiration,' in *Works*, 1:108-9. The humanity of Christ, in light of the fact that 'it can never act out of relation with the Divine nature into conjunction with which it has been brought;' the 'human factors' of Scripture, because 'they have not acted apart from the Divine factors, by themselves, but only under their unerring guidance,' ibid.

103. Packer, *Fundamentalism*, 78-9.

104. Warfield, 'Inspiration,' in *SSW*, 2:628.

105. Augustus H. Strong, *Systematic Theology: A Compendium and Commonplace-Book Designed for the Use of Theological Students* (Philadelphia: Judson, 1907), 208.

mechanical inspiration denies something that plenary, verbal inspiration is concerned to affirm, the genuine humanity of the Bible. But it is not only critics of plenary, verbal inspiration who make this mistake. Even its proponents occasionally misidentify other theologians as advocates of the dictation theory. A. H. Strong, for instance, mistakenly identifies the Free Church theologian, William Cunningham, as a proponent of 'the dictation-theory' because of a single and likely non-technical use of the word 'dictate.'[106] Second, while it is not quite correct to say that the 'dictation theory' is a 'man of straw,' it is decidedly a minority opinion within the tradition of the churches of the Reformation.[107] It has found a few proponents in both the Lutheran and the Reformed traditions, particularly in the seventeenth century, but it does not reflect the mainstream of theological reflection since the Reformation.[108] It is fairer to say that mechanical inspiration likely finds a more congenial home in popular, conservative reflection on the Bible.

Third, it should be noted that 'there are instances when God's communications were uttered in an audible voice and took a definite form of words, and that this was sometimes accompanied with the command to commit the words to writing.'[109] Such instances include Exodus 20:22 with Exodus 20:1-17, and Revelation 19:9. The plausibility of mechanical inspiration arises from the fact that it appears to account for some phenomena of the Scripture. But it is far from being a satisfactory account of the way in which God brought the Scripture as a whole into being. The testimony of the biblical writers, as we have seen, is that the divine activity of the Spirit in the production of Scripture did not obliterate or supersede the personalities of the human authors.[110] The doctrine of plenary, verbal inspiration 'did not necessarily involve an abnormal state of mind on the writer's part, such as a trance, or vision,

---

106. Strong cites Cunningham, 'The verbal inspiration of the Scriptures implies in general that the words of Scripture were suggested or dictated by the Holy Spirit as well as the substance of the matter, and this, not only in some portion of the Scriptures, but through the whole,' *Systematic Theology*, 209.

107. The expression is that of Packer, *Fundamentalism*, 79.

108. For a list of particular proponents, see Warfield, 'Inspiration,' in *SSW*, 2:629.

109. Strong, *Systematic Theology*, 209. The examples that follow come from Strong's discussion.

110. A point that holds even in the case of prophecy, so the careful and extended reflections of Warfield on this point, 'The Biblical Idea of Revelation,' in *Works*, 1:21-6.

or hearing a voice.'[111] On the contrary, inspiration acknowledges the full humanity of the human biblical authors. All that inspiration denies to the compositions of those authors is error.

Inerrancy

We have seen that one of the implications of the doctrine of inspiration for our understanding of the Bible is that the text of the Bible is free from error. That is to say, the Bible is the inerrant Word of God. For much of the twentieth century, the inerrancy of Scripture was a point of considerable debate both inside and outside the church.[112] This debate continues into the present century.[113]

In this section, we will address inerrancy in two ways. First, we will reflect upon the term 'inerrant' and consider the warrant for its application to the Bible. Second, we will briefly consider some of the main lines of objection that have come against the doctrine of inerrancy.

The Bible Is the Inerrant Word of God

What do we mean by the term 'inerrant'? Is it the best word to use to describe the Bible that God has given us or are there better words that are preferable? The words 'inerrancy' and 'infallibility' are often used

---

111. Packer, *Fundamentalism*, 78.

112. These debates generated a considerable literature dedicated to articulating and defending the doctrine. Some of these important volumes include Carl F. H. Henry, ed., *Revelation and the Bible: Contemporary Evangelical Thought* (Grand Rapids: Baker, 1958); Merrill C. Tenney, ed., *The Bible: The Living Word of Revelation* (Grand Rapids: Zondervan, 1968); John Warwick Montgomery, ed., *God's Inerrant Word: An International Symposium on the Trustworthiness of Scripture* (Minneapolis: Bethany Fellowship, 1974); James M. Boice, ed., *The Foundation of Biblical Authority* (Grand Rapids: Zondervan, 1978); Norman L. Geisler, ed., *Inerrancy* (Grand Rapids: Zondervan, 1979); Ronald Youngblood, ed., *Evangelicals and Inerrancy: Selections From the Journal of the Evangelical Theological Society* (Nashville: Thomas Nelson, 1984); Roger R. Nicole and J. Ramsey Michaels, eds., *Inerrancy and Common Sense* (Grand Rapids: Baker, 1980); Gordon Lewis and Bruce Demarest, eds., *Challenges To Inerrancy: A Theological Response* (Chicago: Moody, 1984); John D. Hannah, ed., *Inerrancy and the Church* (Chicago: Moody, 1984); Earl Radmacher and Robert Preus, eds., *Hermeneutics, Inerrancy, and the Bible* (Chicago: Moody, 1984).

113. See, representatively, Craig L. Blomberg, *Can We Still Believe the Bible? An Evangelical Engagement With Contemporary Questions* (Grand Rapids: Brazos, 2014), and Norman L. Geisler and William C. Roach, *Defending Inerrancy: Affirming the Accuracy of Scripture for a New Generation* (Grand Rapids: Baker, 2011).

to describe the Scripture.¹¹⁴ For most of church history, they were used more or less interchangeably. Within the last century, some theologians have claimed that the Bible is 'infallible' but not 'inerrant.'¹¹⁵ We must define each of these terms and consider how or if each appropriately describes the Bible.

The word 'infallible' refers to 'the quality of neither deceiving nor being deceived.' The word 'inerrant' means 'freedom from error of any kind, factual, moral, or spiritual.'¹¹⁶ As John Frame observes, '*inerrant* means that there *are* no errors; *infallible* means that there *can be* no errors.'¹¹⁷ The two terms are very close in meaning, and it is difficult to see how one could cogently affirm the Bible to be 'infallible' without also affirming it to be 'inerrant.' If the Bible is incapable of deceiving us, it must be free from deceptions of any kind.

Those theologians who present infallibility and inerrancy as mutually exclusive ways of describing the Bible operate, however, with a different understanding of infallibility. As Geisler and Roach wryly observe, 'the term "infallible" has been rendered fallible by the intentionalist sense in which it is used by limited inerrantists and noninerrantists.'¹¹⁸ One recent proposal, for instance, restricts infallibility to what God 'intends' by the Bible; it does not see infallibility as a predicate of the text of the Bible.¹¹⁹ Infalliblity, on this view, does not secure the text from error. Such a proposal allows for what Geisler and Roach term 'an infallibly correct error' in Scripture, a supposition that, they

---

114. The following material has been drawn, with some adaptation, from my *What Is the Bible?* (Phillipsburg, NJ: P&R, 2013), 18-25. Used by permission of P&R.

115. See the discussion at Stephen J. Nichols and Eric T. Brandt, *Ancient Word, Changing Worlds: The Doctrine of Scripture in a Modern Age* (Wheaton, IL: Crossway, 2009), 91-2.

116. Packer, *God Has Spoken,* 111. As E. J. Young puts it, 'by the term infallible as applied to the Bible, we mean simply that the Scripture possesses an indefectible authority ... It can never fail in its judgments and statements ... By [inerrant] we mean that the Scriptures possess the quality of freedom from error. They are exempt from the liability of mistake, incapable of error. In all their teachings they are in perfect accord with the truth,' *Thy Word Is Truth,* 113.

117. Frame, *Doctrine of the Word of God*, 533.

118. Geisler and Roach, *Defending Inerrancy,* 163.

119. A. T. B. McGowan, *The Divine Spiration of Scripture: Challenging Evangelical Perspectives* (Nottingham: Apollos, 2007), 49, as cited at Geisler and Roach, *Defending Inerrancy,* 163.

remark, is 'nonsense.'[120] While the term infallible is of itself adequate to describe the Bible that God has given us, its usage among some theologians requires the conjunction of the term 'inerrant' to clarify for contemporary audiences that the Bible's infallibility entails the freedom of the text of Scripture from error.

Both terms, 'infallible' and 'inerrant,' point to the same reality with respect to the text of Scripture. The Bible is free from error. On what basis, then, ought one to make such an affirmation about the Bible? After all, critics have observed, the biblical writers never use the word 'inerrant' in describing the text of Scripture. This observation is true as far as it goes, but it is misleading. The term 'inerrant' faithfully captures what we have already observed the biblical writers to claim about the text of Scripture. The text of Scripture, we have seen, is entirely the work of its Divine Author. God has uttered every word of the Bible. Inerrancy is a 'necessary inference' from the character of the God who authored the Bible.[121]

What precisely is the connection between the Divine Author and the inerrant Word of God? The Bible, we have observed, claims that it is a revelation from God, and was given by inspiration of God. It is in this sense that the church has properly confessed the Bible to be the Word of God. Therefore, what we know of the character of God will necessarily determine our understanding of the character of His Word. John H. Gerstner summarizes the point well.

> There are only two ways by which any person can come to say something that is untrue: either by ignorance or lying ... God suffers from neither limitation, and therefore cannot speak untruth. His message must be true indubitably ... God who is truth, who cannot err, has inspired the Bible, and the Bible is truth and cannot err.[122]

In other words, if the God who cannot be ignorant nor lie has spoken, and if He has given us that Word by inspiration, then that Word cannot

---

120. Geisler and Roach, *Defending Inerrancy*, 163. As they observe, 'the Bible is not merely infallible in its *intentions* and achievements but also in its *affirmations* (and denials),' ibid.

121. The phrase is that of Robert D. Preus, 'Notes on the Inerrancy of Scripture,' quoted at Nichols and Brandt, 89.

122. John H. Gerstner, *Primitive Theology: The Collected Primers of John H. Gerstner* (Morgan, PA: Soli Deo Gloria, 1996), 87, 89.

deceive and cannot be in error. It is both infallible and inerrant, and necessarily so. Conversely, 'to maintain that there are flaws or errors in [the Bible] is the same as declaring that there are flaws or errors in God Himself.'[123] Some have objected to this argument.[124] It is illegitimate, they say, to deduce inerrancy in the manner that we have done. In the absence of an explicit biblical statement of its own inerrancy, we should not speak of the Scripture as 'inerrant.'

This objection can stand only if, in the words of one of these objectors, inerrancy is not a 'legitimate implication' of the doctrine of inspiration.[125] Based upon what we know of the character of God and of the character of His Word, however, inerrancy is a legitimate and inescapable inference. As James Bannerman stresses, '[Scripture] contains God's thoughts; it is the expression of His mind and will; it was produced by His agency; it is characterized throughout by his style of truth; it is marked in all its statements by His infallibility and authority.'[126] It is meaningless to affirm Scripture as the inspired Word of God without also predicating its infallibility and its inerrancy.[127] Positively, the Divine Authorship of Scripture and the inspiration of the text of Scripture afford the reader the utmost confidence of the truth of every one of the Bible's words.

Objections to Inerrancy

One of the most common objections to the inerrancy of Scripture is the allegation that the Bible contains errors. These alleged errors fall into several categories. Some are said to be errors of historical or geographical fact; others, of scientific detail.[128] Others allege that

---

123. E. J. Young, *Thy Word is Truth*, 123, quoted at Nichols and Brandt, 94.

124. McGowan, *Divine Spiration*, 114.

125. ibid.

126. Bannerman, *Inspiration*, 418, cited at Nicholas R. Needham, *The Doctrine of Holy Scripture in the Free Church Fathers* (RSHT; Edinburgh: Rutherford House, 1991), 103. Needham rightly points to this quotation as illustrating Bannerman's conviction that 'plenary inspiration involved an inerrant Bible,' ibid.

127. For a recent and multi-step argument proceeding inferentially 'from inspiration to inerrancy,' see Feinberg, *Light in a Dark Place*, 285-6.

128. Some allege that John's dating of the day preceding and the day of Jesus' death contradicts that provided by the Synoptic Gospels, on which see Andreas J. Köstenberger, *John* (BECNT; Grand Rapids: Baker, 2004), 400, 402, 524, 537-8; and Richard

the way in which the Bible presents miracles and the supernatural compromises any claim that the Bible is a trustworthy, historical record.[129] Some point to what are said to be failed prophecies.[130] Others point to what are thought to be commended immoral actions on the part of God or on the part of His people.[131] Some have argued that the New Testament authors have taken license with the text of the Old Testament in the way in which they quote and apply that text.[132] Some have argued that there are texts in the Bible that were mistakenly attributed to particular authors.[133] Still others point to what are said to be internal contradictions within the Bible, whether concerning specific teachings or particular details.[134]

One could multiply the categories or kinds of errors that have been alleged in the text of Scripture. One could easily fill a book in addressing

---

Bauckham, *The Testimony of the Beloved Disciple: Narrative, History, and Theology in the Gospel of John* (Grand Rapids: Baker, 2007), 100-1. Some have argued that the theory of evolution contradicts the Bible's teachings about the origins of humanity, on which see now the essays in J. P. Moreland, Stephen C. Meyer, Christopher Shaw, Ann K. Gauger, and Wayne Grudem, eds., *Theistic Evolution: A Scientific, Philosophical, and Theological Critique* (Wheaton, IL: Crossway, 2017).

129. It has been common in some quarters of historical-critical scholarship, especially in the nineteenth century, to dismiss the miracles documented in the Gospels and Acts, attributing a naturalistic explanation for them. For a discussion and response, see now Craig S. Keener, *Miracles: The Credibility of the New Testament Accounts* (2 vols.; Grand Rapids: Baker, 2011).

130. As for instance Jesus' prophecy at Mark 9:1 (=Matt 16:28, Luke 9:27), 'Truly, I say to you, there are some standing here who will not taste death until they see the kingdom of God after it has come with power,' on which see the still valuable discussion at Herman N. Ridderbos, *The Coming of the Kingdom* (ed. Raymond O. Zorn; trans. H. de Jongste; Phillipsburg, NJ: P&R, 1962), 503-7.

131. One example is the slaying of the inhabitants of Canaan that God commands Israel to undertake in the days of Joshua, on which see Tremper Longman III, *Confronting Old Testament Controversies: Pressing Questions About Evolution, Sexuality, History, and Violence* (Grand Rapids: Baker, 2019), 123-206.

132. A common example cited is the way in which Matthew quotes and applies Hosea 11:1 at Matthew 2:13-15, on which see the essays in Stanley E. Porter and Beth M. Stovell, eds., *Biblical Hermeneutics: Five Views* (Downers Grove, IL: InterVarsity, 2012).

133. As many historical-critical scholars alleged with respect to at least six letters of Paul (2 Thess., Col., Eph., 1 Tim., Titus, 2 Tim.). For discussion and response, see Carson and Moo, *Introduction*, 337-50, 480-6, 517-21, 536-42, 554-68.

134. As for example the alleged discrepancy between the number of persons who left Egypt according to Genesis and according to Acts, on which see my *The Acts of the Apostles* (Darlington, UK: Evangelical Press, 2015), 179n.19.

and responding to what are said to be errors in the text of the Bible.[135] In what follows, we are not going to approach the question of alleged errors by addressing particular objections. Rather, we are going to address how one ought to approach any accusation of error in the text of Scripture. In other words, what are the presuppositions and expectations that one ought to bring to an informed consideration of such allegations? What should be the approach or method of one who is persuaded of the doctrine of inerrancy to the handling of accusations of error in the text of Scripture?

In the first place, it is critical, prior to handling any such accusation of error, that one formulates the doctrine of Scripture in the proper way. There are two ways in which one may approach the matter. The first is to begin with what the Bible says about itself. 'One ... obtain[s] first the doctrine of inspiration taught by the Bible as applicable to itself, and then testing this doctrine by the facts as to the Bible as ascertained by Biblical criticism and exegesis.'[136] The virtue of this approach is that it respects 'the vast mass of evidence for the general trustworthiness of the Biblical writings as witnesses of doctrine, and for the appointment of their writers as teachers of divine truth to men, and for the presence of the Holy Spirit with and in them aiding them in their teaching (in whatever degree and with whatever effect).'[137] These considerations require us to start with the Bible's own testimony to its inspiration in formulating the doctrine of Scripture and only then proceed to handle difficulties.

Others have argued that one should adopt a different approach to formulating the doctrine of Scripture. One should 'comprehensive[ly] induc[e] from the facts as to the structure and contents of the Bible, as ascertained by critical and exegetical processes, treating all these facts as co-factors of the same rank for the induction.'[138] While this approach

---

135. In addition to Blomberg, *Can We Still Believe the Bible?*, and Geisler and Roach, *Defending Inerrancy*, see, as a starting point, Gleason Archer, 'Alleged Errors and Discrepancies in the Original Manuscripts of the Bible,' in Geisler, ed., *Inerrancy*, 57-82 and, more recently and at greater length Norman L. Geisler and Thomas A. Howe, *When Critics Ask* (Wheaton, IL: Victor, 1992).
136. Warfield, 'Real Problem,' in *Works*, 1:222.
137. ibid.
138. ibid., 1:223.

seems attractive, it suffers from at least two significant problems. The first is that it does not privilege, with respect to the question of the nature of Scripture, the Bible's repeated claims about its own authorship, production, and character. This approach, therefore, is not calculated to arrive at a clear and 'precise' formulation of the Bible's teaching about itself.[139] The second is that it gives undue weight to passages that pose difficulty for the Bible's claims as to its own inspiration. These passages are subjected to an interpretation that is, at best, inadequately informed by the Bible's testimony to its own inspiration. That is to say, this approach fails to set allegations of biblical error within the framework that the Bible itself provides as necessary to address them.

This is not to say that one should ignore or gloss over the difficult passages.[140] It is to say, rather, that one should interpret them within the established framework of the biblical authors' testimony as to the nature of their writings. When faced with a particular difficulty, the benefit of the doubt should be given to the Scripture's testimony to its own inspiration. One should strive to interpret that difficulty in light of that testimony, and not *vice versa*.[141] If the difficulty proves insuperable, then one must conclude that the biblical authors were mistaken in their claims of their own inspiration. But so long as a contradiction cannot be proven, even if doubt or uncertainty remains concerning a particular difficulty, then one may not overturn the established testimony of the biblical authors as to their own teaching.[142]

A second basic consideration concerns what is required for some statement or statements of Scripture to rise to the level of an error or

---

139. ibid.

140. The following summarizes Warfield's argument at 'Real Problem,' in *Works*, 1:223-4.

141. It is 'a settled logical principle that so long as the proper evidence by which a proposition is established remains unrefuted, all so-called objections brought against it pass out of the category of objections to its truth into the category of difficulties to be adjusted to it,' Warfield, quoted at Louis Berkhof, *Introductory Volume to Systematic Theology* (rev. ed.; Grand Rapids: Eerdmans, 1932), 161.

142. It should be stressed at this point that we are not basing these judgments upon the mere assertion of the biblical writers to the inspiration of the texts that they have authored. Rather, we are commending this first way of handling difficulties in light of the fact that the biblical authors are 'trustworth[y] ... as teachers of doctrine,' Warfield, 'Real Problem,' in *Works*, 1:224. In the following chapter, we will present and assess the grounds on which such a judgment may be properly made.

contradiction. It is not enough that a passage presents acute interpretative difficulty to the reader. Nor is it enough even that there is no clear and compelling resolution that presents itself to readers in order satisfactorily to resolve the difficulty. What, then, constitutes an error? According to A. A. Hodge and B. B. Warfield, not fewer than three criteria must be met before we admit the presence of an error in the Scripture:

> Let it (1) be proved that each alleged discrepant statement certainly occurred in the original autograph of the sacred book in which it is said to be found. (2) Let it be proved that the interpretation which occasions the apparent discrepancy is the one which the passage was evidently intended to bear. It is not sufficient to show a difficulty, which may spring out of our defective knowledge of the circumstances. The true meaning must be definitely and certainly ascertained, and then shown to be irreconcilable with other known truth. (3) Let it be proved that, the true sense of some part of the original autograph is directly and necessarily inconsistent with some certainly-known fact of history or truth of science, or some other statement of Scripture certainly ascertained and interpreted.[143]

In other words, any statement in which an error is alleged to occur must be in the original text of Scripture; must be correctly interpreted; and must be proven to contradict a known fact from the world or another correctly interpreted text of Scripture. This is the burden that those who allege errors and contradictions in the Scripture must shoulder. What Hodge and Warfield said in the nineteenth century applies equally to the twenty-first century: 'We believe that it can be shown that this has never yet been successfully done in the case of one single alleged instance of error in the Word of God.'[144]

With this definition of 'error' before us, we may register four observations that relate to allegations of error in the Bible.[145] First, a 'difference' is not necessarily a 'contradiction.' Often, for instance, parallel accounts in the Gospels are not identical. One Gospel account records details or words that are not present in another Gospel account. This state of affairs is precisely what we would expect. Independent

---

143. A. A. Hodge and B. B. Warfield, *Inspiration*, 36. Compare the similar and fuller discussion at A. A. Hodge, *Outlines of Theology* (rev. ed.; 1879: repr., Edinburgh: Banner of Truth, 1972), 76-7.

144. ibid.

145. The first two are mentioned by Berkhof, *Introduction to Systematic Theology*, 161-2.

accounts differ in their retelling of events and discussions. These differences are part of the richness of the Gospels. Each Gospel often gives us a slightly different perspective upon and tells us more than what the parallel account in another Gospel tells us. In fact, if parallel accounts in the Scripture were uniform in detail, our suspicions might be raised. Such uniformity might suggest to us collusion that, in turn, would cast doubt upon the historical worth of the accounts in question. Our Gospels therefore evidence not only their richness as distinct accounts of our Lord, but in so doing demonstrate their credibility as historical witnesses.[146]

Second, the Bible may describe something without approving it. Both Testaments contain examples of the sinful words and actions of individual persons. Sometimes these words and actions go without much comment or even any comment. This relative silence does not constitute the Scripture's tacit or muted approval. For example, Jacob marries two women and takes two more as concubines. Readers of Genesis are sometimes dismayed that there is not an explicit and immediate condemnation of the patriarch's polygamy in that book. Yet, the teaching of the Scripture is clear in setting forth monogamy as the universal and abiding standard for human beings (see Gen. 2:24 and Matt. 19:4-6). Furthermore, it is clear from Genesis that Jacob's polygamy results in a disordered and unhappy home. In this way Moses implicitly disapproves of Jacob's departures from the law of marriage instituted by God at the creation.

Third, as troubling as difficulties that we encounter in the Bible can be, it is important to keep them in proper perspective. Charles Hodge observes that we face a similar situation when contemplating the world.

> The universe teems with evidences of design, so manifold, so diverse, so wonderful, as to overwhelm the mind with the conviction that it has had an intelligent author. Yet here and there isolated cases of monstrosity appear. It is irrational, because we cannot account for such cases, to deny that the universe is the product of intelligence. So the Christian need not renounce

---

146. On the question of the unity and the diversity of the Gospels, generally, and the questions of harmonization that arise from a comparison of their accounts, particularly, see Vern Sheridan Poythress, *Inerrancy and the Gospels: A God-Centered Approach to the Challenges of Harmonization* (Wheaton, IL: Crossway, 2012), and Craig Blomberg, *The Historical Reliability of the Gospels* (2d ed.; Downers Grove, InterVarsity, 2007).

his faith in the plenary inspiration of the Bible, although there may be some things about it in its present state which he cannot account for.[147]

Hodge is making a critical point. In no department of human knowledge do admitted difficulties overturn settled knowledge. Were that the case, skepticism would be the result. What is true for the book of nature holds for the book of Scripture.

Fourth, and relatedly, it is the objector to inerrancy and not the defender of inerrancy who shoulders the burden of proof. This is so because there is a cogent, rational case for the inspiration and inerrancy of the Bible. The premises of this case are true, the reasoning is valid, and therefore the conclusion of the case commands assent. The objector must demonstrate that a contradiction necessarily and unavoidably exists either between two passages of Scripture properly interpreted or between a passage of Scripture properly interpreted and a properly interpreted fact external to the Scripture. By this standard, what appear to be contradictions turn out not to be contradictions at all. It may be that the objector has misread or misinterpreted a certain passage of Scripture, a fact of history, or a fact of science. It may be that the objector has demonstrated a possible but not a necessary contradiction. There may be, in fact, several possible ways to resolve the difficulty that the objector brings forward. The defender of inerrancy does not even have to commit to one possible solution or another. All that he is obligated to do is to show that no contradiction is required.

Perhaps we may understand why two passages of Scripture will never contradict one another. An inerrant book cannot contain statements that necessarily contradict one another. But why may we be confident that a properly interpreted statement of Scripture will never contradict a properly interpreted fact of, say, science? The answer, as J. I. Packer notes, is that 'since the same God is the Author both of nature and of Scripture, true science and a right interpretation of Scripture cannot conflict.'[148] We need to explore, Packer continues, whether 'appearance of contradiction is not due to mistakes and arbitrary assumptions, both

---

147. Hodge, *Systematic Theology*, 1:170.
148. Packer, *Fundamentalism*, 135. Packer's reasoning extends to history and geography, since God is not only the Creator of the world, but He is also its Sovereign Sustainer. The doctrine of providence, in other words, secures our confidence that no fact of history or geography will ever contradict a fact revealed in the Scripture.

scientific and theological, which a closer scrutiny of the evidence will enable us to correct,' and to take heed of 'discounting one or other set of facts or ... locking them into two separate compartments in our minds and refusing to bring them together.'[149] This process is not an easy one and will not always yield immediate results. Whether or not we are able to reconcile these difficulties to the satisfaction of all parties concerned, we may be confident that God's 'Two Books' – Nature and Scripture – will never contradict one another.[150]

In conclusion, we have seen the Scripture's testimony to itself as the inspired Word of God. The inspiration of Scripture is not partial but plenary. It extends down to the very words of the authentic text of Scripture.[151] The text of Scripture is inspired in light of the fact that its Author is divine. To be sure, the Bible was authored by human beings, but the testimony of those authors is that every word that they authored in the biblical text is the very Word of God. God the Spirit so worked in and upon the human authors as to secure a text that was at once fully human and fully divine. Because of the divine authorship of Scripture, the text of Scripture is infallible and inerrant. The text can no more deceive or err than God can. Put positively, Scripture is as trustworthy, reliable, and truthful as its Author.

This chapter has devoted itself to answering the single question of what the Bible testifies about itself. We have yet to consider the warrant for those claims. In the next chapter, we will explore what evidences there are to ground the biblical authors' claims to inspiration and inerrancy. We will also take up the question of the canon of Scripture, that is, which books are rightly counted among the Word of God. But before we look at the canon, we will look at the Spirit's ongoing work

---

149. ibid.

150. In Chapter 8, we will take up a particular challenge to the doctrine of Scripture that has arisen, in part, from scholarship sympathetic to theistic evolution.

151. That is to say, no one claims inerrancy for the errors that surfaced and were transmitted in the copies of Scripture that have been transmitted through the centuries. For classical statements and defenses of the inerrancy of the autographs of Scripture, see Greg L. Bahnsen, 'The Inerrancy of the Autographa,' in Geisler, ed., *Inerrancy*, 151-93, and Douglas Stuart, 'Inerrancy and Textual Criticism,' in Nicole and Michaels, ed., *Inerrancy and Common Sense*, 97-117. For a recent discussion, see Blomberg, *Can We Still Believe the Bible?*, 13-41.

of illumination in the lives of God's people. This work is distinct from the Spirit's work of inspiration, but it is crucial to understanding how God's people may read, interpret, and apply the text of Scripture in the ways that its Divine Author has intended.

Our 'Full Persuasion'

In the previous chapter, we considered the Bible's testimony to itself. The biblical writers claim that the text of Scripture is the inspired and inerrant Word of God. The Bible is unique among human books in that it was fully authored by human beings and fully authored by God.

Christians do not accept these claims on mere or bare assertion. After all, many texts that human beings have authored claim to be or to contain divine revelation.[1] Why, then, do the claims of the biblical authors to inspiration merit the assent, trust, and commitment of their readers? In this chapter we will explore what it is that renders credible the Bible's claim to inspiration. In this connection we will give particular consideration to the witness that the Holy Spirit Himself offers to the Bible. We will then take up a distinct but related question: how do we know that the sixty-six books of the Old and New Testaments are the inspired Word of God? This brings us to the question of the canon of Scripture.

Evidence for the Inspiration of Scripture

The Christian church 'rest[s] the truth of the inspiration of the Scriptures on their own assertions,' but she does not thereby 'reason in a circle.'[2] To see how this is so, we need to explore why it is that

---

1. Two such examples that have influenced, in different ways, both human history and the church include the *Qu'ran* and the *Book of Mormon*.

2. A. A. Hodge, *Outlines of Theology* (rev. ed.; New York: Robert Carter & Bros., 1879; repr., Edinburgh: Banner of Truth, 1972), 69.

the claims of the biblical writers to inspiration are credible. Before we explore that argument, however, we need to address a prior and related question. Why is it that Christians believe the Bible to be the Word of God? A classical and consensus confessional formulation articulates the matter concisely.

> The authority of the Holy Scripture, for which it ought to be believed, and obeyed, dependeth not upon the testimony of any man, or Church; but wholly upon God (who is truth itself) the author thereof: and therefore it is to be received because it is the Word of God. We may be moved and induced by the testimony of the Church to an high and reverend esteem of the Holy Scripture. And the heavenliness of the matter, the efficacy of the doctrine, the majesty of the style, the consent of all the parts, the scope of the whole (which is, to give all glory to God), the full discovery it makes of the only way of man's salvation, the many other incomparable excellencies, and the entire perfection thereof, are arguments whereby it doth abundantly evidence itself to be the Word of God: yet notwithstanding, our full persuasion and assurance of the infallible truth and divine authority thereof, is from the inward working of the Holy Spirit bearing witness by and with the Word in our hearts.[3]

In these paragraphs, the Westminster Divines are making four important claims about how and why we understand the Bible to be the Word of God. First, in response to the claims of the Roman Catholic Church, Westminster affirms that one's deepest confidence that the Bible is the Word of God does not lie in the church's testimony to the Bible.[4] Scripture's authority 'depend[s] ... wholly upon God ... [its] author.'[5] Second, Rome's claims notwithstanding, the church's testimony to the Bible as the Word of God should commend the Scripture to human beings. There is testimony, in other words, external to the Bible that serves the valuable purpose of highlighting the true nature of the Scripture. Third, there is valuable testimony internal to the Bible by which the Bible 'abundantly evidence[s] itself to be the Word of God.'[6] Fourth, while these external and internal evidences afford compelling arguments that the Bible is the Word of God,

---

3. Westminster Confession of Faith, I.4-5.

4. A. A. Hodge, *The Confession of Faith* (Philadelphia: Presbyterian Board of Publication, 1869; repr., Edinburgh: Banner of Truth, 1958), 36.

5. Westminster Confession of Faith, I.4.

6. ibid., I.5.

one's 'full persuasion and infallible assurance of the infallible truth, and divine authority thereof' must come from God Himself, from 'the direct work of the Holy Spirit on our hearts.'[7]

Even a cursory review of the evidences for the Bible would occupy a full volume.[8] The important thing to see, at this initial stage of our discussion, is that the Christian claim that the Bible is the Word of God is a rational one. Since the doctrine of inspiration is of a piece with that claim, it stands to reason that the claim that the Bible is the inspired Word of God is equally a rational one.[9]

What then is the particular case for the inspiration of the Bible? The case, it should be stressed at the outset, assumes the prior 'establish[ment]' of 'theism, the reality of revelation, the authenticity and historical credibility of the Scriptures, the divine origin and character of the religion which they present, and the general trustworthiness of their presentation of it.'[10] Granting each of these points, then, we may give particular attention to the argument for Scripture's inspiration.

Any such argument must begin with the Lord Jesus Christ Himself. Jesus was recognized in His own day as an extraordinary teacher, 'the

---

7. A. A. Hodge, *Confession of Faith*, 36.

8. For a brief survey of these evidences in relation to the teaching of the Westminster Confession of Faith, see William Cunningham, *Theological Lectures on Subjects Connected with Natural Theology, Evidences of Christianity, The Canon and Inspiration of Scripture* (London: James Nisbet, 1878), 269-342. This body of evidence is distinct from the evidences for the truth of the Christian religion, on which see *Theological Lectures*, 175-215.

9. Note here the helpful observation of Benjamin B. Warfield, 'It is necessary ... to discriminate between the several definitions of inspiration. If we are to define it as the correlate of revelation, the evidence for it is the evidence for supernatural religion. If we are to define it as a wide term, including all the divine activities which have entered into the production of the Bible, the evidence for it is the evidence for the general divine origin of the Hebrew and Christian Scriptures ... If, on the other hand, we define inspiration, with exact writers, as the activity of God in producing a divinely safeguarded record of his will in written documents, all this mass of evidence for supernatural revelation and for the divine origin of the Scriptures is presupposed. Inspiration, in its more exact sense, cannot come into discussion until [all this evidence has] been already established,' 'Inspiration,' in *Selected Shorter Writings of Benjamin B. Warfield* (ed. John E. Meeter; 2 vols.; Phillipsburg, NJ: P&R, 1970-3), 2:631-2.

10. Warfield, 'Inspiration,' in *SSW*, 2.631-2. Compare A. A. Hodge, 'we come to this question [of the proof of the inspiration of Scripture] already believing in their credibility as histories, and in that of their writers as witnesses of facts, and in the truth of Christianity and in the divinity of Christ,' *Outlines of Theology*, 69.

crowds were astonished at his teaching, for he was teaching them as one who had authority, and not as their scribes' (Matt. 7:28-9). In fact, John tells us, the crowds of Galilee proclaimed Him 'the Prophet who is to come into the world' (John 6:14, cf. 7:40), likely a reference to the eschatological Prophet of whom Moses spoke in Deuteronomy 18:15.[11]

Jesus was no mere teacher. He not only claimed to come from God (John 3:13), but also uniquely to know the Father and to reveal the Father to human beings.

> All things have been handed over to me by my Father, and no one knows the Son except the Father, and no one knows the Father except the Son and anyone to whom the Son chooses to reveal Him (Matt. 11:27; cf. John 8:19, 10:15)

> Not that anyone has seen the Father except he who is from God; he has seen the Father (John 6:46)

> I know [him who sent me], for I come from him, and he sent me (John 7:29)

Jesus Christ, then, is unlike the prophets who have preceded Him. He does not merely bring a message from God. He is the Son of God and speaks as one who has personal and exclusive knowledge of the Father and the unique prerogative of revealing Him to human beings.

Jesus did not expect people to accept His claims on the basis of mere assertion. This is not because His words were not true. His words are intrinsically true, 'Even if I do not bear witness about myself, my testimony is true, for I know where I came from and where I am going, but you do not know where I come from or where I am going' (John 8:14). Jesus recognizes that the standards of the courtroom apply to the reception of His message, 'in your Law it is written that the testimony of two men is true' (John 8:17).[12] Consequently, Jesus calls witnesses throughout His public ministry to attest to the truth of His message, 'I am the one who bears witness about myself, and the Father who sent me bears witness about me' (John 8:18). In what way or ways does the Father bear witness to Jesus' message? Jesus' miracles

---

11. Craig S. Keener, *The Gospel of John: A Commentary* (2 vols.; Peabody, MA: Hendrickson, 2010), 1:670, 730.

12. On the importance of the courtroom motif to John's Gospel generally, see A. T. Lincoln, *Truth on Trial: The Lawsuit Motif in the Fourth Gospel* (Peabody, MA: Hendrickson, 2000).

are the leading way that the Father attests to the credibility of Jesus as messenger and, therefore, to the truth of His message. This is a point that Nicodemus, notwithstanding his present, spiritual darkness, perceived, '[Nicodemus] came to Jesus by night and said to him, "Rabbi, we know that you are a teacher come from God, for no one can do these signs that you do unless God is with him"' (John 3:2).[13] The 'signs' to which Nicodemus refers are John's preferred designations for Jesus' miracles.[14] Jesus' 'signs' show Nicodemus and others that 'God is with him.' This is so because only God can work a miracle, and, if a genuine miracle has been wrought, that miracle indicates the approving presence of God with the one who worked the miracle. For Nicodemus, Jesus' miracles (and God's presence with Jesus) confirmed that Jesus was 'a teacher come from God.' He correctly reasoned that God would not commend a teacher whose message God found unacceptable.[15] Put positively, Jesus' miracles served to seal or confirm His own teaching as having divine acceptance and approval.

This is not the only instance where we see in Jesus' ministry an acknowledgment that miracles perform this credentialing function. In John 5:36, Jesus says, 'the works that the Father has given me to accomplish, the very works that I am doing, bear witness about me that the Father has sent me.' Here, Jesus identifies His 'works,' that is, His miracles as 'given' to him by 'the Father.' As such, these Father-given works constitute the Father's 'bear[ing] witness' that He has sent Jesus into the world. If the Father has sent Jesus into the world, and if the Father supplies Jesus 'works' to accomplish, it follows that the Father approves of Jesus' teaching. In Matthew 16:1 (compare Matt. 12:38-9), we are told that 'the Pharisees and Sadducees came [to Jesus], and to test him they asked him to show them a sign from heaven,' a request

---

13. In all probability, 'night' here, as elsewhere in this Gospel, is one instance among many in John's Gospel where an historical detail (literal darkness) carries added spiritual significance (the darkness of Nicodemus' own soul, cf. John 3:19), D. A. Carson, *The Gospel According to John* (PNTC; Grand Rapids: Eerdmans, 1991), 186; yet note the reservations of J. Ramsay Michaels, *The Gospel of John* (NICNT; Grand Rapids: Eerdmans, 2010), 178.

14. They are 'signs' because these miracles point beyond themselves to deeper, spiritual realities, Andreas J. Köstenberger, *A Theology of John's Gospel and Letters* (BTNT; Grand Rapids: Zondervan, 2009), 219, 323-35.

15. John H. Gerstner, *Reasons for Faith* (New York: Harper & Row, 1960), 97-105.

that Jesus refuses to grant (Matt. 16:4). Here, the Jewish leadership acknowledges that miracles ('a sign from heaven') serve a credentialing function. Jesus will not perform their bidding, not because He refuses to furnish credentials, but because the credentials He has already furnished are sufficient (16:2-3). The problem, Jesus stresses, is not the lack of credentials. The problem is the unbelief of 'an evil and adulterous generation [that] seeks for a sign' (16:4), being dissatisfied with the signs already available to them.[16]

To summarize, Jesus exclusively knows and is known by the Father, who has sent Him into the world. He is the Prophet of God who uniquely reveals the Father to human beings. The Father credentials the Son so that human beings may know that the Father is with Him and approves His ministry. The way in which the Father credentials Jesus is through the working of miracles or signs. Miracles are acts that, by definition, are only within the power of God to perform (Ps. 72:18). These signs therefore authenticate and confirm that Jesus is sent by and approved by the Father.

How is this set of observations relevant to the question of the Bible's inspiration? In light of His miracles and their relation to His teaching ministry, whatever Jesus teaches has the approval of God the Father. This means, in part, that Jesus' claims to His own deity and equality with the Father are warranted claims. Furthermore, whatever Jesus teaches about the Bible has the Father's commendation. Jesus teaches that the Old Testament is the inspired Word of God, a teaching we surveyed in the last chapter. This teaching necessarily is a teaching approved by the Father. We accept this teaching of the Old Testament's inspiration on the authority of Jesus Christ, whom the Father credentialed as His own messenger. God the Father and God the Son concur in their witness to the inspiration of the Old Testament. As the nineteenth-century Anglican Bishop Christopher Wordsworth observed, 'the New Testament canonizes the Old; the INCARNATE WORD sets His seal on the WRITTEN WORD. The Incarnate Word is God; therefore, the inspiration of the Old Testament

---

16. 'In this manner they also insinuated that the signs that Jesus had been performing in such abundance were, at the least, of doubtful origin,' Herman N. Ridderbos, *Matthew* (trans. Ray Togtman; BSC; Grand Rapids: Zondervan, 1987), 293. See further the reflections of Herman N. Ridderbos, *The Coming of the Kingdom* (trans. H de Jongste; Phillipsburg, NJ: P&R, 1962), 118-19.

is authenticated by God Himself.'[17] The argument for the inspiration of the Old Testament could rest on no surer foundation.

What about the New Testament's inspiration? There is, obviously, no testimony from Jesus during His earthly ministry to the inspiration of the New Testament writings, per se. Here we return to the apostles' testimony about their own authority and teaching and, back of that, Jesus' teaching about the authority that He would grant the apostles. Recall two passages that are crucial to our understanding of the apostles' authority, especially in relation to the books of the New Testament.

> But the Helper, the Holy Spirit, whom the Father will send in my name, he will teach you all things and bring to your remembrance all that I have said to you (John 14:26).

> I still have many things to say to you, but you cannot bear them now. When the Spirit of truth comes, he will guide you into all the truth, for he will not speak on his own authority, but whatever he hears he will speak, and he will declare to you the things that are to come. He will glorify me, for he will take what is mine and declare it to you. All that the Father has is mine; therefore I said that he will take what is mine and declare it to you (John 16:12-15).

Jesus promises these disciples that the Holy Spirit will undertake a particular ministry among them after His resurrection and ascension.[18] This ministry is a teaching ministry. Jesus speaks of this teaching ministry in two respects. First, He tells them that the Spirit will 'teach you all things and bring to your remembrance all that I have said to you' (14:26). Jesus here promises His disciples that the Spirit will ensure that they will comprehensively recall the words of Jesus uttered in His earthly ministry. Second, Jesus tells them that the Spirit will 'speak' or 'declare' 'the things that are to come,' matters that the disciples presently 'cannot bear.' These words will be the words of Jesus (16:12), but it will be the Spirit who conveys those words to the disciples.

These two promises span the range of the New Testament canon. They encompass the inspired records of the words (and deeds) of Jesus

---

17. As cited at Benjamin B. Warfield, 'The Real Problem of Inspiration,' in *The Works of Benjamin B. Warfield* (10 vols.; New York: Oxford University Press, 1932), 1:212.

18. Herman Ridderbos, *The Gospel of John: A Theological Commentary* (trans. John Vriend; Grand Rapids: Eerdmans, 1997), 536-7.

Christ in His earthly ministry – that is, the Gospel accounts. They encompass the ongoing ministry of Christ in His church documented in the Acts of the Apostles.[19] They encompass the apostolic teaching, given by Christ to His church, documented in the Epistles and in the Revelation. They encompass the teaching of Christ concerning the welfare and progress of the church between the first and second comings of Christ, as documented in Revelation. We are not yet at the point where we may show that the twenty-seven books of the New Testament are the specific way in which these promises came to fruition. But we may at this initial stage register the observation that these promises are no less expansive in their range of interest than the New Testament writings.

In the previous chapter, we observed from several passages in the writings of the apostles Paul and Peter that the apostles were conscious of this particular promised ministry of the Spirit (1 Cor. 14:37, 2 Thess. 3:14, 1 Tim. 5:18, 2 Pet. 3:2, 3:15-16). We may now ask the question, what evidence did the apostles afford to serve as credentials for their claim that they were authorized messengers of Jesus Christ and, as such, wrote to the churches by inspiration of the Holy Spirit? What credentialed the apostles is precisely the same as that which credentialed Jesus Christ, namely, miracles.

The New Testament frequently documents the performing of miracles by the apostles. One striking feature of that line of the New Testament's teaching is the way in which the apostolic miracles are patterned after the miracles of Jesus Christ. Acts features the ministries of two apostles, Peter and Paul. It is through the ministry of the apostles, Christ's appointed witnesses to Himself, and particularly through the ministries of Peter and Paul, that the gospel proceeds from Jerusalem to Judea and Samaria to the end of the earth (Acts 1:8). In Acts 1-12, Luke shows how, through Peter, the gospel proceeds from the Jew to the Samaritan and makes first contact with the Gentiles. In Acts 13-28, Luke shows how, through Paul, the gospel extends to the 'end of the

---

19. Note the opening verse of Acts, 'In the first book [i.e., the Gospel According to Luke], O Theophilus, I have dealt with all that Jesus began to do and teach' (1:1). The implication is that this second book [i.e., Acts] documents the continuing deeds and words of Jesus. The narrative clarifies that that ongoing work and teaching transpires through the ministry of the apostles.

earth' (1:8).[20] Strikingly, the inaugural miracle of both Peter and Paul is the same, the healing of a lame man (Acts 3, Acts 14). Luke's accounts of each healing highlight the similarities between the two separate events.[21] While these similarities serve to underscore the complementarity of the two apostles' ministries, there is a deeper significance. The fact that Jesus had performed the same miracle links the ministries of both Peter and Paul to His own. This link accents the way in which the apostles serve as messengers expressly commissioned by Jesus Christ to bring the gospel to the nations and to establish the foundation of the Christian church.

The miracles serve not only to conjoin the ministries of the apostles with the risen Christ, but also to authenticate the apostles as the commissioned messengers of Christ. We may explore four passages, one in Acts, and three in the letters, that help us to see this particular purpose and function of the miracles. The first is Acts 14:3, an account of the ministry of Paul and Barnabas in Iconium, 'So they remained for a long time, speaking boldly for the Lord, who bore witness to the word of his grace, granting signs and wonders to be done by their hands.' Luke mentions that 'signs and wonders' are 'done' by the 'hands' of the apostles. As Luke's syntax makes clear, the apostles are the instruments but not the proper agents of these 'signs and wonders.'[22] It is the 'Lord' Jesus Christ who 'grant[ed]' that these miracles be done through his apostles.[23] There is a purpose, furthermore, in Christ's grant of these miracles. By these signs and wonders, Jesus bears 'witness to the word of his grace.' Strikingly, the word 'witness' is the verbal form of the noun that Jesus uses in His commission to the apostles in Acts 1:8. As the apostles bear 'witness' to Christ through the proclamation of His glorious person and saving work, Christ bears 'witness' to His apostles by granting them miracles to be done through their hands. In this way, Christ credentials His messengers, just as, Peter declares in his

---

20. On the phrase, 'end of the earth' in relation to the ministry of Paul and the structure of Acts, see my 'With a Whimper or a Bang? Acts 28 and the Ending of Acts,' *RTR* 74/1 (2015):1-14.

21. David G. Peterson, *The Acts of the Apostles* (PNTC; Eerdmans, 2009), 407.

22. J. A. Alexander, *A Commentary on the Acts of the Apostles* (2 vols.; New York: Charles Scribner, 1857; repr., Edinburgh: Banner of Truth, 1963), 2:48.

23. So rightly Paton J. Gloag, *A Critical and Exegetical Commentary on the Acts of the Apostles* (2 vols.; Edinburgh: T&T Clark, 1870), 2:46.

Pentecost sermon, God had accredited Jesus during His earthly ministry by 'mighty works and wonders and signs that God did through him ...' (2:22).[24] That the apostles perform miracles proves that their message is from God.

A second passage that reflects the apostle Paul's consciousness of the purpose of miracles in his own apostolic ministry is Romans 15:18-19, 'For I will not venture to speak of anything except what Christ has accomplished through me to bring the Gentiles to obedience – by word and deed, by the power of signs and wonders, by the power of the Spirit of God – so that from Jerusalem and all the way around to Illyricum I have fulfilled the ministry of the gospel of Christ.' In this chapter, Paul is explaining to the Roman Christians his intentions with respect to future ministry (Rom. 15:22-33). In doing so, he gives them an account of his previous sphere of apostolic ministry, a specific work that he deems 'fulfilled' (15:19). Paul's particular calling as an apostle is to bring the gospel to the Gentiles (Rom. 15:18, cf. 1:5, 16:26; Acts 9:15, 22:21, 26:17-18,23). He labors 'by word and deed, by the power of signs and wonders, by the power of the Spirit of God.' As Douglas J. Moo summarizes Paul's point in these two verses, 'Paul has identified the initiator and agent of his apostolic work – Christ; its purpose – "the obedience of the Gentiles"; and its means – "in word and deed, in the power of signs and wonders, in the power of the Spirit".'[25]

Paul points to 'signs and wonders,' undertaken 'in the power of the Spirit' as a hallmark of the apostolic ministry that Christ has assigned him.[26] Why does Paul specifically mention 'signs and wonders' in this context? As Murray notes, 'a miracle is both a sign and a wonder. As a sign it points to the agency by which it occurs and has thus certificatory

---

24. Of the three Greek terms employed by Peter in Acts 2:22, two surface in Acts 14:3 ('signs,' 'wonders'). There is, therefore, a verbal link between these two passages.

25. Douglas J. Moo, *The Epistle to the Romans* (NICNT; Grand Rapids: Eerdmans, 1996), 894. The clause that follows ('so that from Jerusalem and all the way around to Illyricum I have fulfilled the ministry of the gospel of Christ'), Moo continues, expresses the 'results' of that ministry, ibid. On the difficulties presented by the relation of the three clauses, 'in word and deed, in the power of signs and wonders, in the power of the Spirit,' see Moo, *The Epistle to the Romans*, 892-3, and John Murray, *The Epistle to the Romans* (2 vols.; NICNT; Grand Rapids: Eerdmans, 1959, 1965), 2:212-13.

26. On this syntactical relationship between 'signs and wonders' and 'in the power of the Spirit,' see Moo, *The Epistle to the Romans*, 893.

character; as a wonder the marvel of the event is emphasized.'[27] Paul's miracles, then, are done in the power of the Holy Spirit, who is the 'Spirit of Christ' (Rom. 8:9). Paul therefore points to Christ as the One who has wrought these miracles in His ministry (by the Spirit's power, to be sure). Christ's purpose in granting these miracles to be wrought in Paul's ministry was to credential His apostle as an approved messenger or teacher of doctrine. In this way, Paul reasons, Christ was bringing the Gentiles to obedience.

A third passage that helps us to see the credentialing function of miracles in the ministry of the apostles is 2 Corinthians 12:12, 'The signs of a true apostle were performed among you with utmost patience, with signs and wonders and mighty works.' In this portion of 2 Corinthians, Paul is responding to the activity of 'false apostles' in the church in Corinth (2 Cor. 11:13). He describes their activity in terms antithetical to his own. They propose a 'different spirit' and a 'different gospel' (11:4). Their activity is in keeping with Satan (11:3,14).

The false apostles represented themselves as genuine apostles, and have attacked the apostle Paul as unworthy of the apostolic office. In 2 Corinthians 12:12, Paul re-presents his apostolic credentials to the church.[28] In an effort to remind them that he is a 'true' apostle, he points the Corinthians to 'the signs of a true apostle,' namely 'signs and wonders and mighty works.'[29] Paul makes clear that it is God, not he himself,

---

27. Murray, *The Epistle to the Romans*, 2.213. Compare the remarks of Charles Hodge, *Commentary on the Epistle to the Romans* (rev. ed.; New York: A. C. Armstrong & Son, 1896), 693.

28. 'Here Paul reminds his converts of certain distinguishing features of his work at Corinth that showed he was a genuine apostle who was in no way inferior to the Twelve and therefore was worthy of their full endorsement (cf. v. 11). He appeals to what his converts had themselves seen and heard during his founding visit.' Murray Harris, *The Second Epistle to the Corinthians* (NIGTC; Grand Rapids: Eerdmans, 2005), 873.

29. These three terms appear 'together in Acts 2:22; 2 Thessalonians 2:9; and Hebrews 2:4 (cf. Rom. 15:19),' Paul Barnett, *The Second Epistle to the Corinthians* (NICNT; Grand Rapids: Eerdmans, 2007), 581. David Garland rightly notes that 'Paul does not intend to distinguish between three different types of miracles with these words but may have in mind three different effects: miracles that point beyond themselves to spiritual realities, miracles that evoke awe, and miracles that are seen as mighty acts,' *2 Corinthians* (NAC; Nashville: B&H, 1999), 29. On the relation of the three datives ('signs,' 'wonders,' 'mighty works') to the nominative noun 'signs,' see the discussion at Harris, *Second Epistle*, 876.

who is responsible for these miracles.[30] Paul was simply the instrument through whom God wrought these great works. These miracles certainly have redemptive-historical significance.[31] But their significance in the context of Paul's argument in 2 Corinthians 12 is to 'appeal to God's working of miracles during his ministry at Corinth as divine accreditation of his apostleship ... God was testifying to his authentic apostolicity.'[32] The fact that 'they were done over a long period' of time (12:12) indicates that the Corinthians had sufficient exposure to these credentialing signs as to arrive at an informed judgment about the authenticity of Paul's apostleship.[33] Significantly, these 'signs and wonders and mighty works' were so foundational to the identification of a genuine apostle that Paul can appeal to them to distinguish himself from a false apostle. Paul is a messenger of Christ, credited and authenticated by the miracles that God alone can give and has given through his public ministry. The fact that Paul can appeal to the Corinthians' memory of such miracles suggests that the working of miracles was a standing feature of his apostolic ministry, a point that is reinforced elsewhere in the New Testament.[34]

A fourth and final passage that helps us to see the role of miracles in the apostles' ministry is Hebrews 2:3-4, 'How shall we escape if we neglect such a great salvation? It was declared at first by the Lord, and it was attested to us by those who heard, while God also bore witness by signs and wonders and various miracles and by gifts of the Holy Spirit

---

30. Thus, the passive voice of the verb translated 'were performed,' so Garland, *2 Corinthians*, 529.

31. 'The effect of giving this triad as "the signs of the apostle" is to tie the apostle to God's great redemptive event under the new covenant, focused on Christ's death and resurrection. "Signs and wonders" mark the Exodus; "signs, wonders, and miracles" mark the death and resurrection of Jesus as at the first Easter and its apostolic proclamation,' Barnett, *Second Epistle*, 581.

32. Harris, *Second Epistle*, 876. Compare Garland, *2 Corinthians*, 529.

33. Garland, *2 Corinthians*, 530. The Greek phrase 'with utmost patience' renders a Greek word that can carry the sense of the extended duration of time (*hypomonē*). In context, the senses of duration and endurance are not mutually exclusive, Harris, *Second Epistle*, 874-5.

34. The narrative of Acts points to Paul's miracle working, for example, in reference to Paul's ministry in Ephesus (Acts 19:11) and the whole of the First Missionary Journey (Acts 15:12). Paul's statement to the Galatians, 'Does he who supplies the Spirit to you and works miracles among you ...' (Gal. 3:5) suggests that he was the instrument of miracle-working in the churches of Galatia as well.

distributed according to his will.'³⁵ In these verses, Hebrews is issuing the first of several warnings that appear in the letter. The gravity of the warning is commensurate with the 'great' ness of the 'salvation' that is available to believers in Christ. Hebrews explains in these verses what it is that renders this 'salvation' so great. In the first place, 'it was declared at first by the Lord,' that is, the Lord Jesus Himself.³⁶ This 'first phrase of God's final revelation … was succeeded by a second, which consisted of accrediting the word, in the sense of guaranteeing its accuracy … by those who had been witnesses to [Jesus'] word and deed' ('it was attested to us by those who heard').³⁷

After mentioning the witnesses to Jesus, Hebrews turns to the divine accreditation of those witnesses. As 'those who heard' bore witness to the Lord Jesus, so also God 'bore witness' to the witnesses. He did so through 'significant manifestations of power … outward tangible evidence, which served to validate the message delivered to the community.'³⁸ The 'signs and wonders and various miracles,' as in other passages we have considered, served to authenticate the messengers as divinely commissioned witnesses to Jesus Christ.³⁹ This consideration helps us to understand the argument that Hebrews presents in these verses. The writer stresses that 'the message declared by angels proved to be reliable and every transgression or disobedience received a just retribution' (Heb. 2:2). In view is the giving of the Law to Israel on Mt Sinai.⁴⁰ But the message that the Hebrews have received was not 'declared by angels.' It was declared by the Lord Jesus Christ. Therefore,

---

35. The syntax of the sentence presents a number of difficulties to the translator, on which see Paul Ellingworth, *The Epistle to the Hebrews: A Commentary on the Greek Text* (NIGTC; Grand Rapids: Eerdmans, 1993), 142.

36. 'The foundation of the Christian economy is traced to the ministry of the Lord,' William L. Lane, *Hebrews 1-8* (WBC 47A; Dallas: Word, 1991), 39.

37. ibid.

38. ibid.

39. The 'gifts of the Holy Spirit distributed according to his will' may refer to 'the spiritual gifts of the Holy Spirit which God has graciously distributed to his people,' Peter T. O'Brien, *The Letter to the Hebrews* (PNTC; Grand Rapids: Eerdmans, 2010), 90.

40. As commentators often observe, although there is no mention of the presence of angels at the giving of the law in Exodus 19, Deuteronomy 33:2 (and especially LXX Deut. 33:2) affords a textual basis on which to predicate angelic attendance on the giving of the law. Compare the testimony of Galatians 3:19 and Acts 7:38, 53.

Hebrews reasons, 'if the law with its angelic mediation had sanctions that were severe and inescapable, then how much more serious would be the neglect of the message proclaimed by the Son of God who is greater than the angels?'[41] For Hebrews' reasoning to be sound, the message of the witnesses must carry the very same divine authority that the teaching of Jesus Christ carried. It is the credentialing miracles that prove that the teaching of these witnesses was the teaching of God Himself.

In summary, the apostles spoke with the same divine authority that Jesus Christ did, and were attested by God in precisely the same way that Jesus Christ was attested by God – through the miracles that God gave them to do. This means that the apostles are, from God's perspective, credible teachers of doctrine. This fact carries two implications for the doctrine of inspiration. First, their teaching that the Old Testament is the inspired Word of God (2 Tim. 3:16, 2 Pet. 1:19-21) is not the mere opinion of human teachers and guides. It is the teaching of God Himself and, therefore, requires assent. Second, the apostles' claims to the inspiration that Jesus promised by the Spirit in John 14 and John 16 (1 Cor. 14:37, 1 Tim. 5:18, 2 Pet. 3:2, 15-16) are claims that carry divine authority. This is so because God, by the grant of signs and wonders to the apostles, gave His approval to them and to their teaching.[42] Therefore, the church regarded – and continues to regard – the books that Christ gave to her through the hands of the apostles as divinely inspired books. And this is so because apostolic testimony is divine testimony.[43]

The Witness of the Holy Spirit

We have observed that the Bible's claims to inspiration command assent. That is to say, the Bible not only insists that it is the inspired Word of

---

41. O'Brien, *Hebrews*, 85. O'Brien notes that Hebrews 2:1-4 is one example of an *a fortiori* argument, an argument that appears numerous times in the letter, *Hebrews*, 86.

42. 'The fact that the Scriptures are thus inspired is proved because they assert it of themselves; and because they must either be credited as true in this respect, or rejected as false in all respects; and because God authenticated the claims of their writers by accompanying their teaching with "signs and wonders and divers miracles." Heb. ii.4. Wherever God sends his "sign," there he commands belief; but it is impossible that he could unconditionally command belief except to truth infallibly conveyed,' A. A. Hodge, *The Confession of Faith*, 34.

43. 'The weight of the testimony to the Biblical doctrine of inspiration, in a word, is no less than the weight to be attached to the testimony of God – God the Son and God the Spirit,' Warfield, 'The Real Problem of Inspiration,' in *Works*, 1:213.

God, but it also supplies the basis on which one should accept that claim. The apostles are credible teachers of doctrine. What renders them credible are the miracles that they performed. God, who alone can work a miracle, gave the apostles these miracles to be done through their hands. In this way, God authenticates these men as His messengers and witnesses. Their message and teaching is His message and teaching. When the apostles teach that the Bible is the inspired Word of God, we are to receive this teaching as from the mouth of God Himself.

This argument, we have also noted, is the capstone of an extensive body of arguments that demonstrate the existence of God; the historicity, genuineness, and reliability of the Bible; and the coherence and truth of the religion that the Bible inculcates. The argument for the Bible's inspiration is an objective one. That is to say, it rests on claims that are public, historical, and verifiable. As such, they command the assent of all people, whether they are believers in Christ or not.

The Westminster Confession of Faith, we have observed above, points to a certainty that rises higher still. It is the province of the Christian alone. After pointing to multiple 'arguments whereby [the Bible] doth abundantly evidence itself to be the Word of God,' it goes on to say that 'our full persuasion and assurance of the infallible truth and divine authority thereof, is from the inward working of the Holy Spirit bearing witness by and with the Word in our hearts.'[44] There is a Spirit-borne witness and certainty that belongs to every true Christian. It does not pertain to the arguments for inspiration that we have surveyed above, but more fundamentally to the 'truth' and 'authority' of the Bible. Even uneducated Christians who have never studied the arguments for the Bible as the Word of God have warranted confidence in the divine origin, truth, and authority of Scripture.[45]

What, then, is this witness of the Spirit to the Bible?[46] The Westminster Confession of Faith makes some important assertions to help

---

44. Westminster Confession of Faith, I.5.

45. Robert L. Dabney, 'The Bible Its Own Witness,' in *Discussions: Evangelical and Theological, Volume 1* (Richmond, VA: Presbyterian Committee of Publication, 1891; repr., Edinburgh: Banner of Truth, 1967), 116-17.

46. See the classical treatments of Caspar Wistar Hodge, Sr, 'The Witness of the Holy Spirit to the Bible,' *Princeton Theological Review* 11/1 (Ja 1913): 41-84; Charles Hodge, *The Way of Life* (Philadelphia: American Sunday-School Union, 1841; repr., Edinburgh:

stage our reflections. First, the Spirit's witness surpasses, but by no means replaces, the other evidences for the Bible. By these latter evidences, after all, the Bible 'abundantly evidences itself to be the Word of God.' Second, the Spirit's witness is not independent of the Bible. It is, rather, 'by and with the Word.' Third, the Spirit's witness is 'inwardly' wrought, and is seated in the human 'heart.'[47]

Caspar Wistar Hodge, Sr. has defined the Spirit's witness in this way.

> The Witness of the Holy Spirit to the Bible, then, is not objective in the sense of being the mystical communication to the mind of a truth or proposition, nor is it a subjective inference from Christian experience. It is simply the saving work of the Holy Spirit on the heart removing the spiritual blindness produced by sin, so that the marks of God's hand in the Bible can be clearly seen and appreciated.[48]

This witness is part and parcel of the Spirit's work of regenerating the dead soul.[49] Unrenewed sinners are dead in sin and, therefore, their thinking is darkened and corrupt (Rom. 1:18, 21, 25, 28; Rom. 3:11; Eph. 4:18; 2 Cor. 4:4). The Scripture does not teach that sin has utterly destroyed the human mind. The fallen mind continues to function as a thinking faculty, but it functions entirely enslaved to sin and to Satan. It is morally unable to 'see the light of the gospel of the glory of Christ, who is the image of God' (2 Cor. 4:4).

Consequently, the unrenewed mind may and ought to follow and to be persuaded by the arguments that the Bible is the Word of God. But the most to which such a person will attain is 'a merely intellectual or

---

Banner of Truth, 1959), 11-25; Dabney, 'The Bible Its Own Witness,' 115-31; and William Cunningham, *Theological Lectures*, 320-42. More recently, see R. C. Sproul, 'The Internal Testimony of the Holy Spirit,' in Norman L. Geisler, ed., *Inerrancy* (Grand Rapids: Zondervan, 1979), 335-54.

47. 'This operation of the Spirit is here called his inward work, to distinguish it from what has been called his outward work, or the gifts of the Holy Spirit, the miracles wrought by the apostles under his agency, which also afford an evidence of the divine authority of the Scriptures, though some intermediate processes of argument are necessary before, from that outward work of the Spirit, the conclusion is reached,' Cunningham, *Theological Lectures*, 327.

48. C. W. Hodge, 'The Witness of the Holy Spirit,' 63-4.

49. And one crucial and indispensable aspect of the Spirit's work of regeneration is His illumination of the human mind so that the individual may 'spiritually and savingly ... understand the things of God' (Westminster Confession of Faith 10.1; cf. Westminster Larger Catechism 67).

"speculative" faith on the basis of rational arguments or the testimony of the Church.' He 'cannot savingly apprehend God nor see God as He is revealed as the author of Scripture.'[50] Therefore, 'though the unregenerate could rationally grasp the doctrines of the Bible, they would not be grasped *by* them unless enlivened by the Holy Spirit.'[51]

How does the Spirit renew such a person with respect to his thinking? There is a direct, immediate work of the Spirit in which He breaks the dominion of darkness over the soul and, at one and the same time, bestows 'spiritual light, thus enabling and moving him to recognize the marks of God in His Word.'[52] This work of the Spirit is 'internal, supernatural and hence objective to man's consciousness. But it communicates no new truth.'[53] The Spirit does not reveal truth to the mind. The Spirit, rather, sets the mind on the foundation on which alone it will be able 'immediately [to] see in the Bible itself all the marks of its divine authorship,' to 'recognize immediately or behold intuitively the marks of God's hand in the Scripture.'[54]

The Bible testifies to this work on more than one occasion. Relating his apostolic commission to Agrippa, Paul tells the King that Christ sent him to the Gentiles 'to open their eyes, so that they may turn from darkness to light and from the power of Satan to God' (Acts 26:18). Paul can therefore pray for Christians that the Spirit would continue to work in their lives so that they 'may have strength to comprehend with all the saints what is the breadth and length and height and depth' (Eph. 3:18, cf. 3:16).[55] The spiritual blindness that Satan promotes in the thinking of unbelievers and that prevents them from perceiving 'the light of the

---

50. C. W. Hodge, 'The Witness of the Holy Spirit,' 64.

51. John H. Gerstner, 'Warfield's Case for Biblical Inerrancy,' in John Warwick Montgomery, ed., *God's Inerrant Word: An International Symposium on the Trustworthiness of Scripture* (Minneapolis: Bethany Fellowship, 1974), 138. Compare C. W. Hodge who rightly denies that 'the transition from the unregenerate class to the regenerate class can be effected by arguments,' 'The Witness of the Holy Spirit,' 83.

52. C. W. Hodge, 'The Witness of the Holy Spirit,' 64.

53. ibid.

54. ibid., 76, 64.

55. On the referent of 'breadth and length and height and depth,' see the discussion at Harold W. Hoehner, *Ephesians: An Exegetical Commentary* (Grand Rapids: Eerdmans, 2002), 486-8. Hoehner takes the four nouns of Ephesians 3:18 to refer to the 'love of Christ,' 488.

gospel of the glory of Christ...' (2 Cor. 4:4) is dispelled by nothing less than a divine work of new creation, 'For God, who said, "Let light shine out of darkness," has shone in our hearts to give the light of the knowledge of the glory of God in the face of Jesus Christ' (2 Cor. 4:6). There is a particular work of the Spirit (the 'anointing') that seals to believers' minds the truth that they were taught and received by the apostles (1 John 2:20, 27).[56] Only those and all of those who are savingly drawn to Christ by the Father will be 'taught by God' (John 6:45, 44). That is to say, there is a saving apprehension of the truth of God in Christ that is the unique possession of every Christian believer.

How does this work of the Spirit relate to the other evidences that the Bible is the Word of God? In the first place, it should be insisted that these evidences are compelling in themselves to demand speculative assent and persuasion.[57] It is only because of sin that people do not yield to their testimony. Second, the Spirit's testimony is 'by and with the Word.' It does not bypass the Word nor communicate truths in addition to those that the Spirit has already revealed in the words of Scripture. These evidences, then, may and ought to be factored into the Spirit's witness to the Bible. They do so in a particular fashion. The Spirit grants an individual, immediately and intuitively, to see the Bible for what it is, the Word of God. The Spirit does so by removing the impediments posed by sin and by illumining the mind. Caspar Wistar Hodge, Sr likens this experience to the way in which one appreciates an artistic masterpiece.[58]

> It is true that we must be gifted with an aesthetic sense in order to recognize the masterpiece or painting and to discriminate it from that which has no aesthetic value. But given this aesthetic sense, the marks of the master's hand must be present in the work of art or there will be no marks for us to

---

56. On the 'anointing' in 1 John, see my '1 John 2:22 – What Does the Liar Deny?' *PRJ* 8/1 (2016): 29-48.

57. '"Abundant evidence" one must suppose to be sufficient; and objectively it is sufficient and more than sufficient; and this is what the Confession means to affirm. But according to the Reformed theology, man needs something more than evidence, however abundant, to persuade and enable him to believe and obey God's Word; he needs the work of the Holy Spirit accompanying the Word, *ab extra incidens*,' Benjamin B. Warfield, 'The Westminster Doctrine of Holy Scripture,' in *The Works of Benjamin B. Warfield* (10 vols.; New York: Oxford University, 1932), 6:211.

58. Compare here the reflections of C. W. Hodge's father, Charles Hodge, *The Way of Life*, 24-5.

see and recognize. Just so God's Spirit opens the eye of faith, but that eye beholds an object and recognizes the hand of God in the Bible.[59]

The Spirit's witness, then, in no way dispenses either with the evidences that the Bible affords to its own origin and authority nor for the need for arguments that present those evidences to the mind.[60] What the Spirit's witness does is to enable the believer to arrive, immediately and intuitively, at certitude as to the Bible as God's Word. Faith may and ought to embrace the persuasive arguments for the divine origin and authority of the Bible.[61] Even so, 'the ultimate source of faith is the power of the Spirit.'[62]

The Canon of Scripture

We have seen that the inspiration of Scripture is a doctrine taught by the biblical authors. They present themselves as credible teachers of doctrine. Their teaching, generally, and this doctrine, particularly, carries divine authority, an authority that is only savingly apprehended by the Spirit's witness.

It now remains to take up the question, 'which books comprise the Word of God'? Can we be sure that the thirty-nine books of the Old Testament, and the twenty-seven books of the New Testament are God's Word? On what basis can we be certain?

A full discussion of the canon of Scripture is beyond the scope of this chapter.[63] We may undertake a few considerations and questions in

---

59. C. W. Hodge, 'The Witness of the Holy Spirit,' 77. In the pages that follow, Hodge insists that the Spirit's witness does away neither with the need for saving faith nor for the objective evidence to which faith turns and by which faith reaches conviction, 77-9.

60. See here C. W. Hodge's argument against both Kuyper and Bavinck who contend that, in light of the Spirit's witness, 'rational grounds of faith may be dispensed with,' 'The Witness of the Holy Spirit,' 82.

61. 'Faith is not blind, and rational grounds may enter into the grounds of even saving faith, and without some grounds valid for the subject, it cannot arise,' C. W. Hodge, 'The Witness of the Holy Spirit,' 83.

62. ibid. 'The Witness of the Spirit is the efficient cause, and not one of the grounds of faith,' ibid.

63. Classical Reformed treatments of the subject include William Whitaker, *Disputations on Holy Scripture Against the Papists especially Bellarmine and Stapleton* (trans. and ed. William Fitzgerald; 1588; repr., Cambridge: Parker Society, 1849), 25-109; Archibald Alexander, *The Canon of the Old and New Testaments Ascertained, or The*

order to gain clarity about the canon and to assess the degree to which we may be certain that the sixty-six books of the Bible are the Word of God. First, we will offer a definition of canon. In doing so, we will reflect on what the criteria of canonicity are, that is, what the defining and identifying mark or marks of a canonical book are. We will also address an important point of dispute between the Roman Catholic and Protestant churches, namely, the province of the church with respect to the canon of Scripture. Second, we will sketch the case that the thirty-nine books of the Old Testament and the twenty-seven books of the New Testament alone comprise the canon of Scripture.

It is important first to define what one means by 'canon,' and particularly the criteria of canonicity, since there is not a consensus in the literature.[64] The word 'canon' is derived from a Greek word translated 'rule, measure.'[65] Theologians use the word 'canon' to denote a collection of books that is deemed normative and authoritative for the Christian church. There have been different answers, however, to the question how a given book comes to be canonical. The Roman Catholic Church insists that the canon of Scripture is authoritatively settled by

---

Bible Complete Without the Apocrypha and Unwritten Traditions (rev. ed.; Philadelphia: Presbyterian Board of Publication, 1851); William Henry Green, *General Introduction to the Old Testament: The Canon* (New York: Charles Scribner's Sons, 1896); and William Cunningham, *Theological Lectures*, 412-46. For a survey of the Reformation-era debates surrounding the canon of Scripture, see Richard Muller, *Post-Reformation Reformed Dogmatics: The Rise and Development of Reformed Orthodoxy, ca. 1520 to ca. 1725* (4 vols.; Grand Rapids: Baker, 2003), 2:371-96. For more recent conservative or evangelical literature on the canon of Scripture, see, representatively, B. F. Westcott, *A General Survey of the History of the Canon of the New Testament* (6th ed., New York, Macmillan and Co., 1889; repr., Grand Rapids: Baker, 1980); Roger Beckwith, *The Old Testament Canon of the New Testament Church* (London: SPCK / Grand Rapids: Eerdmans, 1986); R. Laird Harris, *The Inspiration and Canonicity of the Scriptures: An Historical and Exegetical Study* (rev. ed.; Greenville, SC: A Press, 1995); F. F. Bruce, *The Canon of Scripture* (Downers Grove, IL: InterVarsity, 1988); Michael J. Kruger, *Canon Revisited: Establishing the Origins and Authority of the New Testament Books* (Wheaton, IL: Crossway, 2012); and John S. Feinberg, *Light in a Dark Place: The Doctrine of Scripture* (Wheaton, IL: Crossway, 2018), 429-564.

64. For recent surveys of discussion concerning the definition and criteria of 'canon,' see Michael J. Kruger, *The Question of Canon* (Downers Grove, IL: InterVarsity, 2013), 27-46, and Feinberg, *Light in a Dark Place*, 429-67.

65. For a brief survey of the lexical history of the Greek word translated 'canon,' see Bruce M. Metzger, *The Canon of the New Testament: Its Origin, Development, and Significance* (Oxford: Clarendon, 1987), 289-93.

the church. This theological conviction gave rise to some extraordinary statements in the period after the Reformation. Johann Eck (1486–1543), one of the earliest disputants of Martin Luther, claimed that 'the Scriptures are not authentic, except by authority of the church.'[66] The Jesuit Guillaume Baile (1557–1620) claimed 'without the authority of the church we should no more believe Matthew than Titus Livy.'[67] Such statements may be extreme, but they are faithful expressions, or at least faithful extensions, of the teaching of the Roman Catholic Church. According to Rome, the authority of the church effectively settles the canon of Scripture.[68] That is to say, we may not know for certain that any particular book of Scripture is canonical unless and until the church first tells us so.[69]

Others have argued that the canon of Scripture was determined and settled by the personalities, movements, and events of the first four centuries of the church's history. In light of that conviction, some have claimed that it is meaningless and inappropriate to speak of 'canon' prior to the fourth century A.D., the date at which the canon of Scripture was

---

66. Johann Eck, *Enchiridion of Commonplaces* 1 (trans. F. L. Battles; Grand Rapids: Calvin Theological Seminary, 1978), 13, as cited at Turretin, *Institutes of Elenctic Theology* (3 vols.; Phillipsburg, NJ: P&R, 1992-7), 1:86.

67. cited at ibid.

68. We set to the side, at this juncture, the doctrine of the Roman Catholic Church, expressed at the Council of Trent, that the apocryphal or deuterocanonical books are part of the Word of God, on which see 'Decree on the Reception of Sacred Books' at Heinrich Denzinger, *Compendium of Creeds, Definitions, and Declarations on Matters of Faith and Morals: Latin – English* (ed. Peter Hünermann; 43d ed.; San Francisco: Ignatius, 2012), §1502. For a classical Reformed refutation of this claim of Rome, see W. H. Green, *General Introduction*, 157-200.

69. As Herman N. Ridderbos notes, 'according to the Roman Catholic view, the Canon *viewed in itself (quoad se)* possesses undoubted inherent authority. But *as it concerns us (quoad nos)*, the recognition of the Canon rests upon the authority of the Church. The Church, as the supposed infallible doctrinal authority, guarantees for its members the authority of the Canon of Scripture,' 'The Canon of the New Testament,' in Carl F. H. Henry, ed., *Revelation and the Bible: Contemporary Evangelical Thought* (Grand Rapids: Baker, 1958), 190. Turretin observes how the sixteenth century Roman Catholic theologians Bellarmine and Stapleton articulate this distinction. They affirm that 'the Scriptures absolutely and in themselves [are] authentic and divine, as coming from God (the source of all truth),' but go on to argue, however, that whatever intrinsic authority the Scriptures have, we are to receive those books as the Word of God only upon the authority of the church, Turretin, *Institutes*, 1.86. But, as Turretin rightly notes, 'Scripture cannot be authentic in itself without being so as to us,' ibid.

allegedly determined by the church. Still others have argued that as soon as a 'book [was] regarded as "Scripture" by early Christian communities,' it arose to the status of canon.[70] On either view, the canon was, at best, fluid and variable and, at worst, non-existent until the church was said to settle the matter officially at the close of the Patristic period.

Protestants in the Reformation tradition have dissented from each of the preceding views of canon. Historically, Protestants view a canonical book as a book that is inherently or intrinsically authoritative, and is to be received as such. That is to say, the recognition of a given book's authority lies ultimately neither in the magisterial authority of the church nor in the decisions of the church councils of late antiquity.

In our study of the inspiration and inerrancy of the Bible, we have seen the claims of the biblical books to be the written Word of God. As such, they carry inherent divine authority. This authority is neither derived from nor bestowed by human beings. Understanding where the authority of a canonical book is properly situated helps us both to define the canon and to ascertain the criteria of canonicity. The canon of Scripture, as Warfield succinctly defines it, is 'a collection of books given of God to be the authoritative rule of faith and practice.'[71] The question of canon, as Cunningham frames it, is 'what are the particular books which are entitled to a place in the collection of sacred writings, which have come from God, are stamped with his authority, and are intended by him to communicate his will?'[72]

For this reason, as Kruger correctly notes, 'books do not *become* canonical – they are canonical because they are the books God has given as a permanent guide for the church.'[73] Therefore, Warfield observes, 'the Canon of the New Testament was completed when the last authoritative book was given to any church by the apostles, and that was when John wrote the Apocalypse, about A.D. 98.'[74]

---

70. Kruger, *The Question of Canon*, 35. Kruger labels this view the 'functional' definition of canon and the view described in the previous sentence the 'exclusive' definition of canon. The views that are being summarized in this paragraph would find expression within the historical-critical tradition.

71. Warfield, 'The Formation of the Canon of the New Testament,' in *Works*, 1:451.

72. Cunningham, *Theological Lectures*, 412.

73. Kruger, *The Question of Canon*, 40.

74. Warfield, 'The Formation of the Canon,' in *Works*, 1:454.

It is the fact of a book having been authored by God and then imposed by God, through His apostles, upon His church that entitles it to membership in the canon of Scripture. The completion of the canon occurred when the last biblical book was authored and subsequently delivered to the church. This state of affairs does not mean, however, that human beings play no role whatsoever with respect to the canon of Scripture. Although humans in no way create the canon, they nevertheless receive or acknowledge the canon.[75] That is to say, the church is tasked with the divine calling of ascertaining which books that God has imposed upon the church as the authoritative rule of faith and practice.

This calling is necessary, in part, because of the circulation of spurious claimants to apostolic literature in the first century.[76] The apostle Paul acknowledges this in his second letter to the Thessalonians, 'Now concerning the coming of our Lord Jesus Christ and our being gathered together to him, we ask you, brothers, not to be quickly shaken in mind or alarmed, either by a spirit or a spoken word, *or a letter seeming to be from us*, to the effect that the day of the Lord has come' (2 Thess. 2:1-2, emphasis added). Paul concludes the argument of the chapter that these verses begin by reminding the Thessalonians, 'so then, brothers, stand firm and hold to the traditions that you were taught by us, either by our spoken word or by our letter' (2 Thess. 2:15). What these statements tell us is that there were circulating in the churches letters ascribed to Paul, some of which were genuine and at least one of which was false. This circumstance had so distressed the church at Thessalonica that Paul himself intervened to reassure these believers. It is little wonder that Paul concluded this letter by saying, 'I, Paul, write this greeting with my own hand. This is the sign of genuineness in every letter of mine; it is the way I write' (2 Thess. 3:17).[77] Paul's remarks in

---

75. 'The canonicity of a New Testament book is not settled by the authority of the Primitive church, but by its testimony.' W. G. T. Shedd, *Dogmatic Theology* (3 vols.; New York: Charles Scribner's Sons, 1888; repr., Grand Rapids: Eerdmans, 1969), 1:142.

76. Leaving aside, for the moment, later literature that claimed to be authored by the apostles Peter and Paul (among others), on which see, for instance, Metzger, *The Canon of The New Testament*, 165-89.

77. The statement that Paul writes a concluding epistolary greeting in his own hand is not unusual (1 Cor. 16:21, Col. 4:18, Gal. 6:11, cf. Philem. 19). It reflects the point at which Paul's amanuensis ceased his secretarial labors with respect to the letter in question,

this closing statement yield an important datum. Paul indicates that his personally inscribed salutation is 'the sign of genuineness in *every letter of mine; it is the way I write*' (emphasis mine). As G. K. Beale has observed, 'his qualification that the *distinguishing mark* of his signature is attached to *all* his *letters* and that he always writes in this manner indicates that the danger of circulating spurious Pauline epistles and the attendant false teaching was more widespread than merely these instances.'[78] Paul took pains, in other words, to ensure that his correspondence bore the marks of authentication. He did this to distinguish his own letters from false letters claiming to be his and thereby to reassure his readers of the genuineness of his correspondence to them.

Paul tells us, then, that there were marks or criteria by which the churches were to identify his letters as genuine. We, of course, do not possess the autographs of any biblical book, and so any criteria peculiar to the autographs are no longer extant.[79] This fact does not mean, however, that God has left His church bereft of any means to ascertain which books He has in fact given to His people. This state of affairs, in turn, raises the question of the criteria of canonicity. Which are the criteria by which the church rightly discerns or recognizes which books are the inspired Word of God, the rule of the church's faith and practice?

Within the Christian church, and in particular among Protestants, there has not been unanimity with respect to the criteria of canonicity. How is one to come to the determination that a given book is or is not canonical?[80] Commonly proposed criteria include one or more of

---

and Paul personally undertook the physical writing of the letter. The fact, however, that Paul appends the statement indicating that his personally signatured greeting is a mark of authenticity is unique to his correspondence. For a dissenting and minority opinion that Paul's greeting is not intended to authenticate his epistle to the Thessalonians, see Jeffrey A. D. Weima, *1-2 Thessalonians* (BECNT; Grand Rapids: Baker, 2014), 637-8.

78. G. K. Beale, *1-2 Thessalonians* (IVPNTC; Downers Grove, IL: InterVarsity, 2003), 269.

79. 'Paul's handwriting ... was, of course, a temporary criterion of authenticity,' Bruce, *The Canon of Scripture*, 256.

80. For discussions of this question, see, representatively, Bruce, *The Canon of Scripture*, 255-9; Metzger, *The Canon of the New Testament*, 251-4; and Lee Martin McDonald, *The Biblical Canon: Its Origin, Transmission, and Authority* (rev. ed.; Peabody, MA: Hendrickson, 2007), 401-21.

the following: orthodoxy, catholicity, apostolicity, and inspiration.[81] Each of these characteristics is plausible as a canonical criterion. Each, however, also poses significant obstacles to serving as a canonical criterion. Orthodoxy appears to have informed the early church's judgments with respect to the canon of the New Testament. That is to say, does the book in question conform to apostolic teaching?[82] It is this criterion, for instance, that led many in the church to reject the *Gospel of Peter* in the third century.[83] The value of this criterion, of course, is that it served to reject from consideration compositions that were at variance with the truth that Christ had revealed through His apostles. This criterion, however, also suffers from a limitation. Orthodoxy *per se* is a necessary but not a sufficient condition of canonicity. In other words, the orthodoxy of a given work does not of itself warrant the conclusion that it is part of the church's rule of faith and practice.

Catholicity was another criterion employed in the early church.[84] This criterion explored how widespread a reception a particular work had received in the Christian church. That is to say, had the work in question merited a place in the worship and practice of the church? This criterion proved useful in rejecting compositions that had not earned the widespread acceptance of the church, and in preserving compositions about which some portion of the church had expressed

---

81. These criteria have surfaced in two recent treatments of the canon of Scripture. John Feinberg, for instance, has recently defined canon (and its criterion) as 'all the literary texts which give evidence of having been produced by both a human and a divine author, i.e., the biblical canon refers to all texts that give evidence of divine inspiration,' *Light in a Dark Place*, 454. Craig L. Blomberg has also recently proposed three criteria of canonicity that informed the judgment of the early church, namely, apostolicity, catholicity, and orthodoxy, *Can We Still Believe the Bible?: An Evangelical Engagement with Contemporary Questions* (Grand Rapids: Baker, 2014), 58-9.

82. This criterion was also applied to reject pseudonymous books, so Bruce, *The Canon of Scripture*, 261.

83. On which, see McDonald, *The Biblical Canon*, 410-11. It is in the context of such discussions that the 'rule of faith' (*regula fidei*) was employed in patristic discussions of the canon of Scripture, on which see Metzger, *The Canon of the New Testament*, 251-2.

84. This criterion is closely related to another but arguably distinct criterion, that of 'use,' or continuous employment in the church. That is to say, 'a church [was unwilling] to be out of step with other churches in regard to which documents were rejected as authoritative,' McDonald, *The Biblical Canon*, 415.

reservation.[85] One drawback to this criterion is the fact that some books, which were ultimately universally received as canonical, took longer than others to win universal acceptance.[86] Other non-canonical books, furthermore, appeared to have enjoyed some measure of ecclesiastical use notwithstanding what would become the church's universal consensus with respect to their non-canonicity.[87]

Another criterion of canonicity that has enjoyed widespread use is that of inspiration. In other words, the inspiration of the text of a given book is understood to be the basis on which the church judges that book to be part of the canon of Scripture. This view has much to commend it. After all, each book that the church ultimately recognized to be canonical is the inspired Word of God. The canonical authority of each book of the Bible rests not in the decisions of human beings but is inherent to the text of book. Because that book is the Word of God it is authoritative for faith and practice.

But it is one thing to observe that every canonical book is inspired and to affirm that the church did not grant the biblical books an authority that they did not already possess as the inspired Word of God. It is another to say that inspiration is the proper criterion of canonicity.[88] One indication that inspiration did not function as such a criterion in the early church is that we know of apostolic compositions that were not included in the canon of Scripture, compositions that may have been penned by inspiration of the Holy Spirit.[89] We cannot

---

85. Bruce notes that the Western church, out of deference to the wider church, preserved the Epistle to the Hebrews, notwithstanding its reservations centering around its authorship, *The Canon of Scripture*, 261.

86. This could be owing to one of a number of reasons. 2 John and 3 John, for instance, likely took longer owing to their comparative brevity and the specificity of their contents.

87. MacDonald, *The Biblical Canon*, 415, referencing *1 Clement, The Shepherd of Hermas, Didache*, and *The Epistle of Barnabas*, as examples.

88. On this distinction, see further Metzger, *The Canon of the New Testament*, 256-7.

89. Paul mentions a letter that he had written to the church in Corinth prior to the composition of 1 Corinthians (1 Cor. 5:9), and a letter to the church in Laodicea in Colossians 4:16. We cannot say for certain whether or not either letter was inspired and we therefore cannot say dogmatically that there were no inspired compositions that were not included in the canon of the New Testament. See here the concurring judgment of Archibald Alexander, 'I am willing to go further and say, that it is possible, (although I know no evidence of the fact,) that some things written under the influence of inspiration for a particular occasion, and to rectify some disorder in a particular church, may have

rule out the possibility that certain inspired compositions were not included in the canon of the New Testament.[90] For this reason, it is doubtful that inspiration *per se* functioned as a canonical criterion in the early church.

A fourth criterion, and one that approximates the criterion set forth by the New Testament, is that of apostolicity. As it is often formulated, apostolicity refers to the conviction that 'a writing was believed to have been produced by an apostle.'[91] As Metzger describes this view, 'the apostolic origin, real or putative, of a book provided a presumption of authority.'[92] This criterion of canonicity appears to have been in operation since the second century, and undergirds two other and 'subsidiary criteria – antiquity and orthodoxy.'[93] It served not only positively to warrant recognition of certain books as part of the canon of Scripture, but also negatively in particular to exclude 'pseudonymous literature,' that is, literature that claimed apostolic authorship but was judged by the church to have done so falsely.

For all of its virtues, the criterion of apostolicity encounters at least two difficulties. The first is that there are books of the New Testament that were not authored by an apostle. Mark's Gospel and Luke's Gospel are two examples. The church navigated this difficulty by underscoring the association of the author of each Gospel with a known apostle, Mark with the apostle Peter, and Luke with the apostle Paul.[94] A second difficulty is the fact that certain books of the New Testament are anonymous. The Epistle to the Hebrews proved challenging on precisely

---

been lost without injury to the Canon. For as much that the apostles preached by inspiration is undoubtedly lost, so there is no reason why every word which they wrote must necessarily be preserved and form a part of the canonical volume,' *The Canon*, 259. Alexander makes these claims in the course of defending his view that 'no canonical book of the New Testament has been lost,' *The Canon*, 258.

90. 'We do not deny that God inspired other writings than those which constitute the canon,' Auguste Lecerf, *An Introduction to Reformed Dogmatics* (1949; repr., Grand Rapids: Eerdmans, 1981), 318, as cited at Metzger, *The Canon of the New Testament*, 257.

91. McDonald, *The Biblical Canon*, 406.

92. Metzger, *The Canon of the New Testament*, 253.

93. Bruce, *The Canon of Scripture*, 259. On the appearance of the criterion of apostolicity in the second century Muratorian Fragment, see Metzger, *The Canon of the New Testament*, 253.

94. Bruce, *The Canon of Scripture*, 259. Tertullian labeled Luke and Mark as 'apostolic men,' *Marc.* 4.2.2, as cited at McDonald, *The Biblical Canon*, 407.

this point.⁹⁵ Although many in the early church attributed the Epistle to the Hebrews to the apostle Paul, this view has not carried the majority of the church since the time of the Reformation.⁹⁶

Given the overwhelming emphasis that the early church placed upon apostolicity, and the difficulties that we have registered, we might be tempted to conclude that the church's settled judgments about the canon of the New Testament were ill-founded. Such a conclusion, however, would be hasty, provided that we give closer attention to the criterion of apostolicity.

The difficulties attending the criterion of apostolicity center upon a narrow definition of apostolicity as apostolically authored. The New Testament, however, testifies to a broader understanding of apostolicity. The criterion presented by the New Testament is not apostolic *authorship* but apostolic *imposition*. That is to say, the church endeavored to recognize those books that the apostles had 'imposed on the infant Church to be its rule of faith and practice.'⁹⁷ It is in this sense that we may say that 'apostolicity thus determines the authority of Scripture; and any book or body of books which were given to the Church by the apostles as law must always remain of divine authority in the Church.'⁹⁸

The apostles, we have seen, were clothed with authority by Jesus Christ to convey instrumentally to the church His own authoritative teaching (John 14:26-7; John 16:12-15). As such, they constituted the redemptive-historical foundation of the New Covenant church (Eph. 2:20). The apostles, we have also seen, wrote in a manner that testified to their consciousness of possessing and exercising this authority in the church (1 Cor. 14:37; 2 Thess. 3:14, 1 Tim. 5:18, 2 Pet. 3:2, 3:15-16). This authority, to be sure, extended to imposing their own teaching upon the first century church. But it also extended to imposing non-apostolically authored compositions on the church. Paul, we have seen, commends Luke's Gospel as Scripture in 1 Timothy 5:18.⁹⁹ Therefore,

---

95. For a brief survey of the Epistle's reception in the early church, see Lane, *Hebrews 1-8*, cl-clv.

96. For an assessment of the difficulties attending the Pauline authorship of Hebrews, see O'Brien, *The Letter to the Hebrews*, 4-6.

97. C. W. Hodge, 'The Witness of the Holy Spirit,' 73.

98. Warfield, 'Authority and Inspiration of Scripture,' in *SSW*, 2:538.

99. Warfield, 'The Formation of the Canon,' in *Works*, 1:455.

Warfield observes, 'the authority of the apostles, as by divine appointment founders of the church, was embodied in whatever books they imposed on the church as law, not merely in those they themselves had written.'[100]

With this principle in mind, the early church's reception of certain books of the New Testament in light of apostolic association becomes clearer. Tertullian, we have observed, labels Luke and Mark as 'apostolic men.' Justin Martyr affirms that 'the Gospel and the Apostles' (referencing the New Testament) were 'written by the apostles and their companions.'[101] Even if many in the early church were mistaken to have concluded that Paul authored the Epistle to the Hebrews, their instincts were correct to observe in the writer a consciousness that 'authoritative apostolic testimony has been entrusted to him and he is now passing it along to his readers.'[102]

In light of what we have seen the New Testament teach about apostolic authority in relation to the church, the importance that the early church assigned to apostolic association is understandable. The early church recognized those books to be the Word of God that were imposed upon them by the apostles. The apostles imposed upon the church books that they, the apostles, had written, on the one hand, and books written by others, known to or associated with the apostles, on the other hand. It is in this sense that we may properly speak of apostolicity as criterion of canonicity, even as we recognize that the early church did not always clearly distinguish apostolic *imposition* from apostolic *authorship* in formulating and applying this criterion.

To affirm apostolic imposition as the criterion of canonicity for Scripture necessarily requires 'historical investigation' in order to settle which particular books are canonical.[103] We may now briefly sketch the

---

100. ibid.

101. For Justin Martyr, see Warfield, 'The Formation of the Canon,' 1.455; for Tertullian, see note 94 on page 141.

102. So Kruger, *The Question of Canon*, 148. Kruger appeals particularly to Hebrews 2:1-3 to warrant this conclusion, and notes that Origen regarded the author to have been 'someone who was part of the apostolic circle, likely a companion and disciple of Paul himself,' ibid.

103. C. W. Hodge, 'The Witness of the Holy Spirit,' 73. Hodge makes this statement in the context of refuting the claim that 'the Witness of the Spirit [is] to the Canonicity of any or all of the Biblical books,' ibid. Not only is the matter one that requires historical inquiry, but the 'Witness' does not consist of 'the communication of any new knowledge

case for receiving the thirty-nine books of the Old Testament, and the twenty-seven books of the New Testament as canonical. We will consider the arguments for the Old Testament and the New Testament separately.

To reiterate a point that we have raised above, our starting point in these discussions is the authority of the Lord Jesus Christ Himself. The pronouncements of Christ, and His appointed witnesses, the apostles, are determinative for the faith and practice of the church. Anything that Jesus and the apostles declare regarding the canon necessarily regulates our understanding of the canon.

What do Jesus and the apostles have to say with respect to the Old Testament canon?[104] We have seen, in the previous chapter, Jesus' and the apostles' recognition of the Scripture or Scriptures as the very Word of God. The New Testament, furthermore, cites numerous books of the Old Testament as 'Scripture.' This manner of citation indicates the New Testament authors' understanding that these particular books belonged to the canon of the Old Testament.[105]

While the New Testament does not give us a canonical list of the Old Testament, it does testify to an accepted three-fold canonical structure. In Luke 24:44, Jesus tells His disciples, 'These are my words that I spoke to you while I was still with you, that everything written about me in the Law of Moses and the Prophets and the Psalms must be fulfilled.' Jesus here offers a summary of His earthly teaching, namely, that His person and work are the fulfillment of 'the Law of Moses and the Prophets and the Psalms.' The next verse clarifies that this three-fold division refers to 'the Scriptures' (24:45). A three-fold division of

---

or matter of fact,' ibid. Compare the concurring comments of Shedd, *Dogmatic Theology*, 1:143.

104. In framing the question in this fashion, we by no means wish to deny that the Old Testament books themselves afford indications of their canonicity. The Law and the Prophets, in multiple places, 'rightful[ly] ... claim to be a revelation of the will of God' and, on this basis, were 'rec[eived] ... into the canon,' W. H. Green, *General Introduction*, 33. For the Old Testament evidence, see Green's discussion at *General Introduction*, 11-18, 31-6.

105. These books include Genesis, Exodus, Leviticus, Deuteronomy, Isaiah, Zechariah, Malachi, several Psalms, Habakkuk, Job, Proverbs, Kings, Hosea, Joel, Amos, Micah, Jonah, and Daniel, Beckwith, *Old Testament Canon*, 72, 76. This list does not include the several Old Testament books that, while cited, nevertheless inform the imagery and wording of Revelation, ibid. Compare the discussion of W. H. Green, *General Introduction*, 141-56.

the Old Testament is attested in the literature contemporary to the New Testament and was tied to the conviction that 'all three sections of the canon [were] closed collections of old books.'[106] Although there is diversity in the manner in which these books were numbered within Jewish literature at the turn of the eras, this diversity is more apparent than real and, in fact, reflects an underlying agreement concerning how many and which books constituted the canon of the Old Testament.[107] In his survey of the Old Testament canon, Beckwith concludes that all but five of the Old Testament books were undisputed within Judaism at the time of the New Testament.[108] 'Disputes' about these five books (Ezekiel, Proverbs, Ecclesiastes, Song of Songs, Esther), Beckwith continues, 'were of limited significance. In most cases they only arose after the recognition of the books as canonical, and they did not seriously interfere with that recognition, which survived the challenge and has continued as before.'[109] In summary, then, at the time of the New Testament there was widespread recognition and consensus within Judaism that the canon of Scripture not only included the thirty-nine books of the Old Testament but also was 'closed.'[110] For all the differences that obtained among Jews and Christians in the first century, the question of which books belonged to the canon of Scripture was not among them.[111] It is this canon that Jesus and the apostles invoke in their public teaching. For this reason, we rightly receive these books as the very Word of God.

---

106. Beckwith, *Old Testament Canon*, 165. See Josephus, *Contra Apionem* 1.8 and the Prologue to Greek Ecclesiasticus, on which, see Beckwith, *Old Testament Canon*, 110.

107. ibid., 262. Beckwith's conclusion follows extensive discussion of the fact that some Jewish writers numbered the Old Testament books at '22,' while others at '24,' *Old Testament Canon*, 235-42.

108. ibid., 274.

109. ibid., 323.

110. ibid., 338. On the non-canonicity of the Pseudepigrapha and the Apocrypha in first century Judaism, see *Old Testament Canon*, 338-408, and, more briefly, R. Laird Harris, *Inspiration and Canonicity*, 178-90. It is worth noting that Beckwith decisively rejects, on historical grounds, the concept of an alleged 'Alexandrian canon' that is sometimes said to have encompassed the Apocrypha, *Old Testament Canon*, 383-6. For older but still valuable discussions of the evidence against the canonicity of the Apocrypha, see Alexander, *The Canon*, 36-83; and Green, *General Introduction*, 119-140, 195-200.

111. Alexander, *The Canon*, 34.

When we come to the New Testament, we do not have the benefit of the inspired testimony of Jesus or the apostles as to which particular books belong to what we have come to call the New Testament.[112] Neither do we have a canonical division of the sort to which Jesus refers in Luke 24:44. How, then, are we to ascertain which books belong to the canon of the New Testament?

To answer this question, we begin by reminding ourselves of three points that we have already surveyed. First, the teaching of Jesus and the apostles is authoritative and normative for faith and practice. Second, Jesus anticipated that, after His resurrection, the apostles would provide inspired accounts of His earthly ministry. He also anticipated that they would provide inspired records of the teaching of the ascended Christ to His church. The apostles, we have observed, were conscious of the authority with which Christ had clothed them, and, at times, reflected awareness that their compositions were the inspired Word of God. Third, the apostles express awareness that 'the "Scriptures" were not a *closed* but an *increasing* canon.'[113] That is to say, to the Scriptures of the Old Testament were being added books of equal authority. These additions were made under the oversight of the apostles. Ultimately, 'the new books thus added were numerous enough to be looked upon as another *section* of the Scriptures,' to which the name 'New Testament' was appended in later centuries.[114]

What, then, does the evidence from the first four centuries of the church's history testify to the church's reception of the books of the New Testament as the Word of God?[115] By the end of the second century, Irenaeus cites nearly all of the New Testament as Scripture.[116] Irenaeus

---

112. Peter's statement in 2 Peter 3:16, referencing a collection of Paul's letters as 'Scripture,' and Paul's probable reference to Luke's Gospel at 1 Timothy 5:18 are about the closest that we come to such declarations.

113. Warfield, 'The Formation of the Canon,' in *Works*, 1:452.

114. ibid., 1:453.

115. For a lengthier discussion of the relevant evidence, see Metzger, *The Canon of the New Testament*, 39-247, and Bruce, *The Canon of Scripture*, 117-240.

116. That is, he references the Gospels, Acts, the Pauline Epistles (except Philemon), Hebrews, James, 1 Peter, 1-2 John, and Revelation as Scripture, Kruger, *The Question of Canon*, 157. Kruger elsewhere speaks of a 'canonical core' that emerged within the second century, a core that 'consisted of the four Gospels, Paul's epistles, Acts, 1 Peter, 1 John, and perhaps a few others,' *Canon Revisited*, 231.

was hardly an outlier in this conviction. Rather, as Kruger has recently shown, extant evidence from throughout the second century shows that 'books were received as Scripture prior to the time of Irenaeus.'[117] The concept of canon was not a late second century invention, but 'gr[ew] naturally and innately out of the earliest Christian movement,' specifically, from the teaching of Jesus and the apostles.[118] Furthermore, the boundaries of the canon had assumed their basic shape early and universally across the post-apostolic church. To be sure, there would be books, as was the case with the reception of the Old Testament canon within Judaism, about which some quarters of the church, for certain periods of time, had reservations. But modern historians can easily exaggerate the depth and extent of these reservations.[119] These books (James, 2 Peter, 2-3 John, Jude, Revelation) were ultimately and universally embraced by the Christian church.[120]

At first glance, the fact that certain books were debated within the church may be unsettling. In reality, this debate should confirm the contemporary church's convictions that each of the books in the canon of the New Testament is the Word of God. This debate shows that the church took great care in its task of examining claimants to the canon of Scripture. The church was not hasty to acknowledge a book as canonical. It was willing to engage in debate, where necessary, to ascertain the credentials of books that claimed to be the Word of God. Furthermore, only a very small proportion of the New Testament was subjected to such scrutiny. Ultimately each of these books was recognized to be the Word of God. What's more, although some sections of the church took longer than others to recognize certain disputed books, 'from the time of Irenaeus down, the church at large had the whole Canon as we now possess it.'[121] For these reasons, the

---

117. Kruger, *The Question of Canon,* 158.
118. ibid., 203.
119. So rightly Kruger, *Canon Revisited,* 265-6. See also the helpful reflections of Ridderbos, 'The Canon of the New Testament,' 199.
120. See the survey at Kruger, *Canon Revisited,* 269-74.
121. Warfield, 'The Formation of the Canon,' in *Works,* 1:455. As Warfield continues, 'And though a section of the church may not yet have been satisfied of the apostolicity of a certain book or of certain books; and though afterwards doubts may have arisen in sections of the church as to the apostolicity of certain books (as e.g. of Revelation):

contemporary church may be well-assured that the post-apostolic church was careful and deliberate as it sought to recognize those books, and only those books, that the apostles had imposed upon the church as the church's rule of faith and practice.

One final question that surfaces concerning the canon of Scripture concerns the authority of the canon understood as the list of sixty-six books formulated by the church from its conviction that these books are the Word of God. Is there authority to the canon, so defined, and, if so, where does it lie? Given that the books of Scripture are infallible, may infallibility be predicated of the canon understood in these narrow terms?[122] To focus the question, is the church's judgment that the sixty-six books of the Bible are the Word of God a fallible or an infallible judgment?

Since the church is not promised infallibility, we are bound to say that the church's canonical judgments are fallible. That is to say, they are capable of error. This is not to say that the church has erred or has likely erred in this matter. It is only to say that even the settled, universal, and undisputed decisions of the church are not infallible.[123] Neither have individual Christians been promised that the Spirit will in some way infallibly reveal or confirm to them the specific or particular contents of the canon of Scripture. There is, we have seen, a distinct witness of the Spirit in relation to the Christian and the Word of God. But that witness does not add verbal or propositional content to the Word of God. Neither does it extend to infallibly settling which books are or are not part of the Word of God. It consists, rather, of the Spirit removing any subjective impediments that might otherwise prevent the believer from seeing God's handiwork in His own Word.

---

yet in no case was it more than a respectable minority of the church which was slow in receiving, or which came afterward to doubt, the credentials of any of the books that then as now constituted the Canon of the New Testament accepted by the church at large. And in every case the principle on which a book was accepted, or doubts against it laid aside, was the historical tradition of apostolicity,' ibid.

122. As John H. Gerstner formulated the question, do we have a fallible or an infallible collection of infallible books?, on which see R. C. Sproul, 'The Establishment of Scripture,' in Don Kistler, ed., *Sola Scriptura! The Protestant Position on the Bible* (Morgan, PA: Soli Deo Gloria, 1995), 66-8.

123. David G. Dunbar, 'The Biblical Canon,' in D. A. Carson and John D. Woodbridge, eds., *Hermeneutics, Authority, and Canon* (Grand Rapids: Baker, 1995), 360.

In affirming the fallibility of the church's recognition, we are not denying that there is genuine authority in relation to the canon of Scripture. The 'authority which guarantees the canon ... is not the Church, but the inspired apostles who gave the sacred books one by one to the Church, thus at once creating and filling up the total contents of the class of sacred books.'[124] The church's role is purely one of 'receiv[ing]' the books that the apostles imposed on it, 'and the authority which validates [the canon] as the law-code of the Church antedates and is the same authority which founded the Church itself.'[125] The reason why it is important to refrain from attributing infallibility to the church's judgment that the sixty-six books of Scripture are the Word of God is to safeguard the church's sole authority, that is, the Word of God imposed upon the church through the apostles.[126] Whatever authority the church possesses is in every way subordinate to that of the Word of God. Even in receiving the Word of God, the church is submissive to the Word of God.

To formulate matters in this way, it is important to stress, in no way relativizes or casts doubt upon the church's judgments in this department. In fact, given what we have observed, we ought to have the highest confidence that no book resides in the canon that is not the inspired, infallible Word of God.[127] But it is to say that our authority, the church's *norma normans*, is the Word of God and the Word of God alone. Seen in this light, the importance of the church's reception of the Word of God becomes clear. As Ridderbos rightly notes, 'the history of the Canon is *the process of the growing consciousness of the Church*

---

124. Warfield, 'Review of Three Books on Inspiration,' in *SSW*, 2:612.
125. ibid., 2:613.
126. 'The point is, whether the Scriptures are a product of the Church, or rather of the authority which founded the Church,' Warfield, 'Authority and Inspiration of Scripture,' in *SSW*, 2:538.
127. 'In part it is left to be determined indirectly from the testimony of the early Church; it being no far cry from the undoubting universal acceptance of a book as authoritative by the Church of the apostolic age, to the apostolic gift of it as authoritative to that Church. But by one way or another it is easily shown that all the books which now constitute our Bible, and which Christians, from that day to this, have loyally treated as their divinely prescribed book of law, no more and no fewer, were thus imposed on the Church as its divinely authoritative rule of faith and practice,' Warfield, 'Authority and Inspiration of Scripture,' in *SSW*, 2:539.

concerning its ecumenical foundation ... It belongs truly to the evidences of the faith, that in the manner in which the Church has accepted the Canon there is seen the fulfillment of the word of the Lord to his apostle: "Thou art Peter, and upon this rock I will build my church" (Matt. 16:18).'[128]

---

128. Ridderbos, 'The Canon of the New Testament,' 198, 201.

The Sufficiency of Scripture

In previous chapters, we have given particular attention to the definition of Scripture. We have seen that God has revealed Himself generally in the creation, and particularly or specially to His people. We have reflected on the necessity and the nature of special revelation. We have closely attended to the claims of Scripture to be the inspired and inerrant Word of God, and have seen how and why these claims are warranted claims.

In the course of our treatment of the Scripture, we have encountered one of the Bible's attributes, namely, its authority. The text of Scripture has divine authority because that text is the very Word of God. As such, the authority of Scripture rests wholly upon its Divine Author. No human being lends or adds any authority to the Scripture.[1] Human beings, rather, are tasked with recognizing the innate or inherent authority of the Bible. Any human being should be able to understand and accept the multitude of internal and external evidences whereby the Scripture 'doth abundantly evidence itself to be the Word of God.'[2] And yet, it is only by the 'Holy Spirit bearing witness by and with the Word in our hearts' that we may come to a 'full persuasion and assurance of the infallible truth and divine authority' of the Scripture.[3]

---

1. See here the testimony of Westminster Confession of Faith 1.4, 'The authority of the Holy Scripture, for which it ought to be believed, and obeyed, dependeth not upon the testimony of any man, or Church; but wholly upon God (who is truth itself) the author thereof: and therefore it is to be received, because it is the Word of God.'

2. Westminster Confession of Faith 1.5.

3. ibid.

In this chapter and in the next chapter, we are going to consider two other attributes of Scripture, the sufficiency of Scripture and the perspicuity (or, clarity) of Scripture. When Reformed Protestants have affirmed Scripture to be sufficient, they are saying that the Bible is sufficient for the purposes for which it was written. In this respect, the Bible does not require supplementation. The perspicuity of Scripture refers to the clarity and accessibility of its basic teaching to the generality of its readership. Christians do not need a priesthood of clergy or scholars mediating its teaching to them in order to understand what God has intended the Scripture to communicate to them.

We will first take up the sufficiency of Scripture. Because this doctrine has been subject to misunderstanding, and because of historic and contemporary disagreements within the church about it, it is important to state clearly what we mean by Scripture's sufficiency. We will then make a specific case for its sufficiency, giving attention to the redemptive-historical shape of Scripture that we observed in Chapters 2 and 4. We will then address two significant objections to the sufficiency of Scripture. The first is the doctrine of the Roman Catholic Church that authoritative, unwritten traditions stand alongside Scripture as Scripture's normative equal. The second is the doctrine that the Holy Spirit continues revelatory activity in the life of the church today. Although this doctrine has assumed many forms in the history of the church, we will give particular attention to those expressions of this doctrine by contemporary theologians who identify themselves as Reformed.

The Sufficiency of Scripture, a Definition

A helpful and classical definition of the sufficiency of Scripture appears in the Westminster Confession of Faith.

> The whole counsel of God concerning all things necessary for His own glory, man's salvation, faith and life, is either expressly set down in Scripture, or by good and necessary consequence may be deduced from Scripture: unto which nothing at any time is to be added, whether by new revelations of the Spirit or traditions of men. Nevertheless, we acknowledge the inward illumination of the Spirit of God to be necessary for the saving understanding of such things as are revealed in the Word: and that there are some circumstances concerning the worship of God, and government

of the Church, common to human actions and societies, which are to be ordered by the light of nature, and Christian prudence, according to the general rules of the Word, which are always to be observed.[4]

This definition makes a number of important claims and qualifications about the sufficiency of Scripture. We will offer a defense of this definition below. For now, we will simply enumerate the claims that Westminster advances in this paragraph. In the first place, everything that human beings need to glorify God; everything that God requires of people to believe and to do is found in Scripture. Scripture is 'the only rule of faith and obedience.'[5] B. B. Warfield comments on the significance of this catechetical expression.

> This, it is to be observed, is to make Scripture something more than *a* rule of faith and practice; something more than *the* rule of faith and practice, in the sense of merely the fullest and best extant rule; something more than even *a sufficient* rule of faith and practice. It is to make it the *only* rule of faith and practice, to which nothing needs to be added to fit it to serve as our rule, and to which nothing is to be added to make it altogether complete as our authoritative law. It contains not only enough to serve all the purposes of a rule of faith and practice, but all that is to be laid as the authoritative law of life on the consciences of Christians.[6]

In matters of faith and practice, then, human beings need go no farther than Scripture to discern what it is that God would have them to believe, and what it is that God would have them to do. The Scripture is 'a total and adequate rule of faith and practice.'[7]

A second and related observation is that Westminster circumscribes the sufficiency of Scripture. The Scripture is not sufficient to all purposes, and is not sufficient in all respects. It is sufficient to guide human beings as to how to glorify God and to be saved. It is sufficient with respect to what human beings are to believe and to do so that they may glorify

---

4. Westminster Confession of Faith, 1.6.

5. Westminster Larger Catechism Q&A 3. Compare the Westminster Shorter Catechism Q&A 2, 'the only rule to direct us how we may glorify and enjoy [God].'

6. Benjamin B. Warfield, 'The Westminster Doctrine of Holy Scripture,' in *The Works of Benjamin B. Warfield* (10 vols.; New York: Oxford University, 1932), 6:225, emphasis original.

7. Francis Turretin, *Institutes of Elenctic Theology* (3 vols.; Phillipsburg, NJ: P&R, 1992-7), 1:135 (=2.16.12).

God and be saved. For this reason, Westminster denies that 'the Bible contains all truth ... Scripture is complete and final only *for the purpose for which it is given*.'[8]

Third, Westminster stresses that the 'teachings and prescriptions' of Scripture come to us in one of two ways.[9] The first is that which is 'expressly set down in Scripture;' the second is that which 'by good and necessary consequence may be deduced from Scripture.' The teaching of Scripture consists not only of express declarations but also of inferences that necessarily follow from the statements of Scripture. Even a 'legitimate inference [is] to be considered as the Word of God.'[10] But Westminster does not guarantee that every reader will infallibly draw such inferences, nor affirm that every conceivable inference from a passage of Scripture is properly to be regarded as the teaching of Scripture.[11] Neither does Westminster say, as Frame has observed, that proper inferences contribute anything to the teaching of Scripture.

> That phrase [i.e., 'good and necessary consequence'] refers to logic done right, ideal logic. When deductive logic is done right, the conclusion of a syllogism does not add to its premises. It rather brings out content already there ... what the syllogism does is to make the implicit content explicit. So (a) the 'content of Scripture' includes all the logical implications of Scripture, (b) the logical implications of Scripture have the same authority as Scripture, and (c) logical deductions from Scripture do not add anything to Scripture.[12]

The human mind, then, is tasked with drawing the meaning that already lies in Scripture, even as it is forbidden from either twisting or adding to that meaning.[13]

---

8. Robert Letham, *The Westminster Assembly: Reading Its Theology In Historical Context* (Phillipsburg, NJ: P&R, 2009), 138, emphasis original.

9. Warfield, 'The Westminster Doctrine,' in *Works*, 6:226.

10. Turretin, *Institutes*, 1:135 (=2.16.3). Warfield notes that Westminster's insistence that 'good and necessary consequences' of Scripture are the Word of God is affirmed in response to Socinians and Arminians, 'The Westminster Doctrine,' in *Works*, 6:226.

11. John M. Frame, *The Doctrine of the Word of God* (Phillipsburg, NJ: P&R, 2010), 222. Warfield observes that the fact that Scripture is given for the salvation of man recognizes the noetic effects of sin, even in the study of the meaning of Scripture, 'The Westminster Doctrine,' in *Works*, 6:227.

12. Frame, *The Doctrine of the Word of God*, 222.

13. As Letham observes, this enterprise of deducing meaning from Scripture is hardly an individualistic enterprise. For Westminster, the public reading and preaching of

Fourth, Westminster stresses that the sufficiency of Scripture excludes two rival claimants of authoritative teaching in the church, 'new revelations of the Spirit' and 'traditions of men.' In the first place, Westminster denies that 'new revelations of the Spirit' may properly stand alongside the teaching of Scripture. In doing so, it in no way countenances those alleged revelations as authentic or authoritative in their own right.[14] In the second place, Westminster denies the parity of 'traditions of men' with the Scripture. It does not, however, thereby deny the legitimacy of tradition, properly defined, for the church.[15]

Fifth, Westminster addresses two areas or respects in which Scripture is <u>in</u>sufficient. First, unless one receives the 'inward illumination of the Spirit of God,' he cannot arrive at 'the saving understanding of such things as are revealed in the Word.' Westminster's phrase 'saving understanding' denotes a particular species of knowledge. It is not merely notional or propositional understanding, to which any reader may attain.[16] It is the knowledge that is 'accompanied with a relish and love for the truth, and leading to a life of holy obedience.'[17] Second, there are 'some circumstances concerning the worship of God, and

---

Scripture is a crucial aspect of the way in which believers are to arrive, in this fashion, at Scripture's meaning, Letham, *Westminster Assembly,* 139.

14. See Westminster Confession of Faith 1.1, 10.

15. That is, it does not 'reject tradition as such,' Letham, *Westminster Assembly,* 141. 'The question is not whether all traditions are to be entirely rejected (for we grant that there may be some use for historical traditions, concerning facts and ritual traditions, concerning rites and ceremonies of free observation). But we here speak only of doctrinal and moral traditions relating to faith and practice, the use of which beside the Scriptures we disapprove,' Turretin, *Institutes,* 1:135 (=2.16.7). In the previous paragraph, Turretin notes that what is in dispute are 'unwritten traditions worthy of as much reverence as the Scriptures …,' ibid. Compare the comments of Petrus van Maastricht who addresses the legitimacy of a distinct set of 'traditions,' 'The Reformed, although they allow as necessary the tradition by means of which the Scripture comes to us, nevertheless do not allow any traditions to become dogmas or commands that are necessary in addition to the Scriptures,' *Theoretical-Practical Theology, Vol. 1: Prolegomena* (ed. Joel Beeke; trans. Todd M. Rester; Grand Rapids: Reformation Heritage, 2018), 1:177; cf. Turretin, *Institutes,* 1.135 [=2.16.8].

16. In this way, Westminster 'steers clear of rationalism,' Letham, *Westminster Assembly,* 141.

17. James S. Candlish, 'The Doctrine of the Westminster Confession on Scripture,' *The British and Foreign Evangelical Review* 26 (1877): 174, as cited at Warfield, 'The Westminster Doctrine,' in *Works,* 6:228.

government of the church, common to human actions and societies' that are not expressly revealed in the Word but to be settled by the church 'by the light of nature, and Christian prudence, according to the general rules of the word.' A circumstance is 'a concomitant of an action, without which it can either not be done at all, or cannot be done with decency or decorum.'[18] The doctrine of circumstances, for instance, clarifies that Scripture's sufficiency does not mean that 'one must have an express text of Scripture for everything he says or does in common life.'[19] An example of a circumstance in the worship of God is the particular hour and location at which a congregation gathers for worship on the Lord's Day. An example of a circumstance in the government of the church is the set of parliamentary rules a church body adopts to govern its formal proceedings. Neither the Spirit's saving illumination nor these circumstances are, of course, without reference to the Word of God.[20] But each serves to illustrate the insufficiency of Scripture in certain respects.

Sixth, it is crucial to understand that Westminster's affirmations about the sufficiency of Scripture apply to the people of God in every age of redemptive history. To be sure, Westminster's particular formulations relating to the sufficiency of Scripture pertain to the Scriptures of the Old and New Testaments and to the people of God under the New Covenant.[21] But Westminster does not thereby deny that the people of God had sufficient revelation prior to the completion of the canon.[22] Its primary concern is to say that now, under the New Covenant, the

---

18. Thomas E. Peck, *Notes on Ecclesiology* (Richmond, VA: Presbyterian Committee of Publication, 1892), 122.

19. Alexander F. Mitchell, quoted at Warfield, 'The Westminster Doctrine,' in *Works*, 6:229.

20. That is to say, the illumination of the Spirit does not supplement revelation, but enables one to a saving understanding of the Word. Furthermore, circumstances must be ordered 'according to the general rules of the Word' (WCF 1.6).

21. And, in this respect, as Turretin notes, there is diversity across redemptive-history, 'the question is not whether the perfection of Scripture has always been the same as to degree (for we acknowledge that revelation increased according to the different ages of the church, not as to the substance of the things to be believed, which has always been the same, but as to the clearer manifestation and application of them),' *Institutes*, 1:135 (=2.16.5).

22. A point that is implied in 1.6 and in the closing words of 1.1 ('those former ways of God's revealing His will unto His people being now ceased').

Scriptures of the Old and New Testaments are a sufficient rule of faith and practice 'without the help of any traditions.'[23]

The Case for the Sufficiency of Scripture

By the sufficiency of Scripture, then, we mean 'that Scripture contained all the words of God he intended his people to have at each stage of redemptive history, and that it now contains everything we need God to tell us for salvation, for trusting him perfectly, and for obeying him perfectly.'[24] Is there a case to be made from the Scripture itself that it is sufficient in the respects that we have argued? We may advance this case in at least two ways. First, we will see that the close of the canon of Scripture carries necessary implications for the sufficiency of Scripture. Second, we will consider some explicit testimonies from Scripture that point to the Bible as a complete rule of faith and practice. After we have made this case, we will show that not only Scripture's express statements but deductions by 'good and necessary consequence' comprise that body of teaching that sufficiently or adequately norms faith and practice.

In the previous chapter, we observed that the canon of Scripture is settled in accordance with the criterion of apostolic imposition. The Word of God has inherent and inalienable divine authority. The church, however, must come to recognize the Word for what it is, and to reject the false claimants to divine teaching that have arisen throughout her history. Her task is to receive those books and only those books that the apostles imposed upon the church.[25] The apostles function in this capacity as the credentialed messengers of Jesus Christ, who was Himself credentialed by the Father as a divinely-approved teacher. It is therefore proper to say that, through the apostles, God in Christ is giving the church her Bible. The fruit of the church's work of recognizing the books that the apostles imposed upon her is what we have come to know as

---

23. Turretin, *Institutes*, 1:135 (=2.16.5).

24. Wayne Grudem, *Systematic Theology: An Introduction to Biblical Doctrine* (Grand Rapids: MI: Zondervan, 1994), 127.

25. 'The complement to apostolic intention … is post-apostolic recognition of the New Testament canon. Furthermore, that process of recognition – because it answers to an apostolic intention – reflects as well, we may say, the intention of Christ. No one less than the exalted Christ himself is the architect of that process,' Richard B. Gaffin, Jr, 'The New Testament as Canon,' in *Inerrancy and Hermeneutic: A Tradition, A Challenge, A Debate* (ed. Harvie M. Conn; Grand Rapids: Baker, 1988), 177.

the canon of the Old and the New Testaments. The church came to recognize the sixty-six books of the Bible relatively early and universally in her history.

Understanding these dynamics of the formation of the canon helps us to appreciate its significance for the sufficiency of Scripture. The office of the apostles and the tasks to which Christ committed them are, by design, not recurring in the life of the church.

> When understood in terms of the history of redemption, the canon cannot be open; in principle it must be *closed*. That follows directly from the unique and exclusive nature of the power the apostles received from Christ and from the commission he gave them to be witnesses to what they had seen and heard of the salvation he had brought. The result of this power and commission is the foundation of the church and the creation of the canon, and therefore these are naturally unrepeatable and exclusive in character.[26]

The canon, in other words, was never intended to be open-ended. The canon is yoked to the office of the apostle, an office that is designedly temporary and foundational to the church. The office of apostle, in turn, is yoked to the work of redemption that Christ accomplished once and for all in His death and resurrection. In accordance with His general pattern of working throughout redemptive history, God's work of redemption in Christ is accompanied by His final and authoritative word of revelation.[27] The 'exaltation of Christ and the founding of the church' mark the commencement of the climactic epoch of redemptive history.[28] All that awaits the church is the return of Christ at the end of the age. Until then, 'the history of revelation is closed' for the simple reason that there will be no advance in the history of redemption until Christ returns.[29]

---

26. Herman Ridderbos, *Redemptive History and the New Testament Scripture* (Phillipsburg, NJ: P&R, 1988), 25, as cited at Michael J. Kruger, *Canon Revisited: Establishing the Origins and Authority of the New Testament Books* (Wheaton, IL: Crossway, 2012), 281, emphasis Ridderbos's.

27. 'The foundational witness of the apostles to the work of Christ brings to light an important characteristic of all verbal revelation – the correlation between redemptive act and revelatory word ... the ongoing history of revelation is a strand within covenant, redemptive history as a whole; the process of verbal revelation conforms to the contours of that larger history,' Gaffin, 'New Testament as Canon,' 178.

28. ibid.

29. ibid., 179. This observation, in turn, necessarily gives definition to the significance of the life and experience of the church within the scope of the history of

For this reason, the canon of Scripture that Christ has given to the church by His apostles does not admit of addition or supplementation. So far as Christ, the Prophet, Priest, and King of His church, is concerned, Scripture is a complete Word to His people. The Scripture is therefore sufficient to the purposes for which He has given it to the church.

The sufficiency of Scripture is demonstrable not only from the redemptive-historical argument from the canon of Scripture, but also from the explicit testimonies of Scripture. To be sure, no one of the passages we are about to survey addresses all sixty-six books of Scripture. But the significance of these passages is the testimony that they give to the inscripturated revelation already in the possession of the people of God. The character of this testimony is such that it applies to the whole of the Bible that God has placed into the hands of the church. In other words, when Scripture testifies to the sufficiency of the Word of God that belongs to the people of God in *any* age, this testimony affirms the sufficiency of the Word of God that belongs to the people of God in *the present* age.

How does Scripture testify to its own sufficiency? We may identify three classes of three passages that testify to Scripture's sufficiency.[30] The first consists of passages affirming the sufficiency of the Word of God as the rule of faith and practice. In 2 Timothy 3:15-17, Paul reminds Timothy of the Scriptures that his mother and grandmother had taught him as a youth, and that he presently proclaims as a minister of the gospel.

> [F]rom childhood you have been acquainted with the sacred writings, which are able to make you wise for salvation through faith in Christ Jesus. All Scripture is breathed out by God and profitable for teaching, for reproof, for correction, and for training in righteousness, that the man of God may be competent, equipped for every good work.

In a previous chapter, we considered the importance of these verses in establishing the inspiration, or God-breathed character, of the text of

---

redemption, 'Ongoing church history, however, is not an extension of redemption. It is not a prolongation in series with Christ's work but the reflex of that work, the application of its benefits. It is not part of the foundation of the church but the building being erected on the finished, once-for-all redemptive foundation laid by Christ,' ibid.

30. The following outline is indebted to the presentation of Turretin, *Institutes*, 1:136-9 (=2.16.13-17).

Scripture. In addition to making this claim, Paul reminds Timothy of the purposes of Scripture, 'which are able to make you wise for salvation through faith in Christ Jesus' (3:15); 'profitable for teaching, for reproof, for correction, and for training in righteousness, that the man of God may be competent, equipped for every good work' (3:16b-17).[31] God has given Scripture for the salvation of His people. In particular, Scripture instructs the church what to believe, and provides practical instruction in living in a way that is pleasing to God.

Paul not only addresses the character and purpose of Scripture in these verses, but he also speaks to its sufficiency. In context, Paul is directing Timothy to the Scripture in the face of the spread of false teaching in the church in Ephesus (2 Tim. 3:1-10). It is significant that Paul sends Timothy to the Scripture and to nowhere else to direct the church's faith and practice. Scripture, in other words, occupies the sole and exclusive role as the norm of belief and life in the face of the spread of error within the church's bounds.[32] That this affirmation is restricted neither to time nor to location is evident from Paul's setting this teaching in the context of the dawn of the 'last days' (3:1). That is to say, the eschatological dawning of the last days in the resurrection of Christ provides the redemptive-historical setting in which Paul declares the Scripture to be sufficient for the faith and practice of God's people.[33] Neither does the fact that 'Scripture,' in the context of Paul's teaching, denotes the Old Testament serve to restrict this affirmation to the Old Testament for the church. As we have seen, the New Covenant books

---

31. Commentators debate the referent of the phrase 'man of God.' Does it refer to the minister or does it refer to every Christian? While the expression 'man of God' likely refers to the minister and not to the Christian, Paul's point in this verse still applies to all believers, William D. Mounce, *The Pastoral Epistles* (WBC 46; Nashville: Thomas Nelson, 2000), 353, 571. The minister, Paul teaches in the Pastoral Epistles, serves as an example for godly living to the people of God (1 Tim. 4:12; Titus 2:7). The teaching of 2 Timothy 3:17, in that circumstance, applies mediately if not immediately to all Christians in the church. As Turretin notes, '[Scripture] can make the man or minister of God perfect in every good work, and what is sufficient for the shepherd must also be so for the sheep,' *Institutes*, 1:136 (=2.16.13).

32. 'Scripture [in Paul's teaching in 2 Timothy 3:16-17] is not merely helpful but is *the* source we turn to for all of life as a Christian,' Matthew Barrett, *God's Word Alone: The Authority of Scripture* (Grand Rapids: Zondervan, 2016), 342, emphasis Barrett's.

33. George W. Knight, *The Pastoral Epistles* (NIGTC; Grand Rapids: Eerdmans, 1992), 428-9.

that the apostles impose upon the church are 'Scripture.'[34] They have the same authority and stand alongside the Old Testament as the very Word of God.

A second passage that testifies to the sufficiency of Scripture as the rule of faith and practice is 2 Peter 1:3-4.

> [God's] divine power has granted to us all things that pertain to life and godliness, through the knowledge of him who called us to his own glory and excellence, by which he has granted to us his precious and very great promises, so that through them you may become partakers of the divine nature, having escaped from the corruption that is in the world because of sinful desire.

In these verses, Peter affirms a divinely provided sufficiency ('all things') with respect to what 'pertain[s] to life and godliness.' This sufficiency is expressly joined to 'the knowledge of [God]' and the 'precious and very great promises' that He has given us. As we have seen Paul argue in 2 Timothy 3:16-17, Peter here affirms that the truth of God is sufficient to guide people in godly living. If we ask where one may find this 'knowledge' and these 'promises,' Peter points us to 'the prophetic word' later in this chapter (1:19, cf. 1:20, 'prophecy of Scripture;' 1:21, 'prophecy').[35] This divine Word continues to guide the faith and practice of God's people under the New Covenant, and will do so until Christ returns ('until the day dawns and the morning star rises in your hearts,' 1:19).[36] We have observed in a previous chapter how Peter conjoins 'the predictions of the holy prophets' with 'the commandments of the Lord and Savior through your apostles' later in this epistle (2 Pet. 3:2). Peter's affirmation of the sufficiency of the Word of God with reference to the Old Testament prophetic writings, then, is not to be restricted to those writings. On the contrary, the principle applies as widely as the extent or boundaries of the whole canon of Scripture.

A third passage that testifies to the sufficiency of Scripture as the rule of faith and practice is Psalm 19:7, the opening sentence of a paragraph that reflects on the nature and attributes of the law of God (19:7-11), 'The law

---

34. See here the argument of Turretin with respect to this point in relation to 2 Timothy 3:16-17, *Institutes*, 1:137 (=2.16.14).
35. Barrett, *God's Word Alone*, 342-3.
36. ibid.

of the LORD is perfect, reviving the soul; the testimony of the LORD is sure, making wise the simple.' David affirms here the truth and perfection of the law of the LORD, which denotes not merely 'God's precepts' but 'God's instruction more generally.'[37] He attributes to the Word of God the capacity to quicken human beings and to make wise those in need of wisdom. As Turretin notes, 'the conversion and restoration of the soul cannot take place unless all things necessary to salvation are known.'[38] The law's 'perfect[ion]' in this context, then, entails a 'full sufficiency' with respect to all that is necessary to be believed and practiced for salvation.[39] It is in light of this sufficient Word that the sinner may be saved and one may attain the wisdom accompanying salvation.

The second class of passages testifies to the sufficiency of Scripture by encompassing certain warnings against either adding to or taking away from the Word of God. These warnings appear in both the Old and the New Testaments.

> You shall not add to the word that I command you, nor take from it, that you may keep the commandments of the LORD your God that I command you (Deut. 4:2).

> Every word of God proves true; he is a shield to those who take refuge in him. Do not add to his words, lest he rebuke you and you be found a liar (Prov. 30:5-6).

> I warn everyone who hears the words of the prophecy of this book: if anyone adds to them, God will add to him the plagues described in this book, and if anyone takes away from the words of the book of this prophecy, God will take away his share in the tree of life and in the holy city, which are described in this book (Rev. 22:18-19).

These warnings threaten readers or hearers of the Word of God with retribution for removing or adding to that Word. These warnings come in the context of three different genres of biblical literature, law (Deut. 4:2),

---

37. John S. Feinberg, *Light in a Dark Place: The Doctrine of Scripture* (Wheaton, IL: Crossway, 2018), 696. The attributes and functions ascribed to the 'law of the LORD' in Psalm 19:7-11 are elsewhere in the Bible attributed more broadly to the Scripture as a whole. To take one example, as the 'law of the LORD ... mak[es] wise the simple,' so too 'the sacred writings are able to make [one] wise for salvation through faith in Christ Jesus' (Ps. 19:7; 2 Tim. 3:15).

38. Turretin, *Institutes*, 1:138 (=2.16.16).

39. ibid.

wisdom literature (Prov. 30:5-6), and prophecy (Rev. 22:18-19). The fact that these warnings not only appear multiple times, but also appear in diverse genres and in books spread across the canon of Scripture suggests that the scope of these warnings should not be limited to the immediate context in which they fall.[40] It is fair to say that these warnings apply to the whole of the Word of God.

These warnings carry with them practical significance. That is to say, they are voiced in contexts where the Word of God's practical influences are mentioned or emphasized. In Deuteronomy, the warning appears alongside an exhortation to keep the commandments of God. The non-addition and non-removal of the Word of God is in order to the observance of God's commands. In Revelation, the adding or removal of words from the 'prophecy of this book' is linked, in the latter case at least, to forfeiture of sharing in 'the tree of life' and 'the holy city.' These latter realities, in the context of Revelation, denote the benefits of salvation and the community of the saved, respectively.[41]

We may draw, then, the following conclusions from these warnings. In the immediate context of these warnings, the Word of God is presented in relation to the commands that God has given His people to obey, and to the saving realities of which the Word speaks and to which the Word points. The warnings threaten adding to or taking from the Word of God. There is, therefore, a sufficiency to the Word of God with respect to matters of faith and practice.

The third class of passages testifies to the sufficiency of Scripture by setting forth the purpose of Scripture.

> But these [signs] are written [in this book] so that you may believe that Jesus is the Christ, the Son of God, and that by believing you may have life in his name (John 20:31).

> I write these things to you who believe in the name of the Son of God that you may know that you have eternal life (1 John 5:13).

> For whatever was written in former days was written for our instruction, that through endurance and through the encouragement of the Scriptures we might have hope (Rom. 15:4).

---

40. See the related observation of Barrett, *God's Word Alone*, 343.
41. G. K. Beale, *The Book of Revelation* (NIGTC; Grand Rapids: Eerdmans, 1999), 1153.

Each of these passages underscores the fundamentally practical purpose of Scripture. That is to say, God intends the Scripture to be the means by which His people enjoy 'eternal life' in the 'name' of Christ.[42] 'Life,' of course, is comprehensive of the saving benefits that belong to God's people in Christ. Scripture is not merely *a* means, nor is it simply God's *preferred* means, but it is *the* exclusively provided means by which one may come to enjoy life in Christ. Furthermore, as Turretin has observed, 'how could that end [i.e., enjoying life in Christ by means of the Scripture] be answered unless they were perfect and contained all things necessary to salvation? They were designed to be the canon and rule of faith.'[43] Were the Scriptures not sufficient with respect to what must be believed and obeyed for salvation, they could not answer the purpose for which God gave them to human beings, namely, to enjoy life in Christ.

We have seen, then, that the biblical writers teach that the Scripture is sufficient as the rule of faith and practice. It makes known all matters that one needs to believe and to do for salvation, for the glory of God. In these respects, nothing needs to be added to the Word. One need not turn anywhere else to receive guidance in these departments. The Westminster Assembly insists, however, that Scripture's sufficiency is not strictly a matter of its express statements. It is also a matter of 'what by good and necessary consequence may be deduced from Scripture.'[44] What the Assembly is denying is the teaching 'that all matters of faith are set down expressly and in so many words of Scripture, and that no matters of faith, at least necessary to salvation, can be built upon consequences drawn from the Scripture.'[45] The deductions of which Westminster speaks are no less the Word of God than the Bible's express statements are the Word of God.

---

42. The passive voice of the verb translated 'written' in Romans 15:4 reflects divine agency. The purpose expressed in Romans 15:4 is, therefore, a divine purpose, James D. G. Dunn, *Romans 9-16* (WBC 38B; Waco, TX: Thomas Nelson, 1988), 839.

43. Turretin, *Institutes*, 1:138 (=2.16.17).

44. Westminster Confession of Faith, 1.6.

45. David Dickson, *Truth's Victory Over Error: A Commentary on the Westminster Confession of Faith* (1684; trans. and ed. John R. De Witt; Edinburgh: Banner of Truth, 2007), 9-10. Dickson was the first sympathetic expositor of the Westminster Confession of Faith. For a brief modern treatment of the historical context of the Assembly's affirmation, see C. J. Williams, 'Good and Necessary Consequences in the Westminster Confession,' in *The Faith Once Delivered: Essays in Honor of Dr. Wayne R. Spear* (ed. Anthony T. Selvaggio; Phillipsburg, NJ: P&R, 2007), 172-4.

It is important to clear this teaching from misunderstanding. First, it needs to be stressed that it is not every or any deduction from a statement of Scripture that may lay claim to be the Word of God.[46] Only deductions 'by good and necessary consequence' from Scripture's express affirmations are entitled to be regarded as God's Word. For a consequence to be 'good,' that 'biblical deduction must be in harmony with other Scripture ... it must be in agreement with the known corpus of truth that Scripture teaches.'[47] For a consequence to be 'necessary,' it 'must be demonstrably certain and not reasonably deniable,' not 'merely possible or conceivable.'[48] These qualifications 'good' and 'necessary' serve, then, to maintain the integrity of biblical teaching from external additions.

Second, it needs to be underscored that this doctrine of deductions in no way adds to the teaching of Scripture. That is to say, it does not supplement biblical doctrine with uninspired human judgments. As Gillespie observes, 'the meaning of the assertion is not that humane reason drawing a consequence from Scripture can be the ground of our belief or conscience. For although the consequence or argumentation be drawn foorth by mens reasons, yet the consequent it self or conclusion is not believed nor embraced by the strength of reason, but because it is the truth and will of God.'[49] Human reason, then, plays a strictly

---

46. As the Scottish Commissioner to the Westminster Assembly, George Gillespie, has observed, 'Now the consequences from Scripture are likewise of two sorts, some necessary, strong, and certain, and of these I here speak in this assertion; others which are good consequences to prove a sutablenesse or agreablenes of this or that to Scripture, though another thing may be also proved to be agreable unto the same Scripture in the same or another place. This latter sort are in diverse things of very use. But for the present I speak of necessary consequences,' *A Treatise of Miscellany Questions: Wherein Many Useful Questions and Cases of Conscience are Discussed and Resolved; for the Satisfaction of Those, Who Desire Nothing More, Than to Search for and Find out Precious Truths, in the Controversies of These Times* (Edinburgh: University of Edinburgh, 1649), 240.

47. Williams, 'Good and Necessary Consequences,' 178. In this connection, Williams rightly notes the importance of the Confession's teaching at WCF 1.9, namely, the principle of *Scriptura Scripturae interpres* ('Scripture interpreting Scripture').

48. Williams, 'Good and Necessary Consequences,' 179. Williams suggestively proposes that 'good and necessary' may correspond, respectively, to the truth of the major and minor premises in a deductive syllogism, and to the validity of the reasoning employed in that syllogism, ibid.

49. Gillespie, *Treatise of Miscellany Questions*, 238-9. Gillespie continues by clarifying that it is not 'corrupt reason' but 'renewed or rectified reason' that is in view in the drawing of good and necessary consequences from the express statements of Scripture, *Treatise of Miscellany Questions*, 239.

instrumental role in deriving deductions from the statements of Scripture. But it in no way contributes to or supplements those statements.

What is the biblical evidence for this doctrine of deductions? We may point to at least four representative examples of passages from Scripture that demonstrate the doctrine. The first comes from the way in which Jesus proves the resurrection to the Sadducees at the end of His public ministry.

> You are wrong, because you know neither the Scriptures nor the power of God … As for the resurrection of the dead, have you not read what was said to you by God: 'I am the God of Abraham, and the God of Isaac, and the God of Jacob?' He is not God of the dead, but of the living (Matt. 22:29, 31-2).

In response to the skepticism of the Sadducees regarding the future, bodily resurrection, Jesus presents an argument for the resurrection from the Scripture. Jesus understands this argument to be the teaching of Scripture itself.[50] The argument comes from God's words to Moses in Exodus 3:6, which Jesus quotes at Matthew 22:32. Jesus understands His reasoning from this text conclusively to prove the bodily resurrection, an understanding that is apparently shared by the crowds (Matt. 22:33). Jesus' reasoning, Matthew observes, even 'silenced the Sadducees' (Matt. 22:34).[51]

Commentators note the complexities of settling precisely how Jesus' appeal to the text of Exodus 3:6 establishes the bodily resurrection.[52] What *is* clear is that the text of Exodus 3:6 does not explicitly state that God will raise the bodies of the dead at the end of the age. The bodily resurrection, rather, is an inference or deduction derived from the text. This inference, furthermore, is one that Jesus and His hearers take to be necessary or compelling. Likely Jesus has in mind the fact that God makes this statement to Moses in the context of God's declared intention

---

50. So Jesus' words, 'you know neither the Scriptures…,' Ryan M. McGraw, *By Good and Necessary Consequence*, (Grand Rapids: Reformation Heritage, 2012), 8.

51. As McGraw notes, the Sadducees 'capitulated under the weight of the Lord's indomitable argument, and they tacitly conceded his point,' *By Good and Necessary Consequence*, 11.

52. See, for instance, R. T. France's discussion at *The Gospel of Mark* (NIGTC; Grand Rapids: Eerdmans, 2002), 470-3, and J. A. Alexander's discussion at *Commentary on the Gospel of Mark* (New York: Charles Scribner & Sons, 1864), 331-2.

to redeem His people from bondage in Egypt (Exod. 3:7-12, cf. 3:15). This purpose to redeem Israel relates to God's covenantal relationship with Abraham and his offspring. It is because of the covenant that God sovereignly made with Abraham and his offspring that God will redeem Israel from their bondage. This temporal redemption typologically points to the greater, spiritual redemption that Christ accomplishes for His people in every age. This redemption, the biblical writers stress, extends to the whole person, body and soul, granting them everlasting life in fellowship and communion with Him.[53] The fact that God declares Himself the God of Abraham, Isaac, and Jacob (who died long before Moses' lifetime) is proof, Jesus reasons, that God will raise their bodies from the dead. Were God not to do so, He would fail His self-imposed purpose to redeem in full all those with whom He has entered into covenant. The bodily resurrection, then, is a deduction drawn, by good and necessary consequence, from the words of God in Exodus 3:6.

A second biblical example of deduction by good and necessary consequence comes from Paul's teaching in 1 Corinthians 10:25-6, 'Eat whatever is sold in the meat market without raising any question on the ground of conscience. For "the earth is the Lord's, and the fullness thereof."' Paul here offers the church in Corinth a command followed by grounds for that command. The command is to eat the meats that they purchase from the pagan meat markets, and not, for conscience's sake, to raise questions about the origin and prior history of the meat.[54] The grounds that Paul supplies for this command is a citation of Psalm 24:1. There is no explicit statement in this Psalm that God's people are free to eat meat sold in the market place. The warrant for the imperative, then, lies in an inference that Paul has drawn from the text of the Psalm. The Psalm declares that God is the proper and rightful owner and possessor of the world and all things in it. The reason that God has claim to the creation is because He is the Creator of all things, a point explicitly drawn in the next verse of the Psalm, but not cited by Paul (Ps. 24:2).

Paul's reasoning appears to be as follows. God has made the world and all things in it. Therefore, the world and all things in it are 'very

---

53. McGraw, *By Good and Necessary Consequence*, 10.

54. Specifically, they were not to inquire whether the meat that they were purchasing had been offered in sacrifice to pagan deities prior to being offered for sale in the market.

good' (cf. Gen 1:31). The meat that Christians find for sale in the marketplace was made by God and is, therefore, good, not evil. As such, neither the meat nor its consumption is inherently sinful. The Corinthian Christians are at liberty to enjoy it, as they would be at liberty to enjoy other works of God's hands.[55] What Paul has done is to deduce the principle of Christian liberty from the doctrine of creation or, more properly, from an implication of the doctrine of creation stated at Psalm 24:1. Paul's reasoning, then, illustrates the fact that deductions by good and necessary consequences from Scripture's teaching are the very teaching of Scripture itself.

A third example of the doctrine of deduction comes from the way in which the apostles demonstrate that Jesus is the Messiah prophesied by the Old Testament. The Old Testament, of course, does not prophesy Jesus of Nazareth by name. Rather, it makes a host of particular prophecies that the New Testament writers argue came to fulfillment in the person and work of Jesus Christ. Matthew, therefore, understands the Isaianic prophecy, 'he took our illnesses and bore our diseases' (Matt. 8:17, Isa. 53:4) to have found fulfillment in the public ministry of Jesus (Matt. 8:13-16).[56] Isaiah does not say, in so many words, that the Servant of Isaiah 53 is Jesus of Nazareth. What Matthew has done is to conclude that the one of whom Isaiah spoke in such particular terms must be and can only be Jesus of Nazareth, whose miraculous activities align seamlessly with the Isaianic Servant.

An even more explicit example of this kind of reasoning is found in Peter's sermon on the day of Pentecost.[57] Quoting a portion of Psalm 16 (Acts 2:25-8), Peter concludes that the words of this Psalm must refer to

---

55. Notice, however, the qualification that Paul appends at 1 Corinthians 10:28-30. Even here, Paul does not forsake the principle he articulates at 1 Corinthians 10:25-6. His stated concern in 1 Corinthians 10:28-30 is not the conscience of the Christian but the conscience of the unbeliever. Paul does not want the believer's consumption of meat that he knows has been offered to an idol to lead the unbeliever to think that Christians approve of other gods and the sacrifices that are made to them, David E. Garland, *1 Corinthians* (BECNT; Grand Rapids: Baker, 2003), 520-1.

56. This passage is but one example of a much larger and pervasive pattern in Matthew's Gospel of pointing to Jesus' person and work as having brought particular prophecies to fulfillment, on which see R. T. France, *Matthew: Evangelist & Teacher* (Downers Grove, IL: InterVarsity, 1989), 166-205.

57. I am grateful to McGraw for calling my attention to this example, *By Good and Necessary Consequence*, 13.

the resurrection of Jesus Christ (Acts 2:24). The reason, Peter explains, is that David 'both died and was buried, and his tomb is with us to this day' (Acts 2:29). In other words, David did not understand the promise of incorruptibility referenced in Psalm 16 to refer to himself.[58] Rather, Peter reasons, David was 'a prophet' and knew 'that God had sworn with an oath to him that he would set one of his descendants on his throne' (Acts 2:30). Therefore, David 'foresaw and spoke about the resurrection of the Christ, that he was not abandoned to Hades, nor did his flesh see corruption' (Acts 2:31). And this Christ is none other than 'Jesus' whom 'God raised up, and of that we are all witnesses' (Acts 2:32). It is by deduction by good and necessary consequence that Peter concludes that David intended to speak of the resurrection of Jesus Christ when he penned Psalm 16.

A fourth and final example of the doctrine of deduction by good and necessary consequence comes from Hebrews 1:6, 'And again, when he brings the firstborn into the world, he says, "Let all God's angels worship him."'[59] This passage, cited from Deuteronomy 32:43, is part of a series of passages cited serially by the author to the Hebrews.[60] This series of citations is intended to prove the superiority of Christ to the angels, not least because of Jesus' deity (Heb. 1:3a). The passage cited in Hebrews 1:6 does not, of itself, declare Jesus' deity. What it does, however, is to declare Jesus Christ to be the object of angelic worship. The unstated assumption, drawn from other statements of the text of Scripture, is that God alone is worthy of His creatures' worship. The fact that Jesus receives the angels' worship proves not only that He is superior to them but also that He is fully God. The author to the Hebrews argues for the deity of Christ, then, by recourse to a necessary deduction from the teaching of Deuteronomy 32:43.

---

58. David Peterson, *The Acts of the Apostles* (PNTC; Grand Rapids: Eerdmans, 2009), 148.

59. This example surfaces not only in Gillespie ('His God head is proved, *Heb:* 1. 6. From these words, *Let all the Angels of God worship him*. Divine worship cannot be due, and may not be given to any that is not God,' *Treatise of Miscellany Questions*, 241), but also in the Minutes of the Westminster Assembly, '*Resolved* upon the Q., Heb. i. 6, "And again, when He bringeth in the first Begotten into the world, he saith, And let all the angels of God worship Him," where it is proved that Christ is the Son of God by a consequence,' as cited at Williams, 'Good and Necessary Consequences,' 186.

60. On the text form of the citation, see William S. Lane, *Hebrews 1-8* (WBC 47A; Waco, TX: Word, 1991), 28.

One reason that the doctrine of deduction by good and necessary consequence is important, as Gillespie acknowledged, is that this doctrine is necessary to establish the Trinity as the teaching of Scripture.[61] The doctrine of the Trinity 'is not the product of a single proof text; rather, it is an authoritative inference based on the premises of many passages, and obviously, it is a central truth of the Christian faith.'[62] In similar fashion, the doctrine of infant baptism rests on the understanding that the deductions by good and necessary consequence of Scripture's teaching are the teaching of Scripture itself.[63] The warrant of women to be admitted to the Lord's Table rests on this doctrine.[64] A considerable portion of biblical doctrine rests on the legitimacy of deductions by good and necessary consequence as the teaching of Scripture itself. Warfield reflects on the implications of denying this doctrine for the Christian faith.

> The reemergence in recent controversies of the plea that the authority of Scripture is to be confined to its expressed declarations, and that human logic is not to be trusted in divine things, is, therefore a direct denial of a fundamental position of Reformed theology, explicitly affirmed in the Confession, as well as an abnegation of fundamental reason, which would not only render thinking in a system impossible, but would discredit at a stroke many of the fundamentals of the faith, such e.g. as the doctrine of the Trinity, and would logically involve the denial of the authority of all doctrine whatsoever, since no single doctrine of whatever simplicity can be ascertained from Scripture except by the use of the processes of the understanding ... If the plea is valid at all, it destroys at once our confidence in all doctrines, no one of which is ascertained or formulated without the aid of human logic.[65]

---

61. 'By which principle [i.e., the denial of good and necessary consequences], if imbraced, we must renounce many necessary truths which the reformed Churches hold against the *Arians, Antitrinitarians, Socinians, Papists,* because the consequences and arguments from Scripture brought to prove them, are not admitted as good by the adversaries,' Gillespie, *Treatise of Miscellany Questions,* 238.

62. Williams, 'Good and Necessary Consequences,' 188.

63. See, representatively, Warfield, 'The Polemics of Infant Baptism,' in *Works,* 9:389-408.

64. '[D]iverse other great absurdities must follow, if this truth be not admitted. How can it be proved that women may partake of the Sacrament of the Lords supper, unlesse wee prove it by necessary consequence from Scripture?' Gillespie, *Treatise of Miscellany Questions,* 243.

65. Warfield, 'The Doctrine of Holy Scripture,' in *Works,* 6:226-7.

We are bound to conclude, then, that the teaching of Scripture is found not only in its 'literal assertion[s]' but also in its 'necessary implication[s].'[66]

The (In)sufficiency of Scripture

Before we conclude our discussion of the doctrine of Scripture's sufficiency, we need to offer further qualification to the doctrine to avoid misunderstanding. We may point to four areas in particular that highlight the limitations of Scripture's sufficiency. To say that the sufficiency of Scripture has limitations is not to attribute a defect to Scripture. It is to say, however, that the Divine Author of Scripture has purposely set certain parameters around what He has designed Scripture to be and to do. It is no defect of Scripture to say that it does not accomplish a purpose that God has not designed for it. The limitations, in other words, are limitations that the all-wise God has set upon His own Word.

We may point to four such limitations. First, Scripture is not in every sense comprehensive with respect to its contents. We may look at this non-comprehensive character of Scripture's contents in two respects. In the first place, Scripture does not offer a complete account or record of the persons and events that it documents. For example, at the close of his Gospel, the apostle John informs his readers, 'Jesus did many other signs in the presence of the disciples, which are not written in this book' (John 20:30).[67] These are details that one might like to know, but that the Holy Spirit has not seen fit to record. This omission is, furthermore,

---

66. Warfield, 'The Doctrine of Holy Scripture,' in *Works*, 6:226. Significantly, Warfield continues by observing, 'the sense of Scripture is Scripture, and that men are bound by its whole sense in all its implications,' ibid. In other words, deductions by good and necessary consequence are the teaching of Scripture because God, in His infinite wisdom, has set them in Scripture. As Gillespie notes, 'If we say that necessary consequences from Scripture prove not a *jus divinum*, we say that which is inconsistent with the infinite wisdom of God, for although necessary consequences may bee drawen from a mans word which do not agree with his minde and intention, and so men are oftentimes insnared by their words; yet (as *Camero* well noteth) God being infinitly wise, it were a blasphemous opinion, to hold that any thing can bee drawne by a certaine and necessary consequence from his holy word, which is not his will. This were to make the onely wise God as foolish man, that cannot foresee all things which will follow from his words. Therefore wee must needs hold, 'tis the minde of God which necessary followeth from the word of God,' *Treatise of Miscellany Question*, 243.

67. As noted by Turretin, *Institutes*, 1:135 (=2.16.2).

owing to a conscious decision of the biblical author. John is well aware of the existence and nature of Jesus' other 'signs,' but he has seen fit not to document them in his Gospel.

Neither does Scripture offer a comprehensive exposition of all the doctrines that it teaches. One question that has long vexed theologians is the origin of sin. As A. A. Hodge frames the question, 'How or why was the existence of sin tolerated in the creation of a God at once eternal, self-existent, and infinite in wisdom, power, holiness, and benevolence?'[68] To this question, Hodge answers, 'It is obvious (a) that God has permitted sin and (b) hence it was right for him to do so. But why it was right must ever remain a mystery demanding submission and defying solution.'[69] In other words, God has revealed enough about the origin of sin to enable us to trust and obey Him. But He has not revealed enough to satisfy all the questions that we may have about the origin of sin. The revelation of God with respect to this question is sufficient for the purposes for which God gave the Scripture to human beings.[70]

A second respect in which the contents of Scripture are non-comprehensive concerns the matters to which the Bible addresses itself. Sufficiency, we have seen, extends to two spheres, faith and practice.[71] Scripture, we have seen above, is a sufficient guide to direct the reader what must be believed and what must be done with respect to salvation and for the glory of God. But Scripture does not claim to be a sufficient guide with respect to other spheres or departments of life. The Bible is not a textbook of philosophy, economics, political science, or biology, to give a few examples. This is not to say that the Bible's teachings do not or should not have bearing on those and other disciplines. But it is to

---

68. A. A. Hodge, *Outlines of Theology* (rev. ed.; 1879: repr., Edinburgh: Banner of Truth, 1972), 319. I owe this reference to David F. Coffin, Jr, 'The Sufficiency of Scripture and Modern Theonomy: An Appreciative Critique and Alternate Course,' in *Written For Our Instruction: The Sufficiency of Scripture for All of Life* (eds. Joseph A. Pipa, Jr and J. Andrew Wortman; Greenville, SC: Southern Presbyterian Press, 2001), 158.

69. ibid.

70. To borrow Feinberg's phrase, the sufficiency of Scripture means that the Bible is 'enough, but not exhaustive,' *Light In A Dark Place*, 686.

71. 'The whole counsel of God concerning all things necessary for His own glory, man's salvation, faith and life is either expressly set down in Scripture, or by good and necessary consequence may be deduced from Scripture ...' (WCF 1.6).

say that God did not intend Scripture to be a sufficient guide to human beings in such areas of inquiry.

One indication of Scripture's awareness of its own delimitations concerns its injunctions regarding wisdom. Scripture commands its readers to pursue and to acquire wisdom (Prov. 23:23). As T. David Gordon notes, the Bible also tells its readers where and how they may acquire wisdom.

> [O]ne acquire[s] wisdom ... by heeding God's commands in holy scripture (Prov. 10:8; Eccles. 12:13). But more commonly, wisdom comes from listening to advice (Prov. 12:15; 19:20), from entertaining the opinion of a variety of people (Prov. 11:14; 18:17; 24:6), by listening to older people (Prov. 13:1), and by observing the natural order itself (Prov. 6:6) ... Solomon promotes listening to parents, elders, a variety of counselors, and even a consideration of ants, badgers, locusts, and lizards (Prov. 30:24-28) ... We will not acquire [wisdom] by simply reading the Bible.[72]

In summary, the Bible itself not only testifies to its sufficiency as the God-given rule of faith and practice, but also explicitly attests to its insufficiency in spheres other than these.

A second limitation to the sufficiency of Scripture concerns the role of tradition and extra-biblical data in one's reading and interpretation of the Bible. The sufficiency of Scripture does not mean that it is inappropriate to access materials outside the Scripture in order to understand better the meaning of Scripture. To be sure, Protestants have rightly insisted that Scripture alone interprets Scripture.[73] But, contrary to popular perception, the magisterial Reformers never called for the church to jettison creeds and confessions or to eschew systematic theological reflection or attention to the historical, geographical, and linguistic contexts of the biblical documents.[74] The Reformers' doctrine

---

72. T. David Gordon, 'The Insufficiency of Scripture,' *Modern Reformation* 11/1 (Jan/Feb 2002), available at www.tdgordon.net. See also James B. Hurley and James T. Berry, 'The Relation of Scripture and Psychology in Counseling from a Pro-Integration Position,' *JPC* 16/4 (1997): 323-45.

73. In the words of the Westminster Confession of Faith, 'The infallible rule of interpretation of Scripture is the Scripture itself: and therefore, when there is a question about the true and full sense of any Scripture (which is not manifold, but one), it must be searched and known by other places that speak more clearly' (1.9).

74. But not only popular perception. See Brad S. Gregory, *The Unintended Reformation: How a Religious Revolution Secularized Society* (Harvard: Belknap, 2012), and

of *sola scriptura* (Scripture alone) must not be confused with *nuda scriptura* (bare or naked Scripture).

Two examples illustrate the point. Contemporary readers are approximately two millennia removed from the language and culture of the original audiences of the New Testament books. We are even farther removed from the original audiences of the Old Testament books. The Bible is not of itself able to overcome or compensate for this deficit. This deficit will only be overcome by the attentive and diligent study of the languages in which, and the cultures into which, the Scriptures were written.[75] The New Testament, for example, alludes to political offices in various municipalities of the first century Eastern Roman Empire (Acts 16:20; 17:6; 19:31,35). It references the names of many of the provinces and officials of the Roman Empire. It alludes to the religious practices of many of the peoples and towns with whom the apostles came into contact. It refers to widely known historical events of the first century (Luke 2:1-3; 3:1-2; Acts 5:36-7; 11:28). Modern students of the Bible may and ought to take advantage of all available resources outside the Bible in order to understand those events, practices, customs, political structures, and historical figures in the way that the first readers of the New Testament would have understood them.

A second example of the propriety of employing materials outside the Bible in order better to understand the Bible's teaching is the creeds and confessions of the church. Creeds and confessions function to summarize the leading teachings of the Scripture.[76] They have been with the church for centuries and arguably originate in the New Testament

---

the helpful evaluation and response of Michael Allen and Scott R. Swain, *Reformed Catholicity: The Promise of Retrieval for Theology and Biblical Interpretation* (Grand Rapids: Baker, 2015), 51-70.

75. See here Robert L. Dabney, 'The Standard of Ordination,' in *Discussions Vol. III: Philosophical* (ed. C.R. Vaughan; 1892; repr., Harrisonburg, VA: Sprinkle Publications, 1992), 557-8. Dabney concludes, 'I confess as to myself that I do not believe that my classical and biblical studies, continued through a long and laborious life have brought me up to the practical level of [a] fortunate Greek mechanic, as to the correct apprehension of the Greek Scriptures,' 558.

76. A classic treatment of the subject is that of Samuel Miller, *Doctrinal Integrity: On the Utility and Importance of Creeds and Confessions and Adherence to our Doctrinal Standards* (Dallas: Presbyterian Heritage Publications, 1989). For a contemporary defense of the propriety of creeds and confessions, see Carl R. Trueman, *The Creedal Imperative* (Wheaton, IL: Crossway, 2017).

itself. Such passages as Romans 1:3-4, Philippians 2:5-11, Colossians 1:15-20, and 1 Timothy 3:16 summarize, in outline form, the apostle Paul's teaching about the person and work of Jesus Christ. They would have provided invaluable help to Timothy and his colleagues in fulfilling the injunction of Paul, 'what you have heard from me in the presence of many witnesses entrust to faithful men who will be able to teach others also' (2 Tim. 2:2). How else would Paul's teaching have been transmitted from generation to generation except through the kinds of topical summaries of that teaching as we find in the apostle's own creedal statements? Neither are such statements unique to the New Testament. The words of Deuteronomy 6:4-5 ('Hear, O Israel: The LORD our God, the LORD is one. You shall love the LORD your God with all your heart and with all your soul and with all your might') have long served believers, under both the Old and New Testaments, in summarizing some of the most central teachings of the Old Testament.

It is important to stress that, in emphasizing the importance of extra-biblical data and creeds and confessions in the interpretation of Scripture, one is not eroding, much less denying, *sola scriptura*.[77] Below, we will engage critically Rome's understanding of tradition as possessing magisterial authority, an authority parallel to that of the Scripture. For now, it is important to distance this Protestant doctrine of tradition from that of Rome. Protestants employ tradition and extra-biblical data not magisterially but ministerially.[78] These materials do not possess an authority equal to that of Scripture.[79] Their authority

---

77. See Keith Mathison, *The Shape of Sola Scriptura* (Moscow, ID: Canon, 2001), 337-43.

78. Barrett, *God's Word Alone*, 346. Allen and Swain provide helpful definitions of these two terms, 'Jesus Christ is the only magisterial authority in the church; the term *magister*, or lord, speaks to his final sovereignty in the church. Inasmuch as the church exercises authority, in particular through the ministry of its officers, this is a ministerial authority; the term "minister," or servant, addresses the executive function of the church's action. The officers of the church do not set principles or policy, but they administer the determinative judgments of Jesus Christ,' *Reformed Catholicity*, 90.

79. The New Perspective on Paul is a recent example of a way in which extra-biblical data can come, in certain respects, to determine the meaning of Scripture. The radical re-evaluation of Judaism proposed by E. P. Sanders eventuated in a corresponding re-evaluation of the teaching of the apostle Paul. Specifically, once scholars came to the conclusion that first century Judaism was a religion of grace (and not a religion of merit), that conclusion prompted a fundamental reinterpretation of the apostle's teaching about

is ministerial, that is to say, they are means to assist the church to enter fully into the meaning of the text of Scripture. They are helps to elucidate what the text says. For this reason, as Allen and Swain have observed, tradition need not stand in antithetical relationship with the authoritative Word of God.

> Principled commitment to biblical authority as the ultimate determining factor for all faith and practice did not lead [among the Protestant Reformers] to diminishing concern for ecclesial authority or waning reception of church traditions. Rather, *sola Scriptura* aided the course of such reception: retrieving the fullness of the catholic past while cognizant of the ever-present need for ongoing reform.[80]

Provided that tradition and extra-biblical data stand in complete submission to the authority of Scripture, they are useful, even necessary, helps to the church to interpret the meaning of the text of Scripture.

A third limitation to the sufficiency of Scripture concerns the practical application of Scripture and the related category of what have been termed 'circumstances.' Scripture issues multiple commands and tasks its readers to implement those commands. The reader, however, must evaluate the specific details of his life and situation in order properly to apply the commands of Scripture. We encounter an example of this in Paul's first letter to the Corinthians. In 1 Corinthians 8:7-13, Paul affirms the liberty of the Christian to eat food that has been offered to a pagan idol. He insists, however, that believers must so exercise that liberty with the governing consideration of the spiritual well-being of their fellow Christians, especially those who are 'weak' (1 Cor. 8:9). In 1 Corinthians 10:28-9, Paul offers similar counsel to a Christian dining with an unbeliever. If the unbeliever tells the believer that 'this [food] has been offered in sacrifice,' then the believer should refrain from eating that food (1 Cor. 10:28). He should refrain from eating out of a consideration to the 'conscience' of the unbeliever and the interests of the gospel (1 Cor. 10:31-3). For a Corinthian church member to know

---

grace, works, and justification. As Robert J. Cara has aptly noted, 'implications from non-canonical Second Temple Judaism texts may be useful, but they are only fallible aids,' *Cracking the Foundation of the New Perspective on Paul* (REDS; Fearn, Ross-shire: Mentor, 2017), 30. See further my *Justification and the New Perspectives on Paul* (Phillipsburg, NJ: P&R, 2004), 151-6.

80. Allen and Swain, *Reformed Catholicity*, 70.

when it was lawful and wise to eat meat that had been offered to a pagan idol, it was necessary for him to read and to understand his situation. In other words, proper application of the apostolic command requires knowledge that falls outside the pages of Scripture.

John Frame offers what for the modern reader is a less complex instance of this same pattern of moral reasoning.

> Stealing is wrong.
> Cheating on your income tax is stealing.
> Therefore, cheating on your income tax is wrong.
>
> The Bible, of course, does not mention the U.S. income tax, though it does mention taxes in general ... In order to evaluate premise 2, we need to know not only these biblical principles, but also some facts not mentioned in Scripture that tell us what the income tax is ... we need some specific information from outside the Bible to warrant the second premise.[81]

In other words, moral reasoning proceeds syllogistically. The major premise is drawn from Scripture; the minor premise draws from data or information that fall outside Scripture; the conclusion must follow from the premises that precede it. One simply cannot undertake the application of Scripture apart from the ingathering of relevant information falling outside the text of Scripture.

There is a distinct sense in which one must access extra-biblical data in order to apply the text of Scripture. Not all commands of Scripture bind Christians in every age. Sometimes, a command is abrogated because of the progression of redemptive history. New Covenant believers, for instance, no longer offer animal sacrifices to God in the way that Old Covenant believers once did. The reason is because Christ's sacrificial death on the cross brought to fulfillment those typological sacrifices. The need for those sacrifices has been removed, and so believers no longer observe them. In other instances, however, a contemporary reader of Scripture does not apply a command that bound even the first readers of the New Testament. Paul tells the church in Thessalonica to 'pray for us' (2 Thess. 3:1). The Thessalonican believers obeyed that command by praying for the Lord to bless the ministry of the apostle Paul. Today, believers no longer pray for the apostle Paul, whose earthly life and

---

81. Frame, *The Doctrine of the Word of God*, 231-2.

ministry has come to its divinely appointed conclusion (2 Tim. 4:6-8). But we do not thereby ignore the command. We apply the command by praying for living individuals who fall into the same category as the apostle Paul, that is, ministers of the Word of God. Our application of this command differs in form from the application of the Thessalonian Christians, but not in substance.

A similar example comes in the command of the apostle to 'greet one another with a holy kiss' (Rom. 16:16). Many Christians do not live in cultures like those of the first century Christians where it was customary to give such a greeting. They do not thereby ignore the command when they do not give such a greeting.[82] Rather, they apply the command by giving a culturally appropriate salutation to one another, one that is expressive of sincere Christian affection.[83]

The point of these examples is to underscore the fact that, in order properly to apply the commands of Scripture, believers must understand their own situation in light of the situation of the original recipients of Scripture. James Bannerman has articulated the matter well in addressing the question whether Scripture examples bind believers today.

> What we learn in both cases alike [precepts and examples] is just this: Thus and thus the Spirit of God commanded certain men to act in certain circumstances. We learn no more in the case of the precept than in the case of the example. The one is as binding upon us as the other, *provided we be in like circumstances* ... The true test of its permanent obligation ... [is to ask] was this command – whether it reaches us in the form in which it was perhaps first given, or whether it is embodied in the obedience which followed – founded on moral grounds, common to all men at all times, in all circumstances, or on local and temporary grounds, peculiar to certain men in certain circumstances, at some given time.[84]

---

82. 'The exercise and manifestation of the feeling [='Christian love'], but not the mode of its expression, are obligatory on us,' Charles Hodge, *Commentary on the Epistle to the Romans* (rev. ed.; New York: A. C. Armstrong and Son, 1896), 714.

83. And, of course, there are certain cultures in the world today in which the form of Christian greeting described in Romans 16:16 is identical with the form of Christian greeting mandated within those cultures.

84. James Bannerman, *The Church of Christ: A Treatise on the Nature, Powers, Ordinances, Discipline, and Government of the Christian Church* (1868; 2 vols.; repr., Edinburgh: Banner of Truth, 1960), 2:408.

Biblical precepts and biblical examples are both binding, Bannerman reasons, provided that we, the contemporary reader, find ourselves in the same set of circumstances in which the original readers found themselves. In order to make that judgment, however, we must ascertain our present circumstances. That is to say, we must access data from outside the Bible.

A related category to that of the application of the commands of Scripture is that of the 'circumstance' in relation to the church's worship and government – a category we had occasion to introduce earlier in this chapter. In addressing the sufficiency of Scripture, the Westminster Divines observe, 'nevertheless, we acknowledge ... that there are some circumstances concerning the worship of God, and government of the Church, common to human actions and societies, which are to be ordered by the light of nature, and Christian prudence, according to the general rules of the Word, which are always to be observed.'[85] A circumstance is 'a concomitant of an action, without which it can either not be done at all, or cannot be done with decency and decorum.'[86] While the circumstances in view in WCF 1.6 fall under certain, specified limitations, the Confession affirms that the church may and must legitimately order such circumstances as they relate to her worship and government.[87] The Bible, for instance, does not stipulate the hour at which a congregation must gather to worship on Sunday. Neither does the Bible prescribe the committee structure of a church's board of elders. These details are left to the church to arrange in submission to the principles both of general and special revelation.

A fourth and final limitation to the sufficiency of Scripture falls in a different category from the other three that we have considered. The other three concern, in one form or another, what matters the Scripture does and does not address on its pages. This fourth limitation transcends, in certain respects, the entirety of the message of Scripture. It finds expression in WCF 1.6, 'nevertheless, we acknowledge the inward illumination of the Spirit of God to be necessary for the saving

---

85. Westminster Confession of Faith, 1.6.

86. Peck, *Notes on Ecclesiology*, 122.

87. And yet, as Warfield notes, Westminster expressly forbids the church from instituting new elements of worship or from adding to the church's government that is set down in Scripture, 'The Doctrine of Holy Scripture,' in *Works*, 6:228-9.

understanding of such things as are revealed in the Word.' Westminster does not say that this illumination of the Spirit is necessary for the understanding of what is contained in the Word, but for the *saving* understanding of what is contained in the Word.[88] As Warfield observes, 'it is not denied that men, in the exercise of their natural powers of understanding, may attain to a knowledge from Scripture of what is revealed in Scripture.' What is affirmed is that the illumination of the Spirit is necessary for that knowledge to be 'accompanied with a relish and love for the truth, and leading to a life of holy obedience.'[89] Importantly, as Barrett observes, 'illumination is not further revelation.'[90] Illumination is the Spirit's work of enabling us savingly to understand what God has revealed in His Word.

Human beings are by nature 'darkened in their understanding, alienated from the life of God because of the ignorance that is in them, due to their hardness of heart' (Eph. 4:18, cf. Rom. 1:21). Because of sin, people 'suppress the truth' (Rom. 1:18). A 'debased mind to do what ought not to be done' is the just penalty of God upon human beings for their rebellion against Him (Rom. 1:28). Satan, furthermore, 'has blinded the minds of the unbelievers, to keep them from seeing the light of the gospel of the glory of Christ, who is the image of God' (2 Cor. 4:4). If the 'gospel is veiled, it is veiled only to those who are perishing' (2 Cor. 4:3). The natural human mind, then, is capable of notionally understanding the propositional contents of Scripture. That mind, however, is governed by a disposition that is hostile to God and does not love the truth that it may apprehend.

In regeneration, however, the Spirit so renews the mind that it can perceive the excellence and glory of God in Jesus Christ who is revealed in the pages of Scripture (Eph. 1:17-19). This work of regeneration is no less than a work of new creation, 'For God, who said, "Let light shine out of darkness," has shone in our hearts to give the light of the knowledge of the glory of God in the face of Jesus Christ' (2 Cor. 4:6). And it is by the continued ministry of the Spirit that the believer

---

88. Robert Letham has observed that 'the word "saving" was added by the Assembly to the committee report,' *Westminster Assembly*, 141.

89. Warfield, 'The Doctrine of Scripture,' in *Works*, 6:227-8. The last phrase is Warfield's citation of the Scottish theologian James S. Candlish.

90. Barrett, *God's Word Alone*, 321.

is able 'to comprehend with all the saints what is the breadth and length and height and depth, and to know the love of Christ that surpasses knowledge, that [we] may be filled with all the fullness of God' (Eph. 3:18-19). This work of the Spirit transpires in conjunction with the Word. Specifically, the reading and preaching of the Word is the occasion of this work of the Spirit. The Spirit so works to enable a person who is under the Word of God to embrace and to relish what he hears from the Word.

While the Word occasions the Spirit's work of illumination, the Word is neither the cause nor even the instrument of that work.[91] It is for this reason that we may point to illumination as an indicator of the insufficiency of the Word. The illumination that leads to a saving understanding of the Bible is the sole prerogative of the sovereign Spirit.[92]

The Sufficiency of Scripture and the Roman Catholic Church

We have surveyed a definition of the sufficiency of Scripture and reflected on the biblical testimony for that doctrine. We have also registered some important qualifications to what Protestants in the Reformation tradition have meant and have not meant when they affirm the Bible to be the sufficient rule of faith and obedience. We may now turn to two challenges to that teaching. The first surfaces from within the Roman Catholic Church. Rome has declared tradition to be authoritative in

---

91. It is here that we may understand the sense in which the Scripture sometimes speaks of the Word doing this work itself. J. I. Packer has collected a number of statements in the Bible that attribute power and efficacy to the Word, 'As in the Old Testament the Word of God is said to go out into the world with power to produce its intended effect (Isa. 55:10f., cf. Jer. 1:9f.) so in the New Testament the Word of God – that is, the Gospel – is declared to be the means whereby God searches hearts (Heb. 4:12), creates faith (Rom. 10:17, cf. John 17:20), effects new birth (James 1:18, 1 Pet. 1:23), cleanses (John 15:3, Eph. 5:26), sanctifies (John 17:17), gives wisdom (Col. 3:16), builds up Christians in faith and brings them to their final heritage (Acts 20:32) – in short, saves their souls (James 1:21),' 'The Necessity of the Revealed Word,' in *Honouring the Written Word of God: The Collected Shorter Writings of J. I. Packer, Volume 3* (Carlisle: Paternoster, 1999), 105. This pattern of speaking does not mean that the Word has intrinsic power to accomplish the ends. Rather, it describes the way in which the Spirit is pleased to work in conjunction with the book that He wrote. In the work of illumination, however, the Spirit's working is immediate (even as the Word is the occasion of that work).

92. Coffin, 'The Sufficiency of Scripture and Modern Theonomy,' 158.

precisely the same sense that the Scripture is authoritative.⁹³ The second arises from the charismatic movement. For all the diversity represented within that movement, charismatics argue that the Spirit continues to reveal Himself to the church even after the close of the apostolic age. We will address each of these teachings, giving particular attention to their implications for the doctrine of Scripture's sufficiency.

At the time of the Reformation, Rome formally articulated the doctrine that ecclesiastical tradition is equally authoritative with the Scripture. In 1546, the Council of Trent issued its 'Decree on the Reception of the Sacred Books and Traditions.'

> [The] gospel was promised of old through the prophets in the Sacred Scriptures; our Lord Jesus Christ, Son of God, first promulgated it from his own lips; he in turn ordered that it be preached through the apostles to all creatures [cf. Mark 16:15] as the source of all saving truth and norms of conduct. The council clearly perceives that this truth and rule are contained in the written books and unwritten traditions that have come down to us, having been received by the apostles from the mouth of Christ himself or from the apostles by the dictation of the Holy Spirit, and have been transmitted, as it were, from hand to hand. Following, then, the example of the orthodox Fathers, it receives and venerates with the same sense of loyalty and reverence all the books of the Old and New Testament – for the one God is the author of both – together with all the traditions concerning faith and practice, as coming from the mouth of Christ or being inspired by the Holy Spirit and preserved in continuous succession in the Catholic Church.⁹⁴

In this decree, Rome is making the following claims. It argues that both 'written books and unwritten traditions' have come down to the church from Christ and His apostles. The church must 'receive and venerate' the Scripture and these traditions alike, presumably because they possess

---

93. Our discussion will concentrate on Rome's confessional statements that are pertinent to this question. For treatments of particularly recent Roman Catholic reflection on Scripture and tradition, see Robert B. Strimple, 'The Relationship Between Scripture and Tradition in Contemporary Roman Catholic Theology,' *WTJ* 40/1 (1977): 22-38; and Matthew Levering, *Engaging the Doctrine of Revelation: The Mediation of the Gospel through Church and Scripture* (Grand Rapids: Baker, 2014), esp. 139-74.

94. 'Council of Trent: Decree on the Reception of Sacred Books,' Heinrich Denzinger, *Compendium of Creeds, Definitions, and Declarations on Matters of Faith and Morals* (eds. Peter Hünermann, Robert Fastiggi, and Anne Englund Nash; 43d ed.; San Francisco: Ignatius, 2012), §1501.

the same authority. The traditions in question are 'unwritten' or 'oral' (AT).⁹⁵ These traditions, according to Trent, have been 'preserved in continuous succession in the Catholic church.' Significantly, while Trent specifies the books that it believes constitute the Scripture, it does not specify which traditions are authoritative.⁹⁶ It does, however, identify them according to the 'criteria' of 'antiquity and catholicity.'⁹⁷

The Roman Catholic Church reaffirmed this doctrine of authoritative tradition at the First Vatican Council in 1870.⁹⁸ It consequently upheld this teaching at the Second Vatican Council in 1965.

> Hence there exists a close connection and communication between sacred tradition and Sacred Scripture. For both of them, flowing from the same divine wellspring (*ex eadem divina scaturigine promanantes*), in a certain way merge into a unity and tend toward the same end. For Sacred Scripture is the Word of God inasmuch as it is consigned to writing under the inspiration of the divine Spirit, while sacred tradition takes the Word of God entrusted by Christ the Lord and the Holy Spirit to the apostles and hands it on to their successors in its full purity, so that led by the light of the Spirit of truth, they may in proclaiming it preserve this Word of God faithfully, explain it, and make it more widely known. Consequently, it is not from Sacred Scripture alone (*non per solam Sacram Scripturam*) that the Church draws her certainty about everything that has been revealed. Therefore both sacred tradition and Sacred Scripture are to be accepted and venerated with the same sense of loyalty and reverence (*utraque pari pietatis affectu ac reverentia*).⁹⁹
>
> Sacred tradition and Sacred Scripture form one sacred deposit of the Word of God (*unum verbi Dei sacrum depositum*), committed to the Church ... [T]he task of authentically interpreting the Word of God,

---

95. 'oretenus a Christo,' rendered 'from the mouth of Christ' at ibid.

96. See Denzinger, *Compendium*, §§1502-3. Trent proceeds to anathematize any who 'knowingly and deliberately rejects the aforesaid traditions' (§1504).

97. Charles Hodge, *Systematic Theology* (3 vols.; New York: Charles Scribner's Sons, 1901), 1:110. Hodge notes that Bellarmine argues for the same criteria.

98. 'Further, this supernatural revelation, according to the universal belief of the Church, declared by the sacred Council of Trent, "is contained in the written books and unwritten traditions that have come down to us, having been received by the apostles from the mouth of Christ himself or from the apostles themselves by the dictation of the Holy Spirit, and have been transmitted as it were from hand to hand,"' *Dei Filius*, Denzinger, *Compendium*, §3006.

99. *Dei Verbum*, Denzinger, *Compendium*, §4212.

> whether written or handed on (*verbum Dei scriptum vel traditum*), has been entrusted exclusively to the living teaching office of the Church, whose authority is exercised in the name of Jesus Christ. This teaching office is not above the Word of God ... It is clear, therefore, that sacred tradition, Sacred Scripture, and the teaching authority of the Church, in accord with God's most wise design, are so linked and joined together that one cannot stand without the others and that all together and each in its own way under the action of the one Holy Spirit contribute effectively to the salvation of souls.[100]

The Second Vatican Council here affirms that both Scripture and tradition constitute 'one sacred deposit of the Word of God.' They proceed 'from the same divine wellspring' and 'in a certain way merge into a unity.' To be sure, the Council recognizes that each plays a different role or function in mediating divine revelation to the church. But they are 'so linked and joined together' that Scripture cannot 'stand without' tradition. For this reason, 'both sacred tradition and Sacred Scripture are to be accepted and venerated with the same sense of loyalty and reverence.'

To be sure, Rome is not claiming that any and every tradition that has circulated in and through the church is authoritative. The Catechism of the Catholic Church draws the distinction between 'Apostolic Tradition and ecclesial traditions.'

> The Tradition here in question comes from the apostles and hands on what they received from Jesus' teaching and example and what they learned from the Holy Spirit. The first generation of Christians did not have a written New Testament, and the New Testament itself demonstrates the process of living Tradition.
>
> Tradition is to be distinguished from the various theological, disciplinary, liturgical, or devotional traditions, born in the local churches over time. These are the particular forms, adapted to different places and times, in which the great Tradition is expressed. In the light of Tradition, these traditions can be retained, modified or even abandoned under the guidance of the Church's magisterium.[101]

---

100. *Dei Verbum*, Denzinger, *Compendium*, §4213, §4214. We will return to Rome's claims regarding the magisterium of the church in the following chapter. We reference this extract in order to show how, for *Dei Verbum*, Scripture and tradition are inextricably joined together.

101. *Catechism of the Catholic Church With Modifications from the Editio Typica* (New York: Doubleday, 1995), §83.

The Catechism gives some indication how Rome defines Tradition in distinction from traditions. It is the Church's magisterium that authoritatively and definitively moderates the distinction between the two. Even so, the Catechism refrains from specifying what constitutes Tradition or pointing the reader to a particular ecclesiastical statement that authoritatively declares what belongs and does not belong to Tradition.[102]

How, then, does Rome support her contention that ecclesiastical Tradition possesses equal authority with the Scripture? One biblical passage to which Roman Catholics have appealed in support of this doctrine is 2 Thessalonians 2:15, 'So then, brothers, stand firm and hold to the traditions that you were taught by us, either by our spoken word or by our letter.'[103] The Catechism, we have seen, understands Tradition, under the supervision of the magisterium, to be in unbroken succession with the New Testament, delivered to the church by the hands of the apostles. In other words, Rome contends, Tradition is the unwritten and seamless complement of the doctrines and practices imposed in writing by the apostles upon the church of the first century.

Rome also stresses the necessity of Tradition in light of what it regards to be the insufficiency of Scripture to regulate the faith and practice of the church. Bavinck summarizes Rome's argument at this point.

> Scripture by itself is insufficient. Aside from the fact that by far not everything has been recorded, various writings by prophets and apostles have been lost as well. Though the apostles were instructed to witness, they were not told to do this in writing. They resorted to writing only in response to circumstances, 'compelled by a kind of necessity.' Their writings, accordingly are mostly occasional writings and fall far short of what is necessary for the teaching and life of the church. For example, we find little or nothing in Scripture about the baptism of women, observance of the Lord's Day, the episcopacy, the seven sacraments, purgatory, the immaculate conception of Mary, the salvation of many Gentiles in the days of the OT, the inspiration and canonicity of several Bible books, and so forth. According to Rome even dogmas like the Trinity, the eternal

---

102. For the way in which one influential Roman Catholic theologian, Robert Bellarmine, sought to define *Tradition*, see the discussion of William Whitaker, *Disputations on Holy Scripture* (1849; trans. and ed. William Fitzgerald; repr., Morgan, PA: Soli Deo Gloria, 2000), 503-11.

103. So *Dei Verbum*, Denzinger, *Compendium*, §4209.

generation [of the Son], the process of the Holy Spirit, infant baptism, and so forth cannot be found literally and explicitly in Scripture. In short: while Scripture is useful, tradition is necessary.[104]

For Rome, then, revelation is sufficient for the church's faith and practice, but Scripture is insufficient. Only when Scripture is coupled with Tradition does the church have the body of revelation that it needs to norm its teaching and morals.

What are we to make of Rome's claims? In the first place, it needs to be stressed that Protestants are not against tradition in every conceivable sense.[105] We have seen above how Protestants since the Reformation have affirmed a positive role for tradition, provided that tradition is properly defined. But Protestants have never understood tradition, in any sense, to have the same authority that the Scripture has. They have insisted that tradition stands in complete submission to the Scripture.[106] That to which Protestants object is the doctrine that tradition – of any kind – is authoritative in precisely the same sense that Scripture is authoritative.

One reason why Rome insists that tradition is authoritative is to remedy what are thought to be certain deficiencies of the Bible's teaching. Rome claims that the Bible is insufficient and, therefore, tradition is necessary to guide the faith and morals of the Church. But Protestants have claimed that the Scriptures of the Old and New Testaments are, as the only rule of faith and obedience, sufficient. As Turretin has noted, the matters that Rome alleges are not contained in Scripture, some of which we registered above, fall into three categories.

---

104. Bavinck, *Reformed Dogmatics* (ed. John Bolt; trans. John Vriend; 4 vols.; Grand Rapids: Eerdmans, 2003), 1:482. For the Roman Catholic authors that Bavinck is summarizing, see 1:482n.64.

105. See, representatively, the testimony cited at Heinrich Heppe, *Reformed Dogmatics* (rev. and ed., Ernst Bizer; trans. G. T. Thompson; 1950; repr., Grand Rapids: Baker, 1978), 30-1.

106. 'The difference between Rome and the Reformation in their respective views of tradition consists in this: Rome wanted a tradition that ran on an independent parallel track alongside of Scripture, or rather, Scripture alongside of tradition. The Reformation recognizes only a tradition that is founded on and flows from Scripture. To the mind of the Reformation, Scripture was an organic principle from which the entire tradition, living on in preaching, confession, liturgy, worship, theology, devotional literature, etc., arises and is nurtured,' Bavinck, *Reformed Dogmatics,* 1:493. See as well the perceptive reflections of Hodge, *Systematic Theology,* 1:113-16.

> What the papists maintain should be received besides the Scriptures either exist in them really – as the Trinity (as to the thing itself), infant baptism …, baptism not necessary to be repeated, the number of the sacraments (at least those enumerated in Scripture), the admission of females to the Eucharist (Acts 2:42; 1 Cor. 11:5, cf. v. 28), the change of the Sabbath to the Lord's Day (Rev. 1:10; 1 Cor. 16:2; Col. 2:16,17); or they are not doctrines necessary to salvation – as the perpetual virginity of Mary even post partum and the ogliation to keep the Passover on the Lord's Day; or they are false and counterfeit – as the local descent of Christ to hell, purgatory, the Mass, the return of Enoch and Elijah, etc.[107]

In other words, some of what Rome alleges to be deficient with respect to Scripture is actually taught by Scripture, provided we understand Scripture's teaching to include matters that may be deduced by good and necessary consequence. Other matters that Rome alleges to evidence Scripture's deficiencies with respect to its guidance of the church in matters of faith and practice are either not necessary to salvation or are teachings contrary to Scripture. In no instance has Rome established the genuine insufficiency of Scripture and the corresponding need for supplemental Tradition to guide the doctrine and life of the Church.

What about the evidence that Rome positively advances for her doctrine of Tradition? Paul's words in 2 Thessalonians 2:15 do not establish that doctrine. The word translated 'traditions' in that verse cannot, in context, convey the sense that Rome understands it to have. The word 'traditions' simply denotes the apostolic teaching of Paul, received by the church in Thessalonica.[108] What Paul enjoins upon the church in Thessalonica is to adhere to his apostolic teaching in whatever form he has transmitted it to them. The form of this tradition, as Paul expresses it in this verse, corresponds to the form of the false teaching that has troubled the church in Thessalonica. This false teaching has come 'either by a spirit or a spoken word, or a letter seeming to be from us, to the effect that the day of the Lord has come' (2 Thess. 2:2). The church in

---

107. Turretin, *Institutes*, 1:140 (=2.16.22).

108. 'Second Thess. 2:15 does not sanction unwritten (*agraphous*) traditions, but designates the twofold method of delivering the same doctrine by the voice and by writing,' Turretin, *Institutes*, 1:140 (=2.16.25). Compare William Cunningham, *Theological Lectures on Subjects Connected with Natural Theology, Evidences of Christianity, the Canon and Inspiration of Scripture* (London: James Nisbet & Co., 1878), 465.

Thessalonica must cling to *authentic* Pauline teaching, in whatever form it comes to them, and reject *spurious* Pauline teaching, in whatever form it comes to them. Paul's words of themselves offer no express ground or warrant for Rome's claims for the existence of unwritten apostolic traditions intended to supplement written Scripture.[109]

Rome also claims that Tradition in the church today is but the transmission of what is said to be the Tradition imposed by the apostles upon the first century church. But the New Testament writers testify to a radical difference between the apostolic and the post-apostolic church with respect to revelation. That difference, we observed in the last chapter, concerns the completed canon of Scripture which, in turn, rests upon the finished mediatorial work of the incarnate Son of God, Jesus Christ. As Bavinck has observed, 'the sufficiency of Holy Scripture results from the nature of the NT dispensation.' 'Christ became flesh and completed all his work. He is the last and supreme revelation of God, who declared to us the Father (John 1:18; 17:4,6); By him God has spoken to us in the last days (Heb. 1:1-2). He is the supreme and only prophet.'[110] Furthermore, as Ridderbos has observed, in light of 'the unique and exclusive nature of the power the apostles received from Christ and from the commission He gave them to be witnesses to what they had seen and heard of the salvation He had brought,' 'the canon cannot be open; in principle it must be *closed*.'[111] In summary, 'the closed nature of the canon thus rests ultimately on the once-and-for-all significance of the New Testament history of redemption itself, as that history is presented by the apostolic witness.'[112]

The subsequent history of the church's reception of the canon confirms the church's understanding and embrace of this fact. The church gathered, compiled, and recognized those writings that had been

---

109. As Michael Horton observes, *'Protestants had no trouble agreeing that there was a time when written Scripture and oral tradition were two media of a unified revelation, but they denied that this situation applies in the post apostolic era.* The critical question for us is whether the noninspired traditions of ordinary ministers of the church can be equated with the revelation given through the extraordinary ministry of prophets and apostles,' *The Christian Faith: A Systematic Theology for Pilgrims on the Way* (Grand Rapids: Zondervan, 2011), 191, emphasis original.

110. Bavinck, *Reformed Dogmatics*, 1:490.

111. Ridderbos, *Redemptive History*, 25, emphasis original.

112. ibid.

imposed upon them by the apostles. Ridderbos draws two important and interrelated implications from this historical process of recognition for the question before us. In the first place, 'the attempt to retain some form of ongoing oral tradition as a supplement to the written canon ... in fact relativizes the latter and makes illusory the church's intention in adopting the canon in the first place.' Second, the very fact of the canon and its recognition by the church acknowledges 'the boundary between the history of redemption and the history of the church,' 'between ... apostolic and ecclesiastical tradition.'[113] When the church acknowledged as the Word of God the entirety of those writings that the apostles had imposed upon them, they were, in principle, shutting the door to any other stream of special revelation, not least in the form of ecclesiastical tradition. And they were, in principle at least, testifying to the radical and qualitative difference between the traditions imposed upon the church by the apostles, and any traditions that would subsequently surface in the church's history, of whatever alleged provenance. The former is what the church has acknowledged to be the infallible, inerrant Word of God, the church's only and sufficient rule of faith and practice. The latter, at least, would be entirely in submission to the former. The origin, significance, and reception of the canon of Scripture, then, testify against Rome's doctrine of Tradition.

Rome's doctrine of Tradition suffers from at least two further objections. First, we have observed a lack of clarity within Rome's confessional statements with respect to the criterion by which Tradition is to be ascertained. Rome acknowledges the distinction between (authoritative) Tradition and traditions that are subject to correction and even rejection by the church. But, as Hodge pointedly asks, 'How shall the line be drawn between the true and false? By what criterion can the one be distinguished from the other?'[114] Roman Catholic theologians have often appealed to the joint criteria of 'antiquity and universality.'[115] The problem for Rome's position, however, is that the Tradition for which she pleads meets neither criterion. Transubstantiation, the

---

113. Ridderbos, *Redemptive History*, 26. The last phrase is cited by Ridderbos from Oscar Cullmann, *Die Tradition als Exegetisches, Historisches und Theologisches Problem* (Zürich: Zwingli Verlag, 1954), 44.

114. Hodge, *Systematic Theology*, 1:122.

115. ibid.; Bavinck, *Reformed Dogmatics*, 1:483.

immaculate conception, and the doctrine of purgatory, for example, are indisputably later developments in the history of the church. Rome's position, furthermore, requires that universality be understood in terms of the official pronouncements of the Roman Catholic Church.[116] This claim to universality, however, is not one that Protestants would grant. Even these professed criteria prove inadequate to set Tradition apart from the traditions of the church's history.

There is, still, a deeper problem. In reality, Protestants object, it is the authority of the Church that is determinative of Tradition. It is beyond the capabilities of untrained people to distinguish Tradition from traditions, and the church has asserted the right authoritatively to declare where Tradition is to be found within the history of the church. As such, Christians are entirely dependent upon the Church in order to know what that Tradition is that God is supposed to have revealed to them.[117] As Turretin notes, 'There is no rule for the distinguishing of traditions which does not bring us back to the testimony and authority of the church.'[118]

A second objection concerns the authoritative weight of Tradition relative to Scripture in the doctrine and practice of the church. We have an illustrative parallel documented in a criticism that Jesus made of the Pharisees in the course of His earthly ministry.

> Then Pharisees and scribes came to Jesus from Jerusalem and said, 'Why do your disciples break the tradition of the elders? For they do not wash their hands when they eat.' He answered them, 'And why do you break the commandment of God for the sake of your tradition? For God commanded, "Honor your father and your mother," and "Whoever reviles father or mother must surely die." But you say, "If anyone tells his father or his mother, 'What you would have gained from me is given to God, he need

---

116. Hodge, *Systematic Theology*, 1:127.

117. 'A rule of faith to the people must be something which they can apply; a standard by which they can judge. But this unwritten revelation is not contained in any one volume accessible to the people, and intelligible by them. It is scattered through the ecclesiastical records of eighteen centuries. It is absolutely impossible for the people to learn what it teaches ... They must take all such doctrines upon trust, *i.e.*, on the faith of the extant church. But this is to deny that to them tradition is a rule of faith. They are required to believe, on the peril of their souls, doctrines, the pretended evidence of which is impossible for them to ascertain or appreciate,' Hodge, *Systematic Theology*, 1:127.

118. Turretin, *Institutes*, 1:139 (=2.16.19).

not honor his father.'" So for the sake of your tradition you have made void the word of God. You hypocrites! Well did Isaiah prophesy of you, when he said, "This people honors me with their lips, but their heart is far from me; in vain do they worship me, teaching as doctrines the commandments of men."' (Matt. 15:1-9).

Jesus is addressing Jewish teachers who regarded both Scripture and 'the tradition of the elders' to be authoritative. Jesus, however, highlights the inherent problem with elevating tradition to the level of Scripture. Because traditions do not derive from Scripture, they will inevitably rival the Scripture. When tradition rivals Scripture, Jesus observes, tradition will trump Scripture ('so for the sake of your tradition you have made void the word of God'). In reality, Scripture and tradition do not stand as equal authorities in the life of God's people. Tradition supplants Scripture and constitutes the primary, if not exclusive, practical authority with respect to the beliefs and practices of the people of God.

We see precisely the same dynamic at work within the Roman Catholic Church. In principle, Rome acknowledges Scripture and Tradition to be derived from the same source, to be equally authoritative in the church. In practice, however, Tradition has come to supplant Scripture both in the teaching and practice of the men and women in the Roman Catholic Church.[119] But it is not simply that Tradition stands over Scripture in the theology and practice of the Roman Catholic Church. Rome teaches that the Word of God is to be received on the authority of the Church, and that it is the Church that effectively determines what is and is not Tradition. In these respects, the Church has placed herself above both Scripture and Tradition.[120]

In summary, Rome claims that the Scripture is insufficient as the rule of the faith and practice of the church. She argues that Tradition supplements those deficiencies and is equally authoritative with the Scripture. In reality, much of what Rome claims for Tradition is contrary to the teaching of Scripture. Scripture, in fact, teaches its own sufficiency as rule of faith and practice. Rome's teaching of Tradition effectively supplants the authority of Scripture with Tradition. And over

---

119. See here the remarks of Bavinck, *Reformed Dogmatics*, 1:492.

120. This observation finds confirmation in the fact that Rome claims to be the infallible interpreter of Scripture, a claim that we will examine in the next chapter.

both Scripture and Tradition stands the authoritative Roman Catholic Church. Although Rome claims that Tradition supplements and complements Scripture, the result or effect of this teaching is to diminish the authority of Scripture and to elevate the authority of humanity in the Church.

The Sufficiency of Scripture and the Charismatic Movement

There is another, and related, challenge to the sufficiency of Scripture in the contemporary church, the charismatic movement's claims to continuing revelation.[121] Such continuing revelation is said to assume the form of tongues and prophecy, not unlike those witnessed on the pages of Acts and First Corinthians. The Roman Catholic doctrine of Tradition has been largely confined to the Roman Catholic Church.[122] The charismatic movement, however, has found a home both within Roman Catholicism and evangelical Protestantism. Furthermore, some Reformed theologians and pastors, while distancing themselves from the

---

121. At the time of the Reformation, the radical wing of the Reformation pressed for continuing revelations of the Spirit. Calvin recognized the fundamental similarity between the challenges that both Rome and the radical Reformation posed to the magisterial Reformation's insistence upon the sufficiency of Scripture, 'We are assailed by two sects [i.e., Rome and the Anabaptists],' although they 'seem to differ more widely from each other ... For when they boast extravagantly of the Spirit, the tendency certainly is to sink and bury the Word of God, that they may make room for their own falsehoods,' 'Reply by John Calvin to Cardinal Sadoleto's "Letter,"' in *Calvin's Tracts and Treatises* (trans. Henry Beveridge; 7 vols.; Grand Rapids: Eerdmans, 1958), 1:36, as quoted at Horton, *Christian Faith*, 192n.29. This association found its way into the Westminster Confession of Faith (WCF 1.6, 'Scripture: unto which nothing at any time is to be added, whether by new revelations of the Spirit or traditions of men;' WCF 1.10, 'all decrees of councils, opinions of ancient writers, doctrines of men, and private spirits...'), so Warfield, *The Westminster Assembly and Its Work*, in *Works*, 6:224, and Gaffin, 'A Cessationist Conclusion,' in *Are Miraculous Gifts For Today? Four Views* (ed. Wayne Grudem; Grand Rapids: Zondervan, 1996), 337-9.

122. There are similar claims within Eastern Orthodoxy, on which see Mathison, *The Shape of Sola Scriptura*, 225-35. For Eastern Orthodox expositions of the doctrine of Scripture, see Georges Florovsky, *Bible, Church, Tradition: An Eastern Orthodox View*, in *The Collected Works 1* (ed. Richard S. Haugh; Vaduz: Büchervertriebsanstalt, 1987), and Archimandrite Chrysostomos and Archimandrite Auxentios, *Scripture and Tradition* (Etna, CA: Center for Traditionalist Orthodox Studies, 1994). Furthermore, forms of Rome's doctrine of Tradition surfaced in the Tractarian movement within the Church of England in the nineteenth century, on which see William Cunningham, *Theological Lectures*, 447-91.

charismatic movement, have embraced claims to continuing revelation in the church.[123] They argue that the gifts of tongues and prophecy encountered in the New Testament have not ceased with the close of the apostolic age, but continue in the church's life today.[124] They do so, however, while consciously intending to uphold the full authority and sufficiency of Scripture.[125] For this reason, these claims merit serious and thoughtful consideration. We may give particular attention to the positions of Wayne Grudem and C. Samuel Storms.

What claims do these theologians advance with respect to the spiritual gifts? Wayne Grudem argues that miracles have not ceased with the apostolic age.[126] It is appropriate for Christians, he insists, to pursue 'miracles for the proper purposes for which they are given by God: to confirm the truthfulness of the gospel message, to bring help to those in need, to remove hindrances to people's ministries, and to bring glory to God.'[127] He is equally open to the continuation of what he calls 'some of the more miraculous gifts (such as prophecy, tongues plus interpretation, and perhaps healing and casting out of demons).'[128] In similar fashion, C. Samuel Storms argues that 'all the gifts of the Holy Spirit are valid for the contemporary church...'[129] These gifts include the gift of prophecy and the gift of tongues.[130]

---

123. Wayne Grudem, for instance, takes care to distinguish his own view from that of 'charismatics' and 'Pentecostals,' *Systematic Theology*, 1031.

124. C. Samuel Storms, 'A Third Wave View,' in *Are Miraculous Gifts for Today? Four Views* (Grand Rapids: Zondervan, 1996); Storms, *Practicing the Power: Welcoming the Gifts of the Holy Spirit in Your Life* (Grand Rapids: Zondervan, 2017); Wayne Grudem, *The Gift of Prophecy in the New Testament and Today* (rev. ed.; Wheaton, IL: Crossway, 2000).

125. See, for example, Wayne Grudem, who asks and answers in the negative the question, 'Would the continuation of prophecy today challenge the sufficiency of Scripture?,' *Systematic Theology*, 1039.

126. ibid., 361-72.

127. ibid., 371.

128. ibid., 1031.

129. Storms, 'Third Wave,' 205. Storms earlier notes that 'when I speak of signs, wonders, and miraculous phenomena available to the church today, I have in mind not the mere potential for rare supernatural activity or surprising acts of providence, but the actual operation of those miraculous gifts listed in 1 Corinthians 12:7-10,' 'Third Wave,' 186.

130. ibid., 207-12, 215-22. In this chapter, Storms adopts Grudem's view of prophecy, 'Third Wave,' 207n.37.

How do Grudem and Storms understand these gifts? Since Storms' view is similar, if not identical, to that of Grudem, we may reflect on Grudem's position.[131] Grudem defines 'tongues' as 'prayer or praise spoken in syllables not understood by the speaker.'[132] He observes that 'sometimes this gift may result in speaking in a human language that the speaker has not learned, but ordinarily it seems that it will involve speech in a language that no one understands, whether that be a human language or not.'[133] Tongues will edify when accompanied by the 'gift of interpretation,' that is, 'reporting to the church the general meaning of something spoken in tongues.'[134] Are tongues revelatory? Grudem understands tongues as a mode of speech 'directed toward God (that is, prayer or praise).' In this respect, tongues are 'unlike the gift of prophecy, which frequently consists of messages directed *from* God toward people in the church.'[135] When tongues are interpreted, they are *like* prophecy in that they edify the church, but *unlike* prophecy in that they are non-revelatory.[136] Unlike tongues, prophecy is revelatory for both Grudem and Storms. Grudem, followed by Storms, has advanced an argument for a different understanding of New Testament prophecy than that shared by many students of the New Testament.[137] Grudem defines prophecy as 'telling something that God has spontaneously brought to mind.'[138] The prophets of the New Testament, however, are not one and the same with the prophets of the Old Testament.[139] The utterances of the New

---

131. Storms sees tongues as a spiritual gift consisting in a person speaking to God in a private prayer language, and thereby edifying himself, 'Third Wave,' 215. For Storms, like Grudem, tongues may or may not be a known human language, 'Third Wave,' 220-1.

132. Grudem, *Systematic Theology*, 1070, emphasis removed.

133. ibid., 1072.

134. ibid., 1076, emphasis removed.

135. ibid., 1071, emphasis original. See Grudem's reflections on the anthropological implications of his view in relation to 1 Corinthians 14:14-15 at *Systematic Theology*, 1073.

136. ibid., 1076.

137. Grudem has argued his view at greatest length in *The Gift of Prophecy*. For Storms, see 'Third Wave,' 207-15.

138. Grudem, *Systematic Theology*, 1049, emphasis removed.

139. 'The New Testament counterparts to Old Testament prophets are New Testament apostles,' Grudem, *Systematic Theology*, 1050.

Testament prophets were not 'equal' in 'authority...to the words of Scripture.'[140] Although the prophets received revelation from God, what they uttered was fallible in content, 'prophecies in the church today should be considered merely human words, not God's words, and not equal to God's words in authority.'[141] In what sense, then, is prophecy from God?

> Paul indicates that God could bring something spontaneously to mind so that the person prophesying would report it in his or her own words. Paul calls this a 'revelation' (1 Cor. 14:30-31) ... Paul is simply referring to something that God may suddenly bring to mind, or something that God may impress on someone's consciousness in such a way that the person has a sense that it is from God.[142]

It is in this sense that Grudem understands prophecy to continue in the church today. Sensitive to the need to emphasize the authority of Scripture in the church, Grudem argues for a comparative inferiority of prophecy to Scripture, 'the church should place even more emphasis [than the gift of prophecy] on the vastly superior value of Scripture as the source to which Christians can always go to hear the voice of the living God. Prophecy is a valuable gift, as are many other gifts, but it is in Scripture that God and only God speaks to us his very words, even today, and throughout our lives.'[143]

Some prominent Reformed theologians have dissented from Grudem's arguments concerning tongues and prophecy.[144] As in Acts, so also in First Corinthians, tongues are revelation given by God to

---

140. Grudem, *Systematic Theology*, 1052, referencing and discussing Acts 21:4, 10-11; 1 Thessalonians 5:19-21; and 1 Corinthians 14:29-38.

141. ibid., 1055.

142. ibid., 1057. Grudem understands 'reveal / revelation' to denote a communication from God to a human being 'that does not result in written Scripture or words equal to written Scripture in authority,' ibid.

143. ibid., 1061.

144. See representatively Richard B. Gaffin, Jr, *Perspectives on Pentecost: New Testament Teaching on the Gifts of the Holy Spirit* (Phillipsburg, NJ: P&R, 1979), 55-87; 'A Cessationist View' in *Are Miraculous Gifts For Today? Four Views*, 25-64; Edmund P. Clowney, *The Church* (Downers Grove, IL: InterVarsity, 1995), 255-68; Sinclair B. Ferguson, *The Holy Spirit* (Downers Grove, IL: InterVarsity, 1996), 212-37; Thomas R. Schreiner, *Spiritual Gifts: What They Are & Why They Matter* (Nashville: B&H, 2018), 123-32. D. A. Carson, while generally agreeing with Grudem, has registered what he terms 'mild dissent' with Grudem's thesis, *Showing the Spirit: A Theological Exposition of 1 Corinthians 12-14* (Grand Rapids: Baker, 1987), 94, 98-100.

human beings in existing human languages that are unknown to the recipient. As such, they are not the devotional utterances of human beings to God.[145] They are 'inspired' and 'thus revelatory' and function to edify the church, provided that they are accompanied by the gift of interpretation.[146]

In similar fashion, prophecy is a revelatory gift.[147] The New Testament writers do not distinguish, principially or functionally, Old Testament prophecy from New Testament prophecy.[148] As such, New Testament prophets not only receive revelation from God, but their utterances are revelatory and inspired as well. These prophets, no less than the Old Testament prophets, speak the very words of God.[149]

As Paul argues in Ephesians 2:20, both the apostles and the prophets of the New Testament constitute the foundation upon which the church is now being built. That is to say, the church's once-for-all foundation is the revelation that God gave to His people in the apostolic age.[150] The implication of this line of teaching of Paul is that all forms of revelation to the church have ceased. The revelatory gifts of tongues and prophecy have served their purpose in contributing to the once-for-all foundation of the New Covenant people of God. As such, they have served their purpose and God has discontinued them in the post-apostolic age.

This observation finds confirmation from the character of special revelation. As Gaffin has observed, revelation is, in the first place, redemptive-historical.

> Revelation is *redemptive-historical*... Since the history of redemption has been *definitively accomplished* and since after Pentecost its ongoing

---

145. 'No gift, including tongues, is integral to true spirituality. The gifts of the Spirit are not "means of grace" indispensable, like God's Word, the sacraments, and prayer, for personal sanctification and growth in grace,' Gaffin, *Perspectives on Pentecost*, 87.

146. ibid., 78.

147. See now Schreiner, *Spiritual Gifts,* 105-117.

148. It is at this juncture that Grudem's exegesis of Ephesians 2:20 has figured prominently in these discussions, on which see R. Fowler White, 'Gaffin and Grudem on Ephesians 2:20: In Defense of Gaffin's Cessationist Exegesis,' *WTJ* 54/2 (1992): 303-20. See also the discussion at Harold W. Hoehner, *Ephesians: An Exegetical Commentary* (Grand Rapids: Baker, 2002), 399-403.

149. 'The words of the prophet are the words of God and are to be received and responded to as such,' Gaffin, *Perspectives on Pentecost*, 72.

150. See Gaffin, *Perspectives on Pentecost,* 93-6.

movement is delayed until Christ's return for the *application* of redemption and the ingathering of the nations to share in the salvation of the covenant, the basis and rationale for new revelations is lacking and revelation has therefore ceased.[151]

Furthermore, 'revelation is "covenantal," [God] reveals himself, not to a mass of undifferentiated individuals, but to his covenant people, in order to build them up and make their number complete as one people.'[152] As such, 'Scripture leaves no place for privatized, localized revelations for specific individual needs and circumstances ... The subject matter of prophecy is "mysteries" (1 Cor. 13:2), always a redemptive-historical category in Paul.'[153]

It is in light of these reasons, then, that one may argue from the Bible that tongues and prophecy have ceased in the church.[154] Tongues and prophecy were revelation from God to His covenant people. By divine intention, they served to contribute to an unrepeatable foundation for the New Covenant church. Once that foundation was laid, these gifts' purposes had been served and they were discontinued in the life of the church. Given the redemptive-historical and covenantal character of revelation, we do not anticipate further revelation of God to His people prior to the return of Christ at the end of the age. What the church does have is the written Word of God which, we have argued, is the sufficient rule of faith and practice under the New Covenant.

It is at this juncture that we may raise a concern about Grudem's understanding of prophecy. Grudem argues for continuing revelation in the church today, albeit in restricted fashion. He does not see ongoing prophecy as verbally revelatory and, therefore, prophecy, as he understands it, does not belong to the same category as the verbal revelation of Scripture. And yet, Grudem maintains a category of continuing revelation in the church. What are the implications of his view for his affirmation of the sufficiency of Scripture?

---

151. ibid., 97-8.

152. ibid., 97.

153. ibid., 98-9. Compare Gaffin, 'The New Testament as Canon,' in *Inerrancy and Hermeneutic*, 180-1.

154. On the appeal made by Grudem to 1 Corinthians 13:8-13, see R. Fowler White, 'Richard Gaffin and Wayne Grudem on 1 Corinthians 13:10: A Comparison of Cessationist and Noncessationist Argumentation,' *JETS* 35/2 (1992): 173-81.

We should certainly acknowledge and express gratitude for Grudem's affirmation of the sufficiency of Scripture, and his desire to safeguard the authority and supremacy of the Scripture in the life of the Christian and in the life of the church. His category of continuing revelation, however, stands at variance with that conviction. Notwithstanding the qualifications that Grudem places upon his understanding of continuing prophecy, not least that its verbal utterances are fallible, Grudem understands two streams of revelation to feed into the church today, Scripture and prophecy. Whenever the people of God have maintained any body of authoritative revelation to stand alongside the written Word of God, the result has been a diminishment of the Scripture in the church's thinking and living.[155] And, as Ferguson has noted, 'if God's special revelation continues in an extra-biblical manner, it is a psychological probability that it will come to exercise a canonical function.'[156]

To say that the Spirit no longer supplies the church with revelation is not to say that the Spirit is absent from the church, not least with respect to the church's faith and practice. Grudem irenically proposes that 'perhaps the Reformed idea of "illumination" allows for what is happening in prophecy today, and may provide a way of understanding it that is not seen as challenging the sufficiency of Scripture.'[157] Illumination, we have seen in a previous chapter, refers to the work of the Spirit in enabling believers to attain to a saving understanding of the matters revealed in the written Word of God. But illumination is not a species of revelation. Illumination is the way in which the Spirit helps readers come to a full and proper understanding of the Bible that the Spirit has authored. Behind Grudem's suggestion may be that much of what is transpiring within quarters of the church that understand revelation to be ongoing reflects a basic confusion of 'illumination' for 'revelation.'[158] What is thought to

---

155. Which is not to say that this result is the intent of advancing what is thought to be additional revelation among the people. But it is its inevitable outcome.

156. Ferguson, *The Holy Spirit*, 233. Ferguson here notes the ironic, if frequently unrecognized, similarity between charismatic Protestant claims of continuing revelation and the Roman Catholic doctrine of continuing revelation in the form of Tradition, ibid.

157. Grudem, *Systematic Theology*, 1042. Compare the reflections of Ferguson, *The Holy Spirit*, 231-5.

158. For similar sentiments, but expressed by cessationist writers, see Ferguson, *The Holy Spirit*, 232-3, 235-6; Gaffin, *Perspectives on Pentecost*, 120.

be continuing revelation or prophecy is in reality 'illumination, fallible insight and contemporary application of biblical truth.'[159] We may be grateful for Grudem's recognition of the distinction between revelation and illumination, and for his concern to safeguard the sufficiency of Scripture in light of claims to continuing revelation. It is puzzling, however, that Grudem fails to see his own doctrine of continuing revelation as in any way jeopardizing the sufficiency of Scripture.

What this confusion underscores is the need for the consistent application of biblical categories to the phenomena of the experiences of Christian people and of the church. These categories derive from a written, final Word that is authoritative and sufficient. At this juncture, Protestantism would do well to take the experience of the Roman Catholic Church as a cautionary tale. As Bavinck has observed, Rome 'first subordinates itself to Christ and his Word, then puts itself on a par with him, later elevates itself above him, to end in the complete replacement of Scripture by tradition, of Christ by the pope, of the church community by the church institution.'[160] This is not to say, of course, that claims to continuing revelation in charismatic quarters of the Protestant church are the equivalent of or interchangeable with Rome's doctrine of Tradition. It is to say, however, that permitting any form of revelation other than that of the written Word of God strikes against the authority and the sufficiency of the Bible.

Making such an affirmation about the Bible, of course, in no way constitutes the categorical rejection of tradition in every sense of the Word. As Bavinck elsewhere rightly observes, the Protestant 'Reformation ... did not reject all tradition as such; it was *reformation*, not *revolution*. It did not attempt to create everything anew from the bottom up, but it did try to cleanse everything from error and abuse according to the rule of God's Word.'[161] Once the Bible was in its proper place in the thinking of the church, then tradition – in the best and proper sense of the term – could serve the church. What Allen and Swain have noted of the church at the time of the Reformation (when

---

159. Ferguson, *The Holy Spirit,* 236. See further John Murray, 'The Guidance of the Holy Spirit' in *Collected Writings of John Murray* (4 vols.; Edinburgh: Banner of Truth, 1976), 1:186-9.
160. Bavinck, *Reformed Dogmatics,* 1.492.
161. ibid., 1:493.

the Reformers recovered the doctrine of *sola Scriptura*) applies no less to the church today, 'Principled commitment to biblical authority as the ultimate determining factor for all faith and practice did not lead to diminishing concern for ecclesial authority or waning reception of church traditions. Rather *sola Scriptura* aided the course of such reception: retrieving the fullness of the catholic past while cognizant of the ever-present need for ongoing reform.'[162]

---

162. Allen and Swain, *Reformed Catholicity*, 70.

The Clarity of Scripture

In the last chapter, we considered one attribute of Scripture, namely, its sufficiency. The Bible is sufficient for the purposes for which its Divine Author intended it. Because the Bible is a sufficient rule of faith and obedience, we do not look outside the Bible to discover what it is that God would have us to believe or to practice with respect to our salvation.

In this chapter, we will consider a distinct attribute of Scripture, namely, its perspicuity or clarity. When we speak of the clarity of Scripture, we are saying that the generality of the Bible's readership is capable of understanding its basic teaching. There is not an obscurity to the fundamental teaching of Scripture. Readers do not require the mediation of clerical or academic authorities in order to ascertain the Bible's message of salvation.

We will first venture a definition of the clarity of Scripture. In doing so, we must clarify what we do and do not understand the doctrine of the clarity of Scripture to teach. Once we have established a working definition, we will show that the Bible teaches its own clarity. Finally, we will consider an influential and historical objection to Scripture's perspicuity, namely, the insistence of the Roman Catholic Church that one requires the mediation of the church in order to understand the basic meaning of the Bible.[1]

---

1. We will not be considering the challenge to the perspicuity of Scripture that has arisen from the ways in which modern and postmodern philosophy and literary theory has challenged the doctrine. For a defense of the clarity of Scripture in light of these objections, see especially Mark D. Thompson, *A Clear and Present Word: The Clarity of*

The Clarity of Scripture: A Definition

Contemporary Protestants in the tradition of the Reformation uniformly affirm the clarity of Scripture. They are not, however, agreed how to define it.[2] Consider the following recent definitions.

> The clarity of Scripture is that quality of the biblical text that, as God's communicative act, ensures meaning is accessible to all who come to it in faith.[3]

> The clarity of Scripture means that the Bible is written in such a way that its teachings are able to be understood by all who will read it seeking God's help and being willing to follow it.[4]

> Scripture is the written word of the living God, God's communicative act, and the Spirit who authored it chooses to continue to speak most directly through it. Therefore we are right to trust that God in Scripture has spoken and continues to speak sufficiently clearly for us to base our saving knowledge of him and of ourselves, and our beliefs and our actions, on the content of Scripture alone, without ultimately validating our understanding of these things or our confidence in them by appeal to any individual or institution.[5]

Each of these definitions affirms the clarity of Scripture, and affirms the doctrine with reference to the text of Scripture. But at least two important differences emerge as well. First, unlike Grudem, Thompson and Ward speak of 'God's communicative act.'[6] Second, each definition

---

Scripture (NSBT 21; Downers Grove, IL: InterVarsity, 2006), 17-47; D. A. Carson, 'Is the Doctrine of *Claritas Scripturae* Still Relevant Today?,' in *Collected Writings on Scripture* (Wheaton, IL: Crossway, 2010), 179-93; and Matthew Barrett, *God's Word Alone: The Authority of Scripture* (Grand Rapids: Zondervan, 2016), 324-9.

2. The following is indebted to the discussion of Philip D. Foster, 'Making Clear the Doctrine of the Clarity of Scripture,' *SBET* 35/2 (2017): 172-85.

3. Thompson, *A Clear and Present Word*, 169-70, as cited at Foster, 'Making Clear,' 183.

4. Wayne Grudem, *Systematic Theology: An Introduction to Biblical Doctrine* (Grand Rapids: MI: Zondervan, 1994), 108, as cited at Foster, 'Making Clear,' 183.

5. Timothy Ward, *Words of Life: Scripture as the Living and Active Word of God* (Downers Grove, IL: InterVarsity, 2009), 126-7.

6. It is with respect to this point that Ward understands Thompson's definition to differ from Grudem's definition, '[the] use of the term "meaning," following on from the reference to Scripture as "God's communicative act", helps to keep the focus rightly on the clarity of God's dynamic presence in and through the words of Scripture. This contrasts

qualifies the beneficiaries of Scripture's clarity, but in different ways. For Thompson, Scripture is clear 'to all who come to it in faith.' For Grudem, 'to all who will read it seeking God's help [and who are] willing to follow it.' For Ward, Scripture's clarity relates to the person who has 'saving knowledge' of the Bible's teaching.

To highlight these differences is not necessarily to affirm incompatibility among these definitions. It is to say that any definition of the clarity of Scripture must address certain basic questions. To what extent is Scripture clear? To whom is Scripture clear? In what manner may an individual arrive at a clear understanding of Scripture?

A classical definition that adequately articulates what Reformed Protestants understand the clarity of Scripture to be is found in the Westminster Confession of Faith.[7]

> All things in Scripture are not alike plain in themselves, nor alike clear unto all: yet those things which are necessary to be known, believed, and observed for salvation, are so clearly propounded, and opened in some place of Scripture or other, that not only the learned, but the unlearned, in a due use of the ordinary means, may attain unto a sufficient understanding of them.[8]

We may pose each of the three questions that we have raised above to this definition. First, to what extent is Scripture clear? The Westminster Divines declare that 'all things in Scripture are not alike plain in themselves, nor alike clear unto all.'[9] This statement denies that clarity may be uniformly predicated of Scripture. It distinguishes what we may term the objective clarity of Scripture from its subjective clarity. Objectively, Scripture's statements vary in their intrinsic 'plain[ness].'

---

with Grudem's more general and potentially more wide-ranging term "teaching,"' *Words of Life*, 125.

7. Speaking with reference to the definitions of Thompson, Ward, and Grudem, Foster concludes that 'all three [of these] modern definitions are less satisfactory than that of the WCF,' 'Making Clear,' 183.

8. Westminster Confession of Faith, 1.7.

9. Note Augustine's reflections with respect to why God has so authored the Scripture, 'Thus the Holy Spirit has magnificently and wholesomely modulated the Holy Scriptures so that the more open places present themselves to [our] hunger and the more obscure places may deter a disdainful attitude. Hardly anything may be found in these obscure places which is not found plainly said elsewhere,' *On Christian Doctrine* (trans. D. W. Robertson, Jr; Indianapolis: Bobbs-Merrill, 1958), 38, as cited at Larry D. Pettegrew, 'The Perspicuity of Scripture,' *TMSJ* 15/2 (Fall 2004): 214.

Some passages of Scripture are simply clearer than others.[10] Subjectively, 'all things in Scripture are not ... alike clear unto all.' What may be clear to one reader may be obscure to another reader. This difference may be attributable to a number of factors, including 'lack of knowledge or education, lack of Christian experience, or deficit of intelligence.'[11]

Westminster, however, delimits a portion of Scripture when it speaks of the clarity of the Bible's teaching. It insists that 'those things which are necessary to be known, believed, and observed for salvation, are so clearly propounded, and opened in some place of Scripture or other, that not only the learned, but the unlearned, in a due use of the ordinary means, may attain unto a sufficient understanding of them.' It is not every teaching of Scripture, but those teachings that touch upon salvation that are said to be clearly taught in the Bible. Westminster's delimitation, furthermore, is not to a particular book or section of Scripture. It is, rather, to the Bible's teaching about what must be 'known, believed, and observed' for salvation.[12] This teaching is 'clearly propounded, and opened in some place of Scripture or other.' Westminster affirms that this clear teaching is present in Scripture, but declines to specify in which particular passage or passages one may locate it.[13] Furthermore, Westminster insists that even this portion of teaching is not subject to exhaustive or comprehensive understanding. Rather, its clarity is such that one may attain to 'a sufficient understanding.'[14]

---

10. To make this claim is not necessarily to say 'that the [human] author may have intentionally been vague,' as Paul Brewster, 'The Perspicuity of Scripture,' *Faith & Mission* 22/2 (Spring 2005): 30.

11. Robert Letham, *The Westminster Assembly: Reading Its Theology In Historical Context* (Phillipsburg, NJ: P&R, 2009), 142.

12. And even here, Westminster declines to specify what those particular teachings are, so rightly William Cunningham, *Theological Lectures on Subjects Connected with Natural Theology, Evidences of Christianity, the Canon and Inspiration of Scripture* (London: James Nisbet & Co., 1878), 504.

13. 'The question is not whether things essential to salvation are everywhere in the Scriptures perspicuously revealed ... The question is whether things essential to salvation are anywhere revealed, at least so that the believer can by close meditation ascertain their truth (because nothing can be drawn out of the more obscure passages which may not be found elsewhere in the plainest terms),' Francis Turretin, *Institutes of Elenctic Theology* (3 vols.; Phillipsburg, NJ: P&R, 1992-7), 1.144 (=2.17.5).

14. 'Nor is it even stated that they all are anywhere so clearly propounded and opened as that they may easily be understood unto perfection; but only so as that "a sufficient understanding of them may be attained,"' Benjamin B. Warfield, 'The Doctrine of Holy

Second, to whom is Scripture clear? Westminster insists that the clarity of Scripture is not dependent upon the educational attainments of the reader. As Grudem notes, 'clarity is a property *of Scripture*, not a property of its readers.'[15] Moreover, Scripture is clear, to the degree that it is clear, both to the 'learned' and the 'unlearned.'[16] As Warfield observes, 'the variety of mental acumen and teachableness of heart brought to the study of Scripture, is sufficiently recognized. But the fact that the Scriptures, despite all their obscurities, are a people's book, is sharply and decisively asserted; and with it the right of the unlearned man to them, and his capacity to make full use of them for the main purpose for which they were given …'[17] The Bible, he concludes, is 'a message to every one of [God's] children.'[18]

Third, in what manner may an individual arrive at a clear understanding of Scripture? While Westminster insists that all manner of persons may attain to a 'sufficient understanding of Scripture,' they insist that this understanding is to be attained 'in a due use of the ordinary means.'[19] These means include the public reading and preaching of the Word, the administration of the sacraments, and prayer.[20] These means are not automatically effective. To understand the clear teaching of Scripture, a 'due use' of these means is necessary. A person must apply himself in order to attain to a clear understanding of Scripture. The clear teaching of Scripture, then, is not appropriated in unmediated fashion. In affirming the necessity of such means, Warfield rightly observes, Rome's insistence upon 'the need of an infallible interpreting Church [is] denied.'[21] Positively,

---

Scripture,' in *The Works of Benjamin B. Warfield* (10 vols.; New York: Oxford University, 1932), 6:233.

15. Grudem, 'The Perspicuity of Scripture,' *Them* 34/3 (2009): 295.

16. 'An unlearned man may be regarded as one who has not access to the Scriptures in the original languages, but only in a translation, who knows no language but his own, and whose mind has not been much cultivated by reading and study,' Cunningham, *Theological Lectures*, 506.

17. Warfield, 'The Doctrine of Holy Scripture,' in *Works*, 6:233.

18. ibid.

19. 'For we hold these means not only to be useful, but also necessary ordinarily,' Turretin, *Institutes*, 1:144 (=2.17.6).

20. Letham, *Westminster Assembly*, 143, citing WSC 88.

21. Warfield, 'The Doctrine of Holy Scripture,' in *Works*, 6:233. Note the concurring comments of Charles Hodge, 'What Protestants deny on this subject, is that Christ has

Westminster affirms 'that Scripture is to be interpreted, as other books are to be interpreted, in the ordinary processes and by means of the ordinary implements of exegesis.'[22] We have here 'the charter of a sound and rational system and method of exposition.'[23]

The definition of the clarity of Scripture proposed by Westminster is careful and nuanced. It is not so nuanced, however, that its primary point is lost. That which must be known, believed, and obeyed for salvation is clearly taught in the Scripture. This teaching is accessible to all sorts of hearers and readers, independently either of any authoritative mediation of the church, or of private or added revelations outside the Scripture. While one may not comprehensively understand the teaching of Scripture, he may, when properly using the ordinary means, arrive at an understanding of this teaching that is sufficient to answer one of the chief purposes for which the Bible was written, that is, to reveal to sinners the way of salvation.

The Biblical Evidence for the Clarity of Scripture

What is the biblical evidence for this understanding of the clarity of Scripture? We may explore the testimony of Scripture along three interrelated lines. First, there are express statements of Scripture that

---

appointed any officer, or class of officers, in his Church to those interpretation of the Scriptures the people are bound to submit as of final authority. What they affirm is that he has made it obligatory upon every man to search the Scriptures for himself, and determine on his own discretion what they require him to believe and to do,' *Systematic Theology* (3 vols.; New York: Charles Scribner's Sons, 1901), 1:184

Warfield also takes the 'ordinary means' to include 'that "inward illumination of the Spirit of God," which is declared to be necessary to the saving understanding of Scripture in section 6 ...,' 6:233. As such, 'all dependence on extraordinary revelations, the "inner light" of the mystical sectaries, and the like, is excluded,' ibid. To invoke the saving illumination of the Spirit in connection with the doctrine of perspicuity is not to deny the inherent or objective clarity of Scripture's teaching with respect to salvation. It is to say, however, that, absent this illumination, one may not obtain a *saving* understanding of this teaching, 'it is not denied ... that all men need the guidance of the Holy Spirit in order to right knowledge and true faith,' Hodge, *Systematic Theology*, 1:183-4; cf. Turretin, *Institutes*, 1:143 (=2.17.2).

22. Warfield, 'The Doctrine of Holy Scripture,' in *Works*, 6:234.

23. ibid. This insight carries a historical dimension as well. '[W]ith the advance of historical and critical knowledge, and by means of controversies, the Church as a community has made progress in the accurate interpretation of Scripture and in the full comprehension of the entire system of truth revealed therein,' A. A. Hodge, *The Confession of Faith* (1869; repr., Edinburgh: Banner of Truth, 1958), 40.

testify to the clarity of the Bible. In Deuteronomy 29:29, Moses addresses Israel at the command of God (see Deut. 29:1), 'the secret things belong to the LORD our God, but the things that are revealed belong to us and to our children forever, that we may do all the words of this law.' These words forbid Israel from attempting to penetrate into 'the secret things' of God, that is the hidden counsel and decree of God. Rather, as Calvin observes, we are 'to look up to God's secret providence with awe.'[24] Positively, God has provided 'the things that are revealed.' These belong to the whole covenant community, including the children of Israel. They are given for the purpose of 'do[ing] all the words of this law.' Whereas Israel is forbidden from delving into the decretal will of God, they are commanded to study, believe, and perform what God has revealed to them in the words of Scripture. This commandment assumes a basic or fundamental clarity to revelation. The words that God has spoken lie within the reach of the whole covenant community, even its children.[25]

In Deuteronomy 30:11-14, God, speaking through Moses, addresses the accessibility of the revelation that He has made to His covenant people.

> For this commandment that I command you today is not too hard for you, neither is it far off. It is not in heaven, that you should say, 'Who will ascend to heaven for us and bring it to us, that we may hear it and do it?' Neither is it beyond the sea, that you should say, 'Who will go over the sea for us and bring it to us, that we may hear it and do it?' But the word is very near you. It is in your mouth and in your heart, so that you can do it.

The commandment of which Moses speaks in verse 11 is that of which he has just spoken in the previous verse – 'when you obey the voice of the LORD your God, to keep his commandments and his statutes that are written in this Book of the Law, when you turn to the LORD your God with all your heart and with all your soul' (30:10). 'This commandment,'

---

24. John Calvin, *Institutes of the Christian Religion* (ed. John T. McNeill; trans. Ford L. Battles; 2 vols.; LCC; Philadelphia: Westminster, 1960), 1:213 (=1.17.2). Compare Calvin's words on the same text at *Institutes*, 2:925 (=3.21.3), 'it is not lawful for mortal men to intrude upon the secrets of God.'

25. On the particularly covenantal character of the Scripture's testimony to its perspicuity, see Barrett, *God's Word Alone*, 303-7. Note as well Turretin's observation that 'the form' of the Scriptures '(because they are to us in place of a testament, contract of a covenant or edict of a king, which ought to be perspicuous and not obscure)' requires the Bible to be perspicuous, *Institutes*, 1:145 (=2.17.11).

refers, then, to the totality of the words that God had spoken to Israel through Moses.[26] In verses 11-14, Moses accentuates the fundamental accessibility of this commandment. It is neither 'too hard' nor 'far off.' It is not out of the intellectual reach of Israel, nor must Israel cross land and sea to access it. God has come near to them and has revealed Himself to them in such a way that they will be able to understand His speech to them. So 'near' is the word to them that 'it is in your mouth and in your heart' (cf. Deut. 6:4-9). The purpose of the nearness and accessibility of the revealed word is practical, 'so that you can do it.' The word could not be applied if it could not first be understood. God has made His word comprehensible to His people so that they might act upon it in faith and obedience.

Significantly, Paul applies these very words of Moses to the gospel that he preached as an apostle of Christ in Romans 10:6-13.[27]

> But the righteousness based on faith says, 'Do not say in your heart, "Who will ascend into heaven?" (that is, to bring Christ down) or "Who will descend into the abyss"' (that is, to bring Christ up from the dead). But what does it say? 'The word is near you, in your mouth and in your heart (that is, the word of faith that we proclaim); because if you confess with your mouth that Jesus is Lord and believe in your heart that God raised him from the dead, you will be saved. For with the heart one believes and is justified, and with the mouth one confesses and is saved. For the Scripture says, "Everyone who believes in him will not be put to shame. For there is no distinction between Jew and Greek; the same Lord is Lord of all, bestowing his riches on all who call on him. For everyone who calls on the name of the Lord will be saved."'

Here, the apostle Paul stresses the fact that the gospel has come to human beings by revelation (cf. Rom. 1:16-17). The grace of justification is not something that one must ascend into heaven or plumb the depths to attain. Through the gospel, it has come near to human beings through the preaching of the gospel (see Rom. 10:14-15), and must be received through faith alone. Paul stresses that this nearness and accessibility is not for some but 'all,' that is, 'Jew and Greek,' or all kinds of people. The 'riches' of the gospel belong to any individual who 'call[s]' upon the

---

26. John D. Currid, *Deuteronomy* (Darlington, UK: Evangelical Press, 2008), 470.

27. Turretin, *Institutes*, 1:145 (=1.17.9). On the hermeneutical and exegetical questions posed by Paul's use of this particular passage of Scripture, see my *The End of Deuteronomy in the Epistles of Paul* (WUNT 2:221; Tübingen: Mohr Siebeck, 2006), 162-85.

Lord Jesus Christ. For one to call upon Christ, however, the revelation about Christ and His grace must be accessible and comprehensible to him. It is this attribute of the revelation that Paul emphasizes here, not in relation to a privileged segment of humanity, but to the full range of humanity, regardless of race or ethnicity.

Psalms 19 and 119 are songs in Israel's inspired hymnal that testify to the truth of the fundamental clarity of the words that God had spoken to them.

> The law of the LORD is perfect, reviving the soul;
> the testimony of the LORD is sure, making wise the simple (Ps. 19:7)
>
> Your word is a lamp to my feet and a light to my path (Ps. 119:105)
>
> The unfolding of your words gives light;
> it imparts understanding to the simple (Ps. 119:130)

The statements of Psalm 119 describe the 'word' or 'words' of God as that which sheds 'light.' That is to say, it has an illuminating character. The word of God carries light, a metaphor surely intended to convey its clarity or lucidity.[28] As a result of this character of the Word, the 'simple' gain understanding or, in the words of Psalm 19, the 'simple' are made 'wise.' This benefit of the law of God, then, is not restricted to the educated or privileged.[29] Furthermore, it is not merely the conveyance of information that is in view in these songs. To be sure, information is transmitted, but it is transmitted in such a way that one becomes 'wise.' The illuminating word of God provides practical guidance and insight to those who benefit from it. This point also surfaces in David's declaration that the word provides light to his 'feet' or 'path' (Ps. 119:105). In other words, the clarity of the Word is particularly related to the practical guidance that it affords to the people of God.[30]

This declaration of the clarity of the Word of God surfaces in the New Testament as well. Peter declares, 'we have something more sure,

---

28. 'The Scriptures are said to be luminous not only because they illuminate the intellect, but because they are in themselves luminous and naturally adapted to illuminate those who look upon them with the eyes of faith. Thus they are luminous formally and effectively because like the sun they emit rays and impress themselves upon the eyes of the beholder,' Turretin, *Institutes*, 1:144-5 (=2.17.8).

29. Allan Harman, *Psalms 1-72* (Fearn, UK: Christian Focus, 2011), 204.

30. J. A. Alexander, *The Psalms* (1864; repr., Grand Rapids: Kregel, 1991), 97.

the prophetic word, to which you will do well to pay attention as to a lamp shining in a dark place, until the day dawns and the morning star rises in your hearts' (2 Pet. 1:19). Peter here reaffirms the clarity of the word of God ('the prophetic word') in terms of its character as 'a lamp shining in a dark place.' In doing so, he testifies that it is no less clear to believers under the New Covenant than it was to its original recipients. The clarity of the word of God is intrinsic to the Word and, therefore, pertains to all generations of its readers. Peter, in fact, stresses that this Word remains clear until the consummation of all things at the return of Christ ('until the day dawns and the morning star rises in your hearts').

We have seen, then, a number of express statements in the Old Testament testifying to the clarity of the Word of God (Deut. 29:29, 30:11-14, Ps. 19:7, Ps. 119:105, 130). Significantly, some of these statements are picked up by the New Testament writers and applied to the church (Rom. 10:6-13, 2 Pet. 1:19). We have seen this clarity affirmed in two areas in particular. The first is the teaching of the Word of God with respect to how it is that the sinner may be saved (Rom. 10:6-13). The second is the teaching of the Word of God with respect to how it is that God expects human beings to live before Him and others (Deut. 30:11-14, Ps. 19:7, Ps. 119:105, 130). We have further seen that the word of God is clear to children and the 'simple' alike (Deut. 29:29; Ps. 19:7). It is not the peculiar province of the mature or the educated.

A second and related line of evidence for the clarity of Scripture is the express purpose statements found in the books of the Bible. We may begin with two purpose statements of the apostle John. First, John wrote his Gospel 'that [readers] may believe that Jesus is the Christ, the Son of God, and that by believing [they] may have life in his name' (John 20:30-1). This purpose is evangelistic in orientation.[31] If readers are to be in a position to believe in Jesus Christ, then the Fourth Gospel must reveal the claims of Christ and the nature and necessity of faith in Christ with sufficient clarity. Second, John wrote his First Epistle 'to you who believe in the name of the Son of God that you may know that you

---

31. On the debate whether John's Gospel is evangelistic in purpose or whether it is primarily intended to promote the discipleship of believers, see D. A. Carson, *The Gospel According to John* (PNTC; Grand Rapids: Eerdmans, 1991), 87-95. Carson aptly observes that to affirm one purpose as John's primary purpose need not preclude other, if subordinate, purposes to the Gospel.

have eternal life' (1 John 5:13). That is to say, John's burden in authoring this letter is that, through the letter's contents, his readers would come to a well-grounded assurance of the life that was theirs through faith in Christ. For the letter to accomplish this practical goal in the lives of its readers, it must clearly communicate the matters that John deemed necessary to that redemptive end.

What John affirms of his Gospel and Epistle, the apostle Paul affirms of the Old Testament writings. Paul does so in no fewer than three of his letters. He tells the Corinthians, 'now these things happened to them as an example, but they were written down for our instruction, on whom the end of the ages has come' (1 Cor. 10:11). Paul here refers to a number of instances from Israel's history in the wilderness (see 1 Cor. 10:1-10). These matters, he insists, were committed to writing to 'instruct' and to serve as an 'example' for the church, the eschatological people of God ('on whom the end of the ages has come'). Given these practical goals set by their Divine Author, the text of Scripture must have a clarity of meaning adequate to those goals. This clarity, Paul insists, extends even to the New Covenant people of God. As such, it is intrinsic to the biblical text.

Paul tells the Roman Christians, 'For whatever was written in former days was written for our instruction, that through endurance and through the encouragement of the Scriptures we might have hope' (Rom. 15:4). In similar fashion to his counsel to the Corinthians, the apostle identifies a particular set of practical outcomes ('endurance' and 'encouragement' leading to 'hope') that is tied to the teaching of the Old Testament Scripture, comprehensively considered ('whatever was written'). Significantly, God has intended this 'instruction' not only for its original recipients ('in former days') but also for the church ('for our instruction'). If the Old Testament Scripture is to be adequate to these practical ends in the lives of God's people, it must clearly convey its teaching to those people.

A third passage appears in Paul's last extant letter, 2 Timothy, 'All Scripture is breathed out by God and profitable for teaching, for reproof, for correction, and for training in righteousness, that the man of God may be competent, equipped for every good work' (3:16-17). Here, Paul not only testifies to what the Old Testament Scripture is ('breathed out by God'), but also what it does. He specifies four purposes that are not only intellectual but also moral and practical in nature ('teaching,' 'reproof,' 'correction,' 'training in righteousness'). The goal of these purposes is that 'the man of God may be competent, equipped for every good work.' There is, then, a sufficiency to the Scripture in rendering the 'man of God' ready to glorify God in all that God has required of him both to believe and do. Even if the 'man of God' refers to the minister or elder and not to non-officers in the church, Paul's words nevertheless apply to all Christians.[32] Paul charges ministers and elders to set a moral example for God's people to emulate (1 Tim. 4:12; Titus 2:7; cf. 1 Pet. 5:3). If Paul is saying here that Scripture equips the minister or elder to be 'competent, equipped for every good work,' he intends that goal to serve the wider goal of the godliness of the congregation whom the minister or elder serves.

We have surveyed several passages that speak to the stated purposes of various parts of the Bible. These purposes are practical in nature and pertain to the congregation generally. In order for the Scriptures in question to meet these purposes, they must communicate their contents in sufficiently clear a manner as to be understood by the whole of their readership in the church. After all, if these Scriptures were unclear to their readers, how could those readers fulfill the biblical authors' aspirations to apply the Scriptures' contents in their own lives? The stated practical purposes of the Scriptures requires that the text of Scripture be clear in relation to those purposes.

We should also note that, while Paul's statements to the Corinthians, Romans, and to Timothy concern the Old Testament, they do not only concern the Old Testament. We may recall from a previous chapter how the New Testament authors understood the canon to be expanding in their day. Alongside the Law and the Prophets were being added those writings that the apostles of Jesus Christ were imposing upon the New Covenant church. As such, the writings of the New Testament are the Word of God and, therefore, possess the same attributes that the writings of the Old Testament possess. If the Old Testament writings, in general, are perspicuous, then the New Testament writings are no less perspicuous.

A third line of evidence testifying to the clarity of Scripture concerns the audiences of the biblical writings. Neither the Law nor the Prophets

---

32. See Chapter 5, note 31.

nor the New Testament writers addressed themselves to segments of the people of God to the exclusion of other segments of the people of God. Their audience was the entirety of the congregation of God's people. Bavinck summarizes the evidence well.

> The torah (*sic*) has been given by God to all of Israel, and Moses conveys all the words of the Lord to all the people ... The prophets, whether by speech or in writing, address themselves to all the people (Isa. 1:10f.; 5:3.; 9:1; 40:1f.; Jer. 2:4; 4:1; 10:1; Ezek. 3:1). Jesus speaks freely and frankly to all the crowds (Matt. 5:1; 13:1, 2; 26:55; etc.), and the apostles wrote to all those called to be saints (Rom. 1:7; 1 Cor. 1:2; 2 Cor. 1:1; etc.) and they themselves took responsibility for the circulation of their letters (Col. 4:16). The written word is recommended to the scrutiny of all (John 5:39; Acts 17:11) ... There is nowhere any indication of withholding Scripture from laypersons. The believers are themselves of age and able to judge (1 Cor. 2:15; 10:15; 1 John 2:20; 1 Pet. 2:9). To them are entrusted the oracles of God (Rom. 3:2).[33]

Across redemptive history, from the Law through the Prophets to the writings of the New Testament, God's spokespersons have always addressed the people of God at large.

The New Testament testifies that, within congregations, no segment of the congregation was omitted much less neglected when the letters of our New Testament were written to them. Paul sometimes addresses the children of the congregation (Eph. 6:1-3; Col. 3:20). Both Paul and Peter address slaves, some of whom may have been educated and some of whom may not have been educated (Eph. 6:5-8, Col. 3:22-5, 1 Tim. 6:1-2, 1 Pet. 2:18-25). Both Paul and James testify to the presence of socially inferior and poor persons among their readership (1 Cor. 1:28; James 2:5-6). The circumstances of at least some of these persons may well have prevented them from acquiring a formal education. Finally, Paul testifies to the fact that, within the church of Corinth, 'not many of [them] were wise according to worldly standards' (1 Cor. 1:26), that is, they lacked the credentials of learning and education that merited respect in the ancient world. Significantly, nowhere do any of the New Testament writers judge the youth, social status, or level of education of

---

33. Herman Bavinck, *Reformed Dogmatics* (ed. John Bolt; trans. John Vriend; 4 vols.; Grand Rapids: Eerdmans, 2003), 1:477-8.

some of their readers to exempt them from the obligation to believe and obey the matters committed to the New Testament writings. Neither do any of the New Testament writings evidence a need for younger or less educated readers to depend upon more mature or more formally educated readers in order to ascertain the meaning of the text of Scripture. This state of affairs testifies to the fact that the New Testament understands itself to be sufficiently clear, for all its intended audiences, with respect to the purposes for which it was written.

One remarkable instance that testifies to the clarity of both the Old Testament writings and the public teaching of the apostle Paul is found in Paul's ministry in Berea.[34] Luke testifies that when Paul came to Berea to preach the gospel, the Jews in the local synagogue, being 'more noble than those in Thessalonica,' 'received the word with all eagerness, examining the Scriptures daily to see if these things were so' (Acts 17:11). These Jews' comparison of the teaching of Paul with the teaching of Scripture points to the fact that both teachings were sufficiently clear to general audiences. Non-specialist members of the synagogue were capable of understanding the teachings of each, and of comparing them to each other to determine if they agreed.

We have seen, then, that the Scriptures of both Testaments are sufficiently clear to all types of readers with respect to what God requires them to understand, believe, and practice for their salvation and for His glory. The text of Scripture, in these matters, is not obscure. Neither is the text of Scripture beyond the reach of some Christians in such a way that they are dependent upon others to tell them what Scripture teaches about salvation. This state of affairs should be no surprise to us. As Barrett correctly notes, 'the clarity of God's Word reflects God himself.'[35] If God Himself is Light, then we expect His Word fully to reflect His character.

Some Qualifications About the Clarity of Scripture

Without withdrawing what we have affirmed about the clarity of Scripture above, it is important to introduce some qualifications about the doctrine. These qualifications serve to prevent misunderstanding about

---

34. Foster, 'Making Clear,' 178.
35. Barrett, *God's Word Alone*, 310.

what Protestants have and have not affirmed regarding the Bible's clarity. We may point to at least five such qualifications.

First, as we have seen, the clarity of Scripture does not touch upon the totality of the contents of its teaching. It concerns those matters that God requires us to know, believe, and obey for salvation. It is precisely in such areas that we have registered Scripture's affirmations of its clarity (Deut. 30:11-14, Rom. 10:6-13, Ps. 19:7).[36] One reason that it is necessary to register this qualification is that there are matters within Scripture that the Scripture itself acknowledges to be intrinsically difficult.[37] Peter testifies to 'some things' in Paul's letters 'that are hard to understand' (2 Pet. 3:16). There are historical, exegetical, and theological difficulties within the teaching of Scripture that have taxed some of the greatest minds in the church's history.[38] This state of affairs should neither surprise nor disturb us. If the works of God in creation, providence, and redemption bear the imprint of His inscrutable and unsearchable wisdom, His words surely, then, will also (see Job 38-41; Rom. 11:33-6).[39] To register these observations, however, in no way compromises or mitigates the basic clarity of Scripture with respect to those matters in reference to which Scripture has said that it is clear. It is, rather, to recognize the richness and depths of the Bible that God has given us.

Second, the clarity of Scripture does not mean that readers will comprehensively understand even the Bible's clear teachings. Neither does it mean that they cannot and will not mature in their understanding of those teachings. There are a significant number of passages commanding

---

36. And yet the doctrine, following Scripture, does not commit us to identify in which particular passage or passages that these matters are revealed with clarity. The Scripture is content to affirm, in the words of the Westminster Confession of Faith, that these matters are 'clearly propounded, and opened in some place of Scripture or other...' (WCF 1.7).

37. For a classical and instructive answer to the question 'why God would have many obscurities in the Scriptures,' see the nine reasons proposed by William Whitaker, *Disputations on Holy Scripture* (1588; repr., Morgan, PA: Soli Deo Gloria, 2000), 365-6.

38. While definitive resolution may not be available for all of those questions, the interpretative labors of generations of Christians has not been without fruit. They demonstrate that, for all the difficulties presented by particular problems in the text of Scripture, no difficulty requires the reader to conclude that there are contradictions or errors within Scripture.

39. Grudem, 'Perspicuity,' 295.

readers to meditate upon the Bible's teachings, 'This Book of the Law shall not depart from your mouth, but you shall <u>meditate</u> upon it day and night, so that you may be careful to do according to all that is written in it ...' (Josh. 1:8); 'I will <u>meditate</u> on your precepts and fix my eyes on your ways' (Ps. 119:15); 'his delight is in the law of the LORD, and on his law he <u>meditates</u> day and night' (Ps. 1:2). After impressing on the Philippian believers the necessity of and motive for perseverance in Christian living, Paul commends a corresponding pattern of thinking, 'let those of us who are mature think this way, and if in anything you think otherwise, God will reveal that to you also. Only let us hold true to what we have attained' (Phil. 3:15-16). In other words, believers must strive to attain to and to preserve mental maturity with respect to the gospel.

Even as there is 'an *initial* level of understanding available to first readers of the Bible and available to some extent to children,' so also 'there are *deeper* levels of understanding that come with further reading and growth in Christian maturity,' as the writer to the Hebrews indicates, 'About this we have much to say, and it is hard to explain, since you have become dull of hearing. For though by this time you ought to be teachers, you need someone to teach you again the basic principles of the oracles of God. You need milk, not solid food, for everyone who lives on milk is unskilled in the word of righteousness, since he is a child. But solid food is for the mature, for those who have their powers of discernment trained by constant practice to distinguish good from evil (Heb. 5:11-14).'[40] The doctrine of perspicuity, then, does not guarantee that all teachings of Scripture are immediately or automatically within the grasp of the new or immature believer.

Third, the clarity of Scripture does not mean that believers have no need of the helps that God supplies to the church in order to understand and to apply Scripture. One way in which all believers are expected to grow or mature in their understanding of Scripture's teaching is through the means of the preaching of the Word of God. The New Testament emphasizes that preaching in the church is the work of those officers whom Christ has gifted and called to that end. Paul emphasizes these points to the Ephesians. After stressing that 'the apostles, the

---

40. ibid., 300. Grudem concludes his observation with a citation of Hebrews 5:14.

prophets, the evangelists, the pastors and teachers' are gifts of the risen and ascended Christ to the church, Paul describes the purpose and result of the work of these gifts in the church (Eph. 4:11). They are 'to equip the saints for the work of ministry, for building up the body of Christ, until we all attain to the unity of the faith and of the knowledge of the Son of God, to mature manhood, to the measure of the stature of the fullness of Christ' (Eph. 4:12-13). Paul stresses that as believers receive the truth from the public ministry of the Word, they in turn 'speak the truth in love' and thus 'grow up in every way into him who is the head, into Christ' (Eph. 4:15). In this way, 'the body grow(s) so that it builds itself up in love' (Eph. 4:16). For the church to mature and to become more like Christ, believers must receive the preached Word and apply that Word in their own lives and in the lives of the church at large.[41]

There is a distinct but related way in which ministers and elders serve the church. Elders together minister the Word of God to the church when they gather in representative councils in order to bring the Word of God to bear on doctrinal difficulties, doubts, and disagreements within the church.[42] One example of such a council is found in the meeting of the apostles and elders in Acts 15.[43] The council has been convened to address a matter that has disturbed the church in Jerusalem and Antioch, and likely other places as well.[44] This matter concerns the gospel of grace. Specifically, the question has arisen whether circumcision is a condition that may be imposed upon Gentiles for their salvation (Acts 15:5). After rational and biblical deliberation, the council univocally repudiates the doctrine of the necessity of circumcision (Acts 15:24, cf. 15:19). They furthermore commend Barnabas and Paul and, by implication, the doctrine of salvation that they proclaimed to the churches. It is not

---

41. And, of course, for ministers to be effective in their work, they must commit themselves to the work of meditating upon the Scripture so that they may correctly interpret and apply it to the people of God (Ezra 7:10, 2 Tim. 2:15), Grudem, 'Perspicuity,' 295.

42. I am grateful to Foster, 'Making Clear,' 179, and Grudem, 'Perspicuity,' 294, for calling my attention to this example.

43. For a discussion of the Council in relation to the polity and life of the church, see my *How Jesus Runs the Church* (Phillipsburg, NJ: P&R, 2011), 126-35.

44. The letter that the council drafts and sends out to the churches reaches the churches of Southern Asia Minor (Acts 16:4-5). This fact suggests that these churches also had been troubled by the issues that had surfaced in the council's deliberations.

that the church was ever in doubt about the terms of salvation. The spread of error within the church, however, had occasioned confusion and troubled the life and witness of the church. It was necessary for the church, through her representative elders, to deliberate upon the teaching of the Old Testament (Acts 15:15-17) and the work of God through the apostles (Acts 15:6-14). Through that deliberation, these elders arrived at a biblical statement of the truth that lent to the church further clarity about the gospel that it embraced and held out to the nations. The clarity of the gospel, therefore, did not and does not militate against the necessity of elders gathering in representative councils in order to address errors that arise in the church in relation to the gospel.

There is another and related matter that the council takes up. Once the terms of salvation have been decisively addressed, the council provides a separate set of instructions for Gentile Christians, '[we] should write to them to abstain from the things polluted by idols, and from sexual immorality, and from what has been strangled, and from blood. For from ancient generations Moses has had in every city those who proclaim him, for he is read every Sabbath in the synagogues' (Acts 15:20-1, cf. 15:28-9). Commentators debate the origin and significance of these four commands.[45] The likeliest solution is that these four commands have in common a deep-seated importance to first century Jewish people. Jews took great offense when they observed Gentiles engaged in these kinds of behavior. The church is counseling Gentile Christians to abstain from practices or behaviors that would give offense to Jews, whether those Jews are within the church or outside it (cf. 1 Cor. 9:19-23).[46] Gentiles are not told to observe these four commands for their justification. Nor are these four commands equally pertinent for a believer's sanctification in any and every age. They are a particular application of the law of love to the situation in which the first century church, comprised of

---

45. See my *The Acts of the Apostles* (Darlington, UK: Evangelical Press, 2015), 362-4; Craig S. Keener, *Acts: An Exegetical Commentary* (4 vols.; Grand Rapids: Baker, 2012-15), 3:2260-77.

46. The principle at work in the council's decision, then, is the application of the law of love to a particular set of circumstances. They are not saying, for example, that 'sexual immorality' is not a moral command (because it is grouped with three non-inherently moral behaviors, namely, partaking of what has been 'sacrificed to idols,' of 'blood' and of 'what has been strangled'). Nor are they pleading for a moral equivalence among these four proscribed activities.

Jews and Gentiles, and set in proximity to active and observant Jewish communities, finds itself.

Significantly, this latter matter that the council addresses, resolves, and sends down to the churches is not one at which the church arrived spontaneously. Her ministers and elders, meeting in a representative, regional assembly adopted these four recommendations after reflection and deliberation. The clarity of the Scripture is not such that assemblies of elders do not need to meet, from time to time, to assist the church in the application of Scripture to the church's particular circumstances.

Fourth, while the elders of the church, severally and jointly, assist the church instrumentally to understand and apply the meaning of Scripture, there is a distinct and immediate work of the Holy Spirit in the lives of believers in relation to the understanding of Scripture.[47] To state the matter another way, the clarity of Scripture does not preclude a reader's need for the Spirit to come to a saving understanding of Scripture. Psalm 119 has several petitions that ask for just such divine assistance in understanding the text of Scripture.[48]

> Open my eyes, that I may behold wondrous things out of your law (Ps. 119:18).
>
> Make me understand the way of your precepts, and I will meditate on your wondrous works (Ps. 119:27).
>
> Give me understanding, that I may keep your law and observe it with my whole heart (Ps. 119:34).
>
> Your hands have made and fashioned me; give me understanding that I may learn your commandments (Ps. 119:73).

These petitions all ask God to provide direct help to the petitioner in order to understand and to observe the Word of God. As Turretin observes, these petitions 'mean that man cannot himself without the aid of grace understand the Scriptures,' but they do 'not thence prove their obscurity …'[49] The reason is because the Spirit's work of illumination

---

47. We addressed the work of the Spirit in relation to the believer's understanding of Scripture in Chapter 4.

48. These passages appear at Grudem, 'Perspicuity,' 298.

49. Turretin, *Institutes*, 1:146 (=2.17.14). Turretin makes this statement in reference to his comments on Luke 24:45. Compare Turretin's earlier remarks, 'Hence if David and

does not render an obscure text suddenly clear.⁵⁰ It is a work of God upon the mind of an individual to enable that person to understand the teaching of Scripture with acceptance, approval, and delight. As such, this work of the Spirit may relate both to passages of Scripture that are clear and those that are obscure.⁵¹ It is entirely possible that one may notionally grasp the teaching of a clear passage without arriving at a saving understanding of that passage. Only the illumination of the Spirit is able to bring a person to that saving understanding.

Fifth, and relatedly, what are we to make of statements in the Bible that speak of Scripture's teaching as hidden or obscured to certain persons? Paul states, for instance, 'And even if our gospel is veiled, it is veiled only to those who are perishing' (2 Cor. 4:3). Does that militate against the perspicuity of Scripture? When we examine such statements, we find that they do not speak directly to the biblical text or meaning of a given passage. They address, rather, the subjective spiritual state of an individual who encounters that passage. Paul goes on to say, in the next verse, that 'the god of this world has blinded the minds of the unbelievers, to keep them from seeing the light of the gospel of the glory of Christ, who is the image of God' (2 Cor. 4:4). Paul stresses that the darkness or obscurity is subjective. It is a condition of the mind of the unbeliever, exacerbated by the influence of Satan, the 'god of this world.' Further, what is obscured to the unbeliever is not the propositional meaning of the text but the 'light of the gospel of the glory of Christ.' Unbelievers are unable to discern the spiritual glory of the Christ revealed in the pages of Scripture. The solution to this state of affairs, Paul continues, is the sovereign grace of illumination, 'For God, who said, "Let light shine out of darkness," has shone in our

---

other believers desire their eyes to be opened that they may see wonderful things out of the law, it does not therefore prove the obscurity of the Scriptures, but only the ignorance of men. The question here is not Do men need the light of the Holy Spirit in order to understand the Scriptures? (which we willingly grant); but Are the Scriptures obscure to a believing and illuminated man?,' *Institutes*, 1:145 (=2.17.13).

50. For this reason, a Christian reader of Scripture should not expect the Spirit immediately to overcome the deficits that may be remedied through careful study, meditation, and interaction with Christians knowledgeable about the meaning of the text of Scripture.

51. For further reflection on the relationship between perspicuity and illumination, see now the discussion at John S. Feinberg, *Light in a Dark Place: The Doctrine of Scripture* (Wheaton, IL: Crossway, 2018), 657-60.

hearts to give the light of the knowledge of the glory of God in the face of Jesus Christ' (2 Cor. 4:6). This solution does not remedy some alleged defect in the text of Scripture. The defect, rather, lies wholly in the 'heart' of the unbeliever.[52] In a work of new creation, God shines saving light into the spiritual darkness of the unbeliever. It is then and only then that this person will be able to perceive, with approbation and delight, the 'knowledge of the glory of God in the face of Jesus Christ.'[53] To the degree that blame for darkness and obscurity is to be placed, it is to be placed solely and squarely upon the mind and heart of the unbelieving reader of Scripture. The Scripture's testimony to Jesus Christ is objectively lucid.

In summary, the testimony of the Bible to itself is that that which is to be known, believed, and obeyed for salvation is clearly taught in some portion of Scripture or another. The five qualifications that we have reviewed in no way mitigate that testimony. They underscore the fact that the Bible is not uniformly clear, and contains certain passages that are difficult to understand. These qualifications remind us that reading and understanding the Scripture requires the diligent use of the minds that our Creator has given us. God has, furthermore, also appointed that we study and apply the Scripture not in isolation from other believers, but in the context of the church, and particularly in the context of the ministry of the Word. And they help us to see our need for the illuminating work of the Holy Spirit, without whose gracious operations we will be unable to perceive the glory of Christ from the pages of the Bible.

A Challenge to the Clarity of Scripture: The Roman Catholic Church

The Roman Catholic Church denies the doctrine of the perspicuity of Scripture. The effect of this denial with respect to what one must know, believe, and obey for salvation is twofold. The first is to emphasize the necessity of Tradition along with Scripture as coordinate authorities in the life of the church and of the Christian.[54] We explored and responded

---

52. In a similar statement, Paul says that the 'minds' of many Israelites of old were 'hardened,' 2 Corinthians 3:14.
53. See further, here, the helpful comments of Barrett, *God's Word Alone*, 317-18.
54. As observed by Turretin, *Institutes*, 1:143 (=2.17.1).

to Rome's claims about Tradition in our previous chapter on the sufficiency of Scripture. The second is to press the need for an infallible interpreter of the Scripture.[55] Rome has identified this interpreter with the Church, particularly the magisterium of the Church. Since Vatican I, Rome has officially identified the papacy as this infallible interpreter. In the remainder of this chapter, we will explore what Rome's claims are with respect to the Church's authority in interpreting Scripture. We will then offer a response to this teaching and a reaffirmation of the Protestant doctrine of Scripture's clarity.

The *Catechism of the Catholic Church* insists that the '"Sacred deposit" of the faith (the *depositum fidei*)' has been 'entrusted ... to the whole of the Church.'[56] But while the Church as a whole possesses this deposit, the interpretation of this deposit belongs to the Church's magisterium.

> 'The task of giving an authentic interpretation of the word of God, whether in its written form or in the form of Tradition, has been entrusted to the living, teaching office of the Church alone. Its authority in this matter is exercised in the name of Jesus Christ.' This means that the task of interpretation has been entrusted to the bishops in communion with the successor of Peter, the Bishop of Rome.[57]

The *Catechism* insists that the magisterium 'is not superior to the Word of God, but is its servant. It teaches only what has been handed on to it ... All that it proposes for belief as being divinely revealed is drawn from this single deposit of faith.'[58] For this reason, 'the faithful receive with docility the teachings and directives that their pastors give them in different forms.'[59]

In one of its early sessions (1546), the Council of Trent responded to the Reformers' affirmation of the clarity of Scripture.[60]

---

55. Bavinck summarizes Rome's view along the following lines, 'Holy Scripture necessarily has to be interpreted. Such interpretation cannot be provided by Scripture itself; Scripture cannot be its own interpreter,' *Reformed Dogmatics*, 1:475.

56. *Catechism of the Catholic Church With Modifications from the Editio Typica* (New York: Doubleday, 1995), §84 (=*CCC*).

57. *CCC* §85. The quoted material is from *Dei Verbum* §10.

58. *CCC* §86.

59. *CCC* §87.

60. A point that Luther vigorously pressed in his dispute with Erasmus, *The Bondage of the Will* (1525), which was published in response to Erasmus's *The Freedom of the Will*

Furthermore, to restrain irresponsible minds, it (='the same holy council') decrees that no one, relying on his own prudence, may twist Holy Scripture in matters of faith and practice that pertain to the building up of Christian doctrine, according to his own mind, contrary to the meaning that Holy Mother the Church has held and holds – since it belongs to her to judge the true meaning and interpretation of Holy Scripture (*cuius est iudicare de vero sensu et interpretatione Scripturarum sanctarum*) – and that no one may dare to interpret the Scripture in a way contrary to the unanimous consensus of the Fathers (*unanimem consensum Patrum*), even if such interpretations are not intended for publication.[61]

Trent, then, denied the Reformers' insistence that individuals could interpret the meaning of Scripture 'in matters of faith and practice' in a way that was 'contrary to the meaning that Holy Mother the Church has held and holds.' The proffered reason for the supremacy of ecclesiastical interpretation of Scripture is twofold. First, it is the right or prerogative of the Church to 'judge the true meaning and interpretation of Holy Scripture.' Second, Trent implies that the Church's interpretation of Scripture is in line with 'the unanimous consensus of the Fathers.' The implication of this statement is the Reformers have departed from this interpretative consensus to which Rome has been faithful and of which she is the privileged guardian.

Significantly, Trent did not specify precisely where or by what specific channels the Church exercised this right of judgment to interpret the Scripture. In its Third Session in April, 1870, the First Vatican Council reaffirmed this teaching with little, if any, alteration.[62]

(1524), on which see the discussions at Thompson, *A Clear and Present Word*, 143-50, and Pettegrew, 'Perspicuity,' 221-3. See also Ulrich Zwingli, *Of The Clarity and Certainty or Power of the Word of God* (1522; trans. and ed. Geoffrey W. Bromiley; Philadelphia: Westminster, 1953).

61. 'Decree on the Vulgate Edition of the Bible and on the Manner of Interpreting Scripture,' Heinrich Denzinger, *Compendium of Creeds, Definitions, and Declarations on Matters of Faith and Morals* (eds. Peter Hünermann, Robert Fastiggi, and Anne Englund Nash; 43d ed.; San Francisco: Ignatius, 2012), §1507.

62. 'Since, however, what the holy council of Trent has laid down concerning the interpretation of the divine Scripture for the good purpose of restraining undisciplined minds has been explained by certain men in a distorted manner, We renew the same decree (*idem decretum*) and declare this to be its sense: In matters of faith and morals, affecting the building up of Christian doctrine, that is to be held as the true sense of Holy Scripture (*pro vero sensu sacrae Scripturae*) which Holy Mother the Church has held and holds, to whom it belongs to judge of the true sense and interpretation of Holy Scriptures

It was in its Fourth Session in July, 1870 that the Council affirmed the infallibility of the Pope. After defining the office, warrant, and scope of the papacy and its authority, the Council addressed the Pope's infallible magisterial authority (*infallibili magisterio*).[63] Much of the opening of the chapter addressing the Pope's teaching authority is an effort to show that the Council's teaching is consonant with prior councils of the church.[64] The Council then defines and delimits papal infallibility. The doctrine does not teach that 'Peter' and his 'successors' may 'disclose a new doctrine by [the Holy Spirit's] revelation, but rather that, with [the Holy Spirit's] assistance, they might reverently guard and faithfully explain the revelation or deposit of faith that was handed down through the apostles.'[65] The purpose of the Spirit's conferral of 'this charism of truth and of never-failing faith' upon the papacy was 'for the salvation of all,' to preserve the church from error and to instruct them in the truth of God.[66]

Although this is a truth that the Council believes has been embraced by the church from the beginning, they reaffirm it in light of the fact that 'not a few are found who disparage its authority.'[67] They therefore teach the following as 'a dogma revealed by God:'

> That the Roman pontiff, when he speaks *ex cathedra*, that is, when acting in the office of shepherd and teacher of all Christians, he defines, by virtue of his supreme apostolic authority, a doctrine concerning faith or morals (*doctrinam de fide vel moribus*) to be held by the universal Church, possess through the divine assistance promised to him in blessed Peter the infalliblity (*infallibilitate*) with which the Divine Redeemer willed his Church to be endowed in defining the doctrine concerning faith or

---

(*cuius est iudicare de vero sensu et interpretatione Scripturarum sanctarum*). Therefore no one is allowed to interpret the same Sacred Scripture contrary to this sense or contrary to the unanimous consent of the Fathers (*unanimem consensum Patrum*),' Dei Filius §2, Denzinger, *Compendium*, §3007.

63. The full chapter heading is *De Romani Pontificis infallibili magisterio*, Denzinger, *Compendium*, 614.

64. *Pastor aeternus*, Denzinger, *Compendium*, §§3065-8.

65. *Pastor aeternus,* Denzinger, *Compendium*, §3070. This paragraph goes on to argue that the church has universally recognized, throughout her history, the fact that 'this See of St. Peter always remains untainted by any error ...,' ibid.

66. ibid., §3071.

67. ibid., §3072.

morals; and that such definitions of the Roman pontiff are therefore irreformable of themselves (*ex sese ... irreformabiles*), not because of the consent of the church.

But if anyone – God forbid – presumes to contradict this Our definition, let Him be anathema (*anathema sit*).[68]

Vatican I, then, affirmed papal infallibility with a few important qualifications. The pontiff's infallibility only applied to his utterances *ex cathedra*, which is said to be 'when, acting in the office of shepherd and teacher of all Christians, he defines, by virtue of his supreme apostolic authority, a doctrine concerning faith or morals to be held by the universal Church.'[69] The scope of papal infallibility, as the citation in the preceding sentence shows, concerns 'faith or morals.' Furthermore, the Pope is not said to have the power of delivering 'a new doctrine by his revelation,' but of 'guard[ing]' and 'explain[ing] the revelation' transmitted by the apostles.[70]

One final document to consider in assessing Rome's doctrine of the magisterial infallibility of the church is the Second Vatican Council's Dogmatic Constitution on divine revelation, *Dei Verbum*. After affirming that 'sacred tradition and Sacred Scripture form one sacred deposit of the Word of God, committed to the church,' the Council addresses the 'teaching authority of the church:'

> But the task of authentically interpreting the Word of God, whether written or handed on (*verbum Dei scriptum vel traditum*), has been entrusted exclusively to the living teaching office of the Church (*soli vivo Ecclesiae Magisterio*), whose authority is exercised in the name of Jesus Christ. This teaching office is not above the Word of God, but serves it, teaching only what has been handed on, listening to it devoutly, guarding it scrupulously, and explaining it faithfully in accord with a divine commission and with the help of the Holy Spirit. It draws from this one deposit of faith (*ex hoc uno fidei deposito*) everything that it presents for belief as divinely revealed.[71]

---

68. ibid., §§3074-5.
69. ibid., §3074.
70. ibid., §3070.
71. *Dei Verbum* §10, Denzinger, *Compendium*, §4214. The final paragraph of this section goes on to say that 'sacred tradition, Sacred Scripture, and the teaching authority of the Church ... are so linked and joined together that one cannot stand without the others and that all together and each in its own way under the action of the one Holy Spirit contribute effectively to the salvation of souls,' ibid.

The Second Vatican Council affirms what Councils since Trent had affirmed, the 'living teaching office of the Church.' Like Trent and Vatican I, Vatican II understands the church's magisterium to concern the interpretation of existing revelation. The magisterium is not the channel much less the source of new revelation. Vatican II, reflecting a similar concern expressed by Vatican I, stresses that this office is 'not above the Word of God' but 'serves' it. That 'Word of God,' of course, includes Scripture but is not limited to Scripture. It includes 'sacred tradition.' Vatican II does not expressly invoke papal infalliblity in its discussion of the magisterium of the church. This silence is not disagreement. We are, rather, to understand this formulation to stand on the foundation laid by the First Vatican Council.

Although Trent, Vatican I, and Vatican II do not explicitly make the connection between the doctrine of perspicuity and the church's magisterial authority, Roman Catholic theologians have done so.[72] The Church's magisterium was virtually necessitated by what was alleged to be the pervasive and inherent obscurity of Scripture's teaching, even on the most fundamental matters of faith and morals. Christians required the church to tell them what their Bibles meant.

The Reformation's affirmations of the clarity of Scripture struck a foundational blow to the edifice of the doctrine of the church's magisterial authority. If the Scripture were clear in the manner for which the Reformers pled, then Rome could not justify its magisterial authority on the grounds of the Bible's obscurity. In light of our reflections on the perspicuity of Scripture, we may close this chapter with some critical reflections on the Roman Catholic Doctrine of magisterial authority.

By way of preface, we should note that Protestants have vigorously contested Rome's claims that its doctrine of magisterial authority finds its origins in the early centuries of the church's history.[73] Already in the sixteenth century, William Whitaker was demonstrating that the

---

72. As, for example, Bellarmine, who denied that Scripture was 'sufficient, without any further interpretation, to determine controversies of the faith.' *De verbo Dei*, III.i, as cited at Richard A. Muller, *Post Reformation Reformed Dogmatics: The Rise and Development of Reformed Orthodoxy, ca. 1520 to ca. 1725* (4 vols.; Grand Rapids: Baker, 2003), 2:329. Compare the remarks of Turretin, *Institutes*, 1:147 (=2.17.21).

73. See the brief, but incisive, reflections of Cunningham, *Theological Lectures*, 516-24.

church fathers had taught the clarity of Scripture.[74] He also showed from the church's history that 'pious bishops never assembled to define a point themselves by their own authority, but by that of scripture.'[75] In the seventeenth century, Turretin showed that some Roman Catholic theologians even denied the infallibility of the church.[76] At the close of the nineteenth century, George Salmon subjected Rome's historical claims to extended and vigorous critical examination.[77] While we will not review those claims or the Protestant response here, it is enough to register that Rome's historical claims have undergone withering criticism.

What, then, are the primary objections to Rome's doctrine of magisterial infallibility? First, we should register a fundamental lack of resolution in Rome's doctrine. Where precisely is the magisterium to be found?[78] The *Catechism of the Catholic Church* declares, 'the task of interpretation has been entrusted to the bishops in communion with the successor of Peter, the Bishop of Rome.'[79] Does interpretation rest ultimately with the bishops or with the papacy? [80] This question is one that Vatican I's affirmation of papal infallibility accentuated but did not resolve. Furthermore, taking the Pope as an example, which are the *ex cathedra* pronouncements of the pontiff? What Salmon observed a century ago remains true today, that there are 'a number of arbitrary rules which have been invented for distinguishing when the pope speaks *ex cathedra* – rules as to which advocates of Infallibility have been able to come to no agreement.'[81] If Rome's doctrine is unable to locate with precision either the source of infallible utterances or the criterion by

---

74. Whitaker, *Disputations*, 393-401.

75. ibid., 434. For the argument that substantiates this claim, see *Disputations*, 434-44.

76. Turretin, *Institutes*, 3:71 (=18.11.4).

77. George Salmon, *The Infallibility of the Church* (4th ed.; London: John Murray, 1914).

78. This was a question already posed and pressed by Turretin, *Institutes*, 3.78-80 (=L.18.11.19-23).

79. *CCC* §85.

80. See here the extended discussion of this question beginning at Salmon, *Infallibility*, 262. Salmon addresses the 'different theories of the Church's infallibility which have been held in the Roman church,' specifically the conciliar theory of infallibility and the papal theory of infallibility, ibid.

81. Salmon, *Infallibility*, 435. See the discussion that follows, *Infallibility*, 435-8.

which infallible utterances are to be observed, then the doctrine is of little practical value, and lacks theological merit.

A second objection to Rome's doctrine of magisterial infallibility is empirical in nature. The Roman Catholic Church has positively erred in her official pronouncements, not least concerning the teaching of the Bible.[82] We surveyed one of those errors at some length in the last chapter, namely, Rome's insistence that Tradition stands alongside the text of Scripture as revelation from God. In this chapter, we are arguing for an additional error, namely, that the *ex cathedra* utterances of the Roman pontiff are infallible. We may add others – Rome's doctrine of justification, of baptismal regeneration, of transubstantiation, of penance, of purgatory, of the veneration of Mary and the saints, to name just a few of the most important ones.[83] Lending gravity to the teaching of some of the errors is that they are sometimes accompanied with anathemas against the corresponding Protestant doctrines.[84]

A third objection is hermeneutical in nature. Even if one grants that the church, in some fashion, infallibly interprets a Bible that is dark and obscure, the church's infallible interpretations must still be interpreted. The allegedly infallible utterances of the Roman Catholic Church are not self-interpreting. They must, in turn, be interpreted, and they must be interpreted by *fallible* interpreters.[85] The only conceivable remedy to this circumstance is an infinite succession of infallible interpreters, for which Rome does not argue. What Rome argues, then, is not as promising as it may seem at first glance. It is, rather, 'sufficient for [the church] to have an infallible rule of faith and practice in the Scriptures, which as long as she observes, she will not wander from the right track.'[86]

A fourth objection concerns the scope of what is alleged to be magisterial infallibility. The First Vatican Council stresses, we have seen, that the doctrine does not mean that the papacy will 'disclose a new doctrine by [the Holy Spirit's] revelation, but rather that, with

---

82. ibid., 225-61.

83. See the discussion at Hodge, *Systematic Theology*, 1:147-9.

84. As, for example, 'Decree on Justification' and 'Canons on Justification,' Denzinger, *Compendium*, §§1520-83.

85. Robert L. Dabney, 'The Bible Its Own Witness,' in *Discussions: Evangelical and Theological, Volume 1* (1891; repr., Edinburgh: Banner of Truth, 1967), 116-17.

86. Turretin, *Institutes*, 3:83 (=18.11.32).

[the Holy Spirit's] assistance, they might reverently guard and faithfully explain the revelation or deposit of faith that was handed down through the apostles.'[87] But at this juncture it is crucial to recall that, for Rome, revelation encompasses both the written Word of God, the Bible, and unwritten Tradition that has allegedly been transmitted by the apostles to the church. We have argued in a previous chapter that the traditions that Rome understands to be apostolic revelation are, from the standpoint of the teaching of Scripture, not revelation at all. Seen in this light, then, papal infallibility does more than simply interpret existing revelation. Papal infallibility is engineered to legislate matters of faith and morals for the church.

A fifth objection to the doctrine of papal infallibility is that it fundamentally misconceives the teaching authority of the church. It is important to stress that there is a legitimate teaching authority that belongs to the church, one that Protestants in the Reformation tradition have affirmed as biblical.[88] But this teaching authority, like all church power, is ministerial and declarative in nature. That is to say, the church, as a servant of God, declares to human beings the revealed will of God in the Scripture.[89] The church has no power to bind the conscience, to legislate matters of faith or practice, or in any way to add or detract from the teaching of Scripture. God alone is the lawgiver and judge of humanity (James 4:12), and every human being must 'stand or fall … before his own master' (Rom. 14:4). Even in relation to a contested matter in the church in Corinth, Paul could tell the Corinthians, 'judge for yourselves …' (1 Cor. 11:13, cf. 10:15).

---

87. *Pastor aeternus,* Denzinger, *Compendium,* §3070. This paragraph goes on to argue that the church has universally recognized, throughout her history, the fact that 'this See of St. Peter always remains untainted by any error …,' ibid.

88. That is, the dogmatic power of the church, on which see Turretin, *Institutes,* 3:281-5 (=L.18.30) and, more briefly, Bavinck, *Reformed Dogmatics,* 1:480-1.

89. One such example of this power is found in Jesus' words in John 20:23, 'If you forgive the sins of anyone, they are forgiven; if you withhold forgiveness from anyone, it is withheld.' Jesus is not granting authority or power to apostles or ministers to forgive sins in their own name. What He grants them is the right to make declarations in particular cases. If an individual professes that he believes in Christ according to the gospel, then a minister may declare to that individual that, through faith in Christ, his sins are forgiven. If an individual remains impenitent in the face of the gospel's proclamation, then a minister may declare to that individual that he does not yet have forgiveness. See D. A. Carson, *The Gospel According to John,* 655-6.

In a later letter to the church in Corinth, Paul insisted that he and his ministerial colleagues did not 'lord it over your faith' (2 Cor. 1:24).[90] On the contrary, Paul commended himself 'to everyone's conscience in the sight of God' (2 Cor. 4:2).

The authority for which Rome pleads, however, is magisterial and, effectively, legislative. It interposes the church between God and the conscience of the individual, and renders the individual dependent upon the church and its teaching. In other words, if the individual is to be saved, then he must be dependent upon the church in order to know those matters he must know and do for salvation. But this teaching not only elevates the church beyond its biblically appointed sphere, but it also derogates from the perfection and sufficiency of the prophetic office of Christ. Furthermore, the individual is deprived of the rights of conscience.[91] He must give an undue deference to the authority of the church, and is prevented from the right of private judgment that the Bible affirms he has.[92]

There is, furthermore, no indication that Christ has promised infallibility to the church, much less to the officers of the church. To be sure, God promises true believers that they will persevere in the truth, such that they will be 'free' from the fatal influence of 'fundamental error.'[93] But this promise of perseverance to elect persons is different from a promise of infallibility to the officers of the visible church. If we should understand the promise of the Holy Spirit in John 16:13 ('When the Spirit of truth comes, he will guide you into all the truth ...') to have application to believers generally, then the Spirit's 'influence ... is not to be understood absolutely and simply as to all truth universally, but with a limitation and relatively with respect to the subject matter (i.e., truth necessary to salvation ...).'[94]

---

90. Contrast the posture of the Pharisees towards Jews in the first century, Matthew 23:8-10.

91. Note Bavinck's observation that the church may lawfully 'bind a person in conscience only to the degree that person recognizes it as divine and infallible,' *Reformed Dogmatics*, 1:481.

92. One practical effect of this teaching, borne out in the experience of the Roman Catholic Church, has been the discouragement of congregants reading the Bible for themselves.

93. Turretin, *Institutes*, 3:72 (=18.21.7).

94. ibid., 3:82 (=18.11.28). Turretin cites 1 Corinthians 1:5 and Acts 20:27 as parallel passages in support of this reading of John 16:13. Compare the similar comments of Hodge, *Systematic Theology*, 1:142.

To be sure, Christ has purposed to 'preserve [the church] from all fundamental error that she may not err totally,' but this preservation from fatal apostasy does not mean that 'he has determined to remove all error from her.'[95] Indeed, to affirm the church's infallibility is to be guilty of an eschatological over-realization. The church, in her present militant state, is imperfect. She is not yet the eschatological bride 'without spot or wrinkle or any such thing ... without blemish' (Eph. 5:27). Because the church's present holiness is imperfect, the church's understanding, embrace, and observance of the truth is correspondingly imperfect. As Charles Hodge has noted, 'as the Church has gone through the world bathed in tears and blood, so has she gone soiled with sin and error. It is just as manifest that she has never been infallible, as that she has never been perfectly holy. Christ no more promised the one than the other.'[96]

Engaging the Roman Catholic doctrine of magisterial infallibility may give the appearance, in the twenty-first century, of beating the proverbial dead horse, of fruitlessly rehearsing a centuries-old dispute. In reality, nothing can be farther from the truth. Reflecting upon this doctrine helps students of the Bible to arrive at clarity about some of the most important aspects of the biblical doctrine of Scripture. How do the individual, the church, and Christ relate to one another in the act of reading, interpreting, and applying the Scripture? What are the rights of the individual in relation to the church? Given the fact that Christ has tasked and gifted the church with teaching the Word of God, what precisely does that work entail and not entail? What, in other words, is the church's authority when it comes to her teaching responsibilities? What promises has Christ made and not made to the church with respect to preservation from error and the maintenance of the truth of God? How are we to understand the church's task of teaching Scripture in light of her present state of eschatological imperfection? The questions posed, then, by the Roman Catholic Church's claims to infallibility touch on a host of matters central to the individual's calling to take up the Bible to read and to apply it, and to the church's calling to teach the nations to observe all that Christ has commanded us (Matt. 28:20).

---

95. ibid., 3:81 (=18.11.25).
96. Hodge, *Systematic Theology*, 1:143.

Karl Barth and Scripture

Introduction

Historians have often observed that the twentieth century began in 1914, when the first shots of World War I were fired. One might argue that the theology of the twentieth century began in 1922, when the second edition of Karl Barth's *Commentary on the Epistle to the Romans* was published. A contemporary reader dubbed this work a bombshell that had fallen on the playground of the theologians.[1] As the First World War shaped the political landscape of the West for much of the twentieth century, so the theology of Karl Barth shaped the theological landscape of the West for much of the twentieth century.

Matching Barth's influence are the overwhelming, at times insurmountable, challenges that his writings present. There is, in the first place, the sheer scale of his output.[2] Barth published over five hundred works, and his *magnum opus*, the 'unfinished' *Church Dogmatics*, is 'over seven thousand pages' long and six million words.[3] Barth himself

---

1. The reader was Karl Adam, a Roman Catholic theologian. For a brief and accessible account of the context and content of Barth's *Römerbrief*, see Bruce L. McCormack, 'The Unheard Message of Karl Barth,' *Word and World* 14/1 (1994): 59-62.

2. '[Karl Barth] has thrown great boulders of books in the path of anyone chasing after him,' J. C. O'Neill, *The Bible's Authority: A Portrait Gallery of Thinkers from Lessing to Bultmann* (Edinburgh: T&T Clark, 1991), 266.

3. J. I. Packer, 'Encountering Present-Day Views of Scripture,' in *Honouring the Word of God: Collected Shorter Writings of J.I. Packer, Volume 3* (Carlisle: Paternoster, 1999), 12. The word count appears at R. Michael Allen, *Karl Barth's Church Dogmatics: An Introduction and Reader* (London: T&T Clark, 2012), 9. Kimlyn J. Bender notes that the

playfully likened the *Church Dogmatics* to 'Moby Dick, the white whale.'[4] Barth's treatment in the *Church Dogmatics* of the Doctrine of the Word of God alone runs in excess of fourteen hundred pages. Such scale intimidates student and scholar alike. For this reason, a number of digests and summaries of Barth's theology have made their way into print.[5] And yet, compounding the frustration of those who labor to understand the theologian, Barth himself decreed that only one who had 'read me completely' was competent to render judgment on Barth's theology.[6]

A second challenge is the sheer complexity of Barth's prose. In Packer's words, 'his teaching is beclouded with mists of ambiguity.'[7] As Rhodes explains, 'Barth's manner of writing [is characterized by] his seemingly interminable dialectical spirals, exhaustively working through

---

prefaces and indices of the *Church Dogmatics* swell this number to over nine thousand pages, *Reading Karl Barth for the Church: A Guide and Companion* (Grand Rapids: Baker, 2019), 2.

4. Karl Barth, 'Foreword to the English Edition,' in Otto Weber, *Karl Barth's Church Dogmatics: An Introductory Report on Volumes I:1 to III:4* (trans. Arthur C. Cochrane; Philadelphia: Westminster, 1953), 7.

5. For an entrée to the *Church Dogmatics* (=*CD*), see particularly Allen, *Karl Barth's Church Dogmatics*. An older and partial summary is that of Otto Weber, *Karl Barth's Church Dogmatics*. For a broader selection of Barth's writings, see now Keith L. Johnson, *The Essential Karl Barth: A Reader and Commentary* (Grand Rapids: Baker, 2019). Barth's own *Evangelical Theology: An Introduction* (New York: Holt, Rinehart and Winston, 1963), consisting of lectures that he delivered in the United States in 1962, capture many of the emphases and themes that characterize his theology at large. Compare also his *Dogmatics in Outline* (New York: Harper & Brothers, 1959), a brief course of lectures delivered in Bonn in 1946. Barth's *Göttingen Dogmatics* constitute a briefer, complete, and earlier statement of his theology. They are the published form of his theological lectures in Göttingen, 1924–5. Unfortunately, they have only been partly translated into English, *The Göttingen Dogmatics: Instruction in the Christian Religion, Volume One* (ed. Hannelotte Reifen; trans. Geoffrey W. Bromiley; Grand Rapids: Eerdmans, 1991).

One useful and accessible summary of the *CD* is Geoffrey W. Bromiley's *An Introduction to the Theology of Karl Barth* (Grand Rapids: Eerdmans, 1979). For a comparable but more extensive and recent treatment of Volume I of the *CD*, 'The Doctrine of the Word of God,' see now Bender, *Reading Karl Barth*. Ben Rhodes offers an admirably concise survey of the contents of *CD* I/2 at 'Barth's Theology of Scripture in Dogmatic Perspective,' in *Freedom Under the Word: Karl Barth's Theological Exegesis* (eds. Ben Rhodes and Martin Westerholm; Grand Rapids: Baker, 2019), 35-49.

6. Karl Barth, 'Foreword to the German Edition,' in Weber, *Karl Barth's Church Dogmatics*, 9, referenced at O'Neill, *The Bible's Authority*, 266.

7. Packer, 'Encountering Present-Day Views of Scripture,' 13.

a theological point only to pivot to consider a different facet of the doctrine from yet another perspective.'[8] The complexity of Barth's prose only tempts the reader, already awed by the sheer breadth of Barth's literary output, to deeper despair.

A third challenge to reading and understanding Barth's theology is the question whether his theology changed or developed over the course of his literary career. Barth's massive theological output, from his *Göttingen Dogmatics* (1924–5) to his *Church Dogmatics* (1935–67) stretches over four decades.[9] May we speak of an 'early Barth' and a 'later Barth'? Or, may we more modestly posit maturation and development with respect to certain themes or emphases of Barth's theology? With respect to Barth's Doctrine of the Word of God (*CD* I/1 and I/2), published in German in 1932 and 1938, some scholars have suggested that later volumes of the *Church Dogmatics* refined or qualified aspects of these earlier volumes.[10] But, notwithstanding these refinements and qualifications, it appears that Barth's doctrine of Scripture remained fundamentally stable over the course of his theological career.[11]

A fourth and final challenge concerns the diversity of interpretation of Barth's writings, both within and outside of evangelicalism. One

---

8. Rhodes, 'Barth's Theology of Scripture,' 35. Rhodes proceeds to defend Barth's manner of writing as purposeful in character, 'This prolix style is meant to indicate the infinite depths of God's perfect triune being as Father, Son, and Holy Spirit and the endless quest for finite and fallen humans to witness to the riches of God's self-revelation, ultimately disclosed in the person of Jesus Christ, who is the object of Scripture's witness, spoken of in the proclamation of the church, as critically tested in the activity of dogmatics,' 'Barth's Theology of Scripture,' 36.

9. On the complexities of the production of the *CD*, see the survey of David L. Mueller, *Karl Barth: Makers of the Modern Theological Mind* (Waco: Word, 1972), 42-8.

10. Katherine Sonderegger argues that Barth provides salutary nuance at *CD* IV/1 to his earlier treatment of the question of faith and history in *CD* I/2, 'The Doctrine of Inspiration and Reliability of Scripture,' in *The Word Is Truth: Barth on Scripture* (ed. George Hunsinger; Grand Rapids: Eerdmans, 2012), 23-6. Other scholars have argued that Barth softens, although does not eliminate, his strident rejection of natural theology in *CD* I/1 and I/2 at *CD* IV/3, Gabriel Fackre, 'Revelation,' in *Karl Barth and Evangelical Theology: Convergences and Divergences* (ed. Sung Wook Chung; Grand Rapids: Baker, 2006), 5-8; and Rhodes, 'Barth's Theology of Scripture in Dogmatic Perspective,' 48n.52. Martin Westerholm discerns a 'new christological emphasis in [the] theology of inspiration' of *CD* IV/3.1, 'Barth's Theology of Scripture in Developmental Perspective,' in *Freedom Under the Word*, 29.

11. For which, see now Westerholm, 'Barth's Theology of Scripture,' in *Freedom Under the Word*, 9-33, esp. 11.

of the first attempts to introduce Barth sympathetically to theological conservatives in the United States was Holmes Rolston, *A Conservative Looks to Barth and Brunner* (1933).[12] Since then, some evangelicals have offered severely critical responses to Barth, while others have been far more appreciative in their assessment.[13] Complicating such assessments is the risk entailed in isolating or extracting certain statements of Barth from the remainder of his writings. Barth, as we shall see, speaks in unvarnished terms of the Bible's fallibility, and of errors alleged to be contained in the books of the Bible. But, scholars have noted, Barth's massive exegetical handling of texts of Scripture in the *Church Dogmatics* consistently treats the biblical texts as though they contain no error.[14] As Clark Pinnock summarizes the matter, 'while preaching the errancy of the Bible, Barth practices its inerrancy.'[15] To draw such an observation is neither to dismiss nor to excuse Barth's statements about the alleged errancy of the Bible. It is, however, to recognize that criticisms directed against Barth's doctrine of Scripture must take account of the totality of the evidence pertinent to that doctrine.

---

12. Holmes Rolston, *A Conservative Looks to Barth and Brunner: An Interpretation of Barthian Theology* (Nashville: Cokesbury, 1933). Rolston dedicated the book to Thomas Carey Johnson, who was Robert L. Dabney's successor at Union Theological Seminary in Richmond, VA. The book's introduction was authored by Ernest Trice Thompson, who would emerge as one of the leading Modernists in the mid-century PC(US).

13. See the recent survey and taxonomy at Kevin J. Vanhoozer, 'A Person of the Book? Barth on Biblical Authority and Interpretation,' in ed. Sung Wook Chung, *Karl Barth and Evangelical Theology*, 27-44. Compare the briefer survey at Michael S. Horton, 'A Stony Jar: The Legacy of Karl Barth for Evangelical Theology,' in *Engaging with Barth: Contemporary Evangelical Critiques* (eds. David Gibson and Daniel Strange; New York: T&T Clark, 2008), 347-8.

14. 'From beginning to end, Barth's *Church Dogmatics* is nothing other than a sustained meditation on the texts of Holy Scripture,' Francis Watson, 'The Bible,' in *The Cambridge Companion to Karl Barth* (ed. John Webster; Cambridge: Cambridge U. Press, 2000), 57, cited at Vanhoozer, 'A Person of the Book?,' 45. Vanhoozer observes that there are 'approximately two thousand extended exegetical sections' in the *CD*, ibid. Note Rhodes's assessment of Barth's exegesis in the *CD*, '[I]t is a virtue of Barth's actual exegetical practice that he does not so shake himself loose from the biblical text. I have nowhere found Barth to identify any detail of Scripture as erroneous in order to dismiss or ignore a difficult passage ... Yet there is nothing in his unitary notion of inspiration that warrants such close attention to these texts, even with an elevated dose of actualism,' 'Barth's Theology of Scripture in Dogmatic Perspective,' 48.

15. Clark Pinnock, 'Three Views of the Bible in Contemporary Theology,' in *Biblical Authority*, (ed. Jack Rogers; Waco: Word, 1977), 57, cited at Packer, 'Encountering Present-Day Views of Scripture,' 14.

Any treatment of the doctrine of Scripture in Karl Barth's theology requires delimitation. In this chapter, we will explore Barth's understanding of the Bible, primarily as it finds articulation in *CD* I/1 and I/2. Before looking at his statements about the Bible, however, we must set his understanding of Scripture within the context of the emphases and concerns that characterize Barth's theological project more broadly. After we have explored his doctrine of Scripture, set in this theological context, we will offer some critical reflections in light of the testimony of the Scripture to itself.

Context

The context for understanding Barth's doctrine of Scripture is two-fold. First, one must come to terms with Barth's settled and wide-ranging epistemological commitments. Second, one must grapple with Barth's ontology, that is, how he conceives being and, in particular, the being of God.

Epistemology

Barth's biographers frequently observe that his theological beginnings were in the nineteenth-century liberalism of his upbringing.[16] By the time that the first edition of his *Römerbrief* had been published in 1918, it was evident that Barth had begun the revolt against liberalism for which he would come to be known. In reality, Barth broke with more than German liberalism. His criticisms of liberalism extended to the classical orthodoxy of the Protestant Reformation. Barth did not call for a return to the old orthodoxy. Instead, Barth advanced a project that was neither liberal nor orthodox. Barth's theology, which came to be termed 'neo-orthodoxy' or 'neo-Reformed,' shared elements in common with each, even as it refused to be identified with either.[17]

The hallmark of Barth's project was his revolt against the anthropocentrism of nineteenth-century liberalism.[18] So far as Barth was

---

16. On which, see the brief sketch at O'Neill, 'Barth,' 269-70. See also, Mark Galli, *Karl Barth: An Introductory Biography for Evangelicals* (Grand Rapids: Eerdmans, 2017), 1-38.

17. On the meaning, propriety, and problematics of the terms, see Gregory G. Bolich, *Karl Barth & Evangelicalism* (Downers Grove, IL: InterVarsity, 1980), 59.

18. Barth's lengthiest analysis of nineteenth century theology is his *Protestant Theology in the Nineteenth Century* (1952; trans. Brian Cozens and Bowden; London: SCM, 2002).

concerned, theological anthropocentrism embraces any 'attempt to establish a pathway to a knowledge of God which by-passes God's self-revelation in Jesus Christ.'[19] This approach to the knowledge of God begins with man as subject and proceeds thence to God as object. As a result, Barth contended, God is objectified and placed under man's control. God becomes, in effect, a projection of human beings.

> Evangelical theology [in the nineteenth century] almost all along the line, certainly in all its representative forms and tendencies, had become *religionistic, anthropocentric,* and in this sense *humanistic*. What I mean to say is that an external and internal disposition and emotion of man, namely his piety – which might well be Christian piety – had become its object of study and its theme ... For this theology, to think about God meant to think in a scarcely veiled fashion about man, more exactly about the religious, the Christian religious man. To speak about God meant to speak in an exalted tone but once again and more than ever about this man – his revelations and wonders, his faith and works.[20]

As Barth's point has been pithily summarized, 'you cannot speak about God by shouting MAN loudly.'[21]

Barth's epistemological criticism extended beyond the liberalism of the nineteenth century. The Roman Catholic Church's doctrine of authoritative tradition, for Barth, was comparable to that of Protestant liberalism.[22] Barth's strident criticisms of natural theology stem from his conviction that natural theology was simply an attempt of human beings to know God in their own way and from their own resources, 'Natural theology is the doctrine of a union of man with God existing outside God's revelation in Jesus Christ. It works out the knowledge of God that is possible and real on the basis of this independent union with

---

Compare also his 'Evangelical Theology in the 19th Century,' in Karl Barth, *God, Grace and Gospel*, (SJTOP 8; trans. James Strathearn McNab; Edinburgh: Oliver and Boyd, 1959), 53-74.

19. Mueller, *Karl Barth*, 53.

20. Barth, *The Humanity of God* (trans. T. Weiser and J. N. Thomas; Richmond: John Knox, 1960), 39-40, as cited at Mueller, *Karl Barth*, 52, emphasis original.

21. As cited at David Wells, *God in the Wasteland* (Grand Rapids: Eerdmans, 1994), 108, referencing *CD* II/1, 339.

22. Barth, *CD* I/1, 295-6. Compare Barth's remarks at *CD* I/2, 688 and *Karl Barth's Table Talk* (SJTOP 10; ed. John D. Godsey; Edinburgh: Oliver and Boyd, 1963), 43.

God, and its consequences for the whole relationship of God, world and man.'[23] As such, natural theology is stillborn. It cannot know much less receive in faith the self-revelation of God.[24]

Barth also accused the post-Reformation Lutheran and Reformed orthodoxies of anthropocentrism. The post-Reformation churches allegedly corrupted and vitiated Luther and Calvin's affirmation that the Bible is the Word of God. They did so by formulating the doctrine of the inspiration of the Bible.[25] In doing so, the seventeenth century church 'transformed ... the statement that the Bible is the Word of God ... from a statement about the free grace of God into a statement about the nature of the Bible as exposed to human inquiry brought under human control. The Bible as the Word of God surreptitiously became a part of natural knowledge of God, i.e., of that knowledge of God which man can have without the free grace of God, by his own power, and with direct insight and assurance.'[26] The God-centeredness of the Reformers lapsed into the man-centeredness of their descendants.[27]

Against the theology of the nineteenth century, Roman Catholicism, natural theology, and the theology of the Post-Reformation Protestant churches, Barth argued that the knowledge of God is altogether objective.[28] As Trevor Hart summarizes Barth at this point, theology must 'locat[e] its final source in a God whose reality and activity utterly

---

23. Barth, *CD* II/1, 168, as cited at Mueller, *Karl Barth*, 88.

24. For a concise discussion of Barth's strictures against natural theology, see George Hunsinger, *How To Read Karl Barth: The Shape of His Theology* (Oxford: Oxford University, 1991), 96-9. For recent evangelical analyses of Barth's critique of natural theology, see Peter Jensen, *The Revelation of God* (Downers Grove, IL: InterVarsity, 2002), 103-5, and Michael Horton, *Christian Faith: A Systematic Theology for Pilgrims on the Way* (Grand Rapids: Zondervan, 2011), 146-9.

25. Barth argues that the alleged development of the doctrine of inspiration in the seventeenth century was paralleled by 'orthodoxy becoming laxer and laxer in relation to natural theology...,' *CD* I/2, 522.

26. Barth, *CD* I/2, 522-3. Barth goes on to claim that the Enlightenment's approach to the Bible not only followed but was in line with seventeenth-century Protestant Orthodoxy's understanding of the Bible, *CD* I/2, 533.

27. Barth, *CD* I/2, 293, 294. '[Theology] fell prey to the absolutism with which the man of that period [the 17th and 18th centuries] made himself the centre and measure and goal of all things ... Originally and properly the sin was one of unbelief ... This later theology thought that it should reckon seriously with man from another standpoint than that of the kingdom and ownership of Christ,' ibid.

28. Hunsinger, *How To Read Karl Barth*, 35-9.

transcends the sphere of the human.'²⁹ Specifically, theology must take as its starting point the self-revelation of God who makes Himself known alone in Jesus Christ, '*God* reveals Himself. He reveals Himself *through Himself.* He reveals *Himself*... This subject, God, the Revealer, is identical with His act in revelation, and also identical with its effect.'³⁰ This state of affairs, as Bromiley notes, means that 'the Triune God [is] the controlling factor in revelation.'³¹ Thus, 'the fact of God's Word does not receive its dignity and validity in any respect or even to the slightest degree from a presupposition that we bring to it. *Its truth for us, like its truth in itself, is grounded absolutely in itself.*'³²

Furthermore, Barth argues, even human beings' reception of divine revelation must be attributed to God Himself, '[Revelation] means that the object becomes the subject. It is not our own work if we receive God's address, if we know God in faith. It is God's work in us.'³³ And this work of reception is the work of God *alone*, 'It is not merely that man lacks something which he ought to be or to have or to be capable of in relation to God. He lacks everything.'³⁴ Thus, as Trevor Hart summarizes Barth's view, God must 'draw us into the circle of his own self-knowing' if we are to come at all to the knowledge of God.³⁵

Ontology

In order to understand adequately Barth's doctrine of revelation, one must understand the ontology that lies back of that doctrine. George Hunsinger has termed this aspect of Barth's thought 'actualism.'

> At the most general level [actualism] means that [Barth] thinks primarily in terms of events and relationships rather than monadic or self-contained substances. So pervasive is the motif that Barth's whole theology might well

---

29. Trevor Hart, 'Revelation,' in *The Cambridge Companion to Karl Barth* (ed. John Webster; Cambridge: Cambridge University, 2000), 41.
30. Barth, *CD* I/1, 296 [2d], emphasis original.
31. Bromiley, *Introduction to the Theology of Karl Barth*, 14.
32. Barth, *CD* I/1, 196 [2d], emphasis mine. Barth advances this formulation against both Thomist and Cartesian conceptions of knowing God, ibid.
33. Barth, *GD* 1:61, as cited at Trevor Hart, 'The Word, the Words and the Witness: Proclamation as Divine and Human Reality in the Theology of Karl Barth,' *TynBul* 46.1 (1995): 83.
34. Barth, *CD* I/2, 257.
35. Hart, 'Revelation,' 42.

be described as a theology of active relations. God and humanity are both defined in fundamentally actualistic terms.³⁶

Barth's actualism lies at the root of his conception of God.

> [W]hen Barth wants to describe the living God in a technical way, he says that God's being is always a being in act. Negatively, this means that God's being cannot be described apart from the basic act in which God lives ... Positively, the description means that God lives in a set of active relations. The being of God in act is a being in love and freedom. God, who does not need us to be the living God, is perfectly complete without us. For God is alive in the active relations of love and freedom which constitute God's being in and for itself. These are the active relations of God's trinitarian self-differentiation.³⁷

Therefore, Hunsinger concludes, 'our relationship to God must be understood in active, historical terms, and it must be a relationship given to us strictly from the outside ... Our relationship to God is ... an event. It is not possessed once and for all, but is continually established anew by the ongoing activity of grace.'³⁸ Actualism, then, informs not only the way in which we understand the being of God and the being of humans, but also the relationships that obtain among God and humans.

Divine revelation to humanity must therefore be understood along these lines. Divine revelation is an event, happening at a particular moment in history.³⁹ Since the creature cannot, of himself, access knowledge about God, God must exercise His sovereignty in revealing Himself to a particular person. Since the creature has no capacity within himself to receive the knowledge so revealed, the Holy Spirit must effect the decisive encounter between the Creator and the creature in the event of revelation.⁴⁰ We are not, therefore, at liberty to understand revelation in terms of a bounded set of propositions.⁴¹ To do so, for Barth, risks

---

36. Hunsinger, *How To Read Karl Barth*, 30.

37. ibid.

38. ibid., 31.

39. Gabriel Fackre, 'Revelation,' in *Karl Barth and Evangelical Theology*, 16-17; Hunsinger, *How To Read Karl Barth*, 67-8.

40. Bruce L. McCormack, *Orthodox and Modern: Studies in the Theology of Karl Barth* (Grand Rapids: Baker, 2008), 110-11.

41. Barth pronounced 'propositions given and sealed once for all with divine authority in both wording and meaning' to be 'theologically impossible,' *CD* I/1, 15, as cited at Hunsinger, *How To Read Karl Barth*, 69.

depersonalizing the entirety of revelation, denying the sovereignty of the self-revealing God, and placing the creature in a position of control over his Creator.

This dynamic approach to revelation informed the manner in which Barth understood God and human beings to interrelate. In an early lecture to fellow ministers, Barth posed a dilemma, 'As ministers we ought to speak of God. We are human, however, and so cannot speak of God.'[42] While many in the church have opted for speaking of God in the way of 'dogmatism' or 'self-criticism,' Barth proposes 'dialectic.'[43] The dialectician must be content to know 'that this Center [i.e., God] cannot be apprehended or beheld, and he will not if he can help it allow himself to be drawn into giving direct information about it, knowing that *all* such information, whether it be positive or negative is *not* really information, but always *either* dogma or self-criticism. On this narrow ridge of rock one can only walk ... There remains only to keep walking ... looking *from one side to the other*, from positive to negative and from negative to positive. Our task is to interpret the Yes and the No and the No by the Yes without delaying more than a moment in either a fixed Yes *or* a fixed No.'[44] Dialectic, in the hands of Barth, permitted him to 'speak in different places, and sometimes even in the same places, in ways which entail contradiction and self-referential incoherence.'[45] The virtue of this mode of discourse for Barth is that it required any person's speech about God to 'point beyond itself to something that it can neither create nor control, that can only happen contingently.'[46]

Later in his life, Barth made a modest retreat from the term dialectic as a descriptor of the mode of humanity's knowing God.[47]

---

42. Barth, *The Word of God and the Word of Man* (trans. Douglas H orton; n.p.: Pilgrim Press, 1928), 186.

43. ibid., 206. For a taxonomy of 'dialectic' in the *Göttingen Dogmatics,* see Daniel L. Migliore, 'Karl Barth's First Lectures in Dogmatics: *Instruction in the Christian Religion,*' in *The Göttingen Dogmatics,* xxviii-xxix.

44. ibid., 206-7, emphasis original. In the material that immediately follows, Barth offers examples of dialectical speech about God.

45. Hart, 'The Word, the Words and the Witness,' 85.

46. Christoph Schwöbel, 'Theology' in *The Cambridge Companion to Karl Barth,* 23.

47. 'I myself was the originator of this unfortunate term ... I have long ago lost interest in the word, however,' Barth, *Table Talk,* 24.

Even so, scholars of Barth recognize its persistence beyond the *Göttingen Dogmatics* into the *Church Dogmatics*. Barth did not so much shed the term as 'demote' it.[48] Alongside and even overshadowing dialecticism was 'analogical predication,' which describes 'the event of correspondence between human word and divine truth, the analogy of truth.'[49] Analogy permitted Barth to 'undertake a rational explication of the content of faith in the form of positive or nondialectical statements.'[50] Even so, as Migliore observes, any speech about God, for Barth, 'must ... be dynamic, self-critical, always open to reform, in continuous movement.'[51] This dimension of speaking about God is required by the fact that God remains hidden, even in His sovereign self-revelation.[52]

The Doctrine of the Word of God in Karl Barth

One of the oft-noted difficulties in Karl Barth is his persistent use of conventional theological language in unconventional ways. That is to say, he uses the terminology of Reformed theology, but does not often define that terminology in the way that classical Reformed orthodoxy has defined that terminology. When Barth speaks, therefore, of 'revelation' and the 'Word of God,' one must take care not to import assumptions about those terms into his use of them. It is critical to allow Barth himself to define these terms. We will now review what Barth understands 'revelation' and the 'Word of God' to be, drawing largely from Part I of the *Church Dogmatics*.

'Revelation'

For Barth, axiomatic to revelation is the inseparability of revelation from God. God's self-revelation is identical with God: 'God's Word is God Himself in His revelation ... *God* reveals Himself. He reveals Himself *through Himself.* He reveals *Himself* ... [T]his subject, God, the Revealer,

---

48. The term is Hunsinger's, *How To Read Karl Barth*, 69.

49. ibid. Migliore argues that at least 'three forms of analogy' are present already in the *Göttingen Dogmatics*, 'Karl Barth's First Lectures,' xxxii. On the difference between Barth's doctrine of analogy and the *analogia entis* of Thomas Aquinas, see Colin Brown, *Karl Barth and the Christian Message* (Chicago: InterVarsity, 1967), 51-4.

50. Hunsinger, *How To Read Karl Barth*, 69.

51. Migliore, 'Karl Barth's First Lectures,' xxxiii, citing *GD* 1.266.

52. ibid., xxviii.

is identical with His act in revelation and also identical with its effect.'[53] Even so, God is dialectically hidden in His revelation and 'human beings are quite incapable of knowing or speaking about God' because of His 'utter transcenden[ce].'[54]

Because revelation is inseparable from God, it is thereby personal.

> God's Word means that God speaks. This implies ... its personal quality. God's Word is not a thing to be described nor a term to be defined. It is neither a matter nor an idea. It is not 'a truth,' not even the very highest truth. It is *the* truth as it is God's speaking person, *Dei loquentis persona*.[55]

And because revelation is personal, it is beyond human control.

> The personal character of God's Word means, not its deverbalising, but the posing of an absolute barrier against reducing its wording to a human system or using its wording to establish and construct a human system. It would not be God's faithfulness but His unfaithfulness to us if He allowed us to use His Word in this way. This would mean His allowing us to gain control over His Word, to fit it in with our own designs, and thus to shut up ourselves against Him to our own ruin.[56]

Precisely because revelation is personal, and because the recipients of revelation are themselves persons, revelation transpires in event or encounter, 'the Word of God must be understood as an event in and to the reality of man.'[57] The fact that human beings receive revelation in no way means that they have 'a predisposition towards this Word, a possibility of knowledge regarding it that is intrinsically and independently native to him.' That would mean that 'God's Word is no longer grace.'[58] This encounter is 'a revelation which man cannot achieve himself, the revelation of something new which can only be told him.'[59]

---

53. *CD* I/1, 296 [2d]. J. K. S. Reid summarizes Barth's concern, 'God's Word is not to be distinguished from God's act, but rather is always God's act,' *The Authority of Scripture: A Study of Reformation and Post-Reformation Understanding of the Bible* (London: Methuen & Co., 1957), 207.

54. Hart, 'The Word, the Words and the Witness,' 96, referencing *CD* I/2, 750.

55. *CD* I/1, 136 [2d].

56. ibid., 139 [2d].

57. ibid., 193 [2d].

58. ibid., 194 [2d].

59. ibid.

It is for this reason that Barth speaks of what he calls objective and subjective revelation. Objective revelation, we shall see below, consists in the Word, Jesus Christ. But there is a second and equally necessary dimension to revelation. This subjective revelation 'occurs in our enlightenment by the Holy Spirit of God to a knowledge of His Word. The outpouring of the Holy Spirit is God's revelation.'[60] Subjective and objective revelation are inseparable, 'subjective revelation can consist only in the fact that objective revelation, the one truth which cannot be added to or bypassed, comes to man and is recognized and acknowledged by man. And that is the work of the Holy Spirit.'[61] Subjective revelation consists, Barth insists, 'only [in] the repetition, the impress, the sealing of objective revelation upon us; or, from our point of view, our own discovery, acknowledgment and affirmation of it.'[62]

Revelation, for Barth, is verbal in nature. '[I]n accordance with the three forms in which we hear this Word [of God] we call it the speech of God. Speech, including God's speech, is the form in which reason communicates with reason and person with person ... The Word of God – and at this point we should not evade a term so much tabooed to-day – is a rational and not an irrational event.'[63] The event or encounter of revelation, therefore, is propositional in character.

How may we describe this 'speech of God'? In keeping with the hidden character of God's self-revelation, God's speech is secular in character, 'When God speaks to man, this event never demarcates itself from other events in such a way that it might not be interpreted at once as part of these other events.'[64] And so, for example, 'The Bible is ... in fact the historical record of a Near Eastern tribal religion and its Hellenistic offshoot. Jesus Christ is also in fact the Rabbi of Nazareth who is hard to know historically and whose work, when He is known, might seem to be a little commonplace compared to more

---

60. *CD* I/2, 203.

61. ibid., 239.

62. ibid. It is in this respect that Barth can argue that 'in its subjective reality God's revelation consists of definite signs of its objective reality which are given by God,' *CD* I/2, 223.

63. *CD* I/1, 135 [2d]. These 'three forms,' for Barth, are preaching, Scripture, and Christ.

64. ibid., 165 [2d].

than one of the other founders of religions and even compared to some of the later representatives of His own religion.'[65]

Thus, God's speech necessarily assumes forms, and these forms are 'garment[s] of creaturely reality ... of fallen man.' 'The form of God's Word, then, is in fact the form of the cosmos which stands in contradiction to God. It has as little ability to reveal God to us as we have to see God in it. If God's Word is revealed in it, is revealed "through it," of course, but in such a way that this "through it" means "in spite if [sic] it."'[66] These secular forms are not a dispensable husk from which the kernel of the Word can be safely extracted. 'This secularity,' rather, 'is in fact an authentic and inalienable attribute of the Word of God itself. If God did not speak to us in secular form, He would not speak to us at all. To evade the secularity of His Word is to evade Christ.'[67]

Before we take up specific consideration of these forms, it is important to reflect further upon the nature of revelation as God's *self*-revelation. To reckon with revelation is, we have seen, to reckon with God, since 'God's Word is God Himself in His revelation.' For Barth, both the Incarnation and the Trinity play a critical role in our understanding the character of revelation. We may look at each in turn.

The 'Incarnation of the eternal Word, Jesus Christ, is God's revelation,' according to Barth.[68] As Trevor Hart has observed of Barth's theology, 'the incarnation is the primary objective condition for the possibility of God's self-revelation in the world.'[69] As 'the outpouring of the Holy Spirit' is

---

65. ibid.

66. ibid., 166 [2d].

67. ibid., 168 [2d], compare *CD* I/1, 175 [2d], where Barth argues that 'the secular form without the divine content is not the Word of God and the divine content without the secular form is also not the Word of God.' Barth, in this same section, also argues for what he calls the 'onesidedness' of God's speech. That is, the Word, in its secular form, comes to us not 'partly veiled and partly unveiled, but either veiled or unveiled, yet without being different in itself, without being spoken and received any the less truly either way.' Such is the 'mystery' of the Word, *CD* I/1, 174, 175 [2d]. The 'full and true Word of God' is heard 'only in faith,' which derives its 'existence' and 'nature' from the 'Word of God.' *CD* I/1, 175, 181 [2d]. And the hearing of the Word in faith 'is the work of the Holy Spirit,' *CD* I/1, 185 [2d].

68. *CD* I/2, 1.

69. Hart, 'Revelation,' 51.

'God's revelation in us,' so 'the incarnation of the Word, with Jesus Christ' is 'God's revelation for us.'[70]

The Incarnation is important because it demonstrates the possibility of revelation. It 'invariably asserts that God can cross the boundary between Himself and us; or expressed in general terms, between His own existence and the existence of that which is not identical with himself.'[71] It is in Christ, furthermore, that the unveiled hiddenness of revelation is vividly manifested. The Word 'by becoming Man at the same time is and remains what He is, the true and eternal God ... We may and must, of course, speak of a veiling of the divine majesty. By becoming flesh the Word enters the hiddenness, the "servant form," which in respect of the knowability of God undoubtedly signifies an "externalisation" (*kenosis*) compared with the "divine form" in which God knows Himself, in which the Father knows the Son and the Son knows the Father.'[72] Therefore, as McCormack has observed, '[the human nature] remains a veil *even as God unveils himself to human eyewitnesses in and through it* – by the testimony of the Holy Spirit to them.'[73]

Inextricably tied to the Incarnation as event or act of revelation is the Triunity of God. The God who reveals Himself is Triune. Revelation therefore necessarily assumes a Triune character. The three forms of the Word of God (preaching, Scripture, Christ), which we shall discuss below, find 'analogy' in the 'doctrine of the triunity of God.' Specifically, Barth argues, 'we can substitute for revelation, Scripture and proclamation the names of the divine persons Father, Son and Holy Spirit and *vice versa*' and that 'in the one case as in the other we shall encounter the same basic determinations and mutual relationships.'[74]

At the commencement of his discussion of 'The Triune God' (*CD* §8-12), Barth briefly but unmistakably testifies to the Triunity of revelation, 'God's Word is God Himself in His revelation. For God reveals himself as the Lord and according to Scripture this signifies for

---

70. *CD* I/2, 1.

71. ibid., 31.

72. ibid., 37, compare *CD* I/2, 159-71.

73. McCormack, *Orthodox and Modern*, 171. McCormack cites in this connection *CD* II/1, 194, 'Knowing the true God in His revelation, we apprehend Him in His hiddenness.'

74. *CD* I/1, 121 [2d].

the concept of revelation that God Himself in unimpaired unity yet also in unimpaired distinction is Revealer, Revelation, and Revealedness.'[75] Similarly, at the commencement of his discussion of 'The Incarnation of the Word' (*CD* §13-15), Barth prefaces his remarks by observing once again how the 'doctrine of God's three-in-oneness' appears in relation to 'the subject of the revelation attested in Holy Scripture.'

> The revelation attested in Holy Scripture is the revelation of the God who, as the Lord, is the Father from whom it proceeds, the Son who fulfills it objectively (for us), and the Holy Spirit who fulfils it subjectively (in us) ... God is the constant Subject of revelation. Neither in His Son in whom He becomes manifest to us, nor in His Holy Spirit in whom He is manifest to us, does He become the predicate or object of our existence or action. He becomes and He is manifest to us. But this very becoming and being is and remains a determination of His existence. It is His act, His work.[76]

The Triunity of God, therefore, sits at the very heart of Barth's doctrine of revelation, not only with respect to the 'content' of that revelation, but also – and particularly – with respect to its 'form.'[77]

One way, we have seen, that the Triunity of revelation evidences itself is in the correspondence of the three forms of the Word of God to Father, Son, and Spirit. We may now take up consideration of what Barth says about those three forms. It is in this discussion that Barth speaks most explicitly to the nature of the Bible.

'The Word of God'

The Word of God, Barth argues, assumes three forms, preaching, the Bible, and Jesus Christ.[78] Barth's discussion of these three forms

---

75. ibid., 295 [2d].

76. *CD* I/2, 1.

77. Hart, 'Revelation,' 51.

78. Robert Brown has argued that 'the term "Word of God" (so popular in volumes I/1 and I/2) tends to be replaced ... in later volumes of the *Dogmatics* ... by explicitly Christological terms, so that any possible ambiguity is removed. The Word of God is not basically the words of a book; the Word of God is Jesus Christ, the Word made flesh,' 'Scripture and Tradition in the Theology of Karl Barth,' in *Thy Word is Truth: Barth on Scripture* (ed. George Hunsinger; Grand Rapids: Eerdmans, 2012), 7. For a concise description of these three forms themselves, see Bolich, *Karl Barth & Evangelicalism*, 144-51.

occupies the whole of *CD* I/2. In §13-18, he discusses the 'Incarnation of the Word' and the 'Outpouring of the Holy Spirit;' in §19-21, 'Holy Scripture;' and in §22-4, the 'Proclamation of the Church.' These sections constitute an elaboration of Barth's discussion in *CD* I/1, §4, 'The Word of God in Its Threefold Form.'[79] We will first briefly consider what these forms are and how they relate to one another in Barth's theology. We will then take up what Barth has to say about these forms in turn.

For Barth, the Word never comes to human beings in unmediated fashion. We do not have direct access to the Word of God. The Word, rather, comes to people through some divinely-appointed form. These forms are not the Word and must not be confused with the Word, '[W]e have [the Word] in a form which as such is not the Word of God and which as such does not even give evidence that it is the form of the Word of God.'[80]

The three forms of the Word of God are alike in some respects, and different in others. Preaching and the Bible stand together as witnesses.

> The Bible is the concrete means by which the Church recollects God's past revelation, is called to expectation of His future revelation, and is thus summoned and guided to proclamation and empowered for it. The Bible, then, is not in itself and as such God's past revelation, just as Church proclamation is not in itself and as such the expected future revelation. The Bible, speaking to us and heard by us as God's Word, bears witness to past revelation, Proclamation, speaking to us and heard by us as God's Word, promises future revelation. The Bible is God's Word as it really bears witness to revelation, and proclamation is God's Word as it really promises revelation. The promise in proclamation, however, rests on the attestation in the Bible.[81]

---

79. Barth notably presents the three forms in *CD* I/2 in the reverse order in which they appear in *CD* I/1 §4. When asked why he did this, Barth replied, 'This is because in this first section [i.e. *CD* I/1 §4] we are in an introduction, and we must start where we are. Thus I begin with analysis and end with synthesis. In this way I can begin with the proclamation of the Word and end with the same, without repeating myself. The first chapter is merely an *approach* to the subject,' *Table Talk*, 25.

80. *CD* I/1, 166 [2d]. These forms, we have seen Barth argue above, are profoundly secular. Thus, Barth says in the sentence immediately preceding this quotation, 'We do not have the Word of God otherwise than in the mystery of its secularity,' ibid.

81. ibid., 111 [2d].

Proclamation and the Bible each serves as a witness to revelation, that is the revelation of God in the incarnate Christ. These witnesses 'point beyond themselves;' find 'authority' only in that to which they point; and must not be equated with 'revelation itself.'[82] That revelation is – 'The Word was made flesh and dwelt among us.'[83]

On the one hand, 'there is no distinction of degree or value between the three forms.' Barth speaks of 'the one Word only in this threefold form,' not 'three different Words of God.'[84] On the other hand, these three forms are not interchangeable. 'The first, revelation, is the form that underlies the other two. But it is the very one that never meets us anywhere in abstract form. We know it only indirectly, from Scripture and proclamation. The direct Word of God meets us only in this twofold mediacy.'[85]

Barth proposes what he calls 'the following brief schedule of mutual relations':

> The revealed Word of God we know only from the Scripture adopted by Church proclamation or the proclamation of the Church based on Scripture. The written Word of God we know only through the revelation which fulfils proclamation or through the proclamation fulfilled by revelation. The preached Word of God we know only through the revelation attested in Scripture or the Scripture which attests revelation.[86]

It is here that Barth's analogy of the Trinity illuminates his understanding of these interrelations.[87] 'Revelation, Scripture and proclamation,' which correspond to 'Father, Son and Holy Spirit,' are three forms of one Word. They are distinct forms, even as they are 'perichoretic,' that is, mutually inhering in their respective functions.[88]

While none of these forms is the Word of God, each of these forms may become the Word of God. In the Incarnation, the Word became

---

82. ibid., 111, 112 [2d].

83. ibid., 119 [2d].

84. ibid., 120 [2d].

85. ibid., 121 [2d].

86. ibid.

87. ibid., 121 [2d], cited above. This analogy immediately follows the quotation cited here.

88. So Hart, 'The Word, the Words and the Witness,' 85.

flesh. He is, we have observed Barth say, revelation. That revelation, of course, is veiled in the very humanity of Jesus Christ and, in any case, the Incarnate Christ is not immediately accessible to human beings. Scripture and preaching, each in its own way, testify to the Word.

> Jesus Christ, very God and very man, is that Word in heaven … The act in which He became the Word of God in His humanity requires neither repetition nor confirmation. But in His eternal presence as the Word of God He is concealed from us who now live on earth and in time. He is revealed only in the sign of His humanity, and especially in the witness of his prophets and apostles. But by nature these signs are not heavenly-human, but earthly- and temporal-human. Therefore the act of their institution as signs requires repetition and confirmation … For if they are to act as signs, if the eternal presence of Christ is to be revealed to us in time, there is a constant need of that continuing work of the Holy Spirit in the Church and to its members which is always taking place in new acts.[89]

It is when the Holy Spirit acts, in conjunction with these witnesses, that Christ reveals Himself in time to human beings. In that sense, Barth says that the witnesses of proclamation and Bible may become the Word of God, even as he distances the two from the Word of God.

For that reason, Barth is prepared to say that the Bible is the Word of God. But he is clear that he does not mean by that proposition what orthodox Reformed Christianity has meant by that proposition.

> That the Bible is the Word of God cannot mean that with other attributes the Bible has the attribute of being the Word of God. To say that would be to violate the Word of God which is God Himself – to violate the freedom and the sovereignty of God. God is not an attribute of something else, even if this something else is the Bible. God is the Subject, God is Lord. He is Lord even over the Bible and in the Bible. The statement that the Bible is the Word of God cannot therefore say that the Word of God is tied to the Bible. On the contrary, what it must say is that the Bible is tied to the Word of God.[90]

We will explore further what Barth understands the relationship between the Bible and the Word of God to be. We may note for the present simply that a bare equation between the two violates, for Barth, the witness

---

89. *CD* I/2, 513.
90. ibid.

character of the Bible as 'form' of the Word of God. Any identification between the two must preserve the distinct nature of each.

To conclude this study of Barth's doctrine of the Word of God, we may explore what Barth has to say about the forms of proclamation and the Bible, respectively. It is not an overstatement to denominate the theology of Karl Barth a 'theology of proclamation.'[91] Barth bookends Part I of the *Church Dogmatics* with extended reflections upon the church's proclamation, which Barth conceives to be 'not merely the formal Sunday sermon from the pulpit but all kinds of Christian witness.'[92] He introduces §§ 3 and 22 with a précis of his understanding of the form of proclamation.[93]

> Talk about God in the Church seeks to be proclamation to the extent that in the form of preaching and sacrament it is directed to man with the claim and expectation that in accordance with its commission it has to speak to him the Word of God to be heard in faith.[94]

> The Word of God is God Himself in the proclamation of the Church of Jesus Christ. In so far as God gives the Church the commission to speak about Him, and the Church discharges this commission, it is God Himself who declares His revelation in His witnesses. The proclamation of the Church is pure doctrine when the human word spoken in it in confirmation of the biblical witness to revelation offers and creates obedience to the Word of God.[95]

As Mueller observes, these summary statements emphasize at least two important aspects of Barth's understanding of the form of proclamation. The first is that proclamation must bind itself to 'the biblical witness to revelation.' In that respect, preaching stands wholly under the Scripture.[96] The second is that, in the event of preaching, and when

---

91. As Trevor Hart, 'The Word, the Words and the Witness,' 81.

92. Colin Brown, *Karl Barth and the Christian Message,* 34. In that respect, dogmatics is an aspect of proclamation, as *CD* I/2 §§ 23-4. O'Neill observes that, when Barth commenced his lectures in Bonn in 1931, he titled them 'Church Dogmatics' rather than 'Christian Dogmatics' in an effort to 'eliminate all philosophical basis for his system and to speak only about the grace of Jesus Christ from a position in the church alone,' *The Bible's Authority,* 271-2.

93. Each is cited at Mueller, *Karl Barth,* 59.

94. *CD* I/1, 47 [2d].

95. *CD* I/2, 743.

96. Mueller, *Karl Barth,* 60.

heard in faith, proclamation becomes the Word of God – 'it is God Himself who declares His revelation in His witnesses.'[97]

It is the task of proclamation to confine itself to the biblical witness to revelation. What, then, does Barth say about the 'form' of the Bible? Like any other form of the Word of God, the Bible is secular in character. Barth insists that, in saying 'that the Bible is the Word of God, we must not compromise either directly or indirectly the humanity of its form and the possibility of the offense which can be taken at it.'[98] Thus, the 'prophets and apostles, as such, even in their office, even in their function as witnesses, even in the act of writing down their witness, were real, historical men as we are, and therefore sinful in their action, and capable and actually guilty of error in their spoken and written word.'[99] The biblical books 'know nothing of the distinction of fact and value which is so important to us, between history, on the one hand, and saga and legend on the other,' and the Bible's 'capacity for error ... also extends to its religious or theological content.' Further, 'there are obvious overlappings and contradictions – e.g., between the Law and the prophets, between John and the Synoptists, between Paul and James.'[100] Unless we are to be 'guilty of Docetism' and 'take away their humanity,' we must recognize that 'within certain limits and therefore relatively they are all vulnerable and therefore capable of error even in respect of religion and theology.'[101]

---

97. ibid.

98. *CD* I/2, 528.

99. ibid., 529. To deny this point, Barth avers later in this paragraph, is to deny the 'miracle that they speak the Word of God.' Rather, 'they have still spoken the Word of God in their fallible and erring human word,' *CD* I/2, 529, 530.

100. In making this point, Barth goes on to say that 'nowhere do we find a rule which enables us to grasp [a synthesis] in such a way that we can make organic parts of the distinctions and evade the contradictions as such. We are led one way, now another – each of the biblical authors obviously speaking only *quod potuit homo* – and in both ways, and whoever is the author, we are always confronted with the question of faith. Again, we must be careful not to be betrayed into taking sides into playing off the one biblical man against the other, into pronouncing that this one or that has "erred". From what standpoint can we make any such pronouncement?,' *CD* I/2, 509-10. In affirming the biblical writers' capacity for errors, and the existence of errors of various kinds within the biblical text, Barth urges restraint both in looking for those alleged errors and in exploiting them once one believes that he has found them in the text.

101. *CD* I/2, 529, 530.

Barth recognizes that such passages as 2 Timothy 3:16 and 2 Peter 1:19-21 lay claim to inspiration with respect to the Scripture. How does Barth understand 'inspiration' here? In an extended discussion of those passages, Barth addresses the claims of each biblical author regarding the text of the Old Testament Scripture.[102] Klaas Runia argues that Barth's observations and conclusions regarding the work of the Spirit in relation to the biblical authors 'teach what Reformed theology has always stated as its doctrine of inspiration.'[103] Even if one does not concur with that assessment, Runia is surely correct to say that Barth's reflections upon what he understands to be present or contemporary inspiration set him at variance with the historical Reformed doctrine.[104] Barth claims that 'the *theopneustia* of the Bible, the attitude of obedience in which it is written, the compelling fact that in it true men speak to us in the name of the true God: this – and here is the miracle of it – is not simply before us because the Bible is before us and we read the Bible. The *theopneustia* is the act of revelation in which the prophets and apostles in their humanity became what they were, and in which alone in their humanity they can become to us what they are.'[105] That is to say, when the Bible is read, 'the same Spirit who has created [this] witness' in turn 'bears witness of its truth to men, to those who hear and read.' 'This self-disclosure,' Barth concludes, 'in its totality, is *theopneustia*, the inspiration of the word of the prophets and apostles.'[106] Inspiration, then, is a work of the Spirit in the lives of present readers no less than in the lives of the biblical writers. Analogously to His work of creating the witness to the Word of God in the biblical writings, the Spirit in turn employs that witness in the present to point readers of that witness to the Word of God.

---

102. ibid., 503-6, cf. *CD* I/2, 514-17.

103. Klaas Runia, *Karl Barth's Doctrine of Holy Scripture* (Grand Rapids: Eerdmans, 1962), 138.

104. We will argue below that Barth's conception of inspiration with respect to the Spirit's work in relation to the biblical writers is contrary to the Scripture's teaching about inspiration.

105. *CD* I/2, 507-8.

106. ibid., 516. Barth proceeds to pronounce the seventeenth century doctrine of biblical inspiration to be 'false doctrine.' 'In [this doctrine] the Word of God could no longer be the Word of God and therefore it was no longer recognized as such. The Bible was now grounded upon itself apart from the mystery of Christ and the Holy Ghost. It became a "paper Pope" ... an instrument of human power,' *CD* I/2, 525.

Given these statements about the Bible and the work of inspiration in relation to the Bible, what, for Barth, is the relationship between the Bible and the Word of God? Barth insists that we may 'hear the Word of God in this book' again and again, but 'the presence of the Word of God itself ... is not identical with the existence of the book itself.'[107] And yet, Barth insists, when the Bible 'is taken and used as an instrument in the hand of God, i.e., it speaks to and is heard by us as the authentic witness to divine revelation,' it 'is therefore present as the Word of God.' It is 'in this event' that 'the Bible shows itself to us ... as the Word of God.'[108] Thus, as it is a witness to the Word of God, the Bible becomes the Word of God.[109] Elsewhere, Barth argues that these two principles of distinction and unity must be held together.

> If we want to think of the Bible as a real witness of divine revelation, then clearly we have to keep two things constantly before us and give them their due weight: the limitation and the positive element, its distinctiveness from revelation, in so far as it is only a human word about it, and its unity with it, in so far as revelation is the basis object and content of this word.[110]

While the Bible may not be strictly identified with the Word of God, it may become the Word of God and, in that respect, we may speak of the Bible as the Word of God.[111] There is an 'indirect identity' of the Bible and the Word of God.[112]

---

107. *CD* I/2, 530.

108. ibid.

109. David Gibson, 'The Answering Speech of Men: Karl Barth on Holy Scripture,' in *The Enduring Authority of Holy Scripture* (ed. D. A. Carson; Grand Rapids: Eerdmans, 2016), 272.

110. *CD* I/2, 463.

111. For a recent treatment of the Bible's becoming the Word of God in Barth's thought, see now Bruce L. McCormack, 'The Being of Holy Scripture Is In Becoming: Karl Barth in Conversation with American Evangelical Criticism,' in *Evangelicals and Scripture: Tradition, Authority, and Hermeneutics* (eds. Vincent E. Bacote, Laura C. Miguelez, and Dennis L. Okholm; Downers Grove, IL: InterVarsity, 2004), 55-75. McCormack argues that this formulation, and back of that its 'relational and actualistic ... theological ontology' is not reflective of Barth's subservience to Kantian philosophy, but of his effort to resolve the 'strictly theological problem of the meaning of divine immutability in relation to the fact of the incarnation,' 74.

112. *GD* I:216. Many students of Barth have adopted this expression to describe this relationship in Barth's understanding of the Bible, Runia, *Karl Barth's Doctrine of Holy Scripture*, viii; McCormack, 'The Being of Holy Scripture Is In Becoming,' 68;

The union between the Bible and the Word of God, McCormack argues, is analogous to the hypostatic union, and may also be spoken of as 'a sacramental union of the divine Word with the sign that is the prophetic and apostolic witness.'[113] It is only in light of this union that we may predicate certain qualities – not of the Bible, but in reference to the Bible. The Bible is true and trustworthy in light of 'its *intrinsic* relationship to the truthfulness and the trustworthiness of the divine self-disclosure speech-act that takes place in Jesus.'[114] When we speak of the Bible as infallible, we are not making an ontological claim about the Bible, for 'ontologically, it is not infallible.' Rather, 'Barth's actualism resolves the matter ... The Scripture ... exists in the act of God's revelation, for God and for man, as the Word of God to man in the words of man himself. Scripture proves itself functionally infallible only in the act of God's gracious opening of human eyes to see Christ ...'[115] We must also speak in similar fashion of authority in relation to the Bible. 'The Church does not claim direct and absolute and material authority for itself but for Holy Scripture *as the Word of God*.'[116] The church has other authorities, but 'Holy Scripture has always in the Church a unique and in its way singular authority' by virtue of the fact that 'it is a record, indeed historically it is the oldest extant record, of the origin and therefore of the basis and nature of the Church.'[117] And yet, Barth stresses, 'the Church cannot evade Scripture. It cannot try to appeal past it directly to God, to Christ or to the

---

Vanhoozer, 'A Person of the Book?', 40; Rhodes, 'Barth's Theology of Scripture in Dogmatic Perspective,' 39, 41.

113. McCormack, 'The Being of Holy Scripture Is In Becoming,' 69, referencing *CD* I/2, 500-1. Compare Trevor Hart, 'The Word, the Words and the Witness,' 87-9.

114. Francis Watson, 'The Bible,' in *The Cambridge Companion to Karl Barth*, 61.

115. Bolich, *Karl Barth & Evangelicalism*, 147-8.

116. *CD* I/2, 538, emphasis added. Later in this discussion, Barth will insist that the 'singular authority' of Scripture in the church is 'still mediate, relative and formal,' where 'mediate means temporal, historical and human,' an 'earthly authority;' where 'relative ... means that like all other authoritative powers in the Church it can only represent the divine authority,' thus 'the Church can and should go beyond the representative and preliminary judgment of Scripture to the supreme and real Judge and Lord;' where 'formal ... means that at bottom and practically Holy Scripture is on a level with other witnesses to divine revelation, simply as witness, as pure form,' *CD* I/2, 540, 541.

117. ibid., 540.

Holy Spirit ... Scripture confronts [the church] commandingly as Holy Scripture ... It obeys Holy Scripture.' It does so by 'serv[ing] the Word of God in the sign and guise of the word of these men [i.e., the prophets and the apostles].'[118]

According to Barth, then, we cannot predicate trustworthiness, infallibility, or authority of the Bible *per se*. We cannot do this for the same reason that we cannot equate the Bible with the Word of God *simpliciter* – the 'presence of God's Word in the Bible is [not] an attribute inhering once for all in this book as such.'[119] Rather, 'it is a matter of this decision and act of God or rather of the actualization of the act of God which took place once and for all in Jesus Christ.' It is in this 'event' that the 'word of man proves itself the Word of God.'[120] And only as such may we speak of the Bible as trustworthy, infallible, or authoritative.

Critical Reflections

There is no question that Barth oversaw a conservative turn in the academic theology of the twentieth century. Originating as a protest against the immanentism of nineteenth-century German theology, Barth's theology trumpeted the transcendence of God. His theology was overtly supernaturalistic. Barth rose to fame as an expositor of Paul's Epistle to the Romans and never left off the work of biblical exegesis in his theological writings. The *Church Dogmatics*, particularly in their lengthy excurses, survey the history of theology from the Fathers to Barth's contemporaries. His expressed sympathies for the Reformers, and particularly for the early Reformed wing of the Protestant Reformation, appeared to augur a return to the confessional orthodoxy of Reformed Protestantism.

Nevertheless, Barth did not return to the orthodoxy of the Protestant Reformation or its heirs. With respect to the doctrine of Scripture, Barth repudiated that orthodoxy. His doctrine of the Word of God is a case in point. At this juncture, we will raise questions and concerns about Barth's doctrine of revelation and the Bible. Although what follows is not a comprehensive response to Barth's formulations about revelation

---

118. ibid., 544.
119. ibid., 530.
120. ibid., 531.

and the Bible, the following four areas touch on some of Barth's most serious departures from the Bible's teaching about itself.[121]

The Bible and the Word of God

First, a cluster of concerns centers around the way in which Barth understands the Word of God. The Word of God, for Barth, necessarily assumes one of three forms. These forms – proclamation, Scripture, and Jesus Christ – exist in set relation even as there is not 'distinction of degree or value between the three forms.'[122] Barth is insistent that the Word is never to be identified with any one of these forms, although each form, in the event of revelation, may *become* the Word of God. We may speak of an *indirect* identity but never a direct identity between the Bible and the Word of God.

To assert that these three forms do not differ in degree or value suggests that, for Barth, preaching, the Bible, and Jesus Christ are comparable to one another. But, as Mark Thompson has noted, Barth sets Jesus Christ in a qualitatively different category from Scripture and preaching.[123] Furthermore, while Barth understands proclamation and Scripture to point beyond themselves to Jesus Christ, Jesus Christ 'is a witness to nothing other than itself.' 'Revelation,' in this instance, 'is not something predicated of it but simply another way of designating it.'[124] There is, therefore, a basic instability in the way in which Barth understands the three forms to relate to one another and to the Word of God.

A related and more substantial problem with Barth's formulation of these three forms is that it unbiblically distances the text of the Bible from the Word of God.[125] To say that the Bible may *become* the Word of God and, in that respect, is the Word of God, is different from

---

121. For instance, we will not here directly engage Barth's denial of general or natural revelation.

122. *CD* I/1, 120 [2d].

123. Mark D. Thompson, 'Barth's Doctrine of Scripture,' in *Engaging with Barth*, 182.

124. ibid., 183. Thompson goes on to observe that Barth establishes a 'direct relation of Jesus Christ and revelation on one hand, but only an indirect relation between revelation and the Bible on the other,' 184.

125. Compare here the reservation of Geoffrey W. Bromiley, 'The Authority of Scripture in Karl Barth' in *Hermeneutics, Authority, and Canon* (eds. D. A. Carson and John D. Woodbridge; Grand Rapids: Baker, 1995), 290.

saying that the Bible *is* the Word of God without qualification. But the biblical writers are not shy in identifying the very words of Scripture with God's own Word. We have seen in a previous chapter how such passages as Exodus 20:1-4, 24:3-4, and the prophetic formulation, 'thus says the LORD' demonstrate the claim of the Old Testament writers that the words of the Old Testament are themselves the very Word of God.[126] Jesus, we observed, teaches the very same point in Mark 12:35-7 and Matthew 19:4-6. His exposition of Psalm 110 and Genesis 2, respectively, positively identify the words of David and of Moses with those of the 'Holy Spirit' and of 'God.' The apostles urge the very same point. Hebrews identifies the words of Psalm 95 with the speech of the Holy Spirit. Peter identifies the words of David in Psalms 69 and 109 with the words of the Holy Spirit. The New Testament writers have no difficulty interchanging 'Scripture' with 'God' in such a way as to require the conclusion that the words written in the Scripture are the very words of God. To cite once again the title of Warfield's article on the subject, '"It Says:" "Scripture Says:" "God Says."'[127] The actualism underlying Barth's formulations is absent from the Scripture formulations, and Barth's concern that identifying the Bible with the Word of God compromised the sovereignty and freedom of God is categorically absent from any of the biblical writers. The Bible speaks with one voice in affirming the words of the biblical writers to be the very Word of God.

Looking particularly at the New Testament, we see that the apostles insist that their own words are the very words of Christ. This is, we have seen, Paul's testimony in 1 Corinthians 14:37 and 2 Thessalonians 3:14. Peter likewise identifies the teaching of the apostles with the teaching of Christ, and likens the authority of the apostles' teaching to that of the Old Testament (2 Pet. 3:15-16). It is true that the apostles are witnesses to Christ, a fact to which they often testify (Acts 1:22, 4:33,

---

126. As Timothy Ward notes, God's commitment in Deuteronomy 18:15-20 underlies precisely this point, '"I will point my words in the mouth of the prophet" (v. 18). The words that the prophets speak are words that come directly from God,' even as Jeremiah 1:9b-10 demonstrates God's commitment in Deuteronomy, 'Now I have put my words in your mouth ...,' 'The Incarnation and Scripture,' in *'The Word Become Flesh': Evangelicals and the Incarnation – Papers from the Sixth Oak Hill College Annual School of Theology* (ed. David Peterson; Carlisle, UK: Paternoster, 2003), 163.

127. Warfield, in *Works*, I:283-332.

1 Cor. 15:1-11; compare Acts 1:8). But the calling of the apostles to be witnesses in no way removes or distances their speech in the writings of the New Testament from the Word of God. In fact, it is precisely in their capacity as witnesses that they bring to the church, in the words of their writings, the very Word of God (see 1 John 1:1-4). This activity constitutes the fulfillment of Jesus' Upper Room promises that the Spirit will bring words from the Father and the Son to the apostles (John 14:25-6; 16:12-15). It is in light of these testimonies that we may ask, with Mark Thompson, 'was Barth really Christological enough?'[128] That is to say, for all of Barth's concerns to uphold the Christocentricity of the Bible, and to safeguard the preeminence of Jesus Christ, the Word of God, he fails to honor the teaching of Jesus Himself – about the words of the Old Testament, and about the words of the apostles who would minister after His resurrection.

The Humanity of Scripture

Second, Barth frequently insists upon the humanity of the Bible. For Barth, the humanity of the biblical writers means that they so reflected their world and age that they had no grasp of the distinction between history and saga or legend. They not only had capacity for error, but even committed errors in the biblical writings. These errors included errors in the department of religion and theology. The biblical writers, furthermore, contradict one another. To deny the preceding, in the manner of Reformation orthodoxy in the seventeenth century, is to deny the very humanity of the biblical authors and to lapse into a form of Docetism.

Barth is right to insist upon the humanity of the biblical authors, but wrong to define humanity in the way that he does. Axiomatic to humanity, in Barth's theology, is that it bears all the marks of its fallen condition, including sin and, in particular, sins of the mind. This commitment is what Bromiley has termed 'a flat equation of humanity and error.'[129]

Barth is fundamentally mistaken here. In the first place, sin cannot be readily identified with humanity *per se*. Adam in his created integrity;

---

128. Thompson, 'Barth's Doctrine of Scripture,' 185.
129. Bromiley, 'The Authority of Scripture in Karl Barth,' 291.

the 'spirits of just men made perfect' (Heb. 12:23); the ingathered righteous on the Day of Judgment; and, preeminently, the humanity of Jesus Christ (Heb. 7:26) all testify to the fact that one may be truly human without sin. Sin is accidental to our present humanity. The hope offered in the gospel is that we will one day be fully and forever freed from sin and all its effects.

In the second place, the biblical writers, as we have seen and will explore once again below, did not write unaided. They wrote by inspiration of the Holy Spirit. The Spirit's operations upon them in producing the text of Scripture did not obliterate their humanity.[130] On the contrary, the humanity of the biblical authors is fully evident in their writings. But that does not mean that there is error in the texts that they authored. The Spirit's work ensured that the human authors' writings would be entirely free from sin, that is to say, free from error and contradiction.[131]

If the Bible is in fact the Word of God – in the sense in which Reformed orthodoxy has affirmed it and not in the sense in which Barth affirms it – then it is categorically impossible for the Scripture to be fallible, for the Scripture to contain errors or contradictions. This is because every word of Scripture is at one and the same time the word of its human author and the word of its Divine Author. The Scripture cannot err because God cannot err.[132] The Scripture must be true in every part and in every word because God is always and only true in His utterances (Titus 1:2; Num. 23:19).

The Divine and the Human in Scripture

Third, Barth speaks of the humanity of the Bible, and he also affirms that the Bible, in the event of revelation, becomes the Word of God. This raises the question how, for Barth, we are to understand the relation of the divine and the human in Scripture. He states that 'in the event

---

130. So, rightly, Runia, *Karl Barth's Doctrine of Holy Scripture*, 65-6. Thompson observes how Barth operates with an 'uncritical acceptance of the nineteenth-century caricature of verbal inspiration as mechanical dictation,' 'Barth's Doctrine of Scripture,' 195.

131. Runia, *Karl Barth's Doctrine of Holy Scripture*, 74.

132. See here the concurring thoughts of Runia, *Karl Barth's Doctrine of Holy Scripture*, 78.

of God's Word revelation and the Bible are indeed one, and literally so ... their union is really an event.'[133] What, then, is the nature of that union or unity?

As McCormack points out, Barth draws an analogy between the relation of the divine and human in Scripture, and the relation of the divine and human in Christ.[134]

> Again it is quite impossible that there should be a direct identity between the human word of Holy Scripture and the Word of God, and therefore between the creaturely reality in itself and as such and the reality of God the Creator. It is impossible that there should have been a transmutation of the one into the other or an admixture of the one with the other. This is not the case even in the person of Christ, where the identity between God and man, in all the originality and indissolubility in which it confronts us, is an assumed identity, one specially willed, created and effected by God, and to that extent indirect, i.e., resting neither in the essence of God nor in that of man, but in a decision and act of God to man. When we necessarily allow for inherent differences, it is exactly the same with the unity of the divine and human word in Holy Scripture ... Even here the human element does not cease to be human, and as such and in itself it is certainly not divine ... That the Word has become Scripture is not one and the same thing as its becoming flesh. But the uniqueness and at the same time general relevance of its becoming flesh necessarily involved its becoming Scripture ... As the Word of God in the sign of this prophetic-apostolic word of man Holy Scripture is like the unity of God and man in Jesus Christ. It is neither divine only nor human only. Nor is it a mixture of the two nor a *tertium quid* between them. But in its own way and degree it is very God and very man, i.e., a witness of revelation which itself belongs to revelation, and historically a very human literary document.[135]

Setting aside the implications of Barth's statements for Christology, how does this incarnational analogy illuminate Barth's understanding of the relationship between the divine and the human in Scripture? Barth does not go so far as to draw a one to one correspondence between the

---

133. *CD* I/1, 113 [2d].

134. As we have observed above, Barth also likens the union of the divine and the human in this instance to the sacramental union.

135. *CD* I/2, 499, 500, 501, a portion of which is cited at McCormack, 'The Being of Holy Scripture Is in Becoming,' 68, and Runia, *Karl Barth's Doctrine of Holy Scripture,* 57, 58.

theanthropic Christ and the Bible. The relationship is an analogous one. In each case, the identity between the human and the divine is an indirect one and is an identity of act or event. Barth insists, furthermore, that the union does not result in the human becoming divine or vice versa. The Bible, then, never ceases to be human in the manner that Barth understands its humanity.

One problem with this formulation is its rejection of the biblical equation between the words of the biblical authors and the words of God. The Old and New Testament writers do not say that God has taken up the words of the human authors and has identified Himself with them for some specific purpose. On the contrary, they insist that God is the author of these words, and that every word of the biblical human authors is the very word of the Divine Author.

A second and related problem with Barth's conception of the divine and the human in the Bible is hermeneutical in nature. We have seen that the biblical authors identify not only the words of the human authors with the words of the Divine Author, but equally the intent of the human authors with that of the Divine Author. That is why, for instance, when David speaks in Psalm 110, Jesus can say that David speaks 'in the Spirit' (Mark 12:36).

Barth's understanding of the unity of the divine and the human in the Bible is unable to sustain this hermeneutical unity.

> What we have in the Bible are in any case human attempts to repeat and reproduce this Word of God in human words and thoughts and in specific human situations, e.g., with reference to the complications of the political position of Israel as a buffer between Egypt and Babylon, or with reference to the errors and confusions in the Christian church at Corinth between A.D. 50 and 60. On the one hand *Deus dixit,* on the other *Paulus dixit.* These are two different things. And precisely because they are not two things but become one and the same thing in the event of the Word of God, we must maintain that it is by no means self-evident or intrinsically one that revelation should be understood primarily as the superior principle and the Bible primarily as the subordinate principle.[136]

Barth entertains a unity between the human words of the Bible and the Word of God. But that unity exists 'in the event.' In themselves,

---

136. *CD* I/1, 113-14 [2d].

the human words of the Bible and the Word of God are 'two different things.' There is the *Deux dixit* (God has said), and the *Paulus dixit* (Paul has said). To put matters this way suggests that God is not bound to respect the intention of the human author when He takes those human words up in the event of the Word of God. As Packer states the implications of Barth's point, 'the divine message of the passage does not always coincide with the human writer's meaning, since God is free in the event of revelation to use the human words any way he pleases.' This approach, Packer continues, 'opens the door to allegorizing and turns God's gift of insight into Scripture into the bestowal of uncheckable private revelations.'[137] Seen from another angle, Barth's formulations call into question God's steadfast faithfulness to the promises that He makes in Scripture. If God is not bound to the intention of the human author, on what basis have God's people expected – or may expect now – His promises in the Bible to come to fulfillment? As Thompson notes, '[Barth] does not appear to consider that God might bind himself to the word he speaks and that he commissions the prophets and apostles to write.'[138] Barth's teaching at this point overturns the settled biblical and Reformed conviction that 'the true and full sense of any Scripture is not manifold, but one.'[139] We are left, in principle, with a plurality of meanings in Scripture – the intention(s) of the human authors, and the divine intention, in principle unpredictable, in the event of revelation.

Third, Barth's understanding of the relationship of the human and the divine in the Bible poses the question, what is it that makes the Scriptures of the Old and New Testaments different from any other human literary production? The Bible, according to Barth, is a thoroughly secular, fallible, human production. God has chosen these books to become the Word of God in the event of revelation. But why, for Barth, has God chosen these books and no other? Why could God not choose other books, religious or not, to become the Word of God in event?

When asked, 'What gives the present canon of Scripture its authority?' Barth replied, 'There is no explanation for authority. The canon is the

---

137. Packer, 'Encountering Present-Day Views of Scripture,' 73.
138. Thompson, 'Barth's Doctrine of Scripture,' 180.
139. Westminster Confession of Faith 1.9.

canon just because it is so.'[140] Barth more fully articulates the point in his *Church Dogmatics*.

> We believe in and with the Church that Holy Scripture has this priority over all other writings and authorities, even those of the Church. We believe in and with the Church that Holy Scripture as the original and legitimate witness of divine revelation is itself the Word of God ... We [do not] have the capacity and competence to ascribe to the Bible this priority, this character as the Word of God, and [to say] that this priority and character of the Bible are immediately clear to us. If we venture to make them, we do so in obedience and therefore not on the basis and according to the measure of an *a priori* understanding and judgment made by us and applied to this object ..., but in obedience to a judgment of God already made in the light of the object, and in preparation for one which has again and again to be made in the light of it.[141]

Barth elsewhere strenuously denies that it is left to individuals to make this canonical determination. The Church, he argues, completed the task of the canon 'about the year 400,' that is, it 'confirm[ed] or establish[ed] it as something which has already been formed and given.' The Church did so 'only to the best of its knowledge and judgment, in the venture and obedience of faith, but also in all the relativity of a human knowledge of the truth which God has opened up to men ... When we adopt the canon of the Church we do not say that the Church itself, but that the revelation which underlies and controls the Church, attests these witnesses and no others as the witnesses of revelation and therefore as canonical for the church.'[142]

Barth argues that the question of canon is one that is settled 'in the venture and obedience of faith, but also in all the relativity of a human knowledge of the truth which God has opened up to men.' The attestation of the Bible as canonical does not derive from itself but from 'the revelation which underlies and controls the Church.' That is to say, the attestation to the Bible as canonical is from a revelation external to the Bible.

Such formulations only accentuate the problem posed by our earlier questions. As Reid has perceptively observed, 'both the Epistle to the

---

140. Barth, *Table Talk*, 26.
141. *CD* I/2, 502.
142. ibid., 473, 474.

Hebrews and the Epistle to Diognetus speak about Jesus Christ; why then does the canon include one and excludes the other?'[143] Elsewhere in his writings, Barth will speak of the biblical witnesses (the 'prophets and apostles') as 'in an absolutely once-for-all and unique position compared to all the rest of us.'[144] But he declines here to proffer any grounds or reasons inherent to those witnesses for their 'unique position.' Barth subsequently speaks of the apostles as 'primary witnesses, who can be succeeded by secondary and tertiary witnesses,' intimating that historical proximity to Christ somehow privileges the apostles as witnesses to Christ.[145] But Barth makes no more of the point in the discussion that follows.

In the end, Barth points to no quality or character inherent in the books of the Bible that would establish or distinguish them as witnesses to Christ. It is the attestation of revelation to faith, an attestation that is external to these witnesses, that settles and determines these witnesses and no other as canonical. It is impossible to escape the conclusion that this is a fundamentally irrational formulation of the criteria of the canon. That is to say, there are no clear, rational grounds on which we may identify the Old and New Testaments as <u>the</u> witnesses of God's choosing. Neither are there clear, rational grounds on which we may exclude other books, especially ancient books that talk about the person and work of Christ, from the canon. Barth's doctrine of the canonicity of Scripture as witness is therefore shot through with subjectivity.

To frame the question of the canon as Barth has done, furthermore, runs counter to the testimony of the biblical books. The New Testament in particular, we have seen in Chapter 4, identifies apostolic imposition as the criterion of the canonicity of the Old and New Testaments. The church early and universally came to recognize and to receive those books that the apostles of Jesus Christ imposed upon the church, books that bore in themselves the marks of the Word of God. While the church's judgment of canonicity is fallible, and was exercised in faith, that judgment is not irrational. That judgment, furthermore, did not concern whether the books of the Bible were *witnesses* to the Word of God, but whether the books of the Bible *were* the Word of God.

---

143. Reid, *The Authority of Scripture*, 201.
144. *CD* I/1, 145 [2d].
145. *CD* I/2, 487.

The Inspiration and (In)errancy of Scripture

Fourth and finally, we may take up two matters that Barth does not conjoin but, for reasons that we have seen in a previous chapter, must be conjoined. These are the inspiration and inerrancy of the Bible. Barth, we observed above, acknowledges that the New Testament teaches inspiration with respect to the Bible. Barth speaks of inspiration both with respect to the past and with respect to the present. With respect to the past, inspiration is God's self-revelation, in which the Spirit renders the prophets and the apostles witnesses to the Word of God. With respect to the present, inspiration is the work of the Spirit in bearing witness to the Word of God, to those who hear and read the Bible.[146]

Past inspiration, Barth insists, 'does not mean the infallibility of the biblical word in its linguistic, historical and theological character as a human word. If [*sic*] means that the fallible and faulty human word is as such used by God and has to be received and heard in spite of its human fallibility.'[147] Thus, inspiration is not an attribute that inheres to the biblical text. It describes, rather, the event of revelation in which the human biblical word becomes the Word of God.[148] Paul's word, *theopneustos*, at 2 Timothy 3:16 means simply 'of the Spirit of God' – the Scripture is 'given and filled and ruled by the Spirit of God, and actively outbreathing and spreading abroad and making known the Spirit of God.'[149] It is in light of this understanding that we may conceive inspiration also to be a present work of the Spirit in the lives of those who hear the Bible. What the Spirit did *then*, He equally does *now*, 'We have to say that we must view inspiration as a single, timeless – or rather, contemporary act of God … in *both* the biblical authors *and* ourselves.'[150] As Hart perceptively summarizes Barth's position, 'In this

---

146. Compare Sonderegger's definition of Barth's doctrine of inspiration, which she pronounces a 'conceptual puzzle': 'the doctrine of Inspiration is the "event" of Spiritual disclosure of human words made conformable with the Divine Word; the relation to text of Divine referent is secured by the miracle of the Holy Spirit's working, the Capable on the incapable, the Truth to the reluctant and wayward human witness,' 'The Doctrine of Inspiration and the Reliability of Scripture,' in *Thy Word is Truth*, 21.

147. *CD* I/2, 533.

148. The term at 2 Timothy 3:16, according to Barth, refers to 'a disposing act and decision of God,' *CD* I/2, 504.

149. *CD* I/2, 504.

150. *GD* 1:225, as cited at Hart, 'The Word, the Words and the Witness,' 101.

single event of the Spirit, then, the biblical witnesses themselves are in a sense made contemporary with us, and we are given to see and hear what they saw and heard for themselves.'[151] There is a sense in which inspiration is incomplete apart from this present work of the Spirit in the hearers of the Bible, 'The circle which led from the divine benefits to the apostle instructed by the Spirit now closes at the hearer of the apostle, who again by the Spirit is enabled to receive as is necessary. The hearer, too, in his existence as such is part of the miracle which takes place at this point ... This self-disclosure [of the Spirit, bearing witness to men of the truth of the witness that he has created] in its totality is *theopneustia*, the inspiration of the word of the prophets and apostles.'[152]

Inspiration, for Barth, is therefore personal, touching on all persons who come into some form of contact with the Spirit's witness, and progressive, continuing as long as the Bible is both read and, by the working of the Spirit, becomes the Word of God. But biblical inspiration, we observed in a previous chapter, does not terminate upon the hearers of the text of Scripture, much less their human authors. Inspiration, according to Paul, is a predicate of the text of Scripture itself (2 Tim. 3:16). For this reason, inspiration is not a dynamic process, a circle to be completed at some point in the future. Inspiration is something that has transpired in the past, at the point in time when the biblical authors, by inspiration of the Holy Spirit, committed the Word of God to writing. Barth is well aware of this doctrine and knowingly rejects it.[153]

How are we to account for Barth's departure from the biblical and Reformed understanding of inspiration? A partial answer lies in his actualistic understanding of the Word of God generally. But we should also register a pattern in Barth's writings to conflate three matters that the Scripture and historical Reformed theology have kept distinct – revelation; inspiration; and illumination.[154] In historical Reformed

---

151. Hart, 'The Word, the Words and the Witness,' 101.
152. *CD* I/2, 516.
153. See his lengthy excursus at *CD* I/2, 514-26.
154. For a sustained defense of these distinctions in relation to Barth's views on inspiration, see Runia, *Karl Barth's Doctrine of Holy Scripture*, 137-68. Note David Gibson's concluding assessment of Barth's 'inspiration thesis,' that it 'is exegetically unproven and historically novel,' 'The Answering Speech of Men,' in *The Enduring Authority of the Christian Scriptures* (ed. D.A. Carson; Grand Rapids: Eerdmans, 2016), 282.

theology, revelation describes God's self-disclosure to human beings, whether that revelation is general or special. Inspiration describes the superintending work of the Spirit that ensures that what is revealed to human authors is in its entirety committed to writing, without error, and thus the Word of God.[155] Illumination describes the work of the Spirit upon the minds of hearers or readers of the Bible such that they savingly understand the contents of Scripture.

But Barth collapses these distinctions upon themselves. Revelation, Barth maintains, is the ongoing activity of the God who reveals Himself in the three forms of proclamation, Scripture, and Jesus Christ. Inspiration captures the same activity from the vantage point of the Spirit. Illumination, furthermore, comes to be caught up into inspiration, to the point that the two terms are virtually indistinguishable.[156] The effect of this conflation is to 'produce further uncertainty about [the] objective authority [of Scripture]. Is it authoritative because God inspired it once for all, or is it authoritative only ad hoc as God inspires it when heard or read?'[157] The leveling of biblical author and biblical reader with respect to the ministry of the Spirit ultimately subjectivizes and destabilizes the Scripture and its authority over the church.

Finally, we may briefly consider Barth's rejection also of the inerrancy of Scripture. For Barth, the humanity of Scripture mandates the fallibility of the biblical documents. Inspiration in no way ensured

---

155. 'The object of revelation is communication of knowledge. The object or design of inspiration is to secure infallibility in teaching. Consequently, they differ, secondly, in their effect. The effect of revelation was to render its recipient wiser. The effect of inspiration was to preserve him from error in teaching,' Hodge, *Systematic Theology*, I:155, as cited at Runia, *Karl Barth's Doctrine of Holy Scripture*, 153.

156. 'If inspiration is co-ordinated into that circle of God's manifestation by the Spirit only for our illumination by the same Spirit, the inspiration of the biblical witnesses which is the link between the two, between God and us, can and must be regarded quite definitely not merely as real but as verbal inspiration,' *CD* I/2, 518. See here the discussion at Thompson, 'Barth's Doctrine of Scripture,' 188-9. Rhodes has attempted to defend Barth's formulation as maintaining a sufficient 'distinction between inspiration and illumination (or enlightenment),' 'Barth's Theology of Scripture in Dogmatic Perspective,' 47. McCormack defends Barth's formulations in relation to Warfield's doctrine of inspiration which McCormack regrettably misrepresents, 'The Being of Holy Scripture Is in Becoming,' 62. Vanhoozer has attempted to narrow, if not bridge, the gap between Barth's formulations and classical formulations by recourse to speech-act theory, 'A Person of the Book?,' 55-9.

157. Bromiley, 'The Authority of Scripture in Karl Barth,' 291.

that the text of Scripture would be inerrant. Consequently, Barth posits the fallibility of Scripture, its susceptibility to err and to contradict itself.

But when inspiration is understood in light of Paul's teaching in 2 Timothy 3:16 and in light of other testimonies in Scripture, an entirely different picture emerges. Without obliterating or compromising the humanity of the biblical authors, the Spirit so superintended the composition of Scripture that the written products were the Word of God. And because they are the Word of God, they are free from error, for the simple reason that God cannot err. The text of the sixty-six books of the Scriptures of the Old and New Testaments, is authoritative because it is the Word of God. The Spirit's work of illumination is necessary for the sinner savingly to perceive what these books already are, the inspired Word of God. There is a needful subjective work of the Spirit in relation to the Bible, but that work terminates upon the mind of the reader. It does not make the Bible something it is presently not.

Conclusion

Karl Barth is one of the most prolific and influential theologians of the twentieth century and, it seems, of the early twenty-first century. He was the unusual combination of a modern theologian who was sympathetically conversant with the past, particularly the Protestant Reformation. For this reason alone, his writings on the doctrine of Scripture merit careful study and thoughtful reflection. Notwithstanding the insights that his writings afford and the questions that they pose, Barth's doctrine of the Word of God suffers from serious liabilities.[158] Not least among these liabilities is its departure from the teaching of the Bible about itself. In the end, Barth's statements about Scripture – like any theologian's statements about Scripture – need to be subjected to the scrutinizing light of Scripture. They stand in submission to the Bible for the simple reason that the Bible 'is and remains the ever-living Word of the ever-living God.'[159]

---

158. With respect to Barth's doctrine of inspiration, see the extensive list of reservations expressed by the self-described 'fallibilist ... in my doctrine of Scripture' at Sonderegger, 'The Doctrine of Inspiration and Reliability of Scripture,' in *Thy Word is Truth*, 22-3.
159. Runia, *Karl Barth's Doctrine of Holy Scripture*, 219.

Peter Enns and the Doctrine of Scripture

One recent and protracted controversy relating to the doctrine of Scripture within contemporary evangelicalism concerns the views of Peter Enns.[1] Enns served as Professor of Old Testament at Westminster Theological Seminary from 1994 to 2008. He exited Westminster after a three-year institutional debate that ensued upon the publication of Enns's *Incarnation and Inspiration: Evangelicals and the Problem of the Old Testament* (Grand Rapids: Baker, 2005).[2]

---

1. This chapter originally appeared as 'Peter Enns and the Incarnational Analogy, Part 1' *RTR* (2019) 78/3: 197-217 and 'Peter Enns and the Incarnational Analogy, Part 2' *RTR* (2020) 79/1: 29-45. Used by permission of *RTR*.

2. David O'Reilly, 'Controversial Theologian,' n.p. [cited 9 March 2020]. *https://www.inquirer.com/philly/news/homepage/20080726_Controversial_theologian.html*. *Inspiration and Incarnation* has since appeared in a second edition, and, unless otherwise noted, it is this edition to which reference will be made in this chapter, *Inspiration and Incarnation: Evangelicals and the Problem of the Old Testament, 10th Anniversary Edition* (2d ed.; Grand Rapids: Baker, 2015).
  Critical responses to *Inspiration and Incarnation* (2005) include Richard B. Gaffin, Jr, 'Observations on a Controversy,' *Reformed Perspectives Magazine* 10 (2008), www.reformedperspectives.org; G. K. Beale, *The Erosion of Inerrancy in Evangelicalism: Responding to New Challenges to Biblical Authority* (Wheaton, IL: Crossway, 2008), 25-122; Bruce K. Waltke, 'Revisiting *Inspiration and Incarnation*,' *WTJ* 71/1 (2009): 83-95, and 'Interaction with Peter Enns,' *WTJ* 71/1 (2009): 115-28; D. A. Carson, 'Three More Books on the Bible: A Critical Review,' *TJ* 27 (2006): 1-62, repr. in D. A. Carson, *Collected Writings on Scripture* (Wheaton, IL: Crossway, 2010), 237-301; Norman L. Geisler and William C. Roach, *Defending Inerrancy: Affirming the Accuracy of Scripture for a New Generation* (Grand Rapids: Baker, 2011), 99-111; and Mark Noll, *Jesus Christ and the Life of the Mind* (Grand Rapids: Eerdmans, 2011), 132-45.

Enns's departure from Westminster in 2008 by no means concluded the controversy surrounding his published views on Scripture. Enns has continued to write on the subject and he has continued to engage evangelical scholarship on the important questions broached by his writings.[3] The issues that have arisen in these discussions are substantive ones touching on the nature, character, interpretation, and application of Scripture. As such, they merit close attention and careful engagement.

In this chapter, we will explore Enns's formulation of what he calls the incarnational analogy.[4] We will see that the particular way in which Enns formulates an analogy between the Bible and the two natures of Christ constitutes a departure from the Bible's teaching about itself. We will give attention to two related topics of interest to Enns, specifically the nature and character of the Old Testament, and the way in which the New Testament writers interpret the Old Testament. We will then explore how Enns conceives his own doctrine of Scripture in relation to the doctrine of inerrancy. Finally, we will offer a critical assessment of Enns's views on Scripture.

The Incarnational Analogy

The incarnational analogy argues for an analogous relationship between the person of Christ and the text of Scripture. The orthodox doctrine

---

Enns's printed responses to some of these critical engagements include 'Response to G. K. Beale's Review Article of *Inspiration and Incarnation*,' *JETS* 49/2 (2006): 313-26; 'Response to Professor Greg Beale,' *Themelios* 32/3 (May 2007): 5-13; and 'Interaction with Bruce Waltke,' *WTJ* 71/1 (2009): 97-114.

3. Enns's publications subsequent to 2008 include *The Evolution of Adam: What the Bible Does and Doesn't Say About Human Origins* (Grand Rapids: Baker, 2012); *The Bible Tells Me So: Why Defending Scripture Has Made Us Unable to Read It* (New York: HarperOne, 2014); *The Sin of Certainty: Why God Desires Our Trust More Than Our 'Correct' Beliefs* (New York: HarperOne, 2016); *How the Bible Actually Works* (New York: HarperOne, 2019). Enns also maintains an extensive library of his own blog posts at www.peteenns.com, including responses to critical reviews of his books.

For Enns's ongoing engagement of evangelical scholarship on questions relating to the doctrine of Scripture, see his 'Fuller Meaning, Single Goal,' in *Three Views of the New Testament Use of the Old Testament* (eds. Kenneth Berding and Jonathan Lunde; Grand Rapids: Zondervan, 2008), 167-217; and 'Inerrancy, However Defined, Does Not Describe What the Bible Does,' in *Five Views on Biblical Inerrancy* (eds. J. Merrick and Stephen M. Garrett; Grand Rapids: Zondervan, 2013), 83-116.

4. Enns, *Inspiration and Incarnation*, 5, et pass. As we will see, the incarnational analogy is not unique to Enns, but has precedent within the Reformed tradition.

of the person of Christ affirms that 'two whole, perfect, and distinct natures, the Godhead and the manhood, were inseparably joined together in one person, without conversion, composition, or confusion' (WCF 8.2). Proponents of an incarnational analogy contend that the Bible is at once fully divine and fully human and therefore is analogous to the incarnate Christ.

Historical Formulations

Some Reformed theologians in the nineteenth century made a general comparison between Christ as divine and human and the Bible as divine and human. Herman Bavinck and Abraham Kuyper, for instance, broadly employed the analogy in order to illustrate the character of Scripture. In doing so, Kuyper particularly emphasized the coordinate character of both Christ and the Bible as 'mystery' and the impossibility of confessing the one mystery without also confessing the other.

> In the union of these two factors [i.e., the divine and the human] now lies the mystery of Holy Scripture. Parallel with the mystery of the incarnation runs the mystery of inscripturation. In both cases the Word of God comes to us, in the manger as Emmanuel in the world where we live, in Holy Scripture as Emmanuel in the world of our thoughts and ideas. Both revelations of the Word belong together, just as our living and the consciousness of that living belong together. Thus both mysteries must either be rejected together or confessed together and, if confessed, then on the same ground.
>
> In Christ and in Holy Scripture we have to do with related mysteries. In the case of Christ there is a union of divine and human factors. The same is true of Scripture; here, too, there is a primary author and a secondary author. To maintain properly the relationship between these two factors is the great work of dogmatics ... Everything depends here on the right insight that the Word has become flesh in Christ and is stereotyped in Scripture. Thus Scripture must be a *graphē theanthrōpeia* [theanthropic writing], truly human and truly divine.[5]

For Kuyper, as Gaffin notes, neither in Christ nor in the Scripture are the divine and the human 'equally ultimate,' since 'the priority and originating

---

5. Abraham Kuyper, *Principles of Sacred Theology* (trans. J. DeVries; 1898; Grand Rapids: Eerdmans, 1954), 1.59, 63, 75, as cited at Richard B. Gaffin, Jr, *God's Word in Servant-Form: Abraham Kuyper and Herman Bavinck on the Doctrine of Scripture* (Jackson, MS: Reformed Academic Press, 2008), 21, 22.

initiative belong to the divine, not the human. Specifically, the Word, in his antecedent identity as the Word, became flesh and God is the primary author of the Bible, in distinction from the secondary human authors.[6]

Kuyper's contemporary, Herman Bavinck, similarly appealed to the incarnation in his explanation of the nature of Scripture.

> In the doctrine of Scripture, [the theory of organic inspiration] is the working out and application of the central fact of revelation: the incarnation of the Word. The Word (*logos*) has become flesh (*sarx*), and the word has become Scripture; these two facts do not only run parallel but are most intimately connected. Christ became flesh, a servant, without form or comeliness, the most despised of human beings; he descended to the nethermost parts of the earth and became obedient even to the death of the cross. So also the word, the revelation of God, entered the world of creatureliness, the life and history of humanity, in all the human forms of dream and vision, of investigation and reflection, right down into that which is humanly weak and despised and ignoble. The word became Scripture and as Scripture subjected itself to the fate of all Scripture. All this took place in order that the excellency of the power, also of the power of Scripture, may be God's and not ours. Just as every human thought and action is the fruit of the action of God in whom we live and have our being, and is at the same time the fruit of the activity of human beings, so also Scripture is totally the product of the Spirit of God, who speaks through the prophets and apostles, and at the same time totally the product of the activity of the authors. 'Everything is divine and everything is human'.[7]

Like Kuyper, Bavinck emphasizes the dual character of Scripture as divine and human. The divinity and humanity of Scripture is not partitive. One may not, in other words, partition Scripture into separate divine and human sections. The divinity and humanity of Scripture is aspectual. Scripture is simultaneously but in distinct aspects divine and human, 'totally the product of the Spirit of God, who speaks through the prophets and apostles, and at the same time totally the product of the activity of the authors.'[8]

---

6. Gaffin, *God's Word*, 22.

7. Herman Bavinck, *Reformed Dogmatics* (ed. John Bolt; trans. John Vriend; 4 vols.; Grand Rapids: Eerdmans, 2003), 1.434-5. Enns cites a portion of this paragraph at Peter Enns, 'Preliminary Observations on an Incarnational Model of Scripture: Its Viability and Usefulness,' *CTJ* 42 (2007): 227.

8. As Gaffin summarizes Bavinck's point, 'Scripture in its entirety – message and medium together and at the same time – is both divine and human,' *God's Word*, 79.

Bavinck joins Kuyper in laying emphatic priority upon the divinity of Scripture when considering the divine and human aspects of Scripture. Just as the 'Word (*logos*) has become flesh (*sarx*),' so also 'the word has become Scripture.' As Bavinck observes elsewhere, 'The revelation of God … does not fly high above us but descends into our situation; it has become flesh and blood, like us in all things except sin … The human has become an instrument of the divine; the natural has become a revelation of the supernatural; the visible has become a sign and seal of the invisible. In the process of inspiration, use has been made of all the gifts and forces resident in human nature.'[9] Bavinck, then, affirms that 'the human has become an instrument of the divine,' but the converse does not hold – he does not here speak of the divine becoming an instrument of the human. The divine is irreversibly prior to the human.

The incarnational analogy has its limitations for Bavinck. To be sure, Christ and Scripture are both divine and human. In each, deity has an irreversible priority to humanity. As Gaffin summarizes Bavinck's view, while Scripture has 'a unique theanthropic character,' Bavinck refrains from positing 'some sort of hypostatic union between divine and human elements.'[10] The analogy, then, is a bounded analogy. There are crucial differences between the way in which we are to understand the divine and the human in Christ, on the one hand, and in Scripture, on the other.

B. B. Warfield, a contemporary of both Bavinck and Kuyper, expresses similar reserve when entertaining the analogy of the incarnation to the character of Scripture.

> It has been customary among a certain school of writers to speak of the Scriptures, because thus 'inspired,' as a Divine-human book, and to appeal to the analogy of Our Lord's Divine-human personality to explain their peculiar qualities as such. The expression calls attention to an important fact, and the analogy holds good a certain distance. There are human and Divine sides to Scripture, and, as we cursorily examine it, we may perceive

---

9. Bavinck, *Reformed Dogmatics*, 1.442-3. Enns cites this portion of Bavinck's discussion at 'Preliminary Observations,' 227n.18.

10. Gaffin, *God's Word*, 101. Gaffin continues, 'Scripture has its distinctive servant-form, not because of its "humanity," generally considered, but because Christ was incarnated, not in a state of glory but of humiliation. The correlate to the sinlessness of Christ is that Scripture is without error,' ibid. Compare Gaffin's concurring comments with respect to Kuyper's understanding of the incarnation and the doctrine of Scripture, *God's Word*, 46.

in it, alternately, traits which suggest now the one, now the other factor in its origin. But the analogy with Our Lord's Divine-human personality may easily be pressed beyond reason. There is no hypostatic union between the Divine and human in Scripture; we cannot parallel the 'inscripturation' of the Holy Spirit and the incarnation of the Son of God. The Scriptures are merely the product of Divine and human forces working together to produce a product in the production of which the human forces work under the initiation and prevalent direction of the Divine: the person of Our Lord unites in itself Divine and human natures, each of which retains its distinctness while operating only in relation to the other. Between such diverse things there can only exist a remote analogy; and, in point of fact, the analogy in the present instance amounts to no more than that in both cases Divine and human factors are involved, though very differently.[11]

Warfield does not categorically object to employing an incarnational analogy to the Scripture. His concern is that this analogy not be 'pressed beyond reason.' 'Incarnation' and 'inscripturation,' he argues, are not 'parallel' for the simple reason that the text of Scripture admits of no hypostatic union. The analogy, for Warfield, is properly a 'remote' one. That is to say, in both the biblical text and the person of Christ we may affirm the 'involv[ement]' of the divine and the human, 'though very differently.' In expressing these reservations, Warfield is not materially disagreeing with either Kuyper or Bavinck. He is, however, urging caution and restraint in the employment of the incarnational analogy with respect to the production and character of Scripture. If Kuyper and Bavinck each offers a modest articulation of the incarnational analogy, Warfield is concerned to make explicit the parameters and limitations of that analogy.

Peter Enns

Enns is aware of at least some of this historical discussion within Reformed theology.[12] We will see, however, that his formulation of

---

11. Benjamin B. Warfield, 'The Biblical Idea of Inspiration,' *The Inspiration and Authority of the Bible*, 162, much of which is cited at Historical and Theological Field Committee (of the Faculty of Westminster Theological Seminary), *'Inspiration and Incarnation*: A Response' (2006), http://www.bible-researcher.com/enns1.html. See the same statement at *The Works of Benjamin B. Warfield* (10 vols.; New York: Oxford University, 1932), 1:108.

12. Enns, 'Preliminary Observations,' 226-8. Enns, however, mistakenly appeals to the category of 'incarnation' to describe the doctrine of Scripture found in A. A. Hodge and B. B. Warfield, *Inspiration* (Philadelphia: Presbyterian Board of Publication, 1881), and

the incarnational analogy departs from this discussion in at least two important ways. First, whereas the comments of Kuyper, Bavinck, and Warfield on the incarnational analogy are spare and brief in comparison with their discussions of the doctrine of Scripture as a whole, Enns has opted to make the incarnational analogy a central plank of his explanation of the character of the Bible. Second, Enns materially departs from the consensus that we have observed in the statements of these three theologians on the subject of the incarnational analogy.

For Enns, the incarnation provides the framework within which one should think about the character of the Bible.

> The starting point for our discussion is the following: *as Christ is both God and human, so is the Bible.* In other words, we are to think of the Bible analogously to how Christians think about Jesus. Christians confess that Jesus is both God and human at the same time ... Jesus is 100 percent God and 100 percent human – at the same time ... In the same way that Jesus is – *must be* – both God and human, the Bible is also a divine and human book.[13]

Enns's interest in the incarnational analogy concerns the way in which it sustains what he understands to be the full and uncompromised humanity of Scripture. Just as the incarnate Christ 'completely assumed

---

Warfield, 'The Divine and Human in the Bible,' 'Preliminary Observations,' 221-4. In the portions that Enns cites, Hodge and Warfield address the relationship between the divine and the human in Scripture. They refrain, however, from invoking the incarnation as an analogy to characterize or explain that relationship. The category they employ, rather, is concursus, '[The] whole of Scripture is the product of the divine activities which enter it, not by superseding the activities of the human authors, but by working confluently with them, so that the Scriptures are the joint product of divine and human activities, both of which penetrate them at every point, working harmoniously together to the production of a writing which is not divine here and human there, but at once divine and human in every part, every word and every particular,' 'The Divine and Human in the Bible,' cited at Enns, 'Preliminary Observations,' 221. As the Historical and Theological Field Committee observe, '*Concursus* is typically discussed within the context of *causality* with respect to God's providence, and is set against such notions as occasionalism and conservationism. Warfield used the word to highlight the fact that God used secondary causes in much of the process of inscripturation, and did not eliminate or override (occasionalism) the human elements, neither did the human elements take precedence (conservationism). *Concursus* is *another model* for thinking of the writing of Scripture, and in that sense is not easily included in an Incarnational analogy,' *Inspiration and Incarnation:* A Response,' emphasis original.

13. Enns, *Inspiration and Incarnation*, 5, emphasis original.

the cultural trappings of the world in which he lived … so too the Bible.' The Bible 'was *connected to* and therefore *spoke to* those ancient cultures. The enculturated qualities of the Bible, therefore, are not extra elements that we can discard to get to the real point, the timeless truths.'[14]

The incarnational analogy, so construed, helps ward off the 'scriptural docetism' that Enns alleges threatens many evangelical understandings of the Bible.[15] Just as orthodox Christology denies that 'Christ only appeared to be human,' the incarnational analogy denies that the 'marks of [Scripture's] humanity are only apparent, to be explained away.'[16] On the contrary, 'that the Bible, at every turn, shows how connected it is to its own world is a necessary consequence of God incarnating himself.'[17] For that reason, 'it is essential to the very nature of revelation that the Bible is not unique to its environment. The human dimension of Scripture is essential to its being Scripture.'[18]

Enns's interest in the incarnational analogy, as he formulates it, overwhelmingly lies in the humanity of Scripture. For the Scripture to be human, according to Enns, it must bear the marks and traits of the culture to which it was tied. Enns elaborates his understanding of Scripture's humanity along two primary lines. The first is the context and message of the Old Testament. The second is the way in which the New Testament writers interpret the Old Testament. We may explore each line in turn.

The Context and Message of the Old Testament

The four books that Enns has authored explaining his understanding of Scripture address dozens of Old Testament passages. We may look at three passages or classes of passages in particular. They will particularly illustrate the way in which Enns conceives the humanity of the Old Testament.

The first passage is the creation account in Genesis 1-2. Noting the similarities between the Genesis creation account and such Akkadian

---

14. ibid.
15. ibid., 6.
16. ibid.
17. ibid., 8.
18. ibid.

texts as *Enuma Elish, Atrahasis,* and *Gilgamesh,* Enns asks 'how can we say logically that the biblical stories are true and the Akkadian stories are false when they both look so very much alike?'[19] He proposes understanding these Ancient Near Eastern accounts and the biblical account as 'myth,' that is, 'an ancient, premodern, prescientific way of addressing questions of ultimate origins and meaning in the form of stories: Who are we? Where do we come from?'[20] We should not thus impose modern and scientific ways of understanding the world upon an ancient and prescientific society. 'God ... allowed his word to come to the ancient Israelites according to standards *they* understood ... the Bible must be understood in light of the cultural context in which it was given.'[21] Genesis, Enns urges, 'reflects an ancient Near Eastern worldview that clearly is significantly older.'[22]

But if Genesis, including its opening chapters, shares the 'worldview categories of the ancient Near East,' what renders it different from *Enuma Elish, Atrahasis,* and *Gilgamesh*? It is that 'the God [to whom Abraham and his seed] are bound to ... is different from the gods around them.'[23] When God, then, 'adopted Abraham as the forefather of a new people ... he also adopted the mythic categories within which Abraham – and everyone else – thought.' But 'God *transformed* the ancient myths so that Israel's story would come to focus on its God, the real one.' [24]

To ask such questions of Genesis as 'whether the days were literal or figurative' or 'whether the flood was local or universal' is to ask questions 'generated by a modern worldview,' and 'borders on modern Western arrogance' in refusing to read Genesis within its own 'ancient contexts.'[25] It overlooks, furthermore, the fact that 'our own theological thinking is wrapped in cultural clothing as well ... the Bible is [not] a timeless, contextless how-to book that we are meant to apply to today's world. Rather, the Bible itself demonstrates the inevitable cultural dimension of

---

19. ibid., 29.
20. ibid., emphasis removed. Enns restates in almost identical terms the definition at *Inspiration and Incarnation,* 39.
21. ibid., 30.
22. ibid., 41.
23. ibid., 41, 42.
24. ibid., 42.
25. ibid., 44.

any expression of the gospel ... Each generation, by the power of God's Spirit, has to make the gospel message its own by wrestling with how the gospel connects with the world in which that generation is living.'[26]

A second group of passages concerns the question whether the Old Testament affirms the existence of one God alone or acknowledges the existence of a plurality of gods, of whom the God of Israel is the greatest. Enns notes that there are many texts in the Old Testament that 'speak of Yahweh alone as God.'[27] But the Old Testament, he argues, 'paints a more varied portrait of God.' The 'ancient Near Eastern people' believed that 'multiple gods ... existed' and 'when God called Israel, he *began* leading them into a full knowledge of who he is, but he started where they were.'[28] For this reason, several Psalms confess God to be 'greater than the gods of the surrounding nations,' and Joshua's well known exhortation to Israel in Josh 24:2, 14-15 assumes the existence of other gods.[29] The message to Israel of Exodus's account of the plagues in Egypt is that 'this god Yahweh, who lives in a desert, who is a god of slaves ... meets these powerful Egyptian gods on their own turf, and ... beats them up.'[30] 'At this point in the history of redemption ... the gods of the surrounding nations are treated as real ... God always speaks in ways that the people understand, not simply to leave them there but to bring them along to deeper knowledge of himself.'[31]

A third group of passages that Enns addresses as illustrative of the humanity of the Bible is the biblical account of the conquest of

---

26. ibid., 56.
27. ibid., 86.
28. ibid., 87.
29. ibid., 87, 88.
30. ibid., 90.
31. ibid., 91. Enns's comments directly follow his reflections upon Exodus 20:1-6. Compare his comments in *The Bible Tells Me So*, 'God allows himself to be talked about, worshipped, and trusted by the Israelites within the boundaries of that ancient horizon ... The Bible reflects diverse views of God because the Bible records Israel's diverse spiritual journey. At some point later on in their journey (we don't know exactly when), the Israelites settled on a final answer to the question: only one God exists. For both Jews and Christians today, that one answer remains true, and the other biblical portrait of God – where he is one among many – is left behind. The portrait of God that the ancient Israelites assumed for much of their history – that he is the best God among the many – is not factually true. And ... God is fine with us drawing that conclusion.' 153, 154.

Canaan, an account that Enns suggests relates the moral equivalent of the terrorist attacks on the United States on September 11, 2001.[32] Enns stresses that 'the extermination of the Canaanites is not an afterthought. According to the Bible, Israel's God planned it from the days of Noah and the flood, and he carries out the plan with bracing determination and precision …'[33] The reason for the extermination of the Canaanites 'wasn't their immorality, but the fact that they (like everyone else) were an immoral people who *occupied the land* God promised to give to the Israelites. To leave any Canaanites alive would (1) contaminate the land and (2) threaten Israel's devotion to their God.'[34]

In point of fact, Enns continues, 'God never told the Israelites to kill the Canaanites. The Israelites believed that God told them to kill the Canaanites.'[35] The Israelites were simply doing what any other culture in their day and age would have done in their circumstances. Complicating matters, furthermore, is that the archaeological record contradicts the biblical account of the conquest, according to Enns. The biblical record is a collection, he concludes, of 'exaggerated stories of Israel's wars against the Canaanites in days of old … the Bible's version of events is not what happened.'[36] The biblical record of the conquest, put positively, 'is the story of God told from the limited point of view of real people living at a certain place and time … part of Israel's story of the past – not a historical account of something God did.'[37] But that 'ancient tribal description of God is *not the last word* … [Their] understanding of God [was] adequate *for them in their time,* but not *for all time.*'[38] The same dynamics are at work generally in the Old Testament's accounts of the creation, the exodus, the monarchy, and the exile – Israel is telling

---

32. Enns, *The Bible Tells Me So*, 31. Enns argues that 'Jesus was against it,' that is to say, the ethic that Jesus promotes in the Sermon on the Mount is diametrically opposed to the ethic evident in the conquest narrative, *The Bible Tells Me So*, 44. For a distinct treatment of the conquest, see Enns, 'Inerrancy, However Defined, Does Not Describe What the Bible Does,' 104-13.

33. ibid., 40.

34. ibid., 53, emphasis original.

35. ibid., 54.

36. ibid., 60.

37. ibid., 62, 70.

38. ibid., 65, emphasis original.

a story about God in familiar cultural categories. They tell this story in order to convey 'meaning for *them* ... [namely,] we are still here, for the God of old, the mighty creator, the one before time, the God of 'back then and up there' is on our side here and now.'[39]

Enns, then, opts to speak of 'what the Bible is doing with the past' as 'storytelling' rather than 'history writing.' In these stories, their Israelite authors inevitably and invariably reflect the cultural milieu of which they are part. But they do not simply echo their culture. They are 'shap[ing] the past' in light of their conviction about Yahweh.[40]

The ensuing diversity of the Old Testament, for Enns, entails that 'portions of the Bible are in tension with each other.'[41] The reason that these tensions, even contradictions, exist in Scripture is because God fully 'participates in history ... he *"incarnates"* himself – in a manner of speaking – throughout Israel's history ... *For God to reveal himself means that he accommodates himself.* [That is], he condescends to the conventions and conditions of those to whom he is revealing himself.'[42]

For Enns, the unity of the Bible does not consist in any harmony of the details, assertions, or even outlook of the Old Testament writers. For Christians, he urges, unity 'should ultimately be sought in Christ himself, the living word.' This unity is 'a broad and foundational theological commitment based on the analogy between Christ and Scripture.' 'The written word bears witness to the incarnate Word, Christ' insofar as 'Christ is the final destiny of Israel's story.'[43]

Seen from this perspective, the diversity of Scripture, as Enns conceives it, is a commendable aspect of the Bible.

> Christ is the ultimate example of how God enters the messiness of history to save his people. He did not keep his distance but became one of us. This is true of Christ, the embodied Word. It is also true of the Bible, the written word. To put it this way is to turn the entire debate on its head: the diversity

---

39. ibid., 126, emphasis original.
40. ibid., 128, 129.
41. Enns, *Inspiration and Incarnation*, 96.
42. ibid., 97, emphasis original. For an example of what Enns understands to be a contradiction internal to the Bible, see *Inspiration and Incarnation*, 80-2. Compare the multiple examples provided at *The Bible Tells Me So*, 160-2.
43. ibid., 98, 99.

of Scripture – and the tensions that this diversity introduces – bears witness to God's revelation rather than detracts from it.⁴⁴

Christians, Enns concludes, should take up the Old Testament and see in its diversity a univocal witness to Christ, in whom the Bible alone finds its unity.

The New Testament's Use of the Old Testament

For Enns, the conviction that Christ is the unifying principle of the Old Testament lies at the heart of the way in which the New Testament writers read, interpreted, and applied the Old Testament. It is when we share the conviction, although not necessarily the methods or even conclusions, of the New Testament writers, that we are interpreting the Old Testament in a manner that is faithful to the New Testament.

Enns summarizes his position under three brief headings.

1. The New Testament authors were not engaging the Old Testament in an effort to remain consistent with the original context and intention of the Old Testament author.
2. They were indeed commenting on what the text *meant*.
3. The hermeneutical attitude they embodied should be embraced and followed by the church today.⁴⁵

The New Testament writers, according to Enns, did not interpret the Old Testament in a manner that was faithful to the 'original context and intention' of the original human author. The reason is because the New Testament writers were Second Temple Jews who employed the same methods and approaches to interpreting the Old Testament books that their Jewish peers and contemporaries did.⁴⁶ Second Temple interpretation, Enns argues, constituted the 'hermeneutical world of Christ and the apostles.'⁴⁷ The New Testament texts, which evidence interpretative diversity among themselves, share the interpretative

---

44. ibid., 99.

45. ibid., 105.

46. Enns claims that these methods and approaches surface, in fact, within the later books of the Old Testament themselves, ibid., 107-10.

47. ibid., 110. See further, Enns, 'Fuller Meaning, Single Goal,' in *Three Views*, 170-80.

methods of their Jewish contemporaries. They also borrow certain traditions current within the Second Temple period – traditions that do not appear in the Old Testament text.[48] What distinguishes the New Testament writers from their Jewish contemporaries is 'their relentless focus on bearing witness to the crucified and risen Christ ... the conviction that Jesus is the climax of God's covenant with Israel.' This distinction is, in a word, 'eschatological' in character.[49]

This similarity of method characterizes the Old Testament interpretation both of Jesus and the apostles. Because 'Jesus was Jewish,' He 'shared with his fellow Jews ... [their] creative approach to handling the Bible.'[50] For this reason, Jesus interprets the Bible in ways, for Enns, that we would not and should not. Whereas Jesus interprets Exodus 3:6 to prove the resurrection, 'no reasonable connection exists between what the burning bush story says and what Jesus says it says.' He is 'engaging in a bit of creative biblical interpretation' that would have been at home within his interpretative culture.[51] What is driving Jesus' interpretation of this text, and of all other Old Testament texts that He interprets, is to show that 'he [is] the Bible's focus.'[52] Similarly, Jesus' reading of Psalm 82 in John 10:34 'isn't what that writer meant,' but 'from the point of view of Jesus' first-century world, creative handling of scripture is what you do.' His concern was to 'make claims about himself,' here, that 'he was superior to David.'[53]

---

48. See Enns, *Inspiration and Incarnation*, 132-41. Enns regards the reference to Jannes and Jambres at 2 Timothy 3:8; the text of Jude 14-15 (paralleled in 1 Enoch 1:9); the references to the law as given through angels at Acts 7:52-3, Galatians 3:19, Hebrews 2:2-3; and Paul's reference to the spiritual rock that accompanied Israel in the wilderness at 1 Corinthians 10:4 as examples of such intertestamental traditions that have made their way into the New Testament. For Enns's interpretation of 1 Corinthians 10:4, see Enns, 'The 'Moveable Well' in 1 Corinthians 10:4: An Extrabiblical Tradition in an Apostolic Text,' *BBR* 6 (1996): 23-38.

49. Enns, 'Fuller Meaning, Single Goal,' 178.

50. Enns, *The Bible Tells Me So*, 169. Jesus is 'fully human,' that is, 'deeply part of the world' of first-century Judea.' For Him to 'handle his Bible in a "fully human" way,' He had to handle it in a 'first-century Jewish' way, *The Bible Tells Me So*, 188.

51. 'The debates of the day were about *how to be flexible and creative*, not whether scripture was still binding. That was the world Jesus was part of,' ibid., 174, emphasis original.

52. ibid., 170.

53. ibid., 178, 179.

The apostles, Enns argues, do precisely the same thing that Jesus does. They adopt the interpretative methods of Second Temple Judaism, but they do so in service of the goal of bearing witness to Jesus from the text of the Old Testament. Matthew, for instance, did not 'respect the historical context of Hosea's words' in Hosea 11:1.[54] The passage, Enns argues, 'is not predictive of Christ's coming but retrospective of Israel's disobedience.'[55] Unbelieving Jews contemporary to Matthew 'would have disagreed with Matthew, but not because their exegetical sensibilities would have been violated. They would have disagreed because they did not share Matthew's faith in Christ.'[56]

Enns reflects upon how Matthew would have arrived at his interpretation of Hosea 11:1.

> Matthew is not reading Hosea 'objectively'. He did not arrive at his conclusion *from* reading Hosea. Rather, he began with the event by which all else is now to be understood. *It is the reality of the risen Christ that drove him to read Hosea in a new way:* 'Now that I see how it all ends, I can see how this part of the OT, too, drives us forward'.[57]

Enns therefore terms the apostolic hermeneutic a 'christotelic' hermeneutic. That is to say, 'to read the Old Testament "christotelically" is to read it *already knowing* that Christ is somehow the *end* to which the Old Testament story is heading.'[58] While a 'grammatical-historical reading of the Old Testament is not only permissible but absolutely vital in that it allows the church to see the varied trajectories set in the pages of the Old Testament itself ... on its own terms, so to speak ... for the church, it is vital to remember that the Old Testament does not exist simply

---

54. Enns, *Inspiration and Incarnation*, 123.

55. ibid.

56. Enns, 'Fuller Meaning, Single Goal,' 200.

57. ibid., 201, emphasis original. Enns is concerned to stress that he does not understand Matthew to be engaging in a 'superficial rummaging through the OT in search of proof texts to hook his Jewish readers. Rather, Matthew's use of Hosea reflects a deep clarity of theological conviction, but one that can only come in light of the reality of Pentecost,' 'Fuller Meaning, Single Goal,' 200.

58. Enns, *Inspiration and Incarnation*, 143, emphasis original. Enns's subsequent claims that apostolic hermeneutics are equally 'ecclesiotelic,' that is, concerned to show how the church, or the people of God, represents the 'fulfill[ment]' of the 'Old Testament story,' *Inspiration and Incarnation*, 144. Compare Enns's comments on christotelic interpretation at 'Fuller Meaning, Single Goal,' 214.

on its own, for its own sake, nor is it the final word. It cannot stand in isolation from the completion of the Old Testament story in the death and resurrection of Christ.'[59]

The apostles' hermeneutic of the Old Testament, therefore, is normative in one respect, and descriptive in another respect. The church is bound to share and adopt the New Testament's 'hermeneutical goal,' that is, 'the centrality of the death and resurrection of Christ.'[60] The apostles' methods, however, need not and often should not be adopted by the contemporary church. Enns hesitates to prescribe a given set of exegetical methods, preferring to insist, rather, that 'we should think of the goal first and recognize that methods exist to serve that goal.'[61] We are faithful to the New Testament when we 'follow … their hermeneutical goal' rather than 'their exegetical methods and interpretative traditions,' both of which are 'a function of their cultural moment.' Because we share their '*eschatological* moment' though not their cultural moment, we therefore adopt the New Testament authors' goal rather than their methods.[62]

Before we conclude this survey of how Enns relates his construal of the incarnational analogy to his understanding of the nature and character of Scripture, we should briefly give attention to Enns's understanding of the goal that serves both as the unifying principle of the Old Testament and as the hermeneutical axiom of the New Testament writers. That goal, of course, is the conviction that Jesus Christ has died and been raised from the dead. 'Israel's story,' Enns argues, 'taken on its own terms, is not adequate to bear the weight of God's surprise move of a crucified and resurrected messiah. It must be reshaped around Jesus.'[63] The New Testament authors, then, '*adapted and transformed* their sacred story to serve the story of Jesus – the story of the future invading the present, of an executed and raised messiah, of a "new creation."'[64] It is the apostle Paul, in particular, who 'transforms a tribal story, of kings,

---

59. ibid., 143.

60. ibid., 148. Enns states the matter emphatically, 'we *must* follow them' in this respect, ibid., emphasis original.

61. ibid., 149.

62. Enns, 'Fuller Meaning, Single Goal,' 216, emphasis original.

63. Enns, *The Bible Tells Me So*, 193.

64. ibid., 199, emphasis original.

land, and the purity of one group of people, into a global story of God's grace and peace to all nations.'[65]

The resurrection of Jesus 'required an act of reimagining God to keep up with this unexpected move. Paul and other New Testament writers had to tie it to Israel's story somehow rather than dismissing it.'[66] Thus, 'the central event of the Christian faith, the resurrection of the Messiah and the defeat of death, isn't part of the Old Testament trajectory. To see God doing such a thing is to radically reimagine what kind of a God we are dealing with.'[67] The New Testament generally, and Paul's epistles particularly, show the outworking of this reimagination with respect to dozens even hundreds of texts of the Old Testament.

But even Paul's words must not be taken to apply wholesale to the twenty-first-century church. Enns has recently argued that Paul's epistles are 'wisdom documents,' applying wisdom in concrete first-century church settings.[68] We must not 'simply graft the words before us onto an entirely different time and place,' but allow ourselves to be 'guided by [the] wisdom' in them and thus 'bring that biblical wisdom into our here and now.'[69] Paul's words, for instance, concerning obedience to the civil magistrate, the institution of slavery, the roles of women in the church, and the morality of same-sex relations may not and ought not be applied directly to the modern church. We must read those words, Enns argues, in light of their 'cultural context,' discovering that 'Paul might mean something other than what we expected.'[70] For instance, Paul's words about 'the role and status of women,' when read in context, lie on a 'wise trajectory' that, in Enns's view, 'Christians today can – and should build on ... and take farther.'[71] He further insinuates that Paul's restrictions on same-sex behavior are not normative for today, given that they 'assume a

---

65. ibid., 218.
66. Enns, *How the Bible* Actually *Works*, 244.
67. ibid., 246.
68. Enns argues, in fact, that the whole of the Bible should be interpreted and understood along these lines, that is, as a book of wisdom, see *How the Bible* Actually *Works*, 3-20.
69. Enns, *How the Bible* Actually *Works*, 256.
70. ibid., 268.
71. ibid., 265.

culture of sexuality different from our own.'⁷² In short, even the New Testament writers' words lie entirely within a first-century context. They ought not therefore to apply wholesale to subsequent generations of readers. Our task, as contemporary readers, is to appropriate the wisdom of the biblical texts for thinking and living today. Like the biblical writers, we too must 'talk about God in a way that is both connected to the tradition and meaningful for today.'⁷³ Like the biblical writers, we must be in 'the business of reimagining God ... following this trajectory laid out for us in Scripture.'⁷⁴

Inerrancy?

Before we conclude our survey of the way in which Enns articulates and develops the incarnational analogy, we should explore how Enns himself characterizes his own doctrine of Scripture. Specifically, we may ask whether he would characterize his view using the term 'inerrancy.' Enns acknowledges that his own views with respect to the propriety of the term have evolved. In the preface to the second edition of *Inspiration and Incarnation*, Enns comments that he drafted the first edition 'firmly and self-consciously in support of a "progressive inerrantist" or "genre inerrantist" point of view.' Progressive or genre inerrancy, for Enns, seeks to distance inerrancy from 'literalistic readings of Scripture.' Positively, inerrancy is 'an expression of faith and trust in God, that *whatever* the Bible does, *no matter* how it might or might not fit into preconceived categories, reflects the "free pleasure of God." Thus, things like historical inaccuracies, myth, and theological diversity in Scripture are not errors needing to be explained away or minimized but, paradoxically, embraced as divine wisdom.' The reason that this is so is because inerrancy 'allow[s]

---

72. ibid., 266.

73. ibid., 275. Even the creeds and confessions of the church's history, Enns claims, are 'monuments to wisdom that we revisit with profit, but dare not hold up as the nonnegotiable high moment of the tradition. That place is taken by Jesus, the true subject that all creeds are trying to put into words,' *How the Bible* Actually *Works*, 274.

74. Enns, *How the Bible* Actually *Works*, 274. 'The Bible does not leave us with one consistent portrait of God, but a collection of ancient and diverse portraits of how the various biblical writers understood God for their times. These biblical portraits of God ... illustrate for us the need to accept the sacred responsibility of asking what God is like for us here and now,' *How the Bible* Actually *Works*, 153.

the biblical phenomena to define the Bible's own framework and for us to adjust our thinking accordingly.'[75] Even so, Enns concludes, he has since shed the term inerrancy because 'the term has accumulated cultural baggage that it seems unable to throw off.' He does not employ the term 'errancy,' and prefers, on balance, the term 'non-inerrancy' to describe his view.[76]

In a separate article on inerrancy, Enns raises vigorous criticisms against the doctrine of inerrancy. Inerrancy is 'an a priori and prescriptive doctrine' that functions as a 'kind of criterion for genuine Christian faith' and 'an identity marker and means of determining who is in and who is out.'[77] Inerrancy arbitrarily seeks to exempt the Bible from 'the advances of modern science and critical study,' and Enns wonders whether 'there is not some sort of Gnosticism inherent in at least some forms of inerrancy.'[78]

On the contrary, Enns argues, one may only 'retain' the 'language of inerrancy' 'as a *descriptive* observation rather than a *prescriptive* declaration.' This 'descriptive approach' constitutes 'a statement of faith on the part of the reader that *no matter what is encountered, the reader is in the presence of the wisdom and mystery of our God.*'[79] It recognizes 'the manner in which God speaks truth, namely, *through the idioms, attitudes, assumptions, and general worldviews of the ancient authors.*' Inerrantist conceptions of truth owe more to modern 'cultural assumptions' than they do to the witness of the biblical text.[80] Inerrancy fails to 'be constrained by the Bible's own witness of God's pattern of working – that God's power is made known in weakness, he reigns amidst human error and suffering, and he lovingly condescends to

---

75. Enns, *Inspiration and Incarnation*, ix, x, emphasis original. The quoted material is from Herman Ridderbos, *Studies in Scripture and Its Authority* (Grand Rapids: Eerdmans, 1978), 26.

76. ibid., x, xn.3.

77. Enns, 'Inerrancy,' 113.

78. ibid., 90, 113. In accusing inerrancy of Gnosticism, Enns alleges that in this doctrine 'the "true" message is somehow lifted off the unfortunate restrictions of the historical page and made to abide in a world of detached dogmatic "universals",' 'Inerrancy,' 90.

79. ibid., 114, emphasis original.

80. ibid., 87, emphasis original. Compare his similar comments at 'Inerrancy,' 91.

finite human culture.'[81] In summary, inerrancy is a 'theory' that cannot 'explain the phenomena of the text.' It should, therefore, 'be amended accordingly' or, preferably, 'scrapped altogether.'[82]

Peter Enns and the Incarnational Analogy: An Assessment

Enns's doctrine of Scripture, formulated in print over a nearly fifteen-year period, places a central and controlling importance upon the incarnational analogy. As both he and his critics have acknowledged, the resulting model of Scripture stands at marked variance with the classical evangelical doctrine of inerrancy.[83] We may now proceed to assess Enns's formulation of the incarnational analogy, particularly as it bears on the doctrine of Scripture.

In doing so, we necessarily bypass engaging the many interpretations that he offers of texts from both the Old and the New Testaments. However, we do not concede to Enns the accuracy of those interpretations. Many critics of Enns, in fact, have constructively and compellingly responded to his exegesis of particular biblical texts.[84] Our concern here, rather, lies in the implications of Enns's published scholarship for the doctrine of Scripture. We may now raise several concerns and objections to Enns's formulation of the incarnational analogy.

The Definition of the Incarnational Analogy

First, it is important to note that, axiomatic for Enns's understanding of Scripture, is what he has termed the 'incarnational analogy.'[85] Kuyper, Bavinck, and Warfield employ the idea in a carefully and modestly delineated fashion, with Warfield going so far as to pronounce it a 'remote analogy' of a general character.[86] Each of these theologians grasped the inherent limitations to the incarnation in explaining or illustrating the character of Scripture. In contrast, Enns's employment

---

81. ibid., 91.

82. ibid., 84.

83. To note one further example, see Enns's comments upon the Chicago Statement on Biblical Inerrancy at 'Inerrancy,' 84-91.

84. See especially Beale, *Erosion*, and Waltke, 'Revisiting.'

85. Enns, *Inspiration and Incarnation*, 5.

86. Warfield, *The Inspiration and Authority of the Bible*, 162.

of the incarnational analogy is not only far-reaching, but it is also fundamentally imprecise, as D. A. Carson has perceptively observed.

> Whenever one makes an entire argument turn on analogy, it is imperative to explain in what ways the two poles of the analogy are alike and unlike ... If the incarnation is to be our model for how we think of Scripture, or even of Scripture's humanness, how do such elementary distinctions [as the humanity of Christ being 'sinlessly perfect'] play out? What might it mean to say that Scripture is composed of thoroughly human, but perfect documents? Or does the analogy break down? If so, why and where? None of this is discussed. 'Incarnation' is merely a rhetorically positive word to approve Enns's argument; it is not a word with real substance that can clarify or illuminate the nature of Scripture by really careful analogical argumentation.[87]

Because Enns fails to advance a formal definition of the incarnation, and a formal comparison of the Incarnate Christ with the text of Scripture, readers are left with no clear guidance as to the precise relationship between the incarnation and the Bible.[88] Enns's analogy neither advances nor illustrates an argument. It stands, rather, as a substitute for an argument.

In the postscript to the second edition of *Inspiration and Incarnation*, Enns signals a preference for the expression 'incarnational model' (or 'incarnational parallel') over 'incarnational analogy.'[89]

> [I prefer 'incarnational model'] since analogies work best if a lesser understood entity is made clearer by analogy with something that is better understood. The problem, of course, is that the incarnation of

---

87. Carson, 'Three More Books,' 269.

88. Enns protests in the Postscript to the Second Edition of *Inspiration and Incarnation* that, in advancing the incarnational analogy, 'I am not thereby suggesting that the Bible is ontologically divine and human – a "hypostatic union,"' 172, emphasis removed. He notes that it is 'correct (and self-evident) ... that a hypostatic union can only be spoken of with respect to Christ, mysterious as it may be,' ibid. But the responsibility for what Enns perceives to be a misreading of his original work is one that Enns must in no small measure shoulder himself. It appears that at least some readers of the first edition have understandably ventured what Enns at that time failed to do – to try to delineate in formal fashion the character of the analogy between Scripture and Christ.

89. In the first edition, Enns suggested a preference for the phrase 'incarnational *parallel* between Christ and the Bible' to the phrase 'incarnational analogy,' *Inspiration and Incarnation: Evangelicals and the Problem of the Old Testament* (Grand Rapids: Baker, 2005), 168.

Christ is itself an unfathomable mystery ... Hence I prefer 'model' to 'analogy' because of how models are used in other disciplines ... Models are mental constructions that try to account for as much data as possible in as economical and pleasing a manner as possible for as many people as possible.[90]

Enns introduces 'incarnational parallel' and 'incarnational model' as alternatives to 'incarnational analogy.' But neither alternative serves to clarify the inherently unclear 'incarnational analogy.' If anything, introducing these terms only compounds the reader's difficulty in understanding precisely how Enns conceives the relationship between the incarnation of Christ and the Bible.

The Divine and the Human in Scripture

When we consider materially the claims that Enns makes about the incarnational analogy, some troubling concerns emerge. The first is the way that Enns understands the relationship between the divine and the human in Scripture. To be sure, Enns disavows – and rightly disavows – conceiving Scripture along the lines of the hypostatic union of the two natures in the one person of Jesus Christ.[91] In doing so, he stands firmly with those nineteenth-century Reformed theologians who employed the analogy in their treatment of the doctrine of Scripture.

What, then, *is* the relationship, positively and constructively, between the divine and the human in Scripture? Enns says little more than that, just as Christ 'is 100 per cent God and 100 per cent human – at the same time,' the Scripture 'in the same way ... is also a divine and human book.'[92] Enns appears largely content to assert the divinity of Scripture. He concentrates virtually all of his attention upon the humanity of Scripture, and does so to such a degree that Scripture's divinity is functionally attenuated in his presentation of the character of the Bible.[93] We may see this by exploring what Enns has to say about the humanity and the divinity of Scripture, respectively.

---

90. Enns, *Inspiration and Incarnation*, 172. Enns goes on to say that 'the incarnational model is by no means the "best" or only useful model for reading Scripture,' *Inspiration and Incarnation*, 173.

91. See note 88 above.

92. Enns, *Inspiration and Incarnation*, 5.

93. See here the perceptive comments of Carson, 'Three More Books,' 269.

The Humanity of Scripture

The way in which Enns conceives Scripture's humanity constitutes a significant departure from the Reformed doctrine of Scripture. Enns properly stresses that the human authors of Scripture inhabited an age and culture very different from our own. Their writings cannot but reflect the stamp of these writers' personalities and the world of which they were part.[94] Enns's claim about the relationship of the biblical texts to their surrounding cultures, however, goes well beyond such a recognition. The Bible, he claims, is 'enculturated' and 'not unique to its environment.'[95] Therefore, the cosmology reflected in Genesis 1-2 is an entirely ancient one, discredited by the findings of modern science. Some Old Testament texts, furthermore, testify to the existence of Yahweh among multiple gods, a reflection of the henotheism of early Israelite culture, but not a 'portrait of God,' Enns concedes, that is 'factually true.'[96] The conquest narratives, like other narratives in the Old Testament, are said to be Israelite 'storytelling' not 'history writing.'[97] Enns has no trouble affirming the existence of factual and theological contradictions within the Old Testament, given the way in which he frames its human character.[98]

Enns understands, then, the humanity of Scripture to entail the biblical text's wholesale reflection of the culture, worldview, and perspective of the world from which it emerged. This dynamic accounts, Enns believes, not only for contradictions internal to the Old and New Testaments, but also for certain claims and assertions made by the biblical writers that modern readers could not accept today. For Enns, these phenomena are not embarrassments to be explained away apologetically. They are, he argues, precisely what we would expect to find in a 'thoroughly encultured product' such as the Bible.[99] Pronouncing such matters to be 'error' simply reflects 'modern expectations rather than the ancient ones.'[100]

---

94. So, rightly, Hodge and Warfield, *Inspiration*, 12-13, 27-8, cited at Enns, 'Preliminary Observations,' 222, 223.

95. Enns, *Inspiration and Incarnation*, 5, 8.

96. Enns, *The Bible Tells Me So*, 154.

97. ibid., 128.

98. Enns, *Inspiration and Incarnation*, 96-7.

99. ibid., 175.

100. ibid.

These enculturated phenomena correspond, for Enns, to the humanity of Christ. 'The mythic nature of Genesis is not analogous to a sinful Jesus (and therefore "error"). Rather, it is analogous to the olive skin, bearded face, and sandaled feet of Jesus of Nazareth, the languages he knew, and his limited knowledge ... Jesus' humanness participates fully in his historical setting; the Bible's "human" qualities likewise participate fully in its various historical settings.'[101] Furthermore, 'when God condescends to embrace myth in Genesis or midrash in Paul, these are to be celebrated and affirmed as *acts of God*, who freely and lovingly steps into the human drama in contextually appropriate ways, a God who is truly Immanuel, "God with us."'[102]

There are at least two related problems with conceiving 'humanity' as Enns does. The first arises from the way that Enns explains away concerns that he understands the text of the Old Testament to contain error. Such concerns, Enns claims, are the preoccupation of modernity and reflect a failure to read the Bible on its own (ancient) terms. But the New Testament writers, to take one example, operate with the very category of truth and error that Enns dismisses as a modern construct.[103] The apostle Peter insists that 'we did not follow cleverly devised myths when we made known to you the power and coming of our Lord Jesus Christ, but we were eyewitnesses of his majesty' (2 Pet. 1:16). Matthew documents the attempt of the Jewish leadership to discredit the resurrection as a fiction crafted by the disciples (Matt. 28:11-15). The New Testament everywhere insists upon the public and verifiable character of the good news about Jesus' death and resurrection that they proclaimed to the world. As Paul said to Agrippa, 'this has not been done in a corner' (Acts. 26:26). Paul goes so far as to say that, were the resurrection anything other than historical fact, then Christian preaching and Christian faith are in vain, and the apostles are guilty of bearing false witness against God (1 Cor. 15:14-15). What's more, when the New Testament authors treat the events recorded in the Old Testament, they treat them as fully

---

101. ibid., 176.

102. ibid., emphasis original.

103. The New Testament writers, in this regard, may be taken as representative of all biblical writers. Enns understands the Old Testament and New Testament writers to be of one mind with respect to their approach toward historical narrative.

historical, true, and non-mythical.[104] The New Testament authors, then, take great pains to distinguish the events they relate from myth or falsehood. They furthermore suspend their message upon the verifiable truth of these events. Modern readers of Scripture are not at liberty to refrain from applying the categories of truth and error to the Bible because of the Bible's antiquity.

Second, Enns's statements draw an analogy between the enculturated text of Scripture, which includes statements and claims that moderns reject, and the enculturated Christ. This analogy suggests that Christ in His humanity was not only capable of erring, but also did actually err. Enns is aware of this objection, but he fails to meet it satisfactorily.[105] He judges the 'mythic nature of Genesis' to be the equivalent not of 'a sinful Jesus (and therefore "error")' but Jesus' skin coloring, clothing, and language. He therefore believes that the incarnational analogy does not necessarily result in a sinful Christ – 'Jesus's humanness participates fully in his historical setting; the Bible's "human" qualities likewise participate fully in its various historical settings.'[106] Enns's reasoning is only persuasive if one accepts his contention that it is a category mistake for a modern reader to attribute error to claims and beliefs that arise from the Bible. But, we have seen, the distinction between truth and error is one that is operative within the biblical text. Enns's formulation of the incarnational analogy is incapable of preventing the legitimate attribution of error to the biblical text. It is equally incapable of preventing the legitimate attribution of error to the man Christ Jesus. Enns's analogy opens the door not only to errors in Scripture but also to errors in the thinking and teaching of the Lord Jesus Christ.

Enns's formulation of the incarnational analogy locks him into a false dilemma. *Either* the Bible is human in the way that Enns insists that it is human, namely, enculturated and, from a modern point of view, mistaken at various points, *or* the Bible is not properly or truly

---

104. See, for instance, the way in which the New Testament handles the opening chapters of Genesis in my 'Theistic Evolution and the New Testament,' in *A Scientific, Theological, and Philosophical Critique of Theistic Evolution: Why No Informed Person Should Believe in Theistic Evolution* (eds. J.P. Moreland, et al., eds.; Wheaton, IL: Crossway, 2017), 879-926.
105. As Enns states the objection, 'Christ's sinlessness invalidates my [i.e., Enns's] use of the incarnational analogy,' *Inspiration and Incarnation*, 171.
106. ibid., 176.

human at all. Enns compels us to choose between a fallible, errant Bible (and, by implication, a fallible, errant Christ) or a docetic understanding of the Bible (and, by implication, a docetic Christology). His published reflections on the Scripture do not seriously entertain the proposition that the Bible may be truly and fully human, without the presence of error in the writings of its authors; that the biblical authors may genuinely reflect their historical and cultural locations, all the while being entirely true and without error in their words and propositions. This is precisely the understanding of the Bible that the historic confessions and leading theologians of the Reformed tradition have upheld. Given Enns's long tenure at Westminster Theological Seminary, one would have expected him to address and to engage this historical position, especially as Reformed writers across the centuries have expounded and defended that position in light of allegations of error and contradiction within the Bible. But it is just such an engagement that is culpably absent from Enns's writings on the nature of Scripture.

The Divinity of Scripture

There is a still deeper problem with Enns's incarnational analogy. Classical Christian formulations of the incarnation affirm not only the full humanity of Christ, but also the full deity of Christ, a fact of which Enns is well aware. If the analogy is to be applied to the Bible, then one must equally affirm the Scripture to be fully divine and fully human, as Enns also recognizes.

The Bible therefore, as a whole and in all its parts, is fully divine. How, then, can Enns meaningfully affirm the Bible to be fully divine if it contains internal contradictions; if it advances claims and beliefs that no modern reader could be expected to espouse? Enns offers a response to questions such as these.

> The divine is ultimate insofar as incarnation initiates from above ... God's initiative has produced something that is irreducible and *sui generis,* an essentially and inextricably divine-human phenomenon not meant to be broken down into its constituent parts to get at some deeper knowledge ... In extending the analogy [of the incarnation] to the Bible, evangelicals tread on dangerous ground if they set aside – even unintentionally – the Bible's 'human dimension' in order to get to the really important matter of its divine dimension. This is a very practical point, for it is on the basis

of the supposed 'perfection' of Scripture (presumed to be a function of Scripture's 'divinity' rather than of its 'incarnate' property) that such things as the presence of significant historical and theological tensions and contradictions are deemed out of bounds; they *need* to be harmonized because a transcendent and logically consistent God would not write that way. For Christians, even the meaning of 'divine' cannot be abstracted from the incarnation, as if we can apprehend the former apart from the latter. Incarnation is the ultimate means by which the divine is mysteriously made known. One cannot get behind the incarnation to get closer to God, to see what God is really like, and then judge Jesus accordingly. Similarly, regarding the Bible, God's word is not truly received by rising above the ancient historical complexities, as if God were saying, 'Now remember, what is really important here is my divine essence, and I want to be sure to maintain its priority. But the best I can do is to give you a divine-human expression of that essence, So your job is to understand the incarnation in order to rise above it, to discern what is "really" going on beyond it, and not linger too long on the diverse, messy ups and downs of human history.' This is a caricature, perhaps, but in my experience, such a borderline gnostic sentiment lurks not too far below a more sophisticated veneer.[107]

Enns's remarks do not so much address the objection as deflect it. He alleges that behind the concern to safeguard the divinity of Scripture is an attempt to detach the knowledge of God from the incarnation. He insinuates that a form of Gnosticism lies behind the objection. Proponents of the classical doctrine of Scripture, of course, vehemently object to such a characterization of their view. If the 'God who never lies' (Titus 1:2) is the author of the Bible, then it necessarily follows, they correctly reason, that the Bible is incapable of deceiving its readers and of containing errors or contradictions.[108]

But neither do Enns's remarks specify precisely how he conceives the Bible to be a fully divine book. To be sure, as he states elsewhere, Enns affirms that 'no matter what is encountered, the reader [of the Bible] is in the presence of the wisdom and mystery of our God.'[109] The '"creatureliness" of Scripture is not an obstacle to be overcome, but *the*

---

107. ibid., 177, 178.
108. See, for instance, Geisler and Roach, *Defending Inerrancy*, 311. Compare Gaffin, 'Observations on a Controversy,' 15, citing WCF 1.4, 'God (who is truth itself) the author thereof.'
109. Enns, 'Inerrancy,' 114, emphasis removed.

very means by which Scripture's divinity can be seen. In fact, Scripture's divinity can *only* be seen *because* of its humanity – God's chosen means – not by looking past it.'[110] Such statements as these, while affirming the Scripture's divinity, fail to show in what sense Enns understands the Bible to be divine.

In a recent publication on the nature of Scripture, Enns addresses how he understands the human and the divine to relate in the Bible and does so in ways that point to his understanding of the divinity of Scripture. The human authors, he argues, give expression to their ideas of God in light of the circumstances in which they find themselves. Jonah portrays God as loving the Ninevites, while Nahum portrays God as hating the Ninevites. Jonah and Nahum relate 'God's attitude toward the Ninevites differently [because] they were written at different times and under different circumstances for different purposes.'[111] Both books 'are works of wisdom, of reimagining God to make sense of current experience in the here and now.'[112] Enns argues that what Jonah and Nahum are said to have done is a project that every biblical writer and every human being necessarily undertakes.

> The God I read about in the Bible is not what God is like – in some timeless abstraction, and that's that – but how God was imagined and then reimagined by ancient people of faith living in real times and places. By 'imagined' I don't mean the biblical writers made up God out of thin air. I believe these ancient people experienced the Divine. But how they experienced God and therefore how they thought and wrote about God were filtered through their experience, when and where they existed ... Reimagining God for one's here and now is what Christians and Jews have been doing ever since there have been Christians and Jews, and invariably so, because we are people ... The sacred responsibility I've been talking about is really a call to follow this biblical lead by reimagining God in our time and place ... We reimagine God in ways that account for and make sense of our experience.[113]

The biblical authors, then, document their experiences of God within a particular time and place. This undertaking, Enns insists, is not unique

---

110. Enns, 'Fuller Meaning, Single Goal,' 204, emphasis original.
111. Enns, *How the Bible Actually Works*, 105, emphasis removed.
112. ibid., 106.
113. ibid., 124-5, 126, emphasis removed.

to a particular culture or age, but is requisite for all human beings. Biblical readers today must 'follow this biblical lead' by 'reimagining God in our time and place,' just as the biblical writers did in their own time and place.

For Enns, then, the biblical writings are specimens of ancient persons' experiences of God within a particular time and place. They are normative in so far as they set a trajectory for readers to mimic or replicate that project in their own time and place. And, as 'scripture itself portrays the boundless God in culturally bound ways of thinking,' so must we.[114] For this reason, we have observed Enns to argue, the statements of Paul about gender and sexuality do not have the normativity that many assign to them. Our task is to 'talk about God in a way that is both connected to the tradition and meaningful for today.'[115]

This state of affairs prompts Enns to reflect on the task of readers of Scripture with respect to its alleged diverse, even contradictory, portrayals of God.

> I'd like to think – and in fact I do think – that the portrait of God in Jonah is closer to what God is like: that God does not rejoice in wiping people out, but desires to commune with people of every tribe and nation. But that's just me. Without a moment's hesitation, I will say that I favor one story over the other, because it makes more sense to me, as that sense is informed by other experiences that I and those I know have had of God and especially given what I understand of God in my time and place as a Christian.[116]

The Scripture, then, is divine in the sense that it is a record of humans' experiences of the divine. It provides the occasion for readers to engage the diverse testimonies to God found within the Bible. In this way, readers may conceive of God in ways that are appropriate to their own 'time[s] and place[s] as Christian[s].'

Enns's understanding of the divinity of Scripture is, of course, a marked departure from the classical Christian understanding of Scripture as the very Word of God. It also raises some important questions. On what basis has Enns privileged the books of the Old and the New

---

114. ibid., 276. Enns stresses that this state of affairs applies even to the way in which the story of Jesus is told in the New Testament, ibid.
115. ibid., 275.
116. ibid., 106.

Testaments as documents of the human experience of God? What sets them apart from any other number of religious texts? Enns indicates that portions of the Bible, such as the record of Jonah's experience of God, resonate with him because of his own experiences of God. Is the criterion of privileging the biblical books their resonance with one's own experience of God? If so, this criterion is entirely subjective, that is, it lies wholly within the realm of the individual. For Enns, however, likely antecedent to this subjective criterion is the Bible's unified witness to Jesus as the Christ. That is to say, one comes to the Bible in order to experience God in light of the Bible's unified testimony to Christ.

Enns, to be sure, repeatedly affirms Christ to be the goal in light of which the New Testament writers interpret the Old Testament. For Enns, it is this goal (and not the apostles' methods) that norms the church's study of the Old Testament. But how did the New Testament writers arrive at this conviction? Enns argues that the New Testament writers did what those before them have done (and what those after them will do), namely, they have 'reimagin[ed] God in view of an unexpected and ground-shifting development – not exile to Babylon, as formative as that was for Judaism, but a Messiah who challenged central elements of Israel's identity (Law, Temple, land), but who also died a shameful, dishonorable, criminal's death and then was raised. The New Testament story is, in other words, one big act of wisdom – a response to God's surprising presence here and now.'[117] This act of reimagination is, of course, in the train of a succession of prior reimaginations of God. But there is no clear reason, in Enns's telling, why *this* act of reimagination should be final or definitive, nor why the twenty-seven books of the New Testament, along with the books of the Old Testament, should be regarded as the complete, final, and sufficient special revelation of God to human beings.

We may press this concern further. On what basis may Enns claim that Jesus Christ is the final and definitive basis upon which people should reimagine God? To be sure, Enns concurs with the apostolic conviction that Christ is the goal or *telos* of God's work in history. But, on Enns's understanding of revelation, how could one preclude God's ongoing or continuing self-revelation to human beings beyond

---

117. ibid., 250.

the first century? Beyond the criterion of one's own experience of God, furthermore, how could one even assess much less verify or falsify a claim to ongoing divine revelation? Enns's position appears to operate on the basis of the conviction of the uniqueness of Jesus Christ in whom God has climactically and completely revealed Himself to human beings. In its sweeping subjectivity, however, Enns's position is not only unable to sustain that conviction, but it also fatally undermines that conviction.

In summary, the incarnational analogy, for Enns, defines the humanity and the divinity of Scripture in ways that are objectionable. For the Scripture to be fully human, Enns contends, it must be a complete expression of the culture in and out of which the human authors lived. As such, he sees Scripture containing claims and employing interpretative methods that modern readers would and should reject. It is impossible to reconcile this construal of the humanity of Scripture with the Bible's testimony to itself as given by inspiration of God (2 Tim. 3:16). Enns affirms in principle the full divinity of Scripture, understanding it to be embedded in the Scripture's humanity. He has recently argued that all of the biblical writers testify to their experience of God. In this latter respect, the Scripture is not so much divine in itself as it is divine as a unique and presumably privileged witness to God, a record of the biblical writers' experiences of God. Modern readers are free to embrace or reject these diverse witnesses to the degree that these witnesses align with their own experiences of God.[118] This construal of the divinity of Scripture stands contrary to the Bible's self-testimony as the infallible, inspired, and inerrant Word of God.

Enns's Method in Formulating the Doctrine of Scripture

Before closing this study of Enns's doctrine of Scripture, we should register an important methodological discrepancy between classically Reformed approaches to Scripture, and that of Enns. All parties acknowledge difficulties and alleged discrepancies in the text of Scripture, and the obligation of students of Scripture to account for

---

118. For Enns, our own experiences of God are subjective but not necessarily individualistic. They form, in part, in relation to the 'experiences [that] … those I know have had of God and especially given what I understand of God in my time and place as a Christian,' ibid., 106.

those difficulties and alleged discrepancies in framing their doctrine of Scripture. Enns opts to begin with those difficulties, even conceding at points that they rise to the level of genuine errors and contradictions. He derives a construal of the humanity of Scripture in light of his conclusions about those difficulties. He then proceeds to address in what respect Scripture is divine. The result, we have seen, is a marked departure from what Christians have historically confessed, namely, that the Bible is the Word of God.

By way of contrast, we may chart the method by which Warfield approached the formulation of the doctrine of Scripture. Warfield neither hid from nor evaded the difficulties. But the difficulties did not control the way in which he came to articulate the doctrine of Scripture. He was, in fact, well acquainted with methods of arriving at the doctrine of Scripture that were not dissimilar to Enns's, and he decisively rejected them.[119]

---

119. Warfield's argument, in full, is as follows: 'There are two ways of approaching the study of the inspiration of the Bible. One proceeds by obtaining first the doctrine of inspiration taught by the Bible as applicable to itself, and then testing this doctrine by the facts as to the Bible as ascertained by Biblical criticism and exegesis. This is good logical procedure; and in the presence of a vast mass of evidence for the general trustworthiness of the Biblical writings as witnesses of doctrine, and for the appointment of their writers as teachers of divine truth to men, and for the presence of the Holy Spirit with and in them aiding them in their teaching (in whatever degree and with whatever effect) – it would seem to be the only logical and proper mode of approaching the question. The other method proceeds by seeking the doctrine of inspiration in the first instance through a comprehensive induction from the facts as to the structure and contents of the Bible, as ascertained by critical and exegetical processes, treating all these facts as co-factors of the same rank for the induction. If in this process the facts of structure and the facts embedded in the record of Scripture – which are called, one-sidedly indeed but commonly, by the class of writers who adopt this procedure, "the phenomena" of Scripture – alone are considered, it would be difficult to arrive at a precise doctrine of inspiration, at the best ... If the Biblical facts and teaching are taken as co-factors in the induction, the procedure ... is liable to the danger of modifying the teaching by the facts without clear recognition of what is being done; the result of which would be the loss from observation of one main fact of errancy, viz., the inaccuracy of the teaching of the Scriptures as to their own inspiration. This would vitiate the whole result: and this vitiation of the result can be avoided only by ascertaining separately the teaching of Scripture as to its own inspiration, and by accounting the results of this ascertainment one of the facts of the induction. Then we are in a position to judge by the comparison of this fact with the other facts, whether this fact of teaching is in accord or in disaccord with those facts of performance. If it is in disaccord, then of course this disaccord is the main factor in the case: the writers are convicted of false teaching. If it is in accord, then, if the teaching is not proved by the accord, it is at least left credible, and may be believed

Warfield took as his starting point the testimony of the Bible to itself. That is to say, he began with what the biblical authors affirmed about their own writings, namely, that they were the very Word of God. He noted that the claims of these authors were well-grounded ones. The biblical writers were competent witnesses, credible teachers of doctrine, and attested and confirmed by the ministry of the Holy Spirit. From this starting point, one is properly positioned to proceed to the remaining phenomena of the biblical books, including any difficulties that they may present to readers.

Warfield highlights two fatal methodological liabilities to the approach that we have seen Enns adopt in formulating the doctrine of Scripture. The first is that one starts with certain 'phenomena' of Scripture and proceeds to construct a doctrine of the Bible on that basis. But one must, Warfield insists, begin with the statements of the Bible about itself, and with the warranted claims that the biblical authors make about themselves. To take these statements and claims as one's starting point in no way militates against an honest and vigorous engagement of the phenomenal difficulties of the Bible. But such a starting point provides the necessary context and framework within which to approach and address these difficulties. If we begin with the 'vast mass of evidence available to prove the trustworthiness of the Scriptural writers as teachers of doctrine,' we find that the 'phenomena' in question do not 'negative this doctrine.' However, if we start with these phenomena, 'classifying and reasoning from them, whether alone or in conjunction with the Scriptural statements, it may easily happen with us, as it happened with certain of old, that meeting with some

---

with whatever confidence may be justified by the evidence which goes to show that these writers are trustworthy as deliverers of doctrine. And if nice and difficult questions arise in the comparison of the fact of teaching with the facts of performance, it is inevitable that the relative weight of the evidence for the trustworthiness of the two sets of facts should be the deciding factor in determining the truth. This is as much as to say that the asserted facts as to performance must give way before the fact as to teaching, unless the evidence on which they are based as facts outweighs the evidence on which the teaching may be accredited as true. But this correction of the second method of procedure, by which alone it can be made logical in form or valid in result, amounts to nothing less than setting it aside altogether and reverting to the first method, according to which the teaching of Scripture is first to be determined, and then this teaching to be tested by the facts of performance,' Warfield, 'The Real Problem of Inspiration,' in *Works*, 1:222-4. Compare Warfield's similar argument at 'Inspiration,' in *SSW*, 2:632-6.

things hard to be understood, we may be ignorant and unstable enough to wrest them to our own intellectual destruction, and so approach the Biblical doctrine of inspiration set upon explaining it away.'[120] Enns, beginning with certain phenomena, finds himself unable to rise to the Bible's own teaching about itself. Had he reversed course and begun with the Bible's explicit statements and testimony to its own character, he would have been better placed to handle the difficulties that he rightly takes up.[121]

The second and related problem, as Warfield astutely notes, is that the Bible's self-testimony – its claims to inspiration, its authors' claims to be spokesmen from God, accredited teachers of doctrine – is in reality among the phenomena of the Bible. These data are no less biblical phenomena than the difficulties with which Enns wrestles over the course of his published reflections on Scripture. But these data play a negligible role in Enns's reflections, and particularly in his construction of the doctrine of Scripture. To the degree that Enns does take up the divinity of Scripture, these lines of teaching are largely absent from that discussion. This lacuna proves, in the end, fatal to Enns's doctrine of Scripture, in so far as he constructs a doctrine that omits data crucial to its formulation. The remaining evidence, furthermore, are not interpreted in light of these omitted data, are subjected to objectionable interpretations, and lead Enns to articulate a doctrine that fundamentally departs from what Christians have historically confessed about the Bible, namely, that it is the very Word of God.

Conclusion

To dissent from Enns's doctrine of Scripture is not to deny the humanity of Scripture. Nor is it to embrace a form of docetism. Neither is it an expression of indifference towards people within and outside the church who sincerely wrestle with difficulties relating to the contents of Scripture. It is, rather, to set and to explore the difficulties of Scripture within their proper context. It is to see the humanity of Scripture,

---

120. Warfield, 'The Real Problem of Inspiration,' in *Works*, 1:224.

121. As Warfield observes, 'what is to the point is to say, that we cannot set aside the presumption arising from the general trustworthiness of Scripture, that its doctrine of inspiration is true, by any array of contradictory facts, each one of which is fairly disputable. We must have indisputable errors – which are not forthcoming,' ibid., 1:225.

properly understood, in light of the Scripture's frequent and clear self-testimony to be the very Word of God. It is, ultimately, to make 'the basis of our doctrine … to be what the Bible teaches' and not 'what men teach.'[122] Here, and here alone, does faith find a firm and settled resting place.

---

122. ibid., 1:226.

Scripture Index

OLD TESTAMENT

Genesis
1-2 .... 278–279, 293–295
1:26-7 15
1:31 168
2 .... 63–65, 259
2:24 .... 87, 111
3:15 .... 62, 66
12:3 88
12:13 49
20:3 47

Exodus
Exodus 68, 280
3:6 .... 166–167, 284
3:7-12 167
3:15 167
9:13 88
9:16 88
17:14 85
20:1-4 .... 85, 259
20:1-17 102
20:22 102
24:3-4 259
24:4 86

Numbers
22-24 47
23:19 261

Deuteronomy
4:2 162–163
4:6-8 49
4:7-8 46
4:32-4 46
6:4-5 175
6:4-9 208
7:6 46
10:15 46
18:15 118
25:4 93
29:1 207
29:29 .... 207, 210
30:10-14 207–208
30:11-14 .... 210, 215
32:43 169

Joshua
1:8 216
24:2 280
24:14-15 280

Esther
Esther 145

Job
38-41 215

Psalms
Psalms 280
1:2 216

16 168–169
19:1-3 41
19:1-4 21–22
19:7 .... 209–210, 215
19:7-11 161–162
24:1 167–168
24:2 167
33:6 80
69 .... 88, 259
72:18 120
82 284
95 .... 87–88, 259
109 .... 88, 259
110 .... 259, 263
110:1 86–87
119:15 216
119:18 219
119:27 219
119:34 219
119:73 219
119:105 209–210
119:130 209–210
147:19-20 46

Proverbs
Proverbs 145
6:6 173
10:8 173
11:14 173

12:15 173
13:1 173
18:17 173
19:20 173
23:23 173
24:6 173
30:5-6 162–163
30:24-8 173

Ecclesiastes
Ecclesiastes 145
12:13 173

Song of Songs
Song of Songs 145

Isaiah
1:10f. 213
5:3 213
9:1 213
11:9 50
40:1f. 213
42:6 49
49:6 49
53 168

Jeremiah
2:4 213
4:1 213
10:1 213

Ezekiel
Ezekiel 145
3:1 213

Daniel
4:1-27 47

Hosea
11:1 285

Amos
3:2 46

Jonah
Jonah 298, 299, 300

Nahum
Nahum 298

Habakkuk
2:14 50

NEW TESTAMENT

Matthew
Matthew 285
5:1 213
7:28-9 118
8:13-17 168
10:10 93
11:27 118
12:38-9 119
13:1-2 213
15:1-9 191
16:1 119
16:2-4 120
16:18 150
19:4-6 ..... 87, 111, 259
22:29 166
22:31-4 166
26:55 213
28:11-15 294
28:18-20 50
28:20 231

Mark
Mark 141
12:35-7 .... 87, 259
12:36 263
16:15 182

Luke
Luke 141–142
2:1-3 174
3:1-2 174
10:7 93
24:25-7 68
24:44 146
24:44-5 144
24:44-9 .... 50, 68

John
1:1-3 61–62
1:1-18 .... 60, 62, 65
1:6 61–62
1:8 61–62
1:9 50
1:14 60–62

1:18 .... 61–62, 188
1:29-42 61
3:2 119
3:13 118
3:16 43
4:22 46
5:36 119
5:39 .... 61, 213
5:46 61
6:14 118
6:44-5 132
6:46 118
7:29 118
7:40 118
8:14 118
8:17-19 118
10:15 118
10:34 284
14 128
14:1-11 60
14:6 32
14:25-6 260
14:26 .... 90, 121
14:26-7 142
16 128
16:12-15 .... 90, 121,
             142, 260
16:13 230
17:4 188
17:6 188
20:19-23 50
20:30 171
20:30-1 210
20:31 163

Acts
Acts 122, 192, 195
1:8 ... 43, 50, 122–123,
              260
1:16 88
1:20 88
1:22 259
2:17 57
2:22 124
2:25-8 168–169
2:29-32 169
2:42 187
3 123
4:12 32

SCRIPTURE INDEX

4:33 259
5:36-7 174
9:15 124
11:28 174
13:47 50
14 123
14:8 26
14:11 26
14:15-17 ...... 26–27, 41
14:16-17 30
15:5 217
15:6-17 218
15:19 217
15:20-1 218
15:24 217
15:28-9 218
16:20 174
17:6 174
17:11 213–214
17:16-34 50
17:22-31 27–28
17:23-8 41
17:24-6 29
17:27 35
19:31 174
19:35 174
22:21 124
26:17-18 124
26:23 124
26:24-6 50
26:26 294

Romans

1 34
1-2 26
1:3-4 175
1:5 124
1:7 213
1:16-17 208
1:16-18 52
1:18 ... 16, 23, 130, 180
1:18-32 .... 24–25, 30
1:19-20 .... 22–23, 41
1:20 .... 29, 46
1:21 ...... 16, 23–24, 34,
                130, 180
1:21-2 33
1:25 .... 33, 35, 130
1:28 .... 33, 130, 180

1:28-32 34
2:1f. 24
2:4 .... 27, 35
2:12 24
2:13 24–25
2:14-15 .. 24–26, 32, 41
2:15-16 .... 30, 35
3:2 .... 47, 213
3:11 130
3:23 16
8:9 125
9:4 47
9:17 88
10:6-13 .. 208, 210, 215
10:13-15 32
10:14-15 208
10:17 41
11:33-6 215
11:36 15
14:4 229
15:4 .... 163, 211
15:9-12 98
15:18-19 124
15:22-33 124
16:16 178
16:25-6 41
16:26 124

1 Corinthians

1 Corinthians. 192, 195
1:2 213
1:20-4 51
1:21 .... 32, 34
1:26 213
1:28 213
2:15 213
8:7-13 176
9:9 93
9:19-23 218
10:1-11 211
10:15 .... 213, 229
10:25-6 167
10:28-9 176
10:31-3 176
11:5 187
11:13 229
11:28 187
12-14 92
13:2 197

14:3-4 48
14:22 48
14:26 91
14:30 91
14:30-1 195
14:37 .... 91, 95, 122,
                128, 142, 259
14:37-8 91
15:1-11 .... 98, 260
15:14 98
15:14-15 294
16:2 187

2 Corinthians

1:1 213
1:24 230
4:2 230
4:3-4 .... 180, 220
4:4 .... 130, 132
4:6 .... 132, 180, 221
11:3-4 125
11:13-14 125
12 126
12:12 125

Galatians

3:1-9 49
3:8 88
3:16 98
4:8 34

Ephesians

1:26 213
2:18-19 181
2:20 .... 66, 142, 196
3:16 131
3:18 131
4 34
4:11-13 217
4:15-16 217
4:17-18 33
4:17-19 180
4:18 .... 16, 130
5:27 231
6:1-3 213
6:5-8 213

Philippians

2:5-11 175

3:15-16 216
3:16 43

Colossians
1:15-20 175
2:16-17 .... 59, 187
3:20 213
3:22-5 213
4:16 213

1 Thessalonians
2:13 79
4:5 34

2 Thessalonians
1:8 34
2:1-2 137
2:2 187
2:15 .... 137, 185, 187
3:1 177
3:6 92–93
3:12 92
3:14 .... 92–93, 95, 142, 259
3:17 137

1 Timothy
3:16 175
4:12 212
4:13 66
5:17-18 93
5:18 .... 122, 128, 142
6:1-2 213

2 Timothy
1:14 66
2:2 .... 66, 175
3:1-10 160
3:15-17 ... 66, 159–160

3:16 . 73, 96, 128, 254, 267–268, 270, 301
3:16-17 .... 80–82, 211–212
4:6-8 178

Titus
1:2 .... 261, 297
2:7 212

Hebrews
Hebrews 141–143, 259, 266
1:1 58
1:1-2 .... 57, 188
1:1-3 82
1:1-4 .... 62, 65, 69
1:3 169
1:3-4 58–59
1:6 169
2:2 127
2:3-4 126–127
3 59
3:7 87
4:7 98
5-10 59
5:11-14 216
7:26 261
9:26 57
12:23 261

James
James 147
2:5-6 213
4:12 229

1 Peter
1:20 58
2:9 213
2:18-25 213
5:3 212

2 Peter
2 Peter 147
1:3-4 161
1:16 294
1:16-18 82
1:19 210
1:19-21 ...... 82–84, 96, 128, 161, 254
2:1-22 83
2:15-16 47
3:1ff. 94
3:2 .... 122, 128, 142, 161
3:15-16 .... 95, 122, 142, 259
3:16 215
15-16 128

1 John
1:1-4 260
2:20 .... 132, 213
2:27 132
4:9 16
5:13 .... 163, 211

2 John
2 John 147

3 John
3 John 147

Jude
Jude 147

Revelation
Revelation 147
1:10 187
7:9-10 50
19:9 102
22:18-19 162–163
22:22 66

Subject Index

NT stands for New Testament;
OT for Old Testament;
RC for Roman Catholic.

A

Abimelech (Biblical person) 47
Abraham (Biblical person) 47, 49, 167, 279
actualism 240–242, 256–257, 259
Adam (Biblical person) 57, 62–65, 87, 260
Agrippa (Biblical person) 50, 131, 294
Akkadian texts 278–279
Alexander, J. A. 21
Allen, Michael 176, 199
angels 53, 127–128, 169
anthropocentrism 237–239, 257
apostles
    apostolic imposition 89–90, 94–96, 141–144, 146, 149–150, 212
    Christ's authority 89–96, 121–122, 128, 259–260
    Holy Spirit 90, 96, 121–122, 124–125
    miracles 86, 122–128
    unique role 90, 158, 188–189, 196

Areopagus (Athens) 27–28, 29
atonement 32, 51
Atrahasis 279
authoritative tradition (RC)
    equal to Scripture 41, 175, 182–186, 238
    Protestant opposition 175–176, 186–192, 199–200

B

Baile, Guillaume 135
Balaam (Biblical person) 47–48
Bannerman, James 106, 178–179
baptism 170, 185–186, 187, 228
Barnabas (Biblical person) 26–27, 123
Barrett, Matthew 180, 214
Barth, Karl
    actualism 240–242, 256–257, 259
    anthropocentrism 237–239, 257
    canon 264–266
    incarnational analogy 262–264
    inspiration 254–255, 267–270
    introduction to 233–237
    proclamation 249–253, 258, 269
    revelation defined 243–248

threefold Word of God..........248–251, 258–260, 269
Bavinck, Herman
    clarity of Scripture 213
    incarnational analogy 273–275, 290
    revelation 14, 22, 36–37, 54, 60, 66
    sufficiency of Scripture...185, 188, 199
Beale, G. K..138
Beckwith, Roger..................................145
benevolence of God..................16, 27, 30, 31, 51, 172
Bible
    (*see:* canon; New Testament authority; Old Testament authority)
Bromiley, Geoffrey W. 240, 260

C

Calvin, John........26, 31, 40–41, 207, 239
canon
    apostolic imposition......89–90, 94–96, 141–144, 146, 149–150, 212
    Barth......................................264–266
    canonicity criteria 136–143
    closed.............157–159, 188–189, 300
    definition 133–137
    early church judgments................136, 143–144, 146–150, 188–189
    OT canon 144–146
Carson, D. A. 291
Catechism of the Catholic Church 184–185, 222, 227
charismatic movement.................192–199
Christ Jesus
    (*see:* Jesus Christ)
Church Dogmatics (Barth) ...233–237, 243, 247–249, 252, 257
circumstances, doctrine of 155–156, 176–179, 185, 197, 219
clarity of Scripture
    audience comprehension........208–209, 212–214, 216–221
    definition 201–206
    for practical living 207–212, 218
    RC denial of clarity................221–226
    RC doctrine opposed 226–231
    for salvation 203–204, 206, 208, 210–211, 214–215
Commentary on the Epistle to the Romans (Barth) 233
communion, humans with God 45, 52, 63–64, 66, 167
concursive operation............54–56, 76–79
conscience 24–26, 30, 35, 86, 153, 165, 229–230
Conservative Looks to Barth and Brunner, A (Rolston) 236
consummation (Christ's return)......58, 62, 64–65, 83, 197, 210
continuing revelation.......64–66, 300–301
    prophesying 44, 91, 193–198
Council of Trent..........182–183, 222–223
covenant........24, 46–50, 56–57, 167, 207
    (*see also:* New Covenant)
creation, medium of revelation 20–23, 26–30, 34, 36–37
creeds 173–175
Cunningham, William 102, 136

D

David (Biblical person).......21–22, 87–88, 162, 169, 209, 259, 263
deduction, doctrine of........154, 164–171, 173, 177–178, 187
depravity, human mind 23–24, 33–35, 40–41, 51–52, 130–132, 180
dialectics...............................234, 242–243
dictation (mechanical inspiration) 101–102
Diognetus, Epistle to..........................266
docetism.............253, 260, 278, 296, 304
dreams................................44, 48, 55, 102

E

Eck, Johann 135
Enns, Peter
    humanity of OT 278–283
    incarnational analogy 272–278, 282, 290–292, 295–296, 301
    inerrancy of Scripture 288–290, 293–297, 301–302
    methodological discrepancies 301–305
    NT use of OT 283–288, 300
    reimagining God 287–288, 298–300
Enuma Elish 279
eternal life 163–164, 167, 211
Eve (Biblical person) 62–63, 87

F

fall 62–64, 66
fallible human words 75–76, 97–98, 100–101
    Barth 246, 253, 260–261, 267, 269–270
false apostles 125–126
false apostolic writings 137–138, 141
false teaching 138, 160, 187–188
Father God
    known through Christ 32, 36, 60–62, 82, 118–120, 128
    sender of Holy Spirit 90, 121
Feinberg, John 98
Ferguson, Sinclair B. 198
First Vatican Council 183, 222–228
Frame, John M. 17, 104, 154, 177

G

Gaffin, Richard B., Jr. 196–197, 273, 275
Garden of Eden 62–64
Geisler, Norman L. 104–105
general revelation
    (*see:* natural (general) revelation)

Gentiles 24–25, 33, 49–50, 124–125, 131, 217–219
Gerstner, John H. 105
Gilgamesh 279
Gillespie, George 165, 170
glorification of God
    goal of revelation 15–16, 21–22, 52–53, 58, 61, 153–154
    Holy Spirit 121, 130–131, 180, 221
gnosticism 289, 297
Gordon, T. David 173
Göttingen Dogmatics (Barth) 235, 243
Grudem, Wayne 88, 91–92, 193–195, 197–199, 202–203, 205

H

Hart, Trevor 239, 240, 246, 267
Heidegger, J. H. 36
Hodge, A. A. 73, 86, 110, 172
Hodge, Caspar Wistar, Sr. 130, 132
Hodge, Charles 75, 111–112, 189, 231
Holy Spirit
    apostles 90, 96, 121–122, 124–125
    Barth 241, 245–248, 250–251, 254, 267–270
    charismatic movement ...193, 198–199
    OT inspiration 82–84, 87–88
    papal infallibility 224–225, 228–229
    (*see also:* illumination of the Spirit)
Hunsinger, George 240–241
hypostatic union 256, 275–276, 292

I

idolatry......................................24, 27–28, 176–177, 218
illumination of the Spirit.............116–117, 129–133, 148, 155, 179–181, 198–199, 219–221
image of God, humans 15–16, 18, 28, 36

Incarnation of Christ....49, 51, 57–62, 68, 246–247, 250–251
incarnational analogy ...99–101, 262–264, 272–278, 282, 290–292, 295–296, 301
inerrancy of Scripture
   alleged errors..........................106–113
   Barth and error.....236, 253, 260–261, 267–270
   definition........................103–106, 113
   Enns....................288–290, 293–296, 297, 301–302
   and inspiration..............72–76, 97–98, 100–101
infallibility of Scripture
   definition........................103–106, 113
   (*see also:* fallible human words)
inspiration
   (*see:* plenary verbal inspiration)
Inspiration and Incarnation (Enns)......271, 288, 291
Irenaeus.......................................146–147
Isaianic prophecy.............49–50, 168, 191
Israel
   covenant ..24, 46–50, 56–57, 167, 207
   first century Jews...........214, 218–219, 283–285
   history in cultural context (Enns) ..279–286, 293, 300
   recipients of law............24, 46–47, 49, 207–208, 213

J

Jacob (Biblical person).........................111
Jesus Christ
   judge..26, 30
   only way to salvation.....32, 44, 51–53, 68, 163–164
   Son of Father God 60–62, 118–120, 128
   (*see also:* apostles, Christ's authority; Incarnation of Christ; redemptive-historical revelation, Christ as goal)

John (Apostle).......................49, 60, 136, 171–172, 210–211
John the Baptist (Biblical person)....61–62
Johnson, Thomas C..............................15
judgment (Last Judgment)..............26, 28, 30–32, 35, 261
Justin Martyr......................................143

K

Kidner, Derek.......................................21
Kruger, Michael J........................136, 147
Kuyper, Abraham 42–44, 273, 276, 290

L

'last days'..................57–60, 68, 160–161, 188, 197, 210
Last Judgment..............26, 28, 30, 31–32, 35, 261
law
   apostolic imposition..............142–143, 149, 212
   Christ as fulfilment 51, 59, 65
   conscience....................24–25, 30, 153
   Israel as recipients 24, 46–47, 49, 207–208, 213
liberalism, 19th century........237–238, 257
Luke (Biblical person) 122–123, 141, 143
Lystra 26–27, 29–30

M

magisterial authority (RC)
   hierarchy with papal authority...................224–225, 227
   interpreting Scripture...........222–223, 225–231
   (*see also:* authoritative tradition (RC))
Mark (Biblical person).................141, 143
marriage 87, 111
Matthew (Apostle) 168, 285, 294
McCormack, Bruce L..........247, 256, 262

mechanical inspiration
  (dictation) 101–102
mercy 31–32, 35–36, 51, 53
Messiah 168, 286–287, 300
Metzger, Bruce M. 141
Migliore, Daniel L. 243
miracles 54–55, 107, 118–120, 168
  apostles 86, 122–128
Moo, Douglas J. 124
Moses (Biblical person) 46, 49, 85–86,
      111, 207–208, 218
  Jesus speaks of 61, 166
Mueller, David L. 252
Murray, John 124
myth 279, 288, 294, 295

N

natural (general) revelation
  definition 18–20, 53
  of God ...21–23, 27–30, 35–37, 44–45
  human depravity 23–24, 33–35
  of human duty to
      God 24–28, 30–32, 35
  limitations................31–33, 36, 40–41
natural theology 19–20, 32, 238–239
Nebuchadnezzar (Biblical person) ...47–48
New Covenant 57–58, 66, 142,
      156, 160–161, 196–197, 210–212
New Testament
  authority 89–96,
      121–122, 128, 259–260
      (*see also:* apostles)
Nicodemus (Biblical person) 119

O

Old Testament authority 61, 80–89,
      120, 128, 144–146, 211

P

Packer, J. I. 51, 68–69, 76, 80–81,
      86, 112–113, 264
papal infallibility 222, 224–229

partial inspiration 97–98, 113
Paul (Apostle)
  apostolic role.....91–95, 122–126, 131,
      137–138, 141–143, 294
  clarity of Scripture 208–209,
      211–217, 220
  inspiration 80–81, 88,
      267–268, 270
  natural revelation 23–28, 29–30,
      33–35
  special revelation 50, 65–66
  sufficiency of Scripture..........159–160,
      167–168, 176–177, 187–188, 196
Pentecost 124, 168–169, 196
personal nature of God.............15–18, 23,
      29–30, 100, 244, 268
perspicuity of Scripture
  (*see:* clarity of Scripture)
Peter (Apostle)
  apostolic role.....94–95, 122–123, 141,
      150, 259, 294
  clarity of Scripture ..209–210, 213, 215
  inspiration and
      Scripture....................82–84, 88, 95
  sufficiency of Scripture...161, 168–169
Peter, Gospel of 139
Pharisees..............................119–120, 190
Pinnock, Clark 236
plenary verbal inspiration
  alternatives to..................96–103, 109,
      111–112, 254–255, 267–270
  concursus 54–56, 76–79
  definition 71–76, 79–81, 113
  NT 89–96, 121–122,
      128, 259–260
  OT.............................80–89, 120, 128
plurality of gods 14, 26–27, 280, 293
pope (pontiff/Bishop of Rome) 199,
      224–225
  infallibility..........................222, 224–229
preaching 50, 65, 123, 216–217

proclamation (Barth)...249–253, 258, 269
priests................................43, 59, 152, 159
probation 62–64
proclamation
  (*see:* preaching)
prophecies
  failed prophecies 107
  fulfilment..................49–50, 144, 159,
    168–169, 191
  NT prophets............48–49, 58, 61–62,
    94, 118, 120
  OT prophets.....46–47, 49–50, 54–58,
    68, 82–86, 94, 161
prophesying
  as continuing revelation 44, 91,
    193–198
  as illumination 198–199
propositional revelation......16–17, 22, 53,
  241–242, 245, 296
Protoevangelium................................62, 66
providence of
  God 27–31, 53, 66, 78, 207, 215

R

'Real Problem of Inspiration, The'
  (Warfield) 71
redemptive-historical revelation
  Christ as goal 51–54, 56–62, 64–66,
    68, 158, 168, 188–189
  epochs..67–69
  pre-redemptive...........................62–64
regeneration 130–131, 180
Reid, J. Nicholas 265–266
reimagining God 287–288, 298–300
repentance................................27, 32, 35
resurrection 98, 158, 160, 166–167,
  169, 286–287, 294
revelation, definition 13–18
Rhodes, Ben 234
Ridderbos, Herman N.................149–150,
  188–189
Roach, William C. 104–105

Rolston, Holmes 236
Roman Catholic Church
  canon....................................134–136
  hierarchy of authority.....224–225, 227
  interpreting Scripture...............43–44,
    222–223, 225–231
  (*see also:*
    authoritative tradition (RC))
Römerbrief (Barth)..............................237
Runia, Klaas 254

S

Sadducees............................119–120, 166
Salmon, George..................................227
salvation
  clear revelation of..........203–204, 206,
    208, 210–211,
    214–215
  Holy Spirit.....130–132, 155, 179–181
  miracles...................................126–127
  natural revelation 31–32, 36, 45
  RC church authority 224, 230
  special revelation 44, 49–53, 66, 68
  sufficient revelation of...........153–154,
    157–160, 162–164, 187
Samaritans.....................................46, 122
Satan 125, 130, 131, 180, 220
Scheid, John 14
Scripture
  (*see:* canon; New Testament authority;
    Old Testament authority)
Second Vatican
  Council..................183–184, 225–226
signs
  (*see:* miracles)
sin
  natural revelation 16, 23–26, 28,
    31–36
  special revelation 40–41, 43–45,
    51–53, 172
  (*see also:* fall; regeneration)
sola scriptura 174–176, 200

sovereignty of God 18, 27–29
special revelation
    covenant audience....24, 46–50, 56–57
    modes 53–56, 58–59
    natural revelation as
        context 20–21, 36–37, 40–45
    salvation............44, 49–53, 64, 66, 68
Storms, C. Samuel......................193–194
Strong, A. H...102
sufficiency of Scripture
    definition 152–157
    doctrine of circumstances......155–156,
        176–179, 185, 197, 219
    doctrine of deduction....154, 164–171,
        173, 177–178, 187
    God-given limitations 171–178
    for practical living 160–162
    for salvation 153–154, 157–160,
        162–164, 187
    (*see also:* authoritative tradition
    (RC); continuing revelation;
    illumination of the Spirit)
Swain, Scott R.............................176, 199

T

Tertullian 143
theophany 54–55
theopneustos 80–81, 254, 267–268
Thompson, Mark D. 202–203,
    258, 260, 264
Timothy (Biblical person) 65–66,
    159–160, 175
Titus (Biblical person) 65–66
tongues, gift of 91, 192–197
Torah 24–25, 213
tradition
    (*see:* authoritative tradition (RC))
Transfiguration of Christ 82–83
Triunity of God................31, 51, 53, 170,
    240, 247–248
Turretin, Francis
    church authority 190, 227

revelation 16, 41
Scripture........162, 164, 186–187, 219

U

unbelievers 33–34, 36, 48, 50,
    131, 220–221

V

Van Til, Cornelius...........................33–34
Vatican I..............................183, 222–228
Vatican II 183–184, 225–226
verbal plenary inspiration
    (*see:* plenary verbal inspiration)
Vos, Geerhardus 62–64

W

Ward, Timothy............................202–203
Warfield, Benjamin B.
    canon.....................................136, 143
    clarity of Scripture 205–206
    incarnational analogy 99, 275–277,
        290
    inerrancy of Scripture.....110, 302–304
    inspiration .71–73, 76–79, 83–84, 259
    revelation 20–21, 44–45, 52,
        54–56, 63, 65
    sufficiency of Scripture...153, 170, 180
Westminster Confession of Faith
    Bible as Word of God..............73, 116,
        129–130, 154–156
    clarity of Scripture 203–206
    Incarnation of Christ 273
    natural revelation 30
    sufficiency of Scripture..........152–156,
        164, 179–180
Westminster Theological
    Seminary........................271–272, 296
Whitaker, William.......................226–227
wisdom 95, 162, 173, 215,
    287–289, 300
wisdom literature.................163, 173, 298
Wordsworth, Christopher....................120
wrath of God.............................23, 31, 52

ISBN 978-1-5271-0391-7

Clash of Visions
Populism and Elitism in New Testament Theology

Robert W. Yarbrough

Each year thousands die for the Jesus they read about in the Bible. At the same time scholars worldwide reject central truths of the Book. Here is an analysis of two contrasting approaches to biblical interpretation: one which has encouraged many to abandon the Christian heritage, the other which has informed the largest numeric increase of professing Christians in world history in recent generations and which is projected to continue.

This is a book that every Christian student should read before studying at a non–evangelical institution. Even those at Bible–believing institutions (including seminaries) will benefit, since they will likely be reading books by 'elitists' and may at some point study under them in graduate school. I found the book riveting and had a hard time putting it down. The two appendices about the life–pilgrimage of two 'populist' theologians are worth the price of the book.

G. K. Beale
Professor of New Testament and Biblical Theology, Westminster Theological Seminary, Philadelphia, Pennsylvania

Christian Focus Publications

Our mission statement —

STAYING FAITHFUL

In dependence upon God we seek to impact the world through literature faithful to His infallible Word, the Bible. Our aim is to ensure that the Lord Jesus Christ is presented as the only hope to obtain forgiveness of sin, live a useful life and look forward to heaven with Him.

Our books are published in four imprints:

CHRISTIAN FOCUS

Popular works including biographies, commentaries, basic doctrine and Christian living.

CHRISTIAN HERITAGE

Books representing some of the best material from the rich heritage of the church.

MENTOR

Books written at a level suitable for Bible College and seminary students, pastors, and other serious readers. The imprint includes commentaries, doctrinal studies, examination of current issues and church history.

CF4•K

Children's books for quality Bible teaching and for all age groups: Sunday school curriculum, puzzle and activity books; personal and family devotional titles, biographies and inspirational stories — because you are never too young to know Jesus!

Christian Focus Publications Ltd,
Geanies House, Fearn, Ross-shire,
IV20 1TW, Scotland, United Kingdom.
www.christianfocus.com